GLOBAL DIPLOMACY

GLOBAL DIPLOMACY

Theories, Types, and Models

ALISON R. HOLMES
Humboldt State University

WITH

J. SIMON ROFE
SOAS, University of London

A Member of the Perseus Books Group

Westview Press was founded in 1975 in Boulder, Colorado, by notable publisher and intellectual Fred Praeger. Westview Press continues to publish scholarly titles and high-quality undergraduate- and graduate-level textbooks in core social science disciplines. With books developed, written, and edited with the needs of serious nonfiction readers, professors, and students in mind, Westview Press honors its long history of publishing books that matter.

Published by Westview Press,
A Member of the Perseus Books Group
2465 Central Avenue
Boulder, CO 80301
www.westviewpress.com

Library of Congress Cataloging-in-Publication Data

Names: Holmes, Alison, author. | Rofe, J. Simon.
Title: Global diplomacy : theories, types, and models / Alison R. Holmes, J. Simon Rofe.
Description: Boulder, Colorado : Westview Press, 2016. | Includes bibliographical references and index.
Identifiers: LCCN 2016003717 | ISBN 9780813345529 (paperback)
Subjects: LCSH: Diplomacy. | International relations. | World politics. | BISAC: POLITICAL SCIENCE / General. | POLITICAL SCIENCE / International
Relations / General. | POLITICAL SCIENCE / International Relations / Diplomacy. | POLITICAL SCIENCE / Government / International. | POLITICAL SCIENCE / History & Theory.
Classification: LCC JZ1305 .H646 2016 | DDC 327.2--dc23 LC record available at http://lccn.loc.gov/2016003717

10 9 8 7 6 5 4 3 2 1

To my students—whose unfailing belief in making a positive difference in the world makes them the most inspiring "global ambassadors" I have had the privilege to know—whatever career path they choose.

~ arh

To Allan; to Jackie and to family.

~ jsr

CONTENTS

ACKNOWLEDGMENTS

From Alison R. Holmes

This project has been longer in the making than was intended, with the inevitable consequence there are more people to thank—and unfortunately more potential to accidentally leave someone out. Official thanks go to University College London Center for the Study of the Americas in London, UK and the Roosevelt Study Center in Middelburg, the Netherlands for short periods of residence that ensured some dedicated time to the writing process. Thanks are also due to the participants of the many Diplomatic Studies Panels of the International Studies Association and the Transatlantic Studies Association who listened patiently and commented sagely on various aspects of my work on these concepts which have been even longer in gestation than the book.

A particular debt is owed to the guest authors: Kenneth Weisbode, Geoffrey Pigman, Giles Scott-Smith, Andrew Dorman, Matthew Uttley and Shaun Riordan, an eclectic group who offered their valuable time and expertise to the odd question posed to them to present the 'history' of diplomacy through 'type'; and of course Simon who has listened longer and more than anyone should have to, to another person's academic fermentation process.

Westview has undergone many changes during this time and while I am grateful to all those who believed the concept might work, Grace Fujimoto 'brought it home' with a judicious mix of encouragement, editorial expertise and sheer determination. I have no doubt this has taken more of her time than she ever feared possible and it is my sincere hope that her unfailing dedication reflects a belief that the end product is worth the considerable effort it has taken to get it out into the world.

Closer to home, and in an effort to keep one's best critics, in this case literally, 'inside the tent', Duncan Burgess has been steadfast in his support and (usually) stoic in the face of my many distractions. Accepting his invitation to come to the west coast and live with him in the redwoods by the sea stands out as one of my best decisions and thus the debt I have incurred with this project is one I will happily pay with interest.

Above all, I want to thank my students at Humboldt State University and specifically, a senior seminar group in the Fall of 2012 who were the original 'guinea pigs' for the ideas in this text. There is no more honest (or terrifying) group of reviewers for a relatively new faculty member and I was deeply touched by their enthusiastic conclusion that every student in every major should be required to take a class in diplomacy—'global' or otherwise.

Three students deserve particular mention in order of their involvement. Jake Walsmith, a Political Science major whose curiosity about diplomats and their stories led to an independent study in 2013 to undertake some research on the 'grand timeline'; Harlee Keller, an International Studies major, whose passionate interest in the Mali Empire and griot culture gained her a student research grant in 2014 and ensured a 'voice' for these oral historians and ancient diplomats here as the basis of a case study; and Doug Smith, also an International Studies major, whose consideration of perhaps becoming an academic himself one day, meant he was willing to read an entire, incomplete, manuscript, provide comments, and undertake some of the last minute research as part of a student grant in 2015. Their intellectual curiosity and earnest, yet infectious, enthusiasm embodies the purpose of this text—and the reason I teach.

From J. Simon Rofe

I would like to take this opportunity to thank the all of those involved in seeing this five-year project through to publication. Particular thanks to Grace Fujimoto at Westview who skillfully piloted the project to its conclusion; to all the contributing authors; and most of all to Alison for her patience, tenacity and commitment.

Introduction

BY ALISON HOLMES

Surely, the first question a text ought to address is why a student might want to study the topic? Does it help them understand a specific issue or the world more generally? Does it explain what has happened in the past or the direction of current events? Is it relevant to daily life or to future plans? Judged in this light, the study of diplomacy may not seem particularly salient. This may be because the term is often used in ways that are either so broad ('she was very diplomatic about her friend's dress') or so far removed from our own experience ('the secretary of state had diplomatic talks with the King of Oman') that we have little sense of the underlying importance and potential significance for diplomacy in today's world. Material from scholarly papers and newspapers, to websites and blogs, use terms such as 'contemporary' or 'globalizing' to describe diplomacy as a whole, or modifiers such as 'dollar,' 'digital,' and 'ping-pong' diplomacy in terms of specific tactics, but these are often designed more for grabbing headlines than for explaining diplomacy's long-term activities or purpose. This leaves little room for understanding what the subject involves out in the world and less for what we might study in a classroom. We hear more about the abstract concept of globalization than we do about the mechanisms that govern us at the international or global level, and the people who operate at that level as diplomats or other agents of change. However, with an interest in globalization, also comes an interest in the connection between issues and the way in which individuals can create impact at the international level. The divisions between the traditional levels of analysis, be it the individual, the state they operate in, or the international arena, seem to be breaking down. This highlights a gap in our understanding of international relations as well as an opportunity to go beyond the more common interpretation of diplomacy as simply the 'peacemakers' or 'peace-keepers' of a system, and examine more carefully the role of diplomacy in a world where power is shifting and politics, economics, and culture are evermore intertwined. Paul Sharp has identified an increase in interest in diplomacy and suggests two reasons for this trend. The first is "the growing sense that the distribution of power and wealth is shifting." The second is a "concomitant sense that the ways in which we represent ourselves to one another are also undergoing change" (Sharp, et. al., 2011, 716). Sharp believes this leads to an interest in diplomacy because it is the institutional means by which societies deal with their sense of uncertainty about change and the way they interact and communicate with others to act on and affect that change. This text agrees and proposes two further points. First, diplomacy is a fundamental activity that has been undertaken throughout history and around the world with a single goal: to mediate the intercultural communication that underlies the connections between all people and all societies. This includes peace and war, trade and exchange, but also a growing awareness of our intercultural interactions at every level. For this reason, it becomes increasingly important also to broaden our ideas of diplomacy and ask ourselves if it isn't actually more accurate to suggest that, rather than a single or monolithic idea of diplomacy, entirely different diploma*cies* are produced by other worldviews as evidenced in their approach to **statecraft** or *the 'art' of politics or the leadership of a country and the conduct of public or foreign affairs.* Second, that diplomacy is all around us. Many different people engage in what can be broadly thought of as 'diplomacy,' from the 'global' to the 'local' level, and these commonly used modifiers challenge us to explore our fundamental notion of who is involved and whether we have been focusing so much on the units or actors involved in the process, that we have not paid enough attention to the importance of the actual relations that influence and shape the units through the process of their interaction. Returning to the question of 'Why study diplomacy?'—the answer proposed here is, because even people who may not be involved in 'official' or 'formal' diplomacy, but who care about global issues such as human rights, the environment, trade, and development, or those who simply love to travel and appreciate foreign cultures and languages, will find that an understanding of the development of diplomacy and its role in our contemporary society will help them to understand, participate in, and change our increasingly global world.

Terminology

Diplomacy is often taught as one element of another course. It may be covered in a week or two in a world politics or international relations class, talked about in a few chapters in an international law class, or condensed in a politics class or an international studies or global studies program. This is because the more formal or academic study of diplomacy is considered to be part of the disciplines of political science or, more specifically, international relations, and both of these fields have some terms and concepts that will be useful to discuss prior to moving forward—not least as many of these concepts will be challenged by the more global approach to diplomacy discussed here.

Paradigms and Theories

Like all disciplines, international relations has a series of theories or *patterns* identified as paradigms. Paradigms are important for the fundamental reason that they have real-world consequences as reflections of an underlying worldview. By understanding **theory** as *a particular worldview and set of rules by which we decide something is important or unimportant in our approach,* and **paradigms** as *a commonly agreed upon set of theories,* we begin to see the significance of theory not only in terms of our framework for various questions, but also to possible solutions and policy outcomes to serious issues. To use a simple analogy, let's say a worldview is like a pair of glasses and theories are different-colored lenses or lenses with different levels of magnification. It is obvious that, even if the frame remains constant, the theories we look through change how, and even what, we see. For international relations, there are two dominant paradigms, **realism** and **liberalism** (sometimes called **pluralism**). If we believe the theorists called **realists**, that human nature is basically selfish and unchangeable and that people will always take every opportunity to maximize their own interests above everything else, our reaction to their behavior might be defensive or even preemptive. A sense of: 'do it to them before they can do it to us' becomes an important part of the decision-making process. On the other hand, if we agree with **liberals** or **pluralists**, who believe in liberal internationalism and that people are basically good and trying to do the best they can, we might respond very differently. We might give them the benefit of the doubt in an unclear situation or allow them extra time to comply with some agreement. Just as our underlying 'theories' about human nature change how we respond to people at the individual level, the argument follows that our 'theories' of the international system as to how actors such as states, inter-governmental organizations and single-issue campaign organizations behave, can fundamentally alter the outcomes in international affairs.

Entities and 'states'

This raises another key assumption of international relations and diplomacy, which is the fact that most of the study in this area has focused on the actor generally considered to be the 'most important,' i.e., the state. However, given that later chapters will argue that the 'state' was not the only form of social organization or source of diplomacy throughout time, it is important to note the use of the term 'entity' and 'polity' rather than 'state' or 'government' in this chapter and elsewhere. These are not elegant words, but they are needed to discuss the infrastructure of all human communities as they have evolved through different forms and social structures or what has been termed a "band-tribe-chiefdom-state model of social complexity" (Crumley, 1995). These take many shapes and can be a group of elders or a council, agencies, bodies or institutions, but uniformly consist of a group with authority 'over' aspects of their society. The crucial point here is that such structures provide the framework for the way a society conceives of, and articulates, power, both over itself and the connections that each society makes to the wider world. The expression of this mediation internally may be called 'government' or 'governance,' while externally, this mediation is most often known as 'diplomacy.' Thus, the terms 'entity' or 'polity' are used as a way to remind ourselves that while these structures were not always 'states' as we understand them today, societies have always had a constant need for the tools and conventions, if not the formal institution, of what we call diplomacy or diploma*cies* of separate international systems.

National Interest and Strategy

Returning to terminology, an understanding of **strategy** as *an overall plan or policy to achieve a primary or fundamental goal (often deemed to be survival, and therefore a term considered to be military in nature)* is also useful, particularly in the more traditional, or more realist, Westphalian/state-centric understanding of politics. This term is also closely related to what is known as **national interest**, a concept that both politicians and scholars believe to be the *overarching and most important driver in determining a course of action of a state's foreign policy.*' These terms are often used interchangeably, which can be confusing, though, in the context of government behavior, 'strategy' is often related to military planning while 'national interest' tends to be so inclusive as to refer to whatever a speaker deems it to mean in a specific instance. For example, the concept of national interest not only frames political debate at home, it can also shape the way states interpret the behavior of others as they ask 'What response is in our best interest?' or 'What do we learn about what that country sees as their *real* national interest by their decision to do X in this situation?' National interest is usually reserved for government purposes, but strategy is commonly used outside these political circles, though no less broadly. Few organizations would admit they have no 'strategy,' but what they perceive it to be, how they agree on one, and how it comes to be implemented are entirely different things.

This idea also raises another important tension as many writers discuss 'diplomacy' and 'foreign policy' as synonymous concepts, while others strongly argue that politicians create strategy or policy, while diplomats merely implement strategy as operators or administrators. This text takes a third position, particularly in light of the traditional 'split' or 'great divide' that many international relations scholars have proposed exists between domestic or national/internal policy and foreign/external policy (Clark, 1999 and Hill, 2003 among many others). This division, while intended to help establish a clear distinction between questions that only matter to 'us' and those that involve 'others,' often creates more difficulties than it resolves. As the interconnected nature of global issues becomes more widely recognized, it is logical to assume that a deeper understanding of the interconnectedness between the 'inside' and the 'outside' of the current political entities known as states is also needed. In other words, diplomats are engaged in the implementation of foreign policy on a daily basis, but what they do in terms of communication also helps to shape and direct strategy as well as to devise policy. Thus, the current dichotomy not only creates a false sense of firm boundaries for the entity, but it also creates an entity of a society within the 'container' of the state and separates two ideas that are entirely dependent on each other for existence while the process itself helps shape the outcome and the institution.

Hierarchy as 'default'

The confusion in the priority or 'order' of these terms also raises a much deeper issue: the pervasiveness of the concept of hierarchy in our understanding of states and their interactions. Simply put, **hierarchy** is *an expression of the relationship between elements where certain factors are deemed to be subordinate to another and may be ranked.* However, and crucially here, it should also be recognized as another frame or worldview that is typically used by thinkers who are seeking to visualize ideas of order and to assert the relative importance of one area over another. Hierarchies can include institutions such as the military or a natural grouping such as a pride of lions that, in the interest of a perceived sense of order, devise a system that is generally respected and adhered to—though not entirely unchallenged—in the pursuit of what is deemed to be for the benefit of all. Such an understanding of power clearly includes different constructed and natural groups, but it is a particular (and culturally specific) way to structure knowledge that has become a default in much western/European thinking. For example, most Americans would 'order' the world powers by putting the United States at, or very close to, the top. One could use a variety of reasoning for this placement, but physical size, military might, and economic strength are likely to feature in the list. Crucially, they also reflect an inbuilt default mechanism that suggests specific ideas about what constitutes power and the desirability of order. To balance this unconscious bias, it is important to consider the alternative to hierarchy, or **heterarchy**, *the idea that the same elements can be ranked or even 'counterpoised' in various ways determined by context and the players involved* (Crumley, 1985). Examples of heterarchy include participants in a community event or leaves on a tree. There is a clear 'order' to the way they behave or interact, but they are not ordered by an external system or ranked in any formal way.

Hierarchy holds an assumed and fundamental default position in the mainstream/Western narrative of diplomacy, which helps to explain the perceived importance of national interest and strategy to be discussed later. Taken in conjunction with the primacy of the idea of **anarchy**—*a situation in which there is no higher authority than the state*—this desire for order puts survival or military issues in a ranking above all others. In contrast, heterarchy allows for different systems of order and opens the possibility that diplomacy is more than the shadow of power, but a shaping power as well.

Substantialist vs Relational

The issues around national interest and hierarchy are directly related to the ideas of scholars such as Patrick Jackson and Daniel Nexon who have argued that the **substantialist** tendency within international relations theory, or *the tendency to conflate an object with the outcomes of its actions,* leads to a focus on the entity itself and not on its processes or interactions with others. They illustrate this problem by quoting Norbert Elias's statement "the wind is blowing," that seems to suggest that somehow the wind could exist separately from its effects (Jackson and Nexon, 1999, 300). In their view, this "substantialist bias" also means that we assume the entity in question existed 'first' "or that entities are already entities before they enter into social relations with other entities rather than being created and shaped by the process of interaction and suggest that the most common of these presupposed entities is 'the state'" (Jackson and Nexon, 1999, 293).

An awareness of this issue may help us form a better appreciation of the problems we encounter when trying to identify the differences between strategy, national interest, foreign policy, and diplomacy and to recognize the default to hierarchy as both reflections of this substantialist tendency involving both theory and practice and almost despite the fact that "…most diplomats know…that world policy is deeply relational. Their job is to make those relations 'work'…" (Adler-Nissen in Sending, Pouliot and Neumann 2105, 286).

To address some of the issues, these authors propose the idea of **Relationalism**, which, like heterarchy, recognizes different forms and *takes as its point of departure the idea that social phenomena making up world politics always develop in relation to other social phenomena.* Thus, for example, "states are not born into this world as fully developed states that then 'exist'; states are made in continuous relations with other states and non-state actors" (Adler-Nissen in Sending Pouliot and Neumann 2015, 286).

These authors, and others like them, are *readjusting the focus* or **problematizing** precisely the point that many simply assert; the increasing interconnectedness of the world requires that we examine the interactions and relations between entities rather than assuming the study of the units involved in the interaction is sufficient. Further, the need for such an adjustment seems clear as the relationship between a government and their own civil society—a government's relationship to another government—and a government's relationship to another country's civil society, and even civil society's relationship with other people in a different society become more visible in our global society. Thus, each relationship or interaction is ultimately part of a larger conversation, though crucially, each level is always seen from its own perspective. In other words, by removing the perception that the state is the only actor/form of governance, and breaking down the hierarchies embedded in statecraft around national interest, it may be possible to see that each of these layers can act and react to any other layer in another location without necessarily going through 'official' channels, or those with the 'authority' granted from a government source, before speaking to others. A more 'global' awareness recognizes that relations create the politics in which the units operate as much as the entities or units create the relations. In much the same way the idea is to broaden the idea of a single form of diplomacy to many diploma*cies*, it will also be possible to expand on this concept of relations at different levels. Perhaps a more concrete example is the case of the European Union as they grapple with issues such as migration or refugees in terms of what is 'domestic' vs what is 'foreign' at three levels: internal diplomacy (each state negotiating with Brussels and then explaining the resulting policy to their own citizens); 'inner-national' (the EU talking across the Union about its supranational activities); and the EU as a whole talking to the 'outside' (the EU talking to the United States or China or to other intergovernmental organizations such as the United Nations or the African Union).

Structure of the Text

In light of these issues, this discussion of global diplomacy is structured in a specific way. First and foremost, the text argues that the essence of diplomacy has not fundamentally changed over time. Its characteristics have been altered by a number of important factors, many of them technological, and that these factors have, in turn, influenced both diplomatic practice and tactics. However, the nature of diplomacy, in terms of mission or strategy, remains communication in its three specifically diplomatic forms: dialogue, representation, and negotiation. Ultimately, the aim is to set out an idea of 'global diplomacy' that recognizes the role of diplomacy as an ancient institution separate, but arguably parallel to, the idea of the form of governance, and constantly evolving to reflect shifts in structure and power. Further, while the role and purpose of diplomacy have not shifted, we have not clearly understood the complexity of the cultural differences and resulting diploma*cies* at work or the institution of diplomacy and the role of diplomats as gatekeepers and guides of the sources of social power that create and recreate our world. The mainstream narrative of diplomacy has created an understanding that is not incorrect, but incomplete. To make that case, four areas must first be explored in the three parts of the text.

First, a new theoretical frame for diplomacy is needed that focuses on the purpose of diplomacy as demonstrated through practice rather than simply as the delivery mechanism of an entity or polity. Thus, different theories of the international system and the role of diplomacy are used to propose a more global perspective.

Second, and unlike many traditional explanations, the argument will be made that diplomacy-as-dialogue goes back to the furthest reaches of history and further, there is evidence of this in the consistency of 'types' of diplomacy over time and in the 'diplomacies of place.'

Finally, the effects of those different worldviews on the diploma*cies* of other regions of the world long before the 'state' or governments as we know them existed, will be examined and different models developed to help us focus on the way global states operate their own forms of diplomacy in today's world.

The result is a more 'global' diplomacy that connects theory and practice by recognizing the relational nature of diplomacy and rejoining dichotomies, rather than reinforcing the differences that have served as the traditional narrative and hindered more than helped our understanding of global relations and diplomacy's role in them.

Decentering the Westphalian State and theories of diplomacy—Part I

The first step is to de-emphasize the state as the sole, or even the main, actor taking part in this dialogue and to re-emphasize the areas of practical diplomatic interaction across time. With scholars Donna Lee and David Hudson, it becomes possible to consider diplomacy as an "open-ended-historical narrative" that sees diplomacy "as a means of connecting cultures, economics and states in order to build and manage social relations at domestic and systemic levels" (Lee and Hudson, 2004, 358). In their work, Lee and Hudson were primarily examining the importance of economic and cultural issues in light of the traditional focus on the political side, but this observation should be significantly expanded so as to create a more holistic approach. To this end, the view of sociologist Michael Mann (identified by Jackson and Nexon as being strongly against substantialism—Jackson and Nexon, 1999, 301) that "human societies are not unitary systems" and that to understand the development of the social world one must examine the "multiple, overlapping, intersecting networks of power" (Mann, 1986, 522), will be pursued.

This idea, combined with the assertion that there is a need to separate the institution of diplomacy from the entity that uses it so as to have a fuller understanding of its purpose and development, results in a more social/interactional approach. This will be done by breaking diplomacy along what Mann identifies as the four "sources" of "social power," or what are called here the four *types* of diplomacy: political, cultural, economic, and military. The proposal is that, by identifying diplomacy more closely with the power sources it guides and directs, it will be possible to see its role and the effect the institution as a whole has on the system.

Types of diplomacy and diplomacies of place—Part II

Second, and with the help of a number of expert authors, the day-to-day interaction of theory and practice will be connected to the four types of diplomacy fundamental to its unchanging nature and mission in terms of communication: dialogue, representation, and negotiation, and put in the context of an awareness of diploma*cies* of place. There are two main reasons for using these types as the fundamental basis for global diplomacy.

First, on a theoretical level, the list of types reflects Michael Mann's observation that "No known state has yet managed to control all relations traveling across its boundaries, and so much social power has always remained 'transnational'" (Mann, 1986, 522), which, he goes on to say, leaves "an obvious role" for "diffusion" (Mann, 1986, 522)—and similarly leaves an equally obvious role for a global diplomacy. This approach also incorporates Adda Bozeman's suggestion that, if diplomacy is the "interplay" of these different sources, a "more complex and dense network of diplomatic systems" is possible in which "diplomacy can be seen in the context of a world history in which non-western cultures are not 'other' but are in fact integral to world society" (Lee and Hudson, 2004, 356).

In other words, there are three main points to consider. First, the state is not a hard and fast entity, but part of a complex web of interactions and relations that are mediated, constructed, and deconstructed by the processes of diplomacy itself. Second, that the focus of most mainstream theory on one area of the world e.g. Europe, or what has been called a **states-system** (more on which later) does not mean that other parts of the world did not continue to develop as entities and evolve their own models of interaction based on their worldviews, even as they participated in, or adapted to, what became the prevailing system. Further, that these 'other' approaches or systems not only played a crucial role in the creation of 'modern', Western/European diplomacy, but are an increasingly important part of the international system in their more traditional forms. For the purposes of this text, these other forms are included as part of the foundation of what is more correctly identified as the global state. Finally, it is possible for different types of states-systems and models of interaction to coexist. One may appear to be dominant, but other diplomacies have been operating and may have more, not less, freedom to operate in an increasingly global world and the expectation should be for more such interactions in the future.

The second reason for outlining these four types is that, at the very simple and basic level of practice, they correspond with the most common divisions in the core activities of diplomats through time. Historically, and in nearly every embassy in the world today, there are positions for 'officers' or 'attachés' whose responsibility is to engage with the issues, organizations, and personalities of politics, culture, economics, and military diplomacy.

The suggestion is that, by separating the story of diplomacy from the story of the relatively recent form of governance known as the 'state,' it will be possible not only to see the way diplomacy has developed in the past, but how it may develop in the future. It may also be possible to look more closely at the interactions of diplomacy that help shape its structure and that of the entities it represents.

Models of interaction for 'Westphalian' States and 'Global' States—Part III

Once an alternative theory is set out and the idea of 'types' have been explored as the constant features or set of activities of diplomacy through time, the current models of diplomacy will be woven into a pattern of global diplomacy.

The obvious place to begin such an examination is the Western/European states system that produced the currently dominant Westphalian form of the state. However, as the state itself has changed, so too has the model of interaction for the states in that states-system. Thus, the argument is that the 'original' or 'classic' Western/European states system has, over time, evolved into two distinct models of interaction for the members of its system: Transatlantic Diplomacy (used by advanced, democratic, and enmeshed, but distinctly sovereign, states as illustrated by UK/US relations) and Community Diplomacy (used in advanced, broadly democratic states, but including a notion of 'pooled sovereignty' as these states increasingly share what had historically been considered to be core functions and essential characteristics of statehood while not entirely bypassing existing state structures).

The next assertion is simply that, while the European states system managed to eclipse others, it could not entirely destroy the ancient alternatives and that at least some features or combination of these prior state-systems still exists. Thus, a 'Relational' model of diplomacy is proposed with the contention that non-Western systems persisted and continued to evolve, even in the 'shadow' of the Western world. However, as states have generally become more porous, non-state actors have become more visible, and the states which operate with this approach become more powerful in the international system, the expectation should be that this Relational model will 'rise' in the sense that it will be more obvious and play a more directly relevant role. This process will, in turn, help to create a more 'global diplomacy' in that states at different levels of development and operating different models of interaction will be more aware of each other and develop ways to coexist more consciously as the global world involves a layering of difference and a focus on interaction as part of the role and process of diplomacy.

Global Diplomacy

Having set out the theories, types, and models, the final step is to bring these different critiques of different ideas and alternative ideas together to create a theory of global diplomacy. The choice of the term 'Global Diplomacy' is deliberate, but differs from other texts in at least four important ways. First, the term 'global' is used here to begin to define a specific understanding of both diplomatic history and international relations theory. For example, international relations' concepts such as 'sovereignty' and 'power' are often used, but not well explained in diplomatic literature. Similarly, and most fundamentally, the 'state' that dominates the literature is implied, but not explicitly demarcated as the state in its 'Westphalian form,' i.e., it is deemed to be equal, universal, and unchanging. These pervasive assumptions have **reified** the state, *shifting it from an abstract concept to a more concrete form.* This has left little room to explore the ways in which asymmetries of power, different cultural histories or diplomacies, and the ways different stages in the state's development as an entity, have affected the institution of diplomacy in its constitutive function for international society or in terms of its own practice and tactics. As John Hoffman argues, "Diplomacy needs to be reconstructed. This involves transforming it into a concept that embodies social relationships which are ordered without the state. A critique of the state itself is essential" (Hoffman, 2003, 526).

'Global' features, not a timeline

However, the term 'global' is not simply in opposition to the domination of the Westphalian state, but a way to help describe the changing features in the development of the state overall. Historians, among others, commonly use terms such as 'early' or 'late modern' to describe a specific set of circumstances and forms of societal interaction. This has led, almost inevitably, to an increasing use of the phrase 'postmodern' in contemporary discussions and is useful for specific understandings of social relations. Yet, in terms of diplomacy, this approach to historical analysis is particularly unhelpful as it quickly becomes overly reliant on the Western/European state and the use of points of conflict or warfare as the primary breakpoints in the narrative.

This text resists this trend by agreeing with the arguments of scholars such as Ian Clark and Martin Shaw who suggest that, by putting 'post' in front of 'modern' is merely to locate the current state form in the time frame *after* modern (Clark, 1999; Shaw, 2000) rather than saying something instructive as to the change that has taken place in the state itself. With these authors, it is possible to begin to identify features that challenge the Westphalian state and could be described as a 'global' form in its own right, which, in turn, has specific implications for diplomacy. Paul Sharp has pointed out that diplomacy is a 'reflection of the state' (Sharp, 2009). From that point, the logical next step posed here is that if diplomacy has always been a reflection of the governing entity, it will include those entities that came before the 'Westphalian' form of the state as well as those that are still to come. Further, that the constantly evolving and increasingly global nature of these governing entities will produce a system that opens the more traditional understanding of diplomacy and will requires the recognition of the coexistence of other kinds of entity operating in the global space.

Second, while appreciating the richness of past diplomatic discourse, there is the issue of the continuing use and abuse of the 'old' vs. 'new' debate that can still dominate current discussion. In ways similar to the discussion of late vs. postmodern above, many diplomatic scholars have tried to mark out specific events as *the* definitive moment of change in diplomacy. For example, the period between World War I and World War II is often held up as the point of great change when the general public began to take a more active part in the discussion of international affairs. Yet such titles of 'old' vs. 'new' are useful only insofar as they identify these moments and put the stages of diplomacy (like the stages of the state) into a rough order, but 'new' and 'old' are so relative as to have little lasting value. They mark out different points in time, but consistent overuse has obscured important issues by periodizing features that are more correctly seen as a continuous evolution. Similarly, the establishment of a continuous or permanent presence by diplomats in other countries or what was termed a 'resident mission' is often pointed to as one of the most significant changes in diplomacy. However, as Jeremy Black and others have made clear, "There was no single moment or cause of the development of permanent diplomatic contacts in Europe, but the major cause seems to have been the need to improve the reporting of foreign states" (Black, 2010, 28). A more persistent example can be found in discussions of the importance of technology. While not wishing to suggest that the cable, telegraph, or Internet have not had a significant impact on the practice and tactics of diplomacy—the idea that technology has somehow altered its fundamental nature is a logical fallacy akin to suggesting that the Gatling gun changed the causes of conflict. The gun undoubtedly made war more effective, at least in terms of 'bang for buck' or lives lost/per dollar spent, but neither the reasons for conflict nor the path towards its resolution are found in the firing mechanisms of a gun; any more than the purpose of global communication and dialogue can be defined by the wonders of Wi-Fi or digitization. As George Shultz, secretary of state under President Reagan put it in his discussion of "virtual diplomacy," "We are in the midst of a revolution. A revolution by definition causes old power structures to crumble and new ones to rise. The catalyst—but not the cause—has always been technological" (Shultz, 1997, 12).

Thus, this text offers an analysis of diplomacy that creates phases in its development by tracking the changes in the political entities as they are reflected by diplomatic practice and statecraft over time. The goal is to identify the underlying causes of change—rather than merely pointing out the order of these changes and the effects of such change on tactics on the ground, discussed below.

The third reason for using the term 'global diplomacy' is to highlight the argument that not only have we arrived at a point at which many states are identifiably 'global' in nature (rather than simply post-Westphalian), but equally, many more have not yet arrived at this 'stage' in their development. This is important because a state's structure (and therefore its overall level of 'development') has a direct impact on their relations, not only with each other, but with the entire international community. Further, the transition currently underway, from state-dominated diplomacy (and based on state-centric ideas) to less hierarchical or linear structures, is likely to be difficult. Indeed, Robert Cooper, a former British diplomat and official in the European Union, argues that one of the biggest challenges is the question of relations between 'premodern' and 'postmodern' states, and while his position takes us some way down a path towards a more nuanced understanding (Cooper, 2003), issues still remain as to his chronologically-biased terminology and the lack of explanation as to what a recognition of this asymmetry between states might mean for diplomacy.

These concerns are undoubtedly shared by Brian Hocking and others of the Clingendael Institute of International Relations as demonstrated in their examination of this exact question. Building on Cooper, they outline what they call three "images" of diplomacy: statist (diplomacy as the processes and structures of bilateral and multilateral relations between sovereign states); globalist (a response to the "first wave" of writing on globalization that focused heavily on the 'demise' of the state as the primary actor); and finally, integrative (a move beyond the first two that is effectively "post-globalization") (Hocking, et al., 2012, 17–18). In so doing, they effectively address the problems of a strict chronology and 'old' vs 'new' by suggesting there is a "layering" in the system, as the practices of one image (or time frame) blend into the next. In their view, the final result is that world politics in the postmodern, "integrative era" are "driven by the logic of mutual interference in each other's domestic affairs, pursuing security through transparency and transparency through interdependence" (Hocking, et al., 2012, 19). This text effectively works on these same issues from the other direction. By recognizing the 'global state' as both a new form and a fact, looking back across time to see continuity rather than disjuncture, and asserting that the processes or interactions of diplomatic practice are the engine of change in the system as a whole, the hope is to arrive at a better position from which to understand the diplomacy between states (or whatever entities are considered significant in any given period of time) as well as the features that determine their relations, and the changes in those patterns that are seen today.

Finally, and perhaps most contentious, is the assertion that diplomacy—its mission and purpose—has not changed. This text defines **diplomacy** as *the mediation of the sources of social power and the systems of organization and mechanisms for communication (specifically dialogue, negotiation, and representation) between social entities*. Given the broadness of this view, it is crucial to make the case clear. The starting point is the straightforward observation that the existence of diplomacy as an institution is not dependent on the existence of the modern state. Diplomacy has mediated between the sources of social power (cultural, economic, political, and military) through time and evolved separately, but in parallel to our governing entities; from the idea of band-tribe-chief-state evolution to a more layered approach of localized tribes and kingdoms, regional frameworks of city-states to regional empires, and finally, nations to nation-states and global empires as technology enabled and enhanced an entity's ability to extend and maintain power further and further away from the base. The modern notion of the state has provided a relatively stable focus for our current system and hence the traditional study of diplomacy, but it is clear that the state per se does not extend back indefinitely. Diplomacy involves the relations between the entities through forms of social power reaching back to the beginnings of time and has shaped and reshaped the governing entities in the process (Sending, Pouliot, Neuman, 2015). The argument is therefore that it is only logical to assume that there is no reason to expect that the state—certainly not the Westphalian form of the state—will continue unchanged into the future. Thus, it is time to examine the current status of the states-system and offer some observations as to the models of interaction currently used or that are under construction as well as to look towards the next stage in this continuous evolution. The aim is to locate diplomacy, both in terms of its unchanging nature and the shifting character of the tools used, along points of a continuum that extends into the past and that may well also provide a guide as to what the future might bring.

This book is dedicated to the exploration of diplomacy, an institution developed to consciously and deliberately define and negotiate the spaces between societies, altering both the entity they represent and the institution itself in that process of interaction. Diplomats are forever caught between the natural, instinctive impulse to reach out and connect, and the equally deep-seated tendency of societies to fear those different from themselves. The institution and those who operate within it are both symbols and tools of power, maintaining a dialogue designed for peace, but often coming into its own during periods of conflict. This text will examine these roles in the hope and expectation that diplomacy will respond to the constant shift in global governance by continuing, through its mission of inter-cultural understanding and communication, to weave a richly patterned tapestry of peoples and societies.

References and Further Reading

Abbott, Andrew. "Things of Boundaries." *Social Research.* Vol. 62. No 4. (1995): 857–882.

Adler-Nissen, Rebecca. "Relationalism or why diplomats find international relations theory strange" in Ole Jacob Sending, Vincent Pouliot and Iver Neumann (eds). *Diplomacy and the Making of World Politics.* Cambridge: Cambridge University Press, 2015.

Black, Jeremy. *A History of Diplomacy.* London: Reaktion Books, 2010.

Bozeman, Adda. *Politics and Culture in International History.* Princeton: Princeton University Press, 1960.

Clark, Ian. *Globalisation and International Relations Theory.* Oxford: Oxford University Press, 1999.

Cooper, Robert. *The Post-Modern State and the World Order.* London: Demos, 1996.

Cooper, Robert. *The Breaking of Nations: Order and Chaos in the Twenty-first Century.* London: Atlantic Books, 2003.

Crumley, Carole L. "Heterarchy and the Analysis of Complex Societies" in *Heterarchy and the analysis of complex societies.* R. Ehrehreich, C. Crumley, and J. Levy (eds). American Anthropological Association Archeological Papers. 6, (1995): 1–6.

Crumley, Carole L. "Pattern recognition in social science." *Social Science newsletter.* Vol. 70, Issue 3, (1985): 176–179.

Hill, Christopher. *The Changing Politics of Foreign Policy.* Basingstoke: Palgrave, 2003.

Hocking, Brian, Jan Melissen Shaun, and Riordan Paul Sharp. *Futures for diplomacy: Integrative Diplomacy for the 21st century.* Clingendael: Netherland Institute of International Relations, 2012.

Hoffman, John. "Reconstructing Diplomacy." *British Journal of Politics and International Relations.* Vol 5. No 4., (2003): 525–542.

Jackson, Patrick and Daniel Nexon. "Relations Before Sates: Substance, Process and the Study of World Politics." *European Journal of International Relations.* Vol. 5 (3), (1999): 291–332.

Lee, Donna and David Hudson. "The Old and New Significance of Political Economy in Diplomacy." *Review of International Studies.* Vol. 30 No 3. (July, 2004): 343–360.

Mann, Michael. *The Sources of Social Power: A history of power from the beginning to A.D. 1760. Volume 1.* Cambridge: Cambridge University Press, 1986.

Neumann. "Euro-centric diplomacy: Challenging but manageable." *European Journal of International Relations.* 18, (2012): 299–321.

Sending, Ole Jacob, Vincent Pouliot and Iver Neumann (eds). *Diplomacy and the Making of World Politics.* Cambridge: Cambridge University Press, 2015.

Sharp, Paul. *Diplomatic Theory of International Relations.* Cambridge: Cambridge University Press, 2009.

Sharp, Paul, Stuart Murray, Geoffrey Wiseman, David Criekemans, and Jan Melisson. "The Present and Future of Diplomacy and Diplomatic Studies." *International Studies Review.* 13, (2011): 709–728.

Shaw, Martin. *Theory of the Global State: Globality as an Unfinished Revolution.* Cambridge: Cambridge University Press, 2000.

Shultz, George. "Diplomacy in the Information Age." Keynote address at the Virtual Diplomacy Conference, United States Institute of Peace, 1997.

Weisbrode, Kenneth. *Old Diplomacy Revisited.* New York: Palgrave, 2014.

Theories of Diplomacy

1 Diplomatic Practice

BY J. SIMON ROFE

One basic challenge in the study of diplomacy is what we call the 'theory *vs* practice' debate. The crux of this discussion is the perception there is a necessary disconnect between academics who often look at things from a broad, abstract perspective (i.e., 'theory') and the ambassador, or any other diplomat, who deals with practical issues on the ground (i.e., 'practice'). However, posing the question of whether theory should 'determine' policy (because big ideas are easier to deal with than complex and contested detail), or if practice is 'more important' (because it's real life), is a false dichotomy as diplomats spend most, if not all of their time crossing the line between theory and practice. In this text, a key point is that 'theory' and 'practice' are not distinct and need to be understood in relation to each other. In other words 'theory' and 'practice' do not exist in sealed boxes, but are terms that should be unpacked so we can see them as separate, but enmeshed aspects of a holistic discussion about the history and purpose of diplomacy.

The meaning of 'practice' as applied here to diplomacy, relies on ideas of *strategy*, *operations*, and *tactics*. Traditionally, this is visualized as a hierarchy with strategy, sometimes called a 'grand strategy,' at the very top. Below that strategic level, lie operations, and below that, we come to tactics. **Practice** as used here is understood to be *a level that effectively connects the 'bottom' of strategy and the 'top' of tactics.* (See Figure 1.1.) This overlapping position is important because practice is both strategy-driven and tactical as the constitutive aspect of operations/implementation.

This chapter introduces the practices of diplomacy to show the ways that diplomacy manifests in the world around us, both in terms of institutional operations and tactics. However, to enhance understanding of these practices, some theoretical concepts, notably the concept of 'power,' are also introduced.

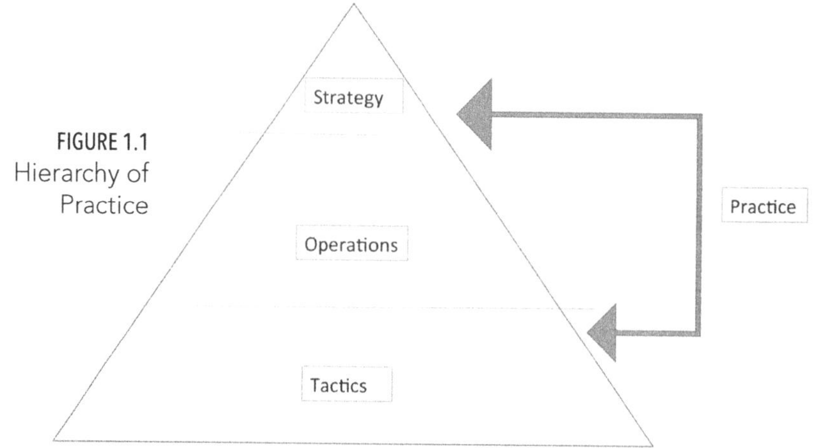

FIGURE 1.1 Hierarchy of Practice

These concepts and practices also serve as important reference points for the theories of diplomacy introduced in later chapters.

'Traditional' Power and Diplomacy

In his memoirs, former US Secretary of State (1982–1988) George P. Schultz stated, "Power and Diplomacy work *together*" (Schultz, 2010, 10). While that may be the ideal case, even a casual look at the way power is understood or operationalized in the world suggests that many consider this pairing unevenly matched. For international politics, power is commonly thought of as being 'over' a territory and/or a people. Hans Morgenthau, a strong realist (the concept of 'realism' will be discussed in greater depth in Chapter 2), long argued for the centrality of power and plainly argued that, "International politics, like all politics, is a struggle for power. Whatever the ultimate aims of international politics, power is always the immediate aim" (Morgenthau, 1978, 29).

Clearly, power is understood in different ways and manifests itself through many different practices and, as we shall see, in different types of diplomacy. While Morgenthau and other realists may consider power to be measured primarily by military might, diplomatic practice relies on other dimensions such as financial strength, cultural resilience, or the power of suasion, which can all go a long way towards achieving one's goals in international politics. Power matters insofar as power, be it perceived or real, can serve to facilitate or hinder the diplomatic process. In these circumstances, power may be about the ability to encourage or cajole parties to a particular outcome rather than to coerce an actor through its use—but whatever the source of power, it is rarely 'neutral.'

Joseph S. Nye recognized at least some aspects of this dilemma as the Cold War was drawing to a close when he promoted the term 'Soft Power' in his 1990 book *Bound to Lead: The Changing Nature of American Power*, and it has become part of the lexicon of statesmen and scholars ever since. Unfortunately, the term's broad use does not reflect its subtleties as it is generally used simply as the alternative/opposite to 'Hard Power,' the latter being the use of military capacity and what the military calls 'kinetic power.' Colloquially, hard power is the ability to blow things up, soft power the skill to achieve a goal without that application of force. The link to our discussion of diplomatic practices is logical if one accepts diplomatic scholar Herbert Butterfield's notion that "diplomacy may include anything short of actual war" (Butterfield, 1966, 10) (Butterfield was a member of the English School who will be discussed in more depth in Chapter 3). Nye's slightly less blunt argument is that "soft power rests on the ability to shape the preferences of others," or the ability to attract others to a particular course of action. Further, that "soft power is not merely influence, though it is one source of influence. Influence can also rest on the hard power of threats or payments. And soft power is more than just persuasion or the ability to move people by argument, though that is an important part of it" (Nye, 2008, 95).

Potentially confusing the relationship between power and diplomacy even further, soft power is often used as a poor synonym for **Public Diplomacy**, which is a tactic discussed later in this chapter. Whatever the corollary, power is clearly a contested subject as there is no single agreement or understanding of its constitutive elements; yet it is fundamental to our understanding of the world as it pervades much of our decision-making. Is power, the power to do something—to make or destroy something or someone? Or is power the power to change people's minds and change their lives? Power, in the abstract, has all of these facets to varying degrees; and while that is little consolation when facing an exam question, or the barrel of a loaded gun, power and diplomacy are distinct aspects of statecraft. The difficulty in terms of our understanding of power as a concept is related to the fact that international relations rarely locates power in a specific source, be it political, economic, military, or cultural. We will return to the point, but in the meantime, an outline of the basic processes and practices of diplomacy are needed to see how these power structures work and how they have evolved.

Fit for Purpose: Process of Diplomacy

A range of scholars have attempted to codify, classify, and catalogue diplomatic process, including Geoff Berridge in *Diplomacy: Theory and Practice* (Berridge, 2015). Nonetheless, in working towards an understanding of global diplomacy there are three activities core to each of the four types of diplomacy to be discussed in Part II: political, military, cultural, and economic. They are Communication, Representation, and Negotiation.

1. **Communication** *is at the heart of diplomatic processes. Being able to communicate in technical terms through appropriate language and symbols, and emotionally with fellow human beings, is vital to ensure messages are conveyed in the way they are intended* (Keller, 1956).

2. **Representation** *in diplomacy is about a group or individual ('a diplomat') representing and communicating on behalf of a constituency, be that a locale or a state, when too many voices risk the message being poorly articulated. In the classic understanding, this means having the endorsement of a state, thus a diplomat can distinguish him or herself from others adopting the term 'diplomat' or 'ambassador.'*

3. **Negotiation** *is the discussion, or conversation, that takes place between those representing a specific position with a view to reaching an agreement, even if the agreement is to keep negotiating.*

The purpose of diplomacy, as demonstrated through these three key activities, does not operate in isolation or in any specific, given sequence, but from this triumvirate emerge specific roles and institutions, and are all interrelated as the activity of one influences the other across types of diplomacy. As tactics become common, they produce practice; as strategy changes, tactics continue to evolve. Diplomacy is derived from these three purposes and is evident throughout all four types of diplomacy we identify, to create both the structures and outcomes of this process.

Diplomats, Embassies, and Ministries of Foreign Affairs

The discussion of diplomatic practice begins with what may be considered the most immediately obvious actors and locations: Diplomats and Embassies and Ministries of Foreign Affairs. These institutions are most commonly associated with the activities of nation-states, but as will be seen, the practice of diplomacy happens at many levels.

Diplomats

Put simply, diplomats are those who implement diplomacy through communication, representation, and negotiation. From ancient times through to the modern era, diplomats have been an elite within society, often those close to the seat of executive power. This access has been critical to their success as diplomats in communicating, representing, and negotiating with their interlocutors. Stereotypically, they are aloof and reserved, 'above politics,' and male. However, while the reality is considerably more complicated than the stereotype, there is a more pointed story that seeks to associate the diplomat with the state. Some scholars, and some diplomats, would argue that a diplomat is someone working on behalf of the state; indeed, this is the clear implication of the *Vienna Convention on Diplomatic Relations* (Bruns, 2014) that codified the roles and responsibilities of diplomatic relations as conducted by those accepted as 'diplomats.' The logic here is that those individuals representing actors other than states are just that—representatives without special standing or privilege.

It is also important to explore the corollary that diplomacy can be conducted by polities that are not states. Intergovernmental organizations such as the United Nations have both individuals as diplomats and to represent the apparatus of diplomacy, as they receive ambassadors and delegations from states, and have a functionally and geographically diverse bureaucracy for a variety of operations. The most important fact here is that the designation of 'diplomat' is essentially the accreditation they carry on behalf of their sovereign, whether that sovereign is a state, an intergovernmental organization, or single-issue campaigning group. This modern version differs in degree, but not entirely, from those conducting diplomacy in the distant past. For example, in the mid-seventeenth century, the representatives who gathered in Lower Saxony to negotiate what became known as the Treaty of Westphalia, covered in greater depth in the next chapter, were 'accredited' by a variety of 'pre'-state actors including princedoms and city-states—often simultaneously. This type of arrangement was typical of those conducting diplomacy in antiquity.

Ambassadors

The most powerful diplomats are Ambassadors as Chief of Mission; that is, they are the single most important individual in a diplomatic Mission, most often an Embassy. Yet the term and the role have evolved considerably from their emergence in the Renaissance (approximately 15-17th centuries). The ranking of diplomats was based on a complex system that essentially relied on the title of the sovereign. The term '*Ambassador*' was the preserve of the great powers of the day such as Spain, England, and France until the nineteenth century and the *Congress of Vienna* in 1815. After this gathering of those who had fought and won against Napoleon's Republican France, the increase in number and sense of 'equality' of status among states meant the term became synonymous for those representatives of one state in another. Those performing the role previously had used the title *Minister Plenipotentiary*—meaning minister with 'full powers' to act on behalf of their sovereign as if they were that sovereign—thus creating a situation in which issues of protocol become highly contentious as the treatment of a Minister Plenipotentiary by a host country was literally considered to be their treatment of the sovereign as a person. However, these two titles are sometimes conflated such as in the case of the Chief of Mission of the United States to the United Kingdom, whose full title is "Ambassador Extraordinary and Plenipotentiary to the Court of St James's"; the role being 'extraordinary' denotes the post as being the individual representative of the US President to the British monarch (Holmes & Rofe, 2012, 14).

The importance of rank in diplomacy is integral to its practice denoting the hierarchy in which diplomats operate. However, the ranking can be complex for at least two reasons. First, not all positions in the hierarchy are permanently filled by each state in relation to each bilateral arrangement. What this means in practice is that it is perfectly possible to have diplomatic relations without the exchange of ambassadors—those at the top of the hierarchy—or, as likely, there may be an exchange of ambassadors, but no military attaché. Second, appointments and longevity in many diplomatic posts, but most especially those at the top, often reflect the politics of the dispatching country. What these two factors mean is that the system is in a permanent state of flux, which allows for a number of exceptions or 'quirks' to the hierarchy.

Nonetheless, at the top is the Ambassador Extraordinary and Plenipotentiary and the hierarchy flows down through the Envoy Extraordinary and Plenipotentiary, and the Resident Minister or Counsellor Minister to the Chargé d'affaires as effectively the chief operating officer (see Figure 1.2). Other ad hoc positions may be created at the behest of a head of state, such as the Special Envoy. A specific example here would be the appointment by the United States of a Special Envoy for Northern Ireland, former Senator George Mitchell, in 1995, at the equivalent rank of Ambassador. With such ad hoc appointments, the question arises as to the longevity of the post. Formality has always been a part of the diplomat's life and is seen throughout the ambassadorial appointment. The process of *accreditation* is the presentation of a letter from the dispatching head of state that the appointee presents physically to the receiving head of state—typically with a great deal of pomp and circumstance. For example, the US Ambassador to the United Kingdom rides from the Embassy in a top hat and morning coat to Buckingham Palace in an open carriage and escorted by the Queen's guard on horseback. This procession makes quite a spectacle through the streets of London, but has become expected as a demonstration of the high regard both countries hold for each other.

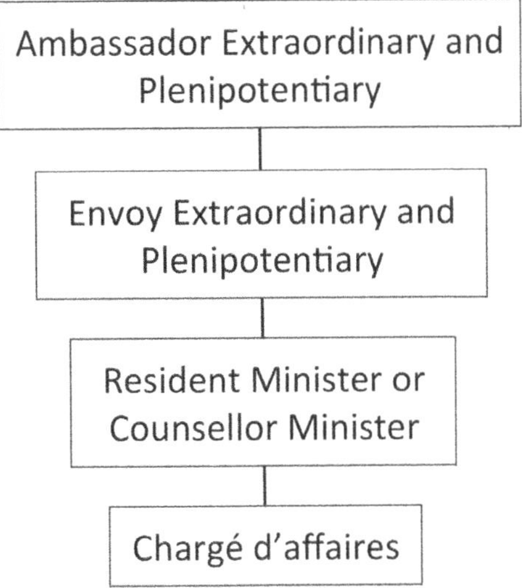

FIGURE 1.2 Hierarchy of Diplomatic Rank

Conducting Diplomacy

Changing the question 'from who they are' to 'what they do,' as Sir Brian Barder has done in his book *What Diplomats Do*, provides another lens through which to view the diplomat. Barder suggests that by the volume of their daily actions and interactions, diplomats (as representatives of a state) are conducting diplomacy—and formulating foreign policy at a micro-level: "foreign policy is being made daily around the world, in the tens of thousands of conversations, speeches, and symbolically pregnant actions of individual diplomats serving away from home" (Barder, 2014). Barder clearly outlines the diplomat's work through the 'day-to-day' application of the processes of communication, representation, and negotiation, rather than through such activities as the grandiose signing of a final agreement between heads of state. It is important to note, therefore, the diplomat's life contains much that is routine and mundane (Sharp, 2015, 40). The requirement to compile daily, weekly, monthly, and annual reports for the home capital; the role of representation requiring attendance of the state; the endless handshaking and photo calls can take their toll on even the most patient and well-trained individuals.

There were forty-five member states of the United Nations at the end of the Second World War, and there are now close to two hundred, each requiring representation. No state accredits a full ambassador to every other state, but there is little doubt that the overall volume of exchange of diplomatic representatives has increased with the increase in number of states.

However, there are others designated as 'ambassadors' and fulfilling the diplomatic processes who do not have any association with the official Foreign Service of a state. The realm of international affairs has become more congested in the late twentieth and into the twenty-first century, with a plethora of actors beyond the state and individuals adopting the title of 'ambassador' alongside the increase in the number of nation-states in the last century.

Diplomats and International Organizations

Indeed, the increasing range of diplomatic activity does not stop with the increasing number of states, as there are an ever-increasing number of non-state actors and civil society organizations through which diplomats operate. Organizations such as the International Committee of the Red Cross (ICRC), *Médecins Sans Frontières* (MSF), the European Union (EU), *Fédération Internationale de Football Association* (FIFA), and the International Olympic Committee (IOC), and many more have entered the stage. The ICRC is an interesting example of the breadth and depth of international organizations, as the ICRC is part of a parent international organization, the 'International Red Cross and Red Crescent Movement,' along with the 'International Red Cross and Red Crescent Societies,' with national societies in almost every state on the planet. In this example, it is clear how the public perception of an international organization has a network of supporting organizations behind it; and this is just one of the increasing number.

The development of international organizations since the mid-nineteenth century means a further tranche of diplomats have emerged. Beginning in 1945, the United Nations Organization (UN) started to receive Ambassadors from each of its member states as a permanent mission, and although the UN does not reciprocate by dispatching ambassadors back to the member states, the organization does have a cadre of its own 'ambassadors' as part of what has been identified as the 'second UN' (Weiss, et al., 2009). The United Nations system is a diverse conglomeration of distinct agencies, funds and programs (see Figure 1.3), and yet many of these components adopt the term 'ambassador' and the institutions of diplomacy. Geoff Wiseman has examined the way that the UN operates and identified a number of other evolving practices now ingrained in UN operations. By way of high-profile example, the former Spice Girl turned fashion designer, Victoria Beckham, became a UNAIDS International Goodwill Ambassador in September 2014, joining her husband, the former footballer, David Beckham, in the UN's ambassadorial ranks, as he has been a UNICEF Goodwill Ambassador since 2005.

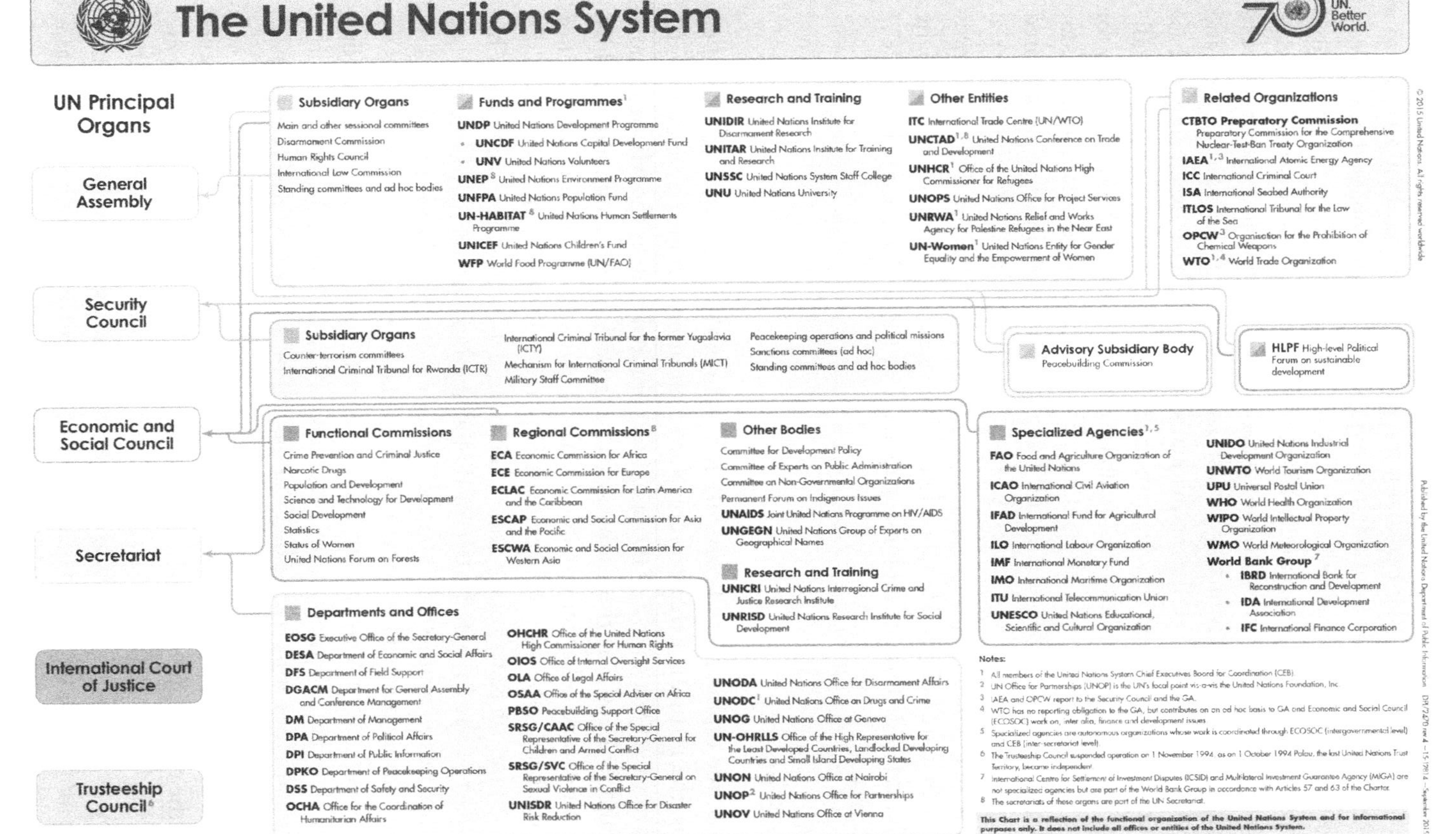

FIGURE 1.3 The United Nations System (Source: United Nations Department of Public Information, © 2015 United Nations. Reprinted with the permission of the United Nations.)

The notion of 'celebrity diplomat' is explored by Andrew Cooper (Cooper, 2007), and while the Beckhams are just two examples, they give rise to a number of questions about what is required to be an ambassador, not least amongst them: Can anyone be an ambassador? In a challenge to state-centric notions of diplomacy, the twenty-first century is an era where other non-state actors have adopted the title ambassador. Multinational corporations and major brands, cities, sporting occasions such as the Olympic Games and FIFA World Cup, as well as individual sports clubs have designated ambassadors, fulfilling at the very least the role of representation. What this indicates is that the term has become ubiquitous in sections of global society for a particular way of transacting affairs. The heritage of the term ambassador and its perceived poise and sound judgment are qualities that are admired and relevant beyond the state. As such, the evolution of the ambassadorial title to apply in multiple contexts says a good deal about the diplomatic processes that are being undertaken beyond the state's purview. It is emblematic of the expanded use of diplomacy in areas of the global society beyond the nation-state.

The Embassy

While the diplomat, and particularly the ambassador, provide an individual focus, the institution that requires particular attention in the conduct of diplomacy over the course of the last three hundred years is the **Mission**, more commonly known as **the Embassy** (see Figure 1.4). Although ambassadors, emissaries, and other representatives have been a feature of interaction since records began, the idea of a **resident or permanent mission** comes from the City-States of Renaissance Italy (Venice and Florence, for example). This was part of the French System of diplomacy, built on the need to carry out the diplomatic processes in a specific place necessitated by the increased flow of mercantile trade. This 'system' required the reciprocal exchange of 'ambassadors' and, given their relative lack of expertise or interest on occasion (due to the fact that their appointment is a function of their relationship to the sovereign), they were increasingly supported by a staff who collectively make up the embassy of today.

The embassy is seen as a physical representation of the diplomatic process with the embodiment of one nation-state on the territory of another. Technically, the buildings that tend to be located in capital cities, and that are often, but by no means exclusively, grandiose, are the **chancery**, and the diplomatic delegation made up of ambassador and ministers constitute the embassy as a whole (Holmes & Rofe, 2012). Equally, the embassy's physical space is not

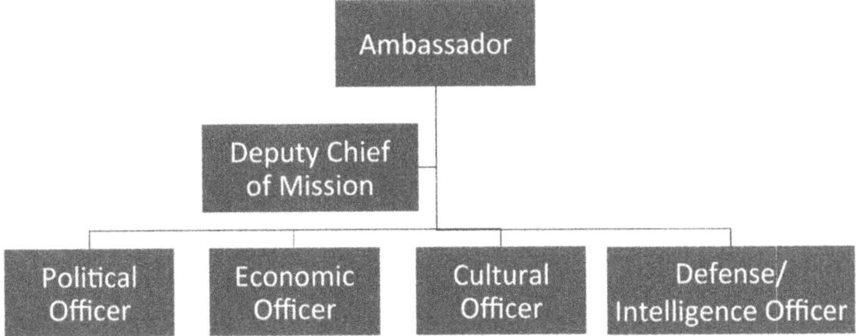

FIGURE 1.4 The Embassy, also known as the 'Country Team'

sovereign to the represented state despite popular assumptions brought about by Hollywood's proclivity to advance their storylines at the expense of accuracy. The symbolism of the chancery buildings and their diplomatic role, explored in Jane Loeffler's *Architecture of Diplomacy* (2010), can be significant if not determinative to the message of a diplomatic mission. For example, in the post-9/11 reappraisal of security for US Embassies around the world, security measures were increased and enhanced. Thus, as American chanceries literally became fortified and inaccessible, the perception of the United States as a warlike, militarized nation rose around the world.

Recent discussion of the embassy as a resident mission has focused upon its demise. Berridge argues, in *The Counter-Revolution in Diplomacy,* that many of the forces that suggest the end of the resident mission have, in fact, reinforced its utility within an environment of increased politicization and securitization of diplomacy while budget cuts have prompted "only generated greater resourcefulness" (Berridge, 2012, 5). The same prerogative for resourcefulness on behalf of the resident mission has also been felt by its partner in diplomatic marriage: the Ministry of Foreign Affairs, which will be discussed below.

Both embassies and consulates, and the diplomats who staff them, form a network that provides for the diplomatic processes of communication, representation, and negotiation. The embassy has assumed a number of roles in diplomacy: a symbolic place representing the nation and, as such, a site of both memorialization and protest; the home to high-level meetings for negotiation and communication; and the venue of many individual exchanges from the visa section to social occasions. These functions are supplemented by those of consulates who are governed by the *Vienna Convention on Consular Relations,* signed in 1963, and whose role is to deal with nationals of the represented state, particularly on matters of trade and visas (see Box 1.1).

BOX 1.1

Passports and Visas

Passports are the common document of international travel and always a form of request. For example, the British passport (also an official document of the European Union) "requests and requires" in "the Name of Her Majesty" that "all those whom it may concern to allow the bearer to pass freely without let or hindrance." The United States passport "hereby requests" that "the person named herein to pass without delay or hindrance."

The term visa is derived from Latin, *chartas visa,* meaning "papers which have been seen" and grants a right of passage for a non-citizen to another nation-state, normally for a specific period of time and purpose such as employment or study. Visas are not always needed for international travel, as states may have negotiated agreements freeing their citizens from such arrangements, such as the 'Schengen Area' comprising twenty-eight states in Europe where border controls have been abolished (in 2015 over 400 million people live in this area).

One of the key diplomatic tasks of embassy and consular staff relates to these important forms of diplomatic documentation, demonstrated by the fact that the word diplomacy has its roots in the Greek for "diploma" or "folded paper" (Black, 2010, 20), used as a way to identify a traveler and the entity they represented.

However, the origin of the term "passport" is disputed. Some suggest it is a medieval document issued by local authorities for passage through the gate ("porte") of a city wall and listed specific towns and cities where the holder was allowed—though they could also be banned (an early version of the 'no fly list'). Others contend the term is a combination of the French term for passage, *passe,* with port referring to sea ports—as open trading points.

The Bible has one of earliest references when Nehemiah, an official serving King Artaxerses I of Persia, asked for permission to travel to Judea. The king gave him a letter addressed "to the governors beyond the river" requesting safe passage. In a slightly different form, a medieval Islamic Caliphate used a *bara'a* or receipt of paid taxes as a passport as only people who had proof of payment could travel.

While most think of a passport as a document of citizenship or residence, its real role is to prove nationality and identity and hence it is closely associated with the nation state. The authority to issue passports is founded on each nation's executive discretion (the sovereign or Crown prerogative) and certain legal tenets follow. First, passports are issued in the name of the

(continues)

(continued)

state; second, no person has a legal 'right' to a passport; third, each nation's government has complete discretion to refuse or to revoke a passport; and fourth, that discretion is not subject to judicial review. There are notable exceptions. For example, the British monarch does not carry papers and while the Vatican has no immigration controls, it does issue passports. The Pope always carries "Passport No 1."

The earliest surviving British reference to such a document was in the reign of Henry V in a 1414 Act of Parliament as a single sheet of folded paper in Latin and English, designed to help his subjects prove themselves while abroad to conduct trade. At that time, such documents could be issued by the king to anyone, regardless of their origin. From 1540, this task became the business of the Privy Council and the oldest surviving British passport was signed by Charles I on June 18, 1641.

The expansion of the railways across Europe from the mid-nineteenth century led to a decline in the use of passports in the thirty years prior to World War I as the speed and number of passengers (and lack of education) made enforcement almost impossible. However, as the war began, spying put passports on the security agenda, especially after the capture and execution in November 1914 of Carl Hans Lody, a German spy living in Britain using a fake US passport. This event also spurred 'The British Nationality and Status of Aliens Act' of 1914. Passports were still a single page, but folded into eight with a cardboard cover including a description and photograph (the spread of photo booths from the 1880s helped standardize them by default).

The format became internationally standardized in 1920 by the League of Nations' *Paris Conference on Passports & Customs Formalities and Through Tickets.* Two further international conferences added requirements on the number and quality of the photos including that they show "full face" and "no hats."

The network as a whole is often referred to as the diplomatic corps—a term based on the idea of *esprit des corps* amongst the group and fostered by the common predicament of diplomats in a particular location. They are 'led' in any given place, by the person known as the 'dean' or 'doyen,' a title granted to an ambassador on the basis of being the longest serving diplomat in that specific place. Intriguingly, this illustrates a quality to diplomacy that favors a temporal dimension over power, particularly hard power, and means that you could have the ambassador from a relatively weak nation-state as the most senior member of a diplomatic corps in a particular nation, rather than the ambassador from what may be perceived to be the most powerful nation. At the end of 2015, for example, Roble Olhaye, the Ambassador of the Republic of Djibouti, a very small country though strategically placed where the Red Sea meets the Gulf of Aden, is the Dean of the Diplomatic Corps in Washington, D.C., by virtue of having been in the post since September 2005. Also key are the increasing number and variety of access points to the network in the globalized society of the late twentieth and early twenty-first centuries.

Ministry of Foreign Affairs

While the evolution of the overseas Resident Mission and its Chief can trace its genealogy to the early Renaissance, the Ministry of Foreign Affairs at home is generally considered a relatively modern invention. The **Ministry of Foreign Affairs (MFA)** is the entity within a government that has responsibility for a nation-state's foreign and diplomatic service, i.e., the organizational and administrative framework in which foreign policy is made and diplomacy conducted. A single date—1626—exists for the creation of the first Ministry of Foreign Affairs in France, yet little fanfare surrounds the date as such ministries have rarely been celebrated or even understood. From that first initiative, there was over a century until the United Kingdom created its Foreign Office in 1782, though the United States followed shortly thereafter by creating the Department of State in 1789, shortly after gaining its independence from the United Kingdom.

The rationale for the creation of the first MFA in 1626 was the desire by **Cardinal Richelieu**, Chief Minister of France, and a post that was the forerunner to the post of Prime Minister, to articulate and pursue *raison d'état*, that is 'reason of state,' or more commonly interpreted as 'national interest,' on behalf of France. The establishment of a Foreign Ministry was due to Richelieu's desire to support his diplomats 'in the field' and his belief that diplomacy required *négociation continuelle* or 'continuous negotiation'—as well as representation and communication—to ensure a constant expression of *raison d'état* through the messages he sent via his extensive network. In this regard, the Ministry of Foreign Affairs began to provide support to the diplomatic service and present a centralized and coordinated means of message dissemination and intelligence gathering.

Long into the twentieth century, a number of states maintained the duality of a ministry looking outward and articulating foreign policy, and a diplomatic service to security national interests overseas (Berridge, 2010) before reconciling them under one administrative roof. A more recent trend has been to incorporate trade, international development, and aid portfolios within the MFA's remit, even when that has meant sharing titles. For

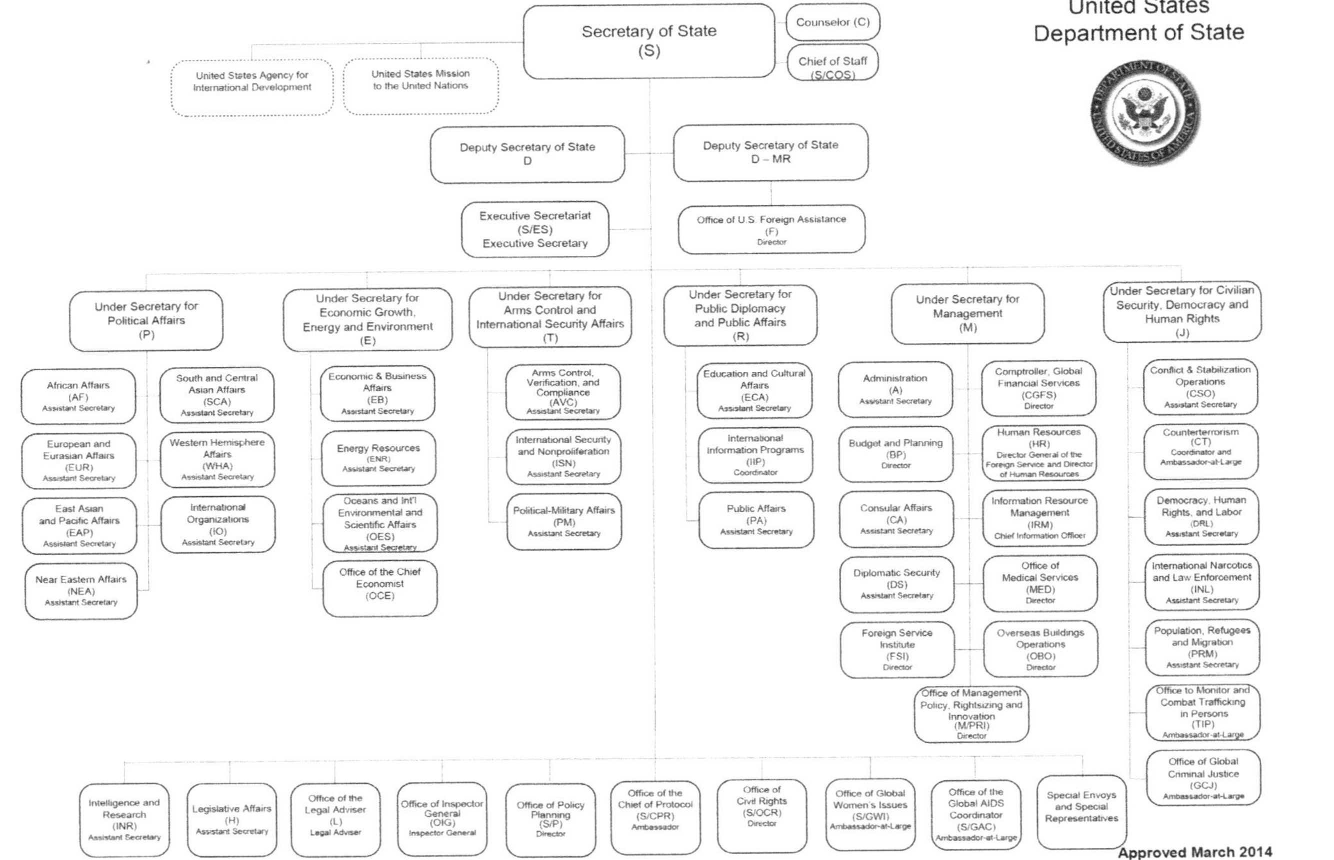

FIGURE 1.5 Structure of the United States' MFA, in this case, the State Department (Source: United States Department of State)

example, the Australian MFA became the Department of Foreign Affairs and Trade in 1987, and the Australian Agency for International Development (Aus AID), after thirty-nine years of independent existence, was folded into DFAT in 2013 (www.dfat.edu.au).

An important point to make is that while the titles and roles of Ambassador and Embassy have been adopted by those in other walks of life, when used by a Ministry of Foreign Affairs, it remains the preserve of the nation-state and therefore logical that the head of the Ministry is the Foreign Minister; and a minister of state with cabinet states within a nation's government. The importance of the Foreign Ministry in safeguarding national interest is seen in the prominence of the post within governments, second only to that of prime minister or president.

Tactics through Time

While an apparatus of diplomacy is manifested in embassies and Ministries of Foreign Affairs and carried out by diplomats, 'tactical' practices are the different ways diplomacy has been deployed over time. Looking back at the hierarchy of practice outlined at the beginning of the chapter (Figure 1.1), the bottom category would be 'pure' **tactics,** *the specific and direct actions taken at a given moment in time as part of an operation and/or in pursuit of a strategy.* However, just because they are a final step or the most direct form of action, they should not be assumed to be small or insignificant. Tactics 'on the ground' can have a dramatic effect on strategy and often become 'standard practice.' For example, when Louis the German and his brother, Charles, of West Frankia, met in 870 to negotiate peace it was more of a tactic in a larger operation in pursuit of a specific strategy. Whereas, by the twelfth century, these meetings between heads of state or 'summits' were more common so the meeting of the main players to resolve a papal issue at the Peace of Venice in 1177 had become part of what could be called diplomatic practice (Black, 2010, 24) and used across many types of diplomacy.

In this section, these 'tactical' practices will be examined, earning diplomacy a number of labels. This is not intended to be a comprehensive list, but four broad categories are offered beginning with 'personal' diplomacy, before looking at 'summit' and 'crisis' diplomacy, then 'conference' or 'track two' diplomacy, and finally, 'public diplomacy.' It is important to be clear that this list is illustrative rather than exhaustive in that there are numerous other activities or tactics that could be included. In fact, the prevalence of prefixes that can be applied to diplomacy raises neatly the question of the ubiquity of the term *diplomacy* if it is not to mean 'everything' and thus 'nothing.' More importantly, these 'tactical' approaches can also map onto each type of diplomacy so that one can identify most readily the elements of 'political' in summit diplomacy, 'cultural' in public diplomacy, and 'economic' in conference diplomacy. Again, there is no prescription; rather an evolution of the practices of diplomacy that allow for greater comprehension.

Personal Diplomacy

The first practice of diplomacy is at the level of the individual, linking the cast of characters discussed above and reflecting diplomacy's intensely personal quality as the core functions of diplomacy: communication, representation, and negotiation ultimately come back to individuals 'talking to each other.' Of course, communication is not always a virtue and history is littered with examples of the meeting of individuals resulting in a deterioration of peace and security. Nonetheless, key aspects of individual or **personal diplomacy** are manifest in the 'diplomats' we encountered at the state level, such as the ambassador or counsellor and, as such, have been deconstructed in recent scholarship. In other words, how important is the individual: How does the personality or psychology of these people influence their ability to fulfill the functions of diplomacy as individuals? (Neumann, 2005; Constantinou, 2006). Clearly, an individual who has held a diplomatic post has his or her own personality—even when they try not to not let it show. Sumner Welles, US undersecretary of state (1937-1943) when acting as presidential envoy to Europe in 1940, was famously reluctant to say anything. He earned the nickname 'Sumner the Silent' from the press and introduced to the world the phrase "no comment." Future British Prime Minister Winston S. Churchill so admired Welles' term that he is supposed to have remarked, "'No Comment' is a splendid expression. I am using it again and again" (Rofe, 2007, 175).

As discussed previously, diplomats are not restricted to state-sponsored individuals, and therefore there is a case to consider an approach to public diplomacy that focuses upon the relationship between civil societies who are connecting with each other and performing, often subconsciously, the functions of diplomacy (Golan, et. al., 2014). Therefore, while diplomacy is traditionally envisaged as being centered on the state and a state-sponsored individual such as an ambassador, we should consider that global diplomacy encompasses these individual actors. The broader cast will be returned to once personal diplomacy has been addressed in its most prominent form by returning to the ambassador.

In contemplating the personal dynamics of diplomacy we encounter a conception of 'power' that foregrounds the individual rather than the state per se. The distinction, such as it is, is with the polity that held and wielded power, usually the state, which, at some level, has to invest its 'power' in an individual; this is why the title of plenipotentiary carries such weight and meaning. However, there is a real tension here for those with plenipotentiary responsibilities and the difference between an ambassador wielding the power of their sovereign and their capacity to wield individual power. In reality, the 'power' given by the sovereign trumps their individual powers in the vast majority of cases across time. In other words, there is little room for their individual agency (Sharp, 2009).

However, the value of exploring the idea of personal diplomacy here is to illustrate there is still some room for maneuver for any 'diplomat' in certain circumstances and at certain times. In this regard, the diplomat has the capacity to exercise 'power,' and because of that they are "morally accountable subjects" (Bjola, 2016, 1). One such example is Sir Henry Wotton (1568-1639), an English scholar and ambassador to Venice during the Renaissance. He is now most famous for his definition of an ambassador as "an honest man, sent to lie abroad for the good of his country." Originally written in Latin—the lingua franca of diplomacy at the time—as *Legatus est vir bonus, peregrè missus ad mentiendum Reipublicae causâ* (Wotton, 1604). His remark became the source of potential controversy both for Wotton's sovereign, King James, and his hosts in Venice. Wotton's first biographer, the English writer Izaak Walton, famous for his work *The Compleat Angler* (1653), recorded that King James thought the slight "to be such an oversight, such a weakness, or worse," for the King to "express much wrath against him." Wotton's response was to illustrate his personal diplomatic qualities. He first composed a public repost to his sovereign's detractors in Italy and Prussia—the quote having been lifted from Wotton's private remarks and published some eight years after Wotton penned them in a colleague's guest book (and the source of his pun on the word 'lie'). Wotton then wrote a private response to the King "so clear, and so choicely eloquent" that, according to Walton, he became "much more confirmed in his Majesty's estimation and favor than formerly he had been" (Walton, 1898). In this instance, Wotton's personal diplomacy was to enhance his individual standing with his sovereign and his host, to the extent he returned to this post in Venice and remained there for a further decade.

Illustrating an alternate manifestation of personal diplomacy, we can look to the case of US Ambassador William C. Bullitt in Paris (1936-1940) at the outbreak of the Second World War in Europe. A Francophile and fluent French-speaker, Bullitt was closely engaged in the highest government circles and close to both Leon Blum and Edouard Daladier, both Prime Ministers during Bullitt's time. Bullitt was also in regular, and personal, contact with US

President Franklin D. Roosevelt to the point that he believed, and relayed to his Parisian interlocutors, that he was acting not only as the president's ambassador to France but to Europe as a whole. This was a notion of his personal importance that the president, unfortunately, did not disabuse him of. As France fell to advancing German forces in the early summer of 1940, the ambassador directly disobeyed an order from the State Department to follow the French government into exile. Instead, he stayed in Paris, believing that an American ambassador should remain in the capital as they had done during the French Revolution (1789–1799), the Napoleonic Wars (1803–1815), and the Franco-Prussian War (1870–71). As the 'de facto Mayor of Paris,' Bullitt oversaw the transfer of the city to German occupation at the Hotel de Crillon: directly next door to the US Embassy. This exercise of 'personal diplomacy' had mixed results. On the one hand, Bullitt's conduct cost him his diplomatic career, as President Roosevelt, his sovereign, personally saw to it that he never held public office again. On the other, Bullitt's assistance as de facto mayor in declaring Paris an 'open city,' with the Germans on the verge of attacking, saved the city from the destruction wrought on Rotterdam and Warsaw by Nazi forces (Bullitt, 1972; Alexander, 1991; Roberts, 2015).

However, there are other instances of personal diplomacy undertaken by those without a direct state portfolio. Since the mid-1990s, Irish rock star Paul Hewson, known as Bono, has held numerous meetings with heads of state including the American and Russian premiers, the Pope, and General Secretaries of the United Nations, and has spoken at the World Economic Forum in Davos and at the G8 (the governmental forum of leading world economies). As part of the hugely commercially successful group U2, he has spoken consistently on the issue of poverty reduction, especially in Africa, and human rights as a 'Celebrity Diplomat' (Cooper, 2007). Bono's commitment in this role, and his advocacy of these issues through diplomatic channels, illustrates his credentials in conducting personal diplomacy as an unofficial ambassador for these causes. In all of these examples, we can see that personal diplomacy depends on the concepts of both credibility and legitimacy and to the related notion of trust.

Trust

In practicing diplomacy, and particularly personal diplomacy, trust matters because, at some level, communication relies on being able to trust the interlocutor. The importance of trust in conducting personal diplomacy is neatly summarized by US Secretary of State James Baker III (1989–1992), explaining how both President George H.W. Bush (1989–1993) and he conceived of trust: "You're always better off if you can trust the guy across the table, but you'll never know that until you test him. If he agrees to some things, if he ever welshes on you or if he ever lies to you, then you've got a problem" (Baker, 2011). Trust therefore becomes part of the practice of diplomacy as it entails dealing with the 'other.' The 'other' being referred to here, draws upon Prussian philosopher Georg Hegel's idea of one's own self-consciousness, requiring an 'other' (Miller, 1977), as such the human condition requires self-awareness in relation to other human beings and entities. For our purpose of exploring the bifurcated relationship between power and trust in diplomacy, we can draw on Constantinou's assertion that diplomacy comprises "an ensemble of practices, power struggles, and truth contestations that develop into a dominant discourse for dealing with the other" (Constantinou, 1996, 110). In other words, diplomatic practice requires trust.

The scholarly work of Reinhard Bachmann (2011a, 2011b) explains how trust manifests itself in trans-organizational relationships and why it is important to comprehend institutional-based trust in relation to individual trust, i.e., the other institutions of diplomacy and diplomats that diplomats encounter. As related specifically to personal diplomacy, Bachmann argues that trust and power "are generated at the interpersonal level" and that "either trust or power dominates the relationship" (Bachman, 2001, 338).

However, trust is difficult to assess: a simple, but notable truth germane to the practice of diplomacy. Baroness Onora O'Neill, in delivering the BBC's Reith Lectures in 2002 under the title of "A Question of Trust?" posited a "crisis of trust" in the modern world (O'Neill, 2002). O'Neill, a student of John Rawls, author of *A Theory of Justice* (1971) and a leading light in political philosophy in the twentieth century, argued that there are more and more reasons not to 'trust' in a globalized world as levels of transparency increase. O'Neill suggested that "A more serious and practical approach to trust . . . would concentrate on showing what we need in order to judge others' honesty, reliability, and competence so that we can place or refuse trust intelligently" (O'Neill, 2009). The essential point O'Neill makes is that trust is always a judgment; it can never be absolute—"trust is needed precisely because all guarantees are incomplete" (O'Neill, 2002). For the diplomat, their practice is to judge where trust can be placed.

Summit Diplomacy

The use of trust in relation to power, and the capacity for mistrust and distrust are evident in a particular form of diplomacy that primarily involves a cast of individuals, but set on the stage of a '**summit**.' The study of summits and summitry entails the gathering of sovereigns and the skills of operating in that environment. Though they have been a feature of diplomatic negotiations for many centuries, summits of political leaders from the world's leading powers held particular sway in the latter half of the twentieth century, as a logical extension of the arrival of conference diplomacy (explained presently) in the nineteenth century. The longer heritage of the summit, or *parlee* or *parley* derived from the French word for 'speaking,' stems from the truces agreed to by warring parties to end conflicts and disputes. Summits were facilitated by improvements in technology, particularly intercontinental air travel, and University of Cambridge Professor David Reynolds' 2007 book, *Summits: Six Meetings That Shaped the Twentieth Century,* gives neat expression to this temporal concentration (Reynolds, 2007). Also important, the prevalence of summits aligns with the period known as the Cold War, as the apogee of realist state-based diplomacy.

The adoption of the term 'summit' can be attributed to British Prime Minister Winston S. Churchill during his second premiership from October 1951 to April 1955. As one of his many other contributions to the English lexicon, Churchill used the term in his pursuit of a gathering of the leaders of the wartime allies (UK, US, USSR, and France) with the endorsement of US President Dwight D. Eisenhower. The president, concerned at the prospect that the Soviet Union would use the event as a propaganda *coup*, declined to take up Churchill's offer. However, Eisenhower acquiesced as Cold War tensions increased and the summit eventually took place in the summer of 1955, in Geneva—though Churchill had resigned on health grounds by that time. The term was adopted by various aspects of the media who later came to apply it specifically to the meetings of US and Soviet leaders, at the same time as there was a global quest to reach the 'summit' of the world's tallest mountain, Mount Everest in Nepal, a feat that was achieved by Sir Edmund Hilary and Tenzing Norgay, his Sherpa guide, on May 29, 1953. A further parallel between the world of diplomacy and that of mountain climbing can be seen in the adoption of the term **sherpa**, i.e., helper, for those individuals who help prepare for a summit. The term was adopted within the European Union and used during intergovernmental conferences, before entering into the parlance of the G-8 and broader governmental circles (the G-8 will be discussed presently), though the increasing number of summits, or at least international gatherings that have adopted the term 'summit,' have gradually called their overall efficacy into question (Dunn, 2004).

Crisis Diplomacy

Diplomacy often captures the attention of politicians and the broader public at moments of high drama and crisis, normally of an acute political nature.

Hence, it is in a crisis that politics, as a type of diplomacy, is most evident. In an important way it can be said that crises arise when diplomacy 'fails': had diplomacy maintained a peaceful equilibrium, then there would have been no crisis. Nonetheless, diplomacy in a crisis does take place, as indeed does diplomacy in war and once again involves the individual/individuals and allows for the exercise of their personal diplomacy. **Crisis diplomacy** also has a relationship with the concepts of marketing communication's 'crisis management' and, in turn, to 'public relations.' These connections, as we shall see, also illustrate the interconnectedness of the tactics of diplomacy included in this chapter, and contribute to our recent understanding of public diplomacy. Nevertheless, 'crisis management' and 'public relations' are distinct concepts; the former relating to an organization's response to a major threat to that organization, and the latter the presentation of an organization to its stakeholders. Parallels with crisis diplomacy are evident insofar as the organization could easily be the nation-state, and one of the functions of diplomacy is of 're-presentation.'

Crises in international affairs come in all shapes and sizes for the nation-state; the threat or reality of invasion by foreign armies; hordes of refugees or natural disaster; or a run on the currency can all provide for acute moments of 'crisis' and necessitate a compressed decision-making timeframe. In direct contrast to the basic notion that diplomacy takes time and trust, crisis diplomacy is characterized by a shortened timespan.

Philip Habib, a Lebanese-American diplomat who served as US President Ronald Reagan's Middle East envoy (1981–1983), described how the method or practice of crisis diplomacy operates: "first of all, you have to decide what it is you want to do, whether you want to do something about it or whether you don't want to do something about it...and that usually does not take very long because if it's a crisis, you've got to get right on to it, then you've got to decide about the mechanics, the methods" (Habib, 1982). These methods are those core functions of diplomacy: communication, representation, negotiation. "They just happen to be concentrated in a tighter time-frame." And generally, Habib goes on to say, "with respect to a very specific problem rather than in terms of broad foreign policy issues." It is therefore little surprise that Habib's prescription for crisis diplomacy resembles closely the remedy diplomats are entrusted with more broadly: "no crisis is resolved unless there is a degree of restraint, unless there's a degree of understanding and agreement, and there usually has to be a degree of compromise" (Habib, 1982).

An example of crisis diplomacy occurred in the late summer of 1938 when British Prime Minister Neville Chamberlain decided he had to do something to address the crisis between Germany and Czechoslovakia (as it was at the time) over the Sudetenland. With strong memories of how Europe, and then the rest of the world, had been drawn into the Great War, Chamberlain sought to negotiate directly with German Chancellor Adolf Hitler before the crisis escalated into conflict. On three occasions in September 1938, Chamberlain took the then-unprecedented step for a prime minister of boarding an airplane and flying to Germany (15th to Berchtesgaden, 23rd to Godesburg, and 29th to Munich). As the likelihood of another war rose and Germany's military forces prepared themselves for combat, the crisis deepened for those seeking to avoid conflict. Chamberlain's crisis diplomacy, blending his personal approach and the constrained timeframe, did bring a resolution in the 'Munich Agreement' dated September 29, 1938, which ceded the Sudetenland to Germany without war. However, his tactics in the 'Sudeten Crisis' were criticized less than a year later (September 1, 1939) for failing to check Hitler's ambitions.

For these purposes, his traveling back and forth to deal with Hitler face to face had two other implications. Firstly, the quick succession of journeys between London and Germany is an early example of what was later termed "Shuttle Diplomacy" in describing US Secretary of State Henry Kissinger's intervention between the protagonists of the Yom Kippur War in late 1973. It has subsequently been applied to other diplomatic episodes, particularly involving the broader Middle East crisis, but also including the trips made by later Secretary of State Alexander Haig to Buenos Aires and London to mediate in the conflict over the Falkland Islands in the early 1980s. The second implication, and one which will be addressed shortly, is the involvement of technology in diplomatic practice. In the case of Chamberlain's diplomacy in 1938, this was the basic airplane; and although the first powered flight had been made in the first decade of the twentieth century, its potential to facilitate diplomacy was not realized until this episode in the late 1930s.

Crises do not just afflict states. In the case of the terrorist attack on the 1972 Olympics, the crisis and the associated diplomacy involved: the city of Munich, the Bavarian regional state authorities, the International Olympic Committee (IOC) as well as the host nation (the Federal Republic of Germany—then West Germany), the victims' country, Israel, and those believed to have supported the Black September organization which carried out the attack (Reeve, 2001). The events that marred the 1972 Summer Olympiad took place on September 5, 1972 and resulted in the death of eleven members of the Israeli Olympic team, a German police officer, and five of the eight terrorists at the Fürstenfeldbruck airfield during a botched rescue.

The absence of the nation-state is notable in the diplomacy surrounding the crisis. While US President Richard M. Nixon was aware of the crisis on

September 5, the administration chose to work through the United Nations, although the speed of events meant the efforts of the UN went unrealized. Even the IOC's own attempts to remain apolitical drew fierce criticism from the broader public, as IOC president Avery Brundage stated in the Olympiastadion Munich on September 6: the "Games must go on" (Ellis, 1972). Thus, despite the fact competition had been suspended for the first time in the history of the modern games, they resumed on September 7.

The broader diplomatic implications were evident in a heightened sense of tension across the Middle East, not helped when Black September sympathizers hijacked Lufthansa Flight 615 on October 29 and demanded the return of the three surviving hostage-takers. Mindful of the denouement in September, West German authorities acquiesced to the demand, and after an exchange of the passengers for the prisoners in Zagreb, the terrorists were offered asylum by General Gadhafi in Libya. More particularly, the aftermath of the crisis included the establishment within Germany, and a range of other countries, of elite anti-terror units, while the Israeli response led to military and intelligence operations against those suspected of involvement. The episode illustrates the fact that diplomacy does not always provide the time necessary or the capacity to work effectively in a crisis.

Conference Diplomacy

Conference diplomacy has gained greater prominence in the post-Cold War era, although its heritage lies in the coming together of the European 'Great Powers' of the nineteenth century (generally deemed to be Austria, Prussia, Great Britain, and France), and therefore pre-dates summitry (Groom, 2013). Johan Kaufmann describes conference diplomacy as "the management of relations between governments and of relations between governments and intergovernmental organizations that takes place in international conferences" (Kaufmann, 1996, 1–2)—a definition that clearly emphasizes the nation-state and its contribution to international affairs.

However, conference diplomacy does not solely involve the nation-state. For example, the International Olympic Committee (IOC) has annual sessions of its hundred elected members, and thirty or so honorary members, to discuss a range of issues such as the awarding of future Olympic Games and any matters arising that affect the IOC's mission. The awarding of the Games—a *summit* in Olympic terms—and the annual sessions have a mimicking quality to that of the United Nations' annual General Assembly meetings each fall, and the *summit* meetings that often characterize the gathering of the Security Council.

Conference diplomacy is largely distinguished from summitry and crisis diplomacy by the absence of particular temporal pressure and an increase in scale either in terms of numbers of participants and/or frequency of meetings. Scholar Volker Rittberger's typology divides conference diplomacy into two: one that is "action-orientated," leading to specific outcomes or agreements; and a second type of "rule-making" which seeks to govern some aspect of the international environment (Rittberger, 1983). Conferences can be regularly scheduled, permanent, or ad hoc and bring together a familiar cast of characters or new polities. Nation-states have traditionally been the main participants, although membership is broadening to include other actors. Whatever their configuration, the altered time frame and scale do not mean serene progress is a feature of conference diplomacy. Conference diplomacy is characterized by adherence to procedure and process, which tends to reinforce the value of the traditional diplomat's role—and the search for alternative forms of diplomacy by those with executive power. Importantly, these diplomats do not always need to be associated states, but can represent transnational bodies themselves (Rittberger, 1983).

While conference diplomacy tends to privilege the political process, the subject of the conference is not restricted to political matters. Indeed, conference diplomacy has evolved since the early 1970s to address economic, humanitarian, environmental, and cultural issues as they have gained an increasing global relevance, reinforcing the processes of globalization. Perhaps the most prominent example is the United Nations Conference on Environment and Development (UNCED) in Rio de Janeiro for two weeks in June 1992, better known as the Rio 'Earth Summit' (and illustrating the coming together of both 'conference' and 'summit' diplomacy). The gathering of representatives from 172 national governments amounted to over 98 percent of the states. Over a hundred of those governments were represented by their head-of-state (the largest ever), while almost two-and-a-half-thousand representatives of non-governmental organizations gathered for the parallel event, the 'Global Forum.' Diplomacy on this scale challenged diplomats to make agreements in ways their predecessors could not have imagined. The conference was able to operate and the efficacy of its agreements—notably the Climate Change Convention which led to the 1997 Kyoto Protocol on greenhouse gas emissions—were debated on the merits of their content rather than the diplomatic practice (Conca and Dabelko, 2014). That the 1992 summit was followed by further conferences in Johannesburg in 2002, and in Rio again in 2012, illustrates that this diplomatic practice has currency across a range of types.

Track Two Diplomacy

Our discussion of diplomatic tactics to this point has encompassed practices that are largely visible to those in the world willing to take an interest in them. That is because they are practices conducted by those seen as diplomats acting on behalf of those entities most associated with being able to conduct diplomacy—nation-states. However, the state has not, and is not, the sole channel for conducting diplomacy. A particular type of non-state diplomacy is '**Track Two**,' 'Track II,' or 'back-channel' diplomacy in contrast to the visible state-based activities known as 'Track One.' This practice is conducted by non-state actors seeking resolution to conflict through dialogue, although it is linked to 'track one' diplomacy being carried out by the state and its official actors, and often with a mediator. Davidson and Montville define track two diplomacy as "unofficial, non-structured interaction. It is always open-minded, often altruistic, and ... strategically optimistic, based on best case analysis. Its underlying assumption is that actual or potential conflict can be resolved or eased by appealing to common human capabilities to respond to good will and reasonableness" (Davidson and Montville, 1981, 155).

The relationship between track one and track two is integral and seen in the case of the Oslo Accords of 1993, which were seen as being a major breakthrough between Israel and the Palestinian Liberation Organisation (PLO). Initially brokered by Norwegian scholars at the beginning of 1993, the dialogue eventually resulted in a handshake between Israeli Prime Minister Yitzhak Rabin and PLO head Yasser Arafat on the lawn of White House in Washington, D.C. in September 1993. More explicit examples of track two diplomacy point to scientific and cultural exchanges, or sporting contests providing for 'Diplomacy as Sport'; that is, the opportunity provided by sport for the conduct of diplomacy. Track two diplomacy challenges traditional delineations between accredited state diplomats and others conducting diplomacy, and between the tools of diplomacy belonging to the state and those that don't. Indeed, its success often depends on distance from the state; and the process is usually ad hoc, a contrast to the procedures that state-to-state diplomacy employs. This kind of diplomacy is underpinned by the notion that the more time protagonists spend together trying to understand each other's position, the less prone they are to conflict.

Public Diplomacy

As with track two diplomacy, **public diplomacy** or 'PD' entails state and non-state engagement. The question here becomes, where does one tactic begin and the other end as public diplomacy consciously looks outward, beyond the state? The basic goal of PD is to engage other publics through non-state actors and transnational civil society so they might look favourably on some aspect of a nation promoting the contact. This is done through a range of activities, some with only a very indirect relationship to the state seeking favor. The tools, or sub-tactical facets of public diplomacy, may include aspects of national culture such as the arts or sport, or particular foods, or iconic industrial centres such as Hollywood and Bollywood, respectively, for the United States and India.

Public diplomacy, according to Nicholas Cull, entails "an international actor's attempt to manage the international environment through engagement with a foreign public" (Cull, 2009, 12). The Center on Public Diplomacy at the Annenberg School at the University of Southern California, considers public diplomacy "the public, interactive dimension of diplomacy which is not only global in nature, but also involves a multitude of actors and networks" (http://uscpublicdiplomacy.org/page/what-pd 2015). The Murrow Center of Public Diplomacy at The Fletcher School Tufts University, named after the famous CBS journalist Edward R. Murrow, considers PD to move "beyond traditional diplomacy" as it deals with "the influence of public attitudes on the formation and execution of foreign policies" (http://fletcher.tufts.edu/murrow/diplomacy). Jan Melissen describes public diplomacy more simply as "the relationship between diplomats and the foreign publics with whom they work" (Melissen, 2005, xix). Definitions proliferate amongst scholars in the field as it has become a prominent, if not fashionable, focus for academics and a sound bite for politicians in contemporary affairs.

The differences between different definitions, which may only appear to be matters of syntax, reflect the diversity of understanding and heritage of public diplomacy. Some see public diplomacy emerging from the propaganda efforts of nation-states, others see PD as having antecedents in the media and communications theories seeking to understand markets and the 'tribes' that inhabit them. Still others retort that, at its heart, public diplomacy is nothing new: it is the latest prefix to diplomacy and will wax and wane as others have in the past. What we can observe with a good degree of certainty is that public diplomacy has evolved. From the modern foundation provided by US State Department career diplomat Edmund Gullion as the first dean of the Murrow Center of Public Diplomacy at Tufts in 1965, the term gained currency through its deployment during the Cold War as a function of the United States Information Agency (1953-1999) (Cull, 2009). As such, it was closely associated with the **propaganda** efforts that typified the Cold War (propaganda being *a form of communication that seeks to influence or change people's outlook towards a particular issue*).

In 2005, Melissen wrote of a "new public diplomacy" as "being an increasingly standard component of overall diplomatic practice and is more than a form of propaganda conducted by diplomats" (Melissen 2005, 11). Public diplomacy did exist beyond the United States and the Cold War and its global purview is perhaps the most striking feature of its modern manifestation. By 2011, according to the same author, public diplomacy had become a "metaphor for the democratisation of diplomacy, with multiple actors playing a role in what was once an area restricted to a few" (Melissen, 2011, 2).

Certainly the scale and reach, in terms of space and time of public diplomacy, are its most intriguing modern features. Joseph Nye gave oral evidence (via phone) to a United Kingdom Parliamentary Select Committee on 'Soft Power and the UK's Influence' in 2013 and argued that, "public diplomacy today is not done from a Government to people but people to people, and that has a very powerful effect" (House of Lords Select Committee, 2013, 750). It is this level of interconnectedness, often facilitated by new technologies and social media, which will be discussed presently, that means vast numbers of people can contribute to the diplomatic practice, given expression by Geoffrey Wiseman as **polylateralism**, meaning *the engagement of state actors with at least one non-state entity* (Wiseman, 2010, 24). The examples provided by responses to the Arab Spring in late 2010 illustrate how individuals and civil society groups can shape the foreign policies of an array of nations, aside from their influence on the internal domestic politics of the states involved.

Giles Scott-Smith, providing written evidence to the same UK House of Lords Select Committee, 'summed up' soft power "as a set of characteristics and values that are associated by others with a particular nation and its people, and which appeal to others in such a way that it can affect their opinion and perhaps their behaviour towards that people and nation in a positive way" (House of Lords Select Committee, 2013, 834). In other words, it uses attraction rather than coercion to encourage a particular point of view. In the realm of public diplomacy, and diplomacy more generally, we can see the link to achieving the desired outcome of the audience—whoever they are—with adopting a point of view that serves to influence policy-makers in their decision-making (Hill, 2014). That said, there are any number of examples of public diplomacy—many will be considered by Giles Scott-Smith in Part II, but the most commonly cited is perhaps educational exchange or 'young leader' programs that involve an embassy in a particular country selecting young people—usually broadly defined to approximately mid-twenties—for either study in a specific place or institution in their home country or a thematic trip around the country to investigate some aspect of the home politics, culture, or economics. Highly selective, such visitors are often encouraged through 'alumni' programs on their return to their own countries to stay in touch and to stay in contact with the embassy. A slow method of influence, but one that is believed to have more long-term effects than with government spokespeople.

Nye's contribution is significant as it serves to highlight the relationship between public diplomacy and the concept of 'Soft Power,' which, like public diplomacy, has enjoyed popular cache in the post-Cold War era since Nye popularized the term in 1990 (Nye, 1990), but remains distinct by virtue of its greater potential scope and its diplomatic purpose.

Technology and Diplomacy

"Will the bleep of the satellite bring people closer together in a common understanding?" (Public Service Broadcasting, 2014). This commentary to the flight to space of the first man-made satellite, *Sputnik,* in 1959, provides an alluring hope that technology has the capacity to enhance the purpose of diplomacy as peaceful relations. That the launch of *Sputnik* by the USSR was a symbol of the Cold War between the Soviet Union and the United States serves to remind us that technology has a long way to go towards achieving the peace. Equally, the discussion of technologies' impact serves to illustrate the capacity for reinvention.

In a discussion of diplomacy, and particularly, diplomatic practices, a familiar refrain is to point to the influence of technology. Claims have regularly been made as to the revolutionary quality of diplomacy of technological change: the telegraph, the telephone, the airplane, and, in the past decade, the digital domain, are often seen as providing a 'silver bullet' to the challenges diplomacy addresses, namely communication, representation, and negotiation.

The allure of technology to diplomats is great. The development of the printing press in the fifteenth century, predating Westphalia, was an opportunity for communication on a scale not seen previously. The advancement of steam power accelerated the rate and range of travel (Hugill, 2007). The roll-out of a local, national, and then international telegraph cable network from the 1830s enabled unprecedented transnational communications (Jones, 2012). In the twentieth century, the telephone, the aircraft and satellite coverage have sped up communications, while in the twenty-first century the mass availability of the Internet/World Wide Web, and accompanying social media has enabled grass-roots movements and individuals to engage on the global stage. Each of these supposed leaps in technology have been heralded as marking out a step-change for the practice—another new 'new' diplomacy. The utility of the telephone would simply do away with the need for (expensive) face-to-face meetings, and when these were deemed necessary, the ease of air-travel would mean the direct flights would undermine the necessity (and costs) of any resident embassy. However, at some point, individuals are still involved in the process and therefore they influence diplomatic practices accordingly. State-endorsed diplomats, and the embassy infrastructures they inhabit, remain. Whether the proliferation of diplomatic practices to non-state actors conducting public diplomacy questions the utility of the state diplomat is perhaps too early to determine, though the resilience of long-standing diplomatic practices is worth noting.

The emergence and development of Information Communication Technology (ICT) would seem to provide explicit support to diplomacy's core functions of communication, representation, and negotiation. The advances in this regard influence the temporal dimension of diplomacy in ways that Cardinal Richelieu could only have dreamed about. "Gains in speed of communication, sometimes eliciting equally quick responses from the partner country are obvious gains" according to former Ambassador from India, Kishan Rana (Rana 2010, 15).

The point to be made here is that all technology—be it the telegraph, the telephone, or the Internet—has a dual capacity either to facilitate or obstruct diplomacy. President George H.W. Bush saw considerable advantage to using the telephone. "I want to be sure [that U.S.-USSR agreements are] real and they're based on fact, not misunderstanding. If [another leader] knows the heartbeat a little bit from talking [with me], there's less apt to be misunderstanding" (Bush, 1998, 10). Bush's penchant for using the phone is seen in the number of calls recorded in his presidential archive. However, not everyone was so enamoured. Henry Kissinger, for example, argues that "the telephone is generally made for misunderstanding. It is difficult to make a good record. You can't see the other side's expressions or body language" (Hoffman and Oberdorfer, 1990). These contrasting points of view about the same technology lend oneself to consider again the value of the individual to the conduct of diplomacy.

Roland Wenzlhuemer's account of the development of a global telegraph network in the nineteenth century illustrates the discourse between the adoption of the technology and the adaption of it to provide utility to the user (Wenzlhuemer, 2013). In other words, technology has the dual capacity to shape diplomacy while simultaneously being influenced by the users of it. It would perhaps be too much to suggest that the twenty-first century development of smartphones and social media such as Facebook and Twitter were conceived of as tools for diplomats, nevertheless, diplomacy has adapted to this new topography. There are a number of high-profile diplomats on Twitter, the micro-blogging service, such as Matthew Barzun, the American ambassador to the Court of St James in the United Kingdom (2012–). He is not alone in that 172 heads of state have Twitter accounts, alongside over four thousand embassies and ambassadors, with thousands of others contributing. This has given rise to the term **Twiplomacy**—*the conduct of diplomacy on Twitter*. The practice of diplomacy that Twitter has the capacity to influence has not directly been that of state to state negotiations necessarily, but rather as a venue for global public opinion via #hashtags that transcend national boundaries in microseconds. To that end, and with the accompanying iconography the medium provides, the opportunity to influence foreign policy does exist. While debate exists about the extent of the influence it has had, social media was significant in the reform movements that comprised the Arab Spring across North Africa, which removed the regimes from Libya and Egypt from late 2010. Further, the imagery of the death of three-year-old refugee Aylan Kurdi, in September 2015, who drowned off the Turkish coast with his mother and brother while trying to escape the conflict in Syria, resulted in a global groundswell of opinion that prompted European political leaders to a swift review and softening of their immigration policies. The longstanding effects of the changes in this case to redress the cause of Europe's 2015 migration crisis, and the influence of social media on policy-makers and diplomacy more broadly, are too soon to gauge, though one is allowed to hope.

Conclusion

In each of the practices addressed in this chapter, diplomacy's key functions of representation, communication, and negotiation have been manifest. That they require the different interpretations seen in these practices is a function of both individual circumstance and their relationship to power and sovereignty. As we have seen, the state has come to monopolize these features of global society. Yet the structures of diplomacy in terms of role and function (immunity and privilege, for example) have been in existence long before the Westphalian state. Arguably, the nation-state has perfected and institutionalized the hierarchy and titles most commonly associated with diplomacy. Yet, diplomats per se, are neither pure policy creators nor simply automatons of implementation. In other words, they have a role to play themselves. For diplomacy to be done well, there is the requirement to constantly exhibit strategic judgment in deploying different diplomatic practices across a spectrum of operational and tactical policy.

The decision to create or seize opportunities for personal diplomacy or the combination of specific people in distinct roles at summits and conferences, as well as the diplomacy undertaken in the glaring headlights of crisis or deep in the shadows of track two, are all part of the equation. Given the importance of power to the success of any of these tactics, a state's endorsement can provide a certain level of credibility and, certainly since the creation of the Westphalian state, has been the focus of diplomatic studies. However, it is also clear that these tactics are not the exclusive property of an entity or a state, but part of the functionality required to engage with another entity in the international system. Each practice is recognizably part of a longstanding history across time and space and demonstrates again that diplomacy has not been the exclusive preserve of the entity of the state, but an institution designed to facilitate dialogue in the form of communication, negotiation, and representation with and to others.

CHAPTER REVIEW QUESTIONS

1. In your own words, who 'practices' diplomacy?
2. What is a diplomatic practice?
3. How do embassies contribute to conducting diplomacy?
4. What constitutes a summit?
5. What characterizes the relationship between public diplomacy and diplomacy writ large?

SEMINAR/ESSAY QUESTIONS

1. To what extent is diplomacy blighted by a plethora of suffixes?
2. What is the difference between 'normal' diplomacy and 'crisis' diplomacy? Give an example.
3. Explain the relationship between at least two different diplomatic practices?
4. "Technology will never surpass the individual in conducting diplomacy." How far do you agree?
5. What does trust mean in diplomacy?

References and Further Reading

Alexander, Martin S. "Safes and houses: William C. Bullitt, embassy security and the shortcomings of the US foreign service in Europe before the Second World War." *Diplomacy & Statecraft*. 2:2 (1991): 187–210.

Bachmann, Reinhard. "At the crossroads: Future directions in trust research." *Journal of Trust Research*. 1:2 (2011 b): 203–213.

Bachmann, Reinhard. "Trust, Power and Control in Trans-Organizational Relations." *Organization Studies.* 22: 337. (2001): 337–365.

Bachmann, Reinhard and Andrew C. Inkpen. "Understanding Institutional-based Trust Building Processes in Inter-organizational Relationships." *Organization Studies.* 32: 281 (2011 b): 281–301.

Baker, James III. Miller Center. "Interview with James A. Baker, III." University of Virginia, March 17, 2011, http://millercenter.org/president/bush/oralhistory/james-baker-2011.

Barder, Brian. *What Diplomats Do – The Life and Work of Diplomats*. Lanham MD: Rowman and Littlefield, 2014.

Benedictus, Leo. "A brief history of the passport: From a royal letter to a microchip." *The Guardian*. November 23, 2006.

Berridge, Geoff. *The Counter-Revolution in Diplomacy and Other Essays*. Basingstoke: Palgrave Macmillan, 2011.

Berridge, Geoff. *Embassies in Armed Conflict*. London and New York: Bloomsbury, 2012.

Berridge, Geoff. *Diplomacy: Theory and Practice,* 5th Edition. New York: Palgrave, 2015.

Bjola, Corneliu. 'Diplomatic Ethics' In, Constantinou, C., Kerr, P. and Sharp, P. (eds.) *SAGE Handbook of Diplomacy*, London: SAGE, 2016.

Black, Jeremy. *A History of Diplomacy*. Chicago: University of Chicago Press, 2010.

Bullitt, Orville H. *For the President Personal and Secret: Correspondence Between Franklin D. Roosevelt and William C. Bullitt*. Boston: Houghton Mifflin Company, 1972.

Bruns, Kai.A Cornerstone of Modern Diplomacy: Britain and the Negotiation of the 1961 Vienna Convention on Diplomatic Relations. London & New York: Bloomsbury, 2014.

Bush, George H.W. and Brent Scowcroft, *A World Transformed*. New York: Vintage, 1998.

Butterfield, Herbert and Martin Wight (eds), *Diplomatic Investigations: Essays in the Theory of International Politics*, London: George Allen and Unwin Ltd,1966

Conca, Ken and Geoffrey D Dabelko. *Green Planet Blues: Critical Perspectives on Global Environmental Politics* 5th Edition. Boulder, CO: Westview Press, 2014.

Cooper, Andrew F. *Celebrity Diplomacy*. Boulder and London: Paradigm, 2007.

Constantinou, C.M. "Before the Summit: representations of sovereignty on the Himalayas" *Millennium: Journal of International Studies* 27 (1) (1998): 23–53.

Constantinou, C.M. "On homo-diplomacy." *Space and Culture* 9 (4) (2006): 351–364.

Cull, Nick. *The Cold War and the United States Information Agency American Propaganda and Public Diplomacy, 1945–1989*. Cambridge: Cambridge 2009.

Cull, Nick. 2007. *Public Diplomacy: Lessons from the Past*. Los Angeles: Figueroa Press, 2007.

Davidson, William D. and Joseph V. Montville. "Foreign Policy According to Freud." Foreign Policy, No. 45, (Winter, 1981–1982): 145–157.

Dunn, David H. "The Lure of Summitry: International Dialogue at the Highest Level", in Langhorne and Jonsson, (eds) *Diplomacy* (3 volumes). London: Sage, 2004.

Dunn, David H. *Diplomacy At The Highest Level: The Evolution of International Summitry*. New York: Macmillan, 1996.

Ellis, Jack. "Games must go on," says Brundage, *Stars and Stripes*. 7 September.

Ghandi, Mahatma. Edited by Louis Fisher, *The Essential Gandhi: An Anthology of his Writings on his Life, Work and Ideas*. New York: Vintage, 2002.

Géraud, Andrew. "Diplomacy Old and New." *Foreign Affairs*, January, 1945.

Golan, Guy, Sung-un Yan, Dennis F. Kinsey. *International Public Relations and Public Diplomacy—Communication and Engagement*. New York: Peter Lang, 2014.

Groom, A.J.R. "Conference Diplomacy" in Andrew F. Cooper, Jorge Heine and Ramesh Thakur, eds. *The Oxford Handbook of Modern Diplomacy*. Oxford: Oxford University Press, 2013.

Habib, Philip. *The Work of Diplomacy*. Conversations with History, Institute of International Studies, UC Berkeley, 1982. http://globetrotter.berkeley.edu/conversations/Habib/

Hegel, G.W.F.; Miller, A.V., Hoffmeister, J., ed. *Force and the Understanding: Appearance and the Supersensible World: Phenomenology of Spirit* (5 ed.). New York: Oxford University Press, 1977.

Hill, Christopher and Sarah Beadle. *The Art of Attraction Soft Power and the UK's Role in the World*. London: The British Academy, 2014.

Hoffman, David and Don Oberdorfer. 1990. Bush Makes Personal Contact Hallmark of his Diplomacy. *The Washington Post*.

Holmes, Alison R. and J Simon Rofe, *The Embassy in Grosvenor Square – American Ambassadors to the United Kingdom 1938–2005*. Basingstoke and New York: Palgrave, 2012.

House of Lords Select Committee, "Soft power and the UK's Influence Written and Oral Evidence—Volume 2," September 2013, 617-994. Parliament.gov.uk

Hugill Peter J. *Global Communications since 1844: Geopolitics and Technology*. Baltimore, MD: Johns Hopkins University Press, 1999.

Jones, Charles. "The Global Cable Network and the International System." Unpublished conference paper, 2012.

Kaldor, Mary. *New and Old Wars: Organized Violence in a Global Era*. London: Polity Press, 1999.

Kaufmann, Johan. *Conference Diplomacy: An Introductory Analysis*. 3rd revised ed. New York: Palgrave, 1996.

Kaufmann, Johan (ed). *Effective Negotiation, Case Studies in Conference Diplomacy*. Dordrecht: Martinus Nijhoff, 1989.

Leguey-Feilleux, Jean-Robert. *The Dynamics of Diplomacy*. Boulder, London: Lynne Rienner Publishers, 2009.

Loeffler, Jane. *The Architecture of Diplomacy: Building America's Embassies*. Princeton, NJ: Princeton Architectural Press, 2010.

Luthi, Lorenz, (ed.). *Nexus Years in the Cold War, Crucial Periods and Turning Points*. Woodrow Wilson Centre & Stanford University Press, 2015.

McConnell, Fiona, Terri Moreau, Jason Dittmer. "Mimicking state diplomacy: The legitimizing strategies of unofficial diplomacies," *Geoforum* 43 (2012): 804–814.

Mackinder, Halford J. "The Geographical Pivot of History." *The Geographical Journal* 23, (2012): 421–444.

Melissen, Jan (ed.). The New Public Diplomacy—Soft Power in International Relations. New York: Palgrave, 2005.

Moomaw, William R. *New Diplomacy*, Discussion Paper, Center for International Environment and Resource Policy The Fletcher School, Tufts University, 2012. http://fletcher.tufts.edu/~/media/Fletcher/Microsites/CIERP/Publications/2012/New_Diplomacy%20 2012.pdf accessed 19.9.15

Morgenthau, Hans J., *Politics Among Nations: The Struggle for Power and Peace*, Fifth Edition, Revised, New York: Alfred A. Knopf, 1978.

O'Neill, Onora. *A Question of Trust: The BBC Reith Lectures 2002*. Cambridge: Cambridge University Press, 2002. http://www.bbc.co.uk/radio4/reith2002/ accessed September 23, 2015.

O'Neill, Onora. "Perverting Trust," Clare Hall Ashby Lecture, May 15, 2009. http://www.clarehall.cam.ac.uk/index.php?id=689 accessed September 20, 2011.

Neumann, I.B. "To be a diplomat." *International Studies Perspectives* 6 (1) (2005): 72–93.

Nye, Joseph S. Jr., House of Lords Select Committee Report, "Soft Power and the UK's Influence." Persuasion and Power in the Modern World. London (2013): 747–760. www.parliament.uk/soft-power-and-uks-influence

Nye, Joseph S. Jr. "Public Diplomacy in a Changing World," *Annals of the American Academy of Political and Social Science*, Vol. 616 (2008): 94–109.

Nye, Joseph S Jr. "Soft Power." *Foreign Policy*. No. 80 (1990): 153–171.

Parkinson, Justin. "How have passport photos changed in 100 years?" *BBC News Magazine* (online). February 5, 2015.

Rana, Kishan. *Diplomacy: A Practitioners Guide*. London: Bloomsbury, 2011.

Reeve, Simon. One Day in September: the Full Story of the 1972 Munich Olympic Massacre and Israeli Revenge Operation "Wrath of God." New York: Arcade publishing, 2001.

Rittberger, Volker. "Global Conference Diplomacy and International Policymaking: The Case of UN Sponsored World Conferences." European Journal of Political Research 11: (1983) 167–182.

Reynolds, David. Summits: Six Meetings That Shaped the Twentieth Century. New York: Basic Books, 2007.

Roberts, Sam. "Paris Saved by a Bullitt—The Ambassador, France and World War II," *Foreign Affairs*, 2015.

Rofe, J. Simon. "Trust between Adversaries and Allies: President George H.W. Bush, Trust and the End of the Cold War" in Martin Klimke, Reinhild Kreis, and Christian Ostermann (eds.) *"Trust, but Verify" The Politics of Uncertainty and the Transformation of the Cold War Order, 1969-1991*. Washington DC: Woodrow Wilson Center Press, 2016.

Rofe, J. Simon. *Franklin D. Roosevelt's Foreign Policy and the Welles Mission*. New York: Palgrave, 2007.

Rittberger, Volker. "Global Conference Diplomacy and International Policy-Making: The Case of UN-Sponsored World Conferences." *European Journal of Political Research* 11 (1983): 167–182.

Schultz, George P. *Turmoil and Triumph: Diplomacy, Power, and the Victory of the American Deal*. New York: Simon and Schuster, 2010.

Scott-Smith, Giles. "Private Diplomacy, Making the Citizen Visible." *New Global Studies*, Vol. 8, No. 1 (2014) 1–7.

Scott-Smith, Giles. Parliamentary Select Committee on Soft Power and the UK's Influence. Persuasion and Power in the Modern World. London, 2013: 834–837 www.parliament.uk/soft-power-and-uks-influence

Sharp, Paul. "Diplomatic theory of international relations," *Clingendael diplomacy papers*. The Hague: Netherlands Institute of International Relations, Clingendael, 2009.

Simpson, Paul. "A Short History of Passports." *Wanderlust Travel Magazine.* Issue 98. October, 2008.

Taylor, P.J. "The state as container: territoriality in the modern world-system." *Progress in Human Geography*, 18, (1994): 151–62.

Wallenstein, Immanuel. *The Politics of the World-Economy.* New York: Cambridge University Press, 1984.

Walton, Izaak. "Lives of John Donne, Henry Wotton, Rich'd Hooker, George Herbert, & C," Project Gutenberg, 1898. http://www.gutenberg.org

Weiss, Thomas G., Tatiana Carayannis, and Richard Jolly. The "Third" United Nations, Global Governance. 15 (2009): 123–142.

Wenzlhuemer, Roland. Connecting the Nineteenth-Century World: The Telegraph and Globalization. New York: Cambridge University Press, 2013.

Westad, Odd Arne. *The Global Cold War: Third World Interventions and the Making of Our Time.* Cambridge: Cambridge University Press, 2011.

Wimmer, A. and Feinstein, Y. "The rise of the nation-state across the world, 1816-2001." *American Sociological Review,* 75, (2010): 764–90.

Wiseman, Geoffrey. "Polylateralism: Diplomacy's Third Dimension." *Public Diplomacy Magazine* 1, Summer, 2010: 24–39.

United Nations Charter, 1945. http://www.un.org/en/charter-united-nations/index.html accessed 29.9.15

2 The Classic Story of Diplomacy

BY J. SIMON ROFE

The practice of diplomacy and statecraft, as demonstrated in the previous chapter, have a great deal to do with the perception and the implementation of power. However, the conception of a 'grand strategy' that can be implemented through various means or practices need not be exclusive to any single type of actor on the international stage. The range of different diplomatic practices including personal diplomacy, summits, conferences, track two, and public diplomacy have been used by a range of individuals, groups, and entities through time. Yet, the most common narrative of diplomacy focuses on the Ministry of Foreign Affairs as well as on the embassy and the ambassador as the official channels of diplomacy being conveyed through communication, representation, and negotiation. Indeed, international law and other bodies and groups are designed specifically so as to exclude non-state actors so as to protect the state's power and the underlying notion of sovereignty. It is perhaps not surprising then, that the main focus of the study of diplomacy has been on the centrality of the state as its primary source and the diplomat as the primary channel of implementation. In order to enhance the understanding of diplomacy, it is useful to explore the relationship between the nation and the state, beginning with the centrality of the state. This chapter begins with an exposition of the state, its nature and emergence, before turning to a discussion of key moments in diplomatic history, followed by the core theoretical concepts that underpin both diplomacy and international relations. The goal of this chapter is to set out the classical or traditional way in which the conduct of diplomacy has been currently framed.

The State of the State

The nation-state is seen as the prime, accepted, and undisputed starting point—*sine qua non* ('without which it cannot be')—for most discussions in the realm of diplomacy and international relations. John Agnew states clearly in "The Territorial Trap" that "[t]he field of international relations has been defined by the notion of a world divided up into mutually exclusive territorial states" (Agnew, 1994). Specifically, Agnew's notion of international relations pertains to the academic discipline of International Relations (IR) founded in the aftermath of the First World War, most notably at the University of Wales Aberystwyth with the endowed Woodrow Wilson Chair of International Politics. (Note the distinction from International Relations: this distinction provides an insight into the field's internal discourse about its own parameters. This post was first held by Sir Alfred Zimmerman, and subsequently by globally renowned International Relations Scholars E.H. Carr, Ken Booth, and Andrew Linklater.) The field was established in a coming together of historians, political scientists, and, importantly, practitioners such as lawyers, soldiers, statesmen, and diplomats as the study of relationships between—'inter'—nations and drawing a sharp distinction between external relations of states and internal or domestic politics. Thus, 'internal/external' separation or the 'Great divide,' as it is often called, gave a logical focus to International Relations generally and Diplomacy in particular from the outset, on what has become the nation-state. It is important to acknowledge in this the use of the words 'Diplomacy' and 'International Relations' as surrogates, while they do have distinct if overlapping meanings. "Diplomacy in its widest sense easily becomes a synonym for international relations in general," Paul Sharp sagely notes (Sharp 2002, 1). In the course of this section, these uses of language will be clearly separated and explained. In most books written about Diplomacy and IR, the author(s) try to tackle the challenge of providing a meaningful explanation and definition of the entity known today as a nation-state. This text will follow suit presently, but it does so in full recognition that there are many other entities in the international system usually known as non-state actors or civil society.

The trouble in providing a definition of the nation-state is that it is a 'contested' term. Many would start with the notion of a people being referred to as 'nation.' Then a polity that has some form of governance can be considered a 'state'; and when peoples are governed, a nation-state emerges (Bobbit, 2002). To add to the complexity, much of the literature written on the subject often uses three words interchangeably: nation, state, and nation-state. **Nation** is defined in dictionary terms as *an aggregate of people united by common descent, history, culture, or language* (OED, 1999). **State** is *the entity that symbolizes the nation with the conflation of* *the two words—at least with a classical, Eurocentric focus*—as the **nation-state.** The interchangeability in the use of these words, is part of the topography in addressing diplomacy and a lesson in dealing with the ambiguity of diplomatic practice.

Put simply, there is no universally accepted understanding of the nation-state beyond which all discussion is closed. This is despite various concerted efforts to establish 'statehood' in documents such as the *Montevideo Convention on the Rights and Duties of States of 1933* which determined a state had "(a) a permanent population, (b) a defined territory, (c) government, and (d) capacity to enter into relations with other States" (Article 1). Instead, there have been multiple interpretations provided by scholars, commentators, and policy-makers. Many overlap and draw on similar language, but none should be considered conclusive. Students need to be aware that each definition is ultimately the product of its author's environment: be that political persuasion, the regime in which they work, or, more broadly, the 'times' in which they lived. In terms of diplomacy, one needs to reconcile oneself to the lack of absolute clarity on one of its most basic terms. There are, however, congruent features of the nation-state which in recent times are closely associated with the state in its Westphalian guise. They are important to consider as the story moves on to explaining diplomacy's practical role in the world.

The most common features of the Westphalian nation-state are as follows:

1. Some form of political association (the polity or entity);
2. Defined geographical territory;
3. Recognized population;
4. Legitimate form of government;
5. Capacity to exercise legitimate use of force on behalf of that government.

This list is not exhaustive and some might argue that part of a nation-state's function is to utilize whatever their attributes to create common cause and identity amongst its inhabitants, often drawing on notions of nationalism and ethnic identity. In order to illustrate the continuing reappraisal of the nation-state, some authors forming a 'post-modern' school of thought, have suggested that the state is just an abstract, a construct of the human condition that has assumed an importance and character beyond any relation to its physical attributes (Kukathas, 2008).

Following the features of the nation-state above and despite the fact they are constantly evolving, a set of second order questions that logically flow from any list of features of the nation-state would be: states as defined by whom, recognized by whom, legitimated by whom? It is here important to acknowledge that it is, in large part, states themselves who adjudicate on their territories, recognize their populations, legitimate each other, and communicate with each other. This idea of mutual recognition is a constitutive aspect of the system of states that has proliferated since at least the mid-seventeenth century. The self-replicating nature of modern state-ness, regardless of location or political persuasion, allows us to observe the features outlined above across the planet and long periods of time (McConnell et al., 2012). However, students of diplomacy, should be ready to recognize that this idea of the *state* was not always as prevalent. So what happened to facilitate all this 'mimicking'?

Treaty of Westphalia

The answer that nearly all international relations scholarship points to is the Treaty of Westphalia of 1648, an event now synonymous with the *start* of the state system, the "Westphalian system," the European or Western idea of state. It is considered by some to be a 'big-bang' moment of international relations in that, from apparently *nothing* with no antecedents, *something* emerged. This overstates the particular importance of the particular date, or the particular location, and overlooks the fact there was not just one, but at least two, *treaties*, but the perception of the date is what matters in the understanding of the classical story as it has become code for the recognition of the principle of what is called **sovereignty** in the study of international relations.

The focus on 1648 in broad international relations scholarship is a result of a series of peace treaties that were signed that year in the Westphalia region of what is now modern-day Germany. The Peace of Münster brought to an end the Eighty Years' War (1568–1648) between the Dutch Republic and the Kingdom of Spain ratified in May, while the Treaty of Munster (October) reconciled the Holy Roman Emperor and France; and the Treaty of Osnabrück (October) rectified matters between the Holy Roman Empire, including the Kingdoms of Germany, Italy, and many of the princedoms of central Europe, and France and her respective allies, to bring the Thirty Years' War (1618–1648) to a close. These diplomatic agreements replaced the disorder and competition that characterized the late Middle Ages as monarchs and princedoms raised their own armies and struggled for power.

These diplomatic agreements were brought together as a result of the gathering, in 1643, of delegations from up to a hundred polities—that is, kingdoms, republics, and princedoms—comprising the major if nascent power entities of: France, Spain, Sweden, the Netherlands, and the princes and emperor of the Holy Roman Empire. The delegations were made up of representatives fulfilling a diplomatic role in negotiating on behalf of their sovereigns, and were a significant steppingstone on the way to establishing Congress/Conference Diplomacy (ref). Five years later, in 1648, the result of their separate and collective deliberations, the treaties emerged recognizing the principles of self-determination and sovereignty for their time. That meant the component entities of the Holy Roman Empire were able to determine the religious denomination of their own people, which in turn reinforced the idea of sovereignty of those who ruled over their territory without interference. In practical terms, the Westphalian settlement did not create overnight change. It would be another two hundred or more years before the forces of nationalism and social democracy emerged to shape Europe's map into the countries we see today as the monarchs who had previously ruled, retained their power, and, in some senses, saw it enhanced with this agreement. The point of difference was the recognition that their power was tied to territory, and that meant it had a finite end rather than being bequeathed from a deity. This also serves to reinforce mutual acceptance of their legitimacy to exercise power in *their* territory. As such, what the particular terms of the Westphalian settlement set out are not as important as the recognition of sovereignty for the distinct political entities that flowed from it.

Sovereignty

The concept of sovereignty is integral to understanding the state; and hence to conceptualizing diplomacy. Sovereignty allows for the supreme political authority in any given state to exercise power over its territory and population, while simultaneously excluding external foreign influence (Mashiro, 2008). This seemingly simple, but at the same time complex, dualism goes a long way to help explain the proliferation, longevity, and evolution of the state seen today.

States have come under existential threat of course, through wars between states and groups of states, but since 1648, and drawing on the historical analysis of ancient Greece from the likes of Plato and Aristotle, sovereignty is the concept by which sovereigns as leaders (including present-day presidents and prime ministers) fulfill their roles. Sovereignty has come to be seen as the means by which leaders are charged with enacting, and acting within, an agreed body of norms or laws that rest on the features of the nation-state listed above. That the concept is permanently evolving, as the nation-state is, illustrates the intimate relationship between the Westphalian, Eurocentric form of 'state' and diplomacy as a whole.

In practical terms, sovereignty is a political attribute of the state as well as a legal status recognized in the evolution of international law. The legality of the state in the eyes of international law reveals the customary nature of international law—and the mutuality of the system of states, given that it is only when a political entity is able to adhere to the criteria outlined above, that it can enter into the activities and privileges accorded to similarly recognizable entities. States therefore form a mutually reinforcing 'club' that guards its membership closely, allowing 'in' only those that look like the existing membership.

According to Amelia Hadfield, "the first systematic study of sovereignty" is provided by sixteenth century French jurist, Jean Bodin (1530–1596) in *De la république* (1576). Bodin posits that sovereignty is evident as one central force within a state: *"la puissance absolue et perpetuelle d'une Republique"*; in translation: "the absolute and perpetual power of a Republic." Bodin argues that to secure power is an ongoing challenge for sovereigns. Bodin's work was widely read at the time and his influence evident in the treaties of Westphalia which followed fifty-two years after his death as they applied the principles of sovereignty over territory. His ideas pre-date 1648 and lend credence to the idea that there were important precedents to any notion that Westphalia can be considered a 'big-bang' moment. While a celebrated, and much cited example of the thinking underpinning the development of sovereignty, he was not alone, as there were others thinking along similar lines before the seemingly seminal year of 1648.

'New' Diplomacy

Many, particularly in the academic field of international relations, which, as McConnell et al. observe has been the home to the 'theorization of diplomacy' (McConnell et al., 2012, 805), point to the Peace of Westphalia in 1648 as a 'big-bang moment' that inaugurated a 'new' era of diplomacy because it established the principle of sovereignty and thus, the apparent importance of the nation-state in diplomacy. In addition to Westphalia, there were a number of points in time that scholars have identified as the beginning of a 'new' diplomacy (Eban 1983, Nicholson 1963, Weisbrode 2014) that are often attributed to a specific event such as war or shifts in the balance of geopolitical power recognized in significant treaties. Other moments that are said to mark the beginning of a 'new diplomacy' include the Congress of Vienna in 1815, the Treaty of Versailles in 1919, the emergence of the United Nations in 1945, and the end of the Cold War after 1991. Leaving aside for a moment whether or not these events truly lead to a 'new diplomacy,' they nonetheless represent important points in the classic story of diplomacy.

Congress of Vienna

One could point to the **Congress of Vienna 1814–15** as heralding 'new' diplomacy. Following the continent-wide destruction of the Napoleonic wars (1799–1815), the great powers of the day, Russia, Prussia, Austro-Hungary, and the United Kingdom, met for the first time to consider the shape of Europe after the impact of the French Revolution and the Napoleonic Wars. The diplomatic innovation stemmed not only from this meeting of ambassadors, but also from the 'Congress system' that provided a measure of regularized governance to the relationship between states of continental Europe for the majority of the next century by engaging those in high position in systemic meetings. Yet the Revolutions of 1848 that started in Italy and then moved to France and eventually much of Europe, the Crimean War (1853–56), the Franco-Prussian War (1870–71), and any number of imperial conflicts across Africa and Asia, puncture the coherence of something new here.

The Treaty of Versailles and the Interwar Period

The interwar period started at the end of the First World War (1914–18) and lasted for some twenty years. This period is characterized by one of hope and expectation flowing from the end of the Great War through the Great Depression of the 1930s, which traumatized the global economy, and the series of crises culminating in the Second World War. What made the diplomacy of the period new is in part its contrast to what came before it. The First World War was seen as the culmination of a series of alliances that enmeshed Europe's major nation-states, and hence, by virtue of the empires, they controlled vast numbers of the world's peoples, into a war that could and should have been avoided. This thinking underpinned many of the 'peace groups' that pledged to prevent war in the future, and the 'Inquiry' United States' President Woodrow Wilson set up in September 1917. This group of scholars, lawyers, and informed journalists sought to prepare for the postwar peace conference which would eventually meet in early 1919 at Versailles near Paris (an example of conference diplomacy).

The novelty to the system, which warrants it being conceived of as a 'new' diplomacy, that was inaugurated at Versailles, rested on a number of features of that settlement which officially terminated the war with Germany. The agreement to conduct 'open' diplomacy—that is, not to undertake secret agreements—was coupled with an agreement to formally limit armaments; and the inauguration of the **League of Nations**—an international intergovernmental organization designed to keep order and peace amongst its members—the nation-states. The ramifications of the new system were not limited to a particular moment in Versailles in 1919 either. Further conferences, such as the 1921–22 Washington Naval Conferences sought to limit armaments, not just for those who had been defeated in the Great War, but for the victors. Importantly also, this supposedly new era of open diplomacy recognizing that public opinion could have an influence on policy-makers—itself novel to diplomacy also—was coupled with a new conceptual approach to understanding international affairs known as liberal internationalism or pluralism that will be discussed later in this chapter.

However, this new dawn did not deliver on all its promises. Not all agreements made after Versailles were 'open' as emerged later; limitations on armaments were unenforced when challenged during the 1930s by those nation-states with aggressive intent; and the League proved unable to match the hopes of its founders as Europe and then the world hurtled towards a second global conflict within a generation. This is not just a post-facto assessment taken from the twenty-first century. It is important to recognize that any sense of old and new is determined by its own context. French commentator, Andre Géraud, gave neat expression to what he saw as the distinction between the old and new diplomacies in 1945. "The system of alliance set up by France, England and Russia to ward off the German danger in the decade before 1914 is dubbed 'old diplomacy.' The system of so-called international security which took shape in the League's Covenant of June 1919, and afterward regulated or was supposed to regulate the relations of the fifty-odd states of the world, is labelled 'new diplomacy.'" (Géraud, 1945). Little did Géraud know when he wrote these words in 1945, that what many would consider a further new age of diplomacy was in the process of being born.

World War II Aftermath and the United Nations

In the aftermath of the Second World War there emerged what some scholars consider a 'new' diplomacy. The rationale for this diplomacy stems from a number of features including: the huge increase in the number of nation-states as a result of the de-colonization movement which accompanied the demise of the once-powerful European powers; the acceptance of the 'Convention on the Prevention and Punishment of the Crime of Genocide (CPPCG)' which came into effect on January 12, 1951; and the inauguration of vast number of international organizations and particularly the United Nations that had a remit to "save succeeding generations from the scourge of war" on behalf of "we the peoples" (UN Charter, 1945). It is the latter phrase that is crucial in any assessment of 'new,' as it is noticeable that the charter did not say the nation-states of the world. Suffice to say that its preeminence was challenged by the emphasis on human security and the publication of the United Nation's Universal Declaration of Human Rights in December 1948. However, the influence of this version of 'new' diplomacy can be questioned by the onset of the Cold War with its emphasis on the nation-state; human rights abuses that have proliferated; and the moral bankruptcy of the United Nations in the face of genocides in Cambodia, Rwanda, and the former Yugoslavia. As such, any assessment of this era inaugurating a fundamentally new form of diplomacy rests with the reader of these events.

End of the Cold War

A further era of 'new' diplomacy is identified by some with the end of the Cold War after 1991. The demise of the Soviet Union and the communist bloc, and the nuclear standoff with the United States, meant an end to the bipolar conflict, and what then-US President George H.W. Bush pronounced to the United Nations as a "New World Order" on September 11, 1990. The president was deliberately recalling President Wilson's language in terms of the 14 points to suggest that the collapse of the Soviet Union had produced a profound shift in the overall balance of power in the world that would provide more opportunities for collaboration and cooperation on a global scale—even if there was no suggestion that the sovereign state would be superseded or replaced by new global structures of governance. By the end of the decade, certain governments under the aegis of the United Nations were holding other nation-states to account for the treatment of their populations in what became known as humanitarian intervention operations. Yet others suggest that the end of the Cold War is not the disjuncture it would at first appear to be, as the conflicts it supposedly governed continued and intensified; states remained wedded to serving national interest and millions continue to live below the poverty line (Kaldor 2008; Westad 2012; Luthi, 2015).

Thus, the significance of looking at 'new' and 'old' diplomacy is that it provides a framework for understanding contemporary global analysis. This dichotomy doesn't have a framework that has neatly defined parameters or one that will provide absolute answers, but it is nonetheless valuable in asking us to reflect on what constitutes diplomacy. In other words, it is the *'plus ça change'* ('the more it changes, the more it stays the same') that one needs to consider: as writing from the vantage point of 1945, Géraud was already looking back on the interwar period when he mused "[t]he terms 'old diplomacy' and 'new diplomacy' have been in common use for twenty-five years or more" (Géraud, 1945).

Classic Theories of Diplomacy

In addition to the historical timeline, the classic story of diplomacy involves theories of international relations as applied to diplomacy. Although there are two main classic theories, liberalism, also known as pluralism, and realism, the latter has dominated much of the theoretical discourse related to diplomacy in the late twentieth and early twenty-first centuries. Understanding the basic tenets of realism—whether or not one agrees with them—opens the door to understanding, and perhaps even formulating, critiques and alternatives to the theory.

Liberalism/ Pluralism

The founding conceptual theory or approach to understanding international relations at the end of the First World War (1914–1918) is known as liberalism, sometimes called pluralism or liberal internationalism.

Liberalism as a theory or paradigm posits a number of characteristics of international affairs that determine and simultaneously govern international affairs:

1. The character—both moral and physical—of states and their populations matters for the conduct of international affairs;
2. Conflict in international relations can be mitigated by cooperation amongst individuals and states to curb the excesses of power politics;
3. Democratic states are more peaceful, leading to the proposition of "Democratic Peace Theory," which argues that democracies do not go to war with each other (Doyle, 1983a, 1983b, 1986);
4. Self-determination, free trade, and human rights are worth defending proactively because they have the potential to enhance the fabric of all states.

These characteristics are again not universally agreed upon, but held particular sway amongst vast swaths of the world's population in the aftermath of the First World War. The logic follows that if states would only behave reasonably and with self-restraint, then the horrors of global conflict could be avoided. However, attributes of liberalism, as was the case before 1648 with sovereignty and power, existed before the term was added to the vernacular of the academic discipline in the aftermath of the Great War. Certain nation-states may be said to have 'liberal internationalist' traits, particularly at certain points in time. The United States, for the majority of its 200-plus years of history, may be said to be one, but equally, aspects of ancient Greek society can be considered in this light. In stark contrast, the Khmer Rouge regime that ruled Cambodia between 1975 and 1979, and oversaw the death of 25 percent of its own population, may be said to be the antithesis of a liberal internationalist state.

Liberalism is closely associated with the thinking of the United States president of the time, Woodrow Wilson (1913–1921) (hence the concept is sometimes called Wilsonianism or Wilsonian Internationalism). Wilson, formerly a Princeton professor before becoming a politician, gave rhetorical expression to liberalism in his famous "14 Points Address" to the US Congress in January 1918 (www.ourdocuments.gov). These included as its first point "open covenants of peace, openly arrived at," the notion that treaties and agreements between nation-states would be open; that they would be accessible beyond the small number of people in the room and those they represent is considered revolutionary, and marked a supposed point of 'new diplomacy.' In other words, the world's populations could observe the diplomatic process of negotiation, representation, and communication; the press would be able to report on it and people read about it in their newspapers. The immediate clamor for this was the disclosure at the end of the First World War of the number of secret, closed agreements that countries had entered into which traded territory and the people who lived there.

Yet, in articulating the "14 Points," Wilson, a scholar himself, was drawing upon longer antecedents than simply the relief and euphoria of the end of the First World War. Evident in the genealogy of Wilson's speech are the ideas of John Locke (1632–1704), Jacques Rousseau (1712–1778), Immanuel Kant (1724–1804), and Norman Angell (1872–1967). These four liberal thinkers, and there were a number of others one could point to, transcend three hundred years, and serve to illustrate that the regime that came into being after 1919 did not arrive out of the blue. In other words students should question the extent of any disjuncture from what had gone before. The "14 Points" did form the basis of the Treaty of Versailles which brought to an end the First World War between the Allied Powers of Great Britain, France, and Italy, the Associated Powers including the United States, and Imperial Germany. (Other peace treaties brought the conflict to a close with Germany's allies.)

The articulation of the "14 Points" and the hope they embodied created an expectation that international affairs and therefore the conduct of diplomacy, would be fundamentally different. It is why much of the literature on diplomacy would consider the post-1919 regime as a distinct 'big-bang' moment. In some regards, there was a new era; the calling for the freedom of the seas, the removal of barriers to free trade, the call for disarmament, and the right to self-determination—or the population of a region determining their own governance. The implications for diplomats at the time were potentially great. The fourteenth of Wilson's points was perhaps the most revolutionary as it called for the inauguration of a "general association of nations," that became known as the League of Nations by the time it first met in Geneva in January 1920. As an intergovernmental international organization, the League sought to order the affairs of states and resolve disputes between them. Its initial successes, and the conference diplomacy its existence sponsored, gave rise to a period known as the 'Locarno Honeymoon' following on from the Locarno Treaty of 1925. This treaty, on the basis of mutual agreement between Germany, France, and the United Kingdom, Europe's leading powers, confirmed their adherence to the terms of the Treaty of Versailles, and the collaborative 'Spirit of Locarno' flourished until the end of the decade.

However, by the 1930s the honeymoon was over, and for reasons that many historians have articulated (Hobsbawm, 1994), liberal internationalism was widely perceived to have 'failed' to address the conflictual nature of international relations as Europe slid towards another continental and then global conflict in the late 1930s. At the same time, just as Wilson had been the focal point in articulating the liberal internationalist approach to world affairs, another charismatic and astute political leader, Vladimir Ilyich Ulyanov Lenin, instigated a communist regime in Russia. In the early 1930s, the Union of Soviet Socialist Republics (USSR) looked like an attractive alternative to liberalism. Equally, the failure to address the 'real' nature of conflict was addressed in E. H. Carr's *The Twenty Years' Crisis*, and post-Second World War rise of realism as the dominant explanatory tool of international relations.

Realism

Theories do not emerge from the ether, and by the same token they do not exist in isolation, as no single universal theory has emerged that addresses all of the planet's challenges. It should therefore be of little surprise that both an alternative to liberal internationalism emerged, and that, like diplomacy, it has antecedents that predate the study of international relations. So **Realism** is the yin to Liberalism's yang and this dichotomy is certainly the way that many international relations books seek to explain global politics. Though much debated, realism as a theoretical approach to international politics is widely considered to have been the preeminent conceptual approach during the past century. Equally, its antecedents can be seen in Richelieu's concentration of *raison d'être,* or Prussian and then-German Chancellor Otto von Bismarck's *realpolitik* of the late nineteenth century.

Realism's key features are:

1. a focus on existential survival for the state as the most important actor in international affairs;
2. that, above all else, states pursue their national interest where moral and ethical considerations are subordinated, and will engage all means available to do this (including building up military resources);
3. there is anarchy amongst the constituent elements of the international arena, i.e., states;
4. the conflictual nature of that arena where one party's loss is another's gain in a zero-sum calculation.

What is known as Classical Realism, nomenclature that immediately reveals that the term realism is contested, emerged in the aftermath of the Second World War, particularly in the writings of Hans Morgenthau in his seminal work *Politics Amongst Nations* (1948). Morgenthau argued that international politics reflected human nature, and that because humans were fallible and inherently flawed, conflict would arise between nations as it did between individuals. As seen in the previous chapter, he also felt strongly that power was a, if not the main, driving force in statecraft, with all the built-in bias towards hierarchy, coercion, and the military that entails.

Like liberalism in spanning a number of centuries, prominent realists include **Thucydides** (460–400 BC), **Niccolò Machiavelli** (1469–1527), *Thomas Hobbes* (1588–1679), **Carl Von Clausewitz** (1780–1831), *Otto Von Bismarck* (1815–1898), each with their own articulation of what became known as realism. Add to these in the twentieth century Carr and Morgenthau, and you have a cast of characters who may be considered foundational to the Realist school of thinking (it should also be clear that 'realism' existed before the term was coined in the 1930s). Subsequent to the Second World War, the influence of both Carr and Morgenthau seemed to provide an explanation to the onset of the Cold War (1948–1989) between 'The East,' states under the influence of the Union of Soviet Socialist Republics (USSR), and 'The West,' those under the influence of the United States and Western Europe.

The implication of the authority of the state is that no other entity exercises authority over them. In other words, states exist in **anarchy**; that is, *there is no higher authority that the state has to observe other than itself.* And the logical consequence to this for states in their conduct of their diplomacy is the principle of non-interference in the affairs of other states and that power would determine the balance of the entire system with those 'in power' or the 'great powers,' as they have been known at various points in history, leading a clear hierarchy of states. This idea was then codified by the United Nations Charter under Article 2, stating: "Nothing contained in the present Charter shall authorize the United Nations to intervene in matters which are essentially within the domestic jurisdiction of any state" (1945).

There is an ironic, or at least a cautionary, point to make here. The United Nations, in many ways a legacy of Kantian liberalist thinking, also exhibits realist thinking that reinforces the preeminence of the nation-state. The consequences of this can be tragic, as other nation-states have adhered to this principle while governments have committed crimes against humanity upon their own peoples, such as in the case of the central African nation of Rwanda where, in 1994, a genocide of approximately 800,000 Tutsis was carried out by the Hutu majority. The influence of Article 2, in a Charter to which the world's nations have signed on to, upon the conduct of diplomacy is thus critical to contemporaneous debates about global diplomacy and diplomatic practice. Equally critical is the evidence of 'interventions' by states in the affairs, and the territories (Morgenthau, 1967).

Like liberalism, the theory of realism has not stood still. It has evolved and reinvented itself through discourse with other approaches into 'neo-realism,' also known as 'structural realism,' which is closely associated with the work of Kenneth Waltz in his book, *Theory of International Politics* (1979). This approach has incorporated critical responses to realism and posits that the structural constraints provided by the international system govern behavior in international relations, even when these constraints may occasionally lend themselves to inter-state cooperation. A further iteration of realism can be identified in the work of neoclassical realists. They respond to neorealism acceptance of structure as determinative by seeking to explain policy variables.

More recent proponents of what can be termed liberalism include John Rawls (1921-2002), Anne-Marie Slaughter (1958–), and G. John Ikenberry (1954–); they co-exist in the same scholarly and public spaces as contemporary realists such as William Wohlforth (1959–), John J. Mearshimer (1947–), Stephen Walt (1955–), and prominent realist statesmen George F. Kennan (1904–2005), Henry Kissinger (1923–), and Brent Scowcroft (1925–). What this suggests is that no concept is without its own internal discourse, or fractures in what might at first seem coherent from the outside. That is as true for the discourse, within the academic discipline of international relations as it approaches its centenary, as it is for the longer running discussion on diplomacy.

This brief account of liberalism and realism provides insight into the contended and contentious nature of issues such as the nation-state, sovereignty, and power, which can be likened to Miles' law: "Where you stand depends on where you sit." Coined by Assistant Secretary in US administrations from Harry Truman to Lyndon Johnson, Rufus Miles, the maxim suggests that our understanding of any subject is determined by our own perspectives and is useful here in terms of the role of diplomacy in international affairs. This is because clear start and end dates are not always applicable; instead, the prevalence of different approaches illustrates an ebb and flow, a cognitive dissonance that facilitates the mutual co-existence of such seemingly diverse approaches as liberalism and realism.

Conclusion

This chapter has provided a specific perspective on diplomacy, recognizing the need to be mindful of how diplomatic processes can be seen from multiple viewpoints: historical, conceptual, and a blend of both. While there is clearly a need to start somewhere, it is by adopting a longitudinal and panoptical approach that it becomes possible, indeed preferable, to question the default focus on the state and particularly the state at the specific point in time of the mid-seventeenth century. The focus here, instead of the Westphalian moment of 1648, falls on the evolution of diplomacy, diplomats, diplomatic roles, and their likely continual evolution, into the future. The 'big-bang' moments such as 1648, 1815 and the Congress of Vienna, 1919 and the Treaty of Versailles, or 1945 and the emergence of the United Nations system, remain critical to our understanding, but they are no longer seen as 'breaks' in diplomacy as between old and new, but rather as points of recognition by the international actors themselves that something significant has changed in the governance and self-regulation of the anarchical system. By investigating the institution's continuity rather than change, alternatives to hierarchy and linear thinking emerge with the potential for a narrative where themes, activities, and trends matter as much as individuals and events.

The concept of sovereignty is central in the Westphalian states-system and more generally to inter-state relationships. Equally, the idea of power so dominates conceptions of international affairs that the word is simply incorporated into titles such as the **great powers** or the **superpowers**. These two concepts find a home in the principal theoretical framework for the study of international relations: realism and pluralism, but as global realities force a deeper and broader recognition of what interconnectivity actually means, these concepts are challenged (or redefined) along with subsequent challenges to the dominance of the nation-state. So while the state's longevity and supreme importance has been increasingly questioned in a globalized world, suggesting the demise of the state-based diplomat, the Foreign Ministry, and diplomacy writ large (and the field of Diplomatic Studies) is also premature, and the fact they all remain is a testament to their ability to evolve in ways that have yet to be fully explored.

In the past twenty-five years, or post–Cold War era, scholars such as Paul Sharp, Jan Melissen, Brian Hocking, Richard Langhorne, Alan K. Henrikson, and Erik Goldstein have contributed to a rich, if underreported, debate of diplomatic theory (Hocking, 2011). However, their contributions have not been sufficient to mark a step-change—or big-bang—in either the study of diplomacy, or what continues to be considered 'new diplomacy.' They do, however, seek to be on the leading edge of the reconciliation of states and diplomatic history and what might be global diplomacy.

CHAPTER REVIEW QUESTIONS

1. What characterizes the Westphalian state?
2. What happened in 1648?
3. Who is sovereign?
4. Why was the Congress of Vienna considered important?
5. Define 'new' diplomacy.

SEMINAR/ESSAY QUESTIONS

1. To what extent is diplomacy dependent on the state?
2. Explain the relationship between the state and sovereignty?
3. How far do you agree that the conduct of diplomacy requires a resident embassy?
4. "Those arguing for the demise of the diplomat have failed to understand the evolution of diplomacy since antiquity." Discuss.
5. Explain Realism and Liberalism, and their relevance to diplomacy.

References and Further Reading

Agnew, John. "The territorial trap: the geographical assumptions of international relations theory." *Review of International Political Economy*, 1 (1994): 53–80.

Agnew, John. *Globalization and Sovereignty*. Lanham MD: Rowman and Littlefield, 2009.

Berridge, Geoff. *Diplomacy: Theory and Practice*, 4th Edition. Basingstoke: Palgrave Macmillan, 2010.

Berridge, Geoff. *The Counter-Revolution in Diplomacy and Other Essays*. Basingstoke: Palgrave Macmillan, 2011.

Berridge, Geoff. *Embassies in Armed Conflict*. London and New York: Bloomsbury, 2012.

Barder, Brian. *What Diplomats Do—The Life and Work of Diplomats*. Boulder CO: Rowman and Littlefield, 2014.

Bobbit, Phillip. *Shield of Achilles: War, Peace and the Course of History*. London: Penguin, 2002.

Bodin, Jean *Les Six Livres De La Republique*, 1576, available at the Biblotteque nationale de France http://gallica.bnf.fr/ark:/12148/bpt6k6546272j

Butterfield, Herbert and Martin Wight. *Diplomatic Investigations*. Cambridge MA: Harvard University Press, 1966.

Burns J. H.(ed). *The Cambridge History of Political Thought 1450–1700*. Cambridge: Cambridge University Press, 1991.

Carr, E H. *The Twenty Year Crisis: 1919–1939: An Introduction to the Study of International Relations*. New York: Perennial, 1939.

Cooper, Andrew F. *Celebrity Diplomacy*. Boulder and London: Paradigm Press, 2007.

Doyle, Michael W. "Kant, Liberal Legacies, and Foreign Affairs". (a) *Philosophy and Public Affairs* 12 (Vol. 12, No. 3. (Summer, 1983)): 205–235.

Doyle, Michael W. "Kant, Liberal Legacies, and Foreign Affairs, Part 2". (b) *Philosophy and Public Affairs* 12 (Vol. 12, No. 4. (Autumn, 1983)): 323–353.

Doyle. M, "Liberalism and World Politics," *The American Political Science Review*, 80: 4 (1986): 1151–1169.

Géraud, André. 'Diplomacy, Old and New'. *Foreign Affairs*, January 1945.

Hobsbawm, Eric. *The Age of Extremes: The Short Twentieth Century 1914–1991*. New York: Random House, 1994.

Hocking, Brian, Jan Melissen, Shaun Riordan, and Paul Sharp. "Futures for Diplomacy: Integrative Diplomacy in the 21st Century." Clingendael, Netherlands Institute of International Relations, 2012. http://www.clingendael.nl/sites/default/files/20121030_research_melissen.pdf

Kaldor, Mary. *New and old wars: organized violence in a global era*. Cambridge: Polity Press, 2006.

Keller, Suzanne. "Diplomacy and Communication, " *The Public Opinion Quarterly*. Vol. 20, No. 1, Special Issue on Studies in Political Communication (1956): 176–182.

Keohane, Robert. *After Hegemony: Cooperation and Discord in the World Political Economy*. Princeton, N.J.: Princeton University Press, 1984.

Kukathas, Chandran (LSE), "A Definition of the State." http://philosophy.wisc.edu/hunt/A%20Definition%20of%20the%20State.htm

Layne, Chris. "Kant or Cant: The Myth of the Democratic Peace." *International Security*, 19: 2 (1994): 5–49.

Luthi, Lorenz. (ed). *Nexus Years in the Cold War, Crucial Periods and Turning Points*. (Stanford: Stanford University Press, 2015.)

Mearshimer, John J. "Hans Morgenthau and the Iraq War: realism versus neo-conservatism." *Open Democracy—free thinking for the world.* 2015. https://www.opendemocracy.net/democracy-americanpower/morgenthau_2522.jsp

Mearshimer, John J. *The Tragedy of Great Power Politics*. New York: W.W. Norton & Company, 2001.

Miles, Rufus, "The Origin and Meaning of Miles' Law," *Public Administration Review*, September—October 38(5) (1978): 399–403.

Miyoshi, Masahiro. "Sovereignty and International Law." Aichi University, Japan, 2008. https://www.dur.ac.uk/resources/ibru/conferences/sos/masahiro_miyoshi_paper.pdf

Morgenthau, Hans J. "To Intervene or Not To Intervene." *Foreign Affairs* 45 (April, 1967).

Morgenthau, Hans. *Politics Among Nations: The Struggle for Power and Peace*, Fifth Edition, Revised, New York: Alfred A. Knopf, 1978.

Nye, Joseph Jr. "Public Diplomacy and Soft Power." *Annals of the American Academy of Political and Social Science*. Public Diplomacy in a Changing World. Vol. 61 (2008): 94–109.

Sharp, Paul. "Practitioners, Scholars and The Study of Diplomacy." *The Foreign Service Journal*. January–February, 2015.

Sharp, Paul. "*Diplomatic Theory of International Relations.*" Cambridge Studies in International Relations. Cambridge: Cambridge University Press, 2009.

Sharp, Paul. "The English School, Herbert Butterfield and Diplomacy." Netherlands Institute of International Relations, Clingendael: Netherlands Institute of International Relations. November, 2002.

Sharp, Paul. "For Diplomacy: Representation and the Study of International Relations." *International Studies Review*, Vol.1., No.1, (1999): 33–57.

United Nations Charter http://www.un.org/en/documents/charter/chapter1.shtml

Waltz, Kenneth. *Theory of International Politics*. New York: McGraw-Hill, 1979.

Waltz, Kenneth. *Man, the State, and War: A Theoretical Analysis*. New York: Columbia University Press, 1959.

Weiss, Thomas G., Tatiana Carayannis, and Richard Jolly. The "Third" United Nations, *Global Governance*. 15 (2009): 123–142.

Westad, Ode Arne. The Global Cold War. Cambridge: Cambridge University Press, 2006

Williams, Andrew, Amelia Hadfield, J. Simon Rofe. *International History and International Relations*. London: Routledge, 2012.

Wiseman, Geoff. "Diplomatic Practices at the UN." *Cooperation and Conflict*, (2015):1–18.

3 A Different Kind of 'New' Diplomacy

BY ALISON HOLMES

In previous chapters, the center of attention has been the 'standard' story of the evolution of diplomacy up to the twenty-first century. For many reasons, this explanation focuses on the state, especially in the period after the Treaties of Westphalia when these international actors became the main mediators of the relationships between societies. While developed in Europe, nations, nation-states, or states became the fundamental unit of the international system while sovereignty, territory, and equality—the key features of the Westphalian system—became the basis of statehood and both international trade and legal structures. This 'Western' or 'Western European' form of the state also had a direct impact on the way we understand and practice diplomacy. It is not surprising, therefore, that this perspective eventually came to dominate the way we look at international relations as a whole. However, as the international arena has changed, and as we examine the processes of globalization more closely, the traditional ways of looking at states, and consequently, the way we look at diplomacy, has begun to shift.

'New' Diplomacy and Its Problems

As discussed in previous chapters, there were a number of points in time that scholars have identified as the beginning of a 'new' diplomacy, points often associated with developments in technology or, more fundamentally, a shift in the nature of the governing entities themselves. However, over a longer time frame, the term 'new' becomes problematic in five ways. First, 'new' is generally judged only in the context of the immediate past. Second, the actual features that made diplomacy appear 'new' are often not well explained, making it difficult to discern whether they are real innovations or perhaps a reemergence of older practices and traditions. Third, such loose language also means that the bigger story, namely a picture of the broader development in the structure of the state (or the governing entities that preceded it) has been largely overlooked. There is a tendency to tell history as the story of the 'victor'—in this case, the state in its Western/European form and the actors associated with that model—with the result that the contributions from other diplomatic traditions, such as those found in India or China, are not regularly explored. Fourth, and more practically, a constant overuse of the term 'new diplomacy' can become confusing to the student trying to understand diplomacy over time. By asserting so many points in time as a major shift, it is easy to miss deeper trends and patterns, or mistake fashion for substance, as we regularly stumble over a kind of shallow advertising language where everything is 'new,' 'improved,' or both. Finally, and most worrying for the study of contemporary diplomacy, is the fact that the tendency to focus almost exclusively on the state may be hindering our understanding of the direction of events in international affairs today. Marking moments of change without understanding their underlying causes can make it more difficult to see how the increasing number of actors on the international stage create, and become part of, diplomatic practice. Not exploring these relational or causal connections also makes it more difficult to see how the changes in the structure of states themselves are both driving, and being driven by, larger forces.

Diplomacy without the (Westphalian) State

This chapter will look at three approaches taken by different scholars or schools of thought and the way they have organized the same information to set out different narratives and explanations as to the purpose and goals of diplomacy. Of course, there are many points of view in any story, and while international relations is traditionally understood to have two primary paradigms, realism and liberalism (or pluralism), there are many other 'critical approaches,' so-called because they critique the state-centricity of these mainstream ideas. These different perspectives are constantly developing, but many are now considered part of the main concerns of the discipline.

For example, **Structuralism,** often associated with Marxism, argues that states are not necessarily the primary actors, but that economic issues and an understanding of class are crucial to international affairs. **Feminism** argues that the hierarchical/state model is a male analysis of international activity and therefore a very narrow perspective. More recently,

post-colonialism (or **postcolonialism**—with the absence of the hyphen used to indicate a difference in perspective) make a strong case that the views of many societies are not reflected in the discipline as a whole due to the legacy of colonialism and disempowerment of many parts of the world at the international level. Like all critiques, there is a pattern of response as scholars react to events and the corresponding shifts in social, political, moral, and normative values. However, as the goal of this text is primarily to explore the traditional narrative of diplomacy and the impact of changes within the prevalent governing structures, the focus is on three approaches that begin with, and are based on, the idea of the state—although the alternatives offered in the course of the text may ultimately address some of the concerns of other critiques as well.

These approaches were chosen to perform three specific tasks. The first is to attempt an explanation as to where the state came from—widely agreed to be in the year 1648—and what went before. This will enable clearer thinking about the role and purpose of diplomacy and not simply the way diplomacy has operated in a system dominated by Westphalian states. The second task is to identify approaches that have opened the door to more historical or sociological perspectives of diplomacy, or rather, approaches that try to bring in a longer-term historical view and ask questions of social order, social disorder, and change—even if the originators of some of these ideas didn't fully explore these aspects themselves. The third is to create the foundation for a combined approach that identifies features of continuity as well as of change.

The goal is to better understand what happens if we try to tell the story of diplomacy 'without the state,' or at least downgrade the state's status to one actor among many, while resisting the English School's view that what is identified as the Westphalian or European/Western style of diplomacy is the pinnacle or most 'advanced' stage of diplomacy. To do this, the story needs to be started again, but this time the focus will be on two things. First, the idea of states-systems and their continuing role in international affairs, and second, the tasks and themes of diplomacy through the idea of 'types' of diplomacy and the sources of social power (political, military, cultural, and economic) rather than the dominant form of governance such as the state. By looking at these theoretical alternatives, the argument is that the state is *not* the most important actor in the diplomatic world, not least because, for much of our history, the state as understood today, did not exist. The hope is that by anchoring the story from different vantage points, it will be easier to understand the challenges and problems in international affairs today.

Purpose and Types Through Time

As indicated in the Introduction, the argument is that there are four basic 'types' of diplomacy: political, cultural, economic, and military; categories that shape and define the major areas of communication between entities as well as the practical activities of diplomats during any period of time. This fact is clearly reflected in the organizational structure of embassies and Ministries of Foreign Affairs (MFAs) around the world. In this chapter, the focus will be on wider patterns to see how societies have organized power and how that has affected the way they communicate with others. In other words, the goal is a theory that helps frame and explain the essential and relational nature of diplomacy in terms of communication with dialogue, representation, and negotiation at the core of its purpose.

Before looking back and thinking about shifts in the international system, it is also important to remind ourselves just how recently we have been able to see so much of the world. In contrast, and for literally thousands of years, even the 'whole world' for most people was a relatively small and local place, specific to individuals and the societies in which they lived. There were few reliable maps and, amazingly, even the vast Roman Empire was built on military advances of no more than ninety miles at a time (Mann, 1986, 320). This makes it even more impressive to realize that, despite the distances, hardships, and lack of information, people traveled relatively long distances in their effort to communicate and conduct trade (as well as our usual sense that they went to conquer and control) the other peoples of their world.

Finally, it is important to remember that history is often effectively told 'backwards' from a specific point in time. This means there is a tendency to recall, and subsequently to retell, the story of history from a single point of view and, crucially, as if that single point of view or the way things are today was somehow inevitable. Events and the roles people play in those events are given a 'directionality' by the way we frame a story, making it appear that there was only one possible 'outcome' of history. **Historiography**, or *the study of the dominant themes and points of view found in the writing of history,* has changed dramatically as we learn more about the world and about the way we perceive ourselves in the world. It is important to appreciate that, to tell any story is to have a specific point of view, but conversely, to try and tell the story of 'everything about everything' would obviously take forever and lack depth. For diplomacy, this has resulted in a tendency to leave out, or investigate less fully, those parts of the story that do not connect to a state-centric approach primarily because that approach is itself built on concepts of hierarchy, anarchy, and a linear approach to history. The traditional frame has made it particularly difficult to see certain kinds of difference which means students should always try to be aware of what authors are leaving out as rigorously as they examine what they include. It is also important to be aware of the danger of addressing the problem of state-centric storytelling by repeating the mistake and concluding that 'globality' was the only, or the inevitable, outcome.

Alternative Views

While contested, most discussions of international relations or world affairs understand the **state** as an entity that is *a territorially bounded legal entity, sovereign and equal in the world of states,* but answering to no higher authority and therefore operating in a state of anarchy. This essentially Westphalian view is useful, but looking back through time it becomes clear that 'state-like' entities existed long before this particular definition and further that, during the periods of **prehistory** *before written records* and **protohistory,** *a time between prehistory and when cultures had no written records of their own, but we know of them through other societies,* many groups had processes and practices we understand as diplomacy. This raises the question as to where to begin our alternative narrative if we do not have the usual starting point of 1648 and the birth of the 'state.' (See Box 3.1.)

Many scholars have discussed the origins of diplomacy and it is instructive to note the features they highlight as well as how their histories are framed to support their point of view. The 'traditional' approach, which usually builds on, or departs only slightly from, the diplomatic history narrative set out by scholars such as Sir Harold Nicolson (1964) or Geoffrey Berridge (2015), has already been set out. These authors consistently and almost exclusively focus on diplomacy in the period after the state became the dominant feature of the international system and, whether by default or design, it becomes clear these authors are not investigating diplomacy as a whole, but the rich history and development of diplomacy as reflected by this specific form of governance. It is entirely logical then, that they do not examine earlier traditions or practices in any great detail and give only passing notice to the changes linked specifically to the different forms of the 'state.'

Unfortunately, this approach misses important features of diplomatic engagement in pre-state or protohistorical societies that are arguably becoming relevant as the state is changing its fundamental shape. In contrast this chapter will focus on three approaches that offer different views of the overall narrative of diplomacy. Some of the scholars remain firmly rooted in the more traditional perspective, while more recent efforts have begun to offer a critique as to the usefulness—or necessity—of the Westphalian state in

BOX 3.1

Diplomacy in the Mali Empire 1230 – 1600 CE

While the traditional narrative often acknowledges the idea that nascent states existed prior to the Westphalian model, there is generally little exploration of the form and function of diplomacy in the societies of protohistory who, while not quite contemporaries of European states, relied on an oral tradition (and who we have only been able to investigate primarily through the written records of others). The Mali Empire in Western Africa, also historically known as the *Manden Kurufaba,* falls into this category, demonstrating both a complex and consistent structure of diplomatic practice long before the state. The Mandinka/Bambara Empire (1230–1600 CE) that spread primarily along the Niger River was both large and wealthy. Founded in what is today Mali and northern Guinea, it began as a confederation of tribes called the *Manden Kurufaba* whose ruler was known as a *mansa.*

Mansa Musa I, the most well-known ruler of the empire from approximately 1280-1340 CE, was largely responsible for an expansion which, at its peak, included an army of over 100,000 men, 10,000 cavalry, more than 400 towns and villages and 20 million people across the modern-day countries of Senegal, southern Mauritania, Mali, northern Burkina Faso, western Niger, the Gambia, Guinea-Bissau, Guinea, the Ivory Coast and northern Ghana. For the sake of comparison, only the Mongol Empire in China was larger at this point. By some reports, Mansa Musa I took 60,000 men and 12,000 slaves to make a pilgrimage to Mecca—each slave carried a gold bar and 80 camels carried gold dust that was distributed to the poor he met along the route. He brought back Arab teachers and architects to build mosques and schools in the cities of Timbuktu and Gao.

The Mali Empire offers an interesting perspective on diplomatic practice in that it supports the assertion that many of the practices we may think of as 'European' are clearly ancient and originated elsewhere in the world. Also, and more importantly, this example demonstrates the fact that the role and the tasks of the diplomat as the official and privileged voice of the sovereign, negotiator and keeper of records and alliances, and 'storyteller' has been the purpose of diplomacy for centuries.

This negotiated federation of tribes was made up of the 'three freely allied states' of Mali, Mema and Wagadou plus what were called the 'twelve doors of Mali' or the conquered territories and allies of the Mansa who pledged their allegiance to the empire and were, in return, named as *farbas* or a kind

(continues)

(continued)

of commander. The empire was ruled through a great assembly or *Gbara* (until 1645 three years before Westphalia) and administration was very decentralized and based on a constitution known as the *Kouroukan Fouga*. This was effectively a contract between the clans, despite the fact it did not exist in written form. Key to this oral, but highly structured governance, was the position of the griot (a derivative of the French word *guiriot* though also known as *gewel, jali, gawlo, jeli* etc depending on region) – a person who might be readily be identified as a diplomat or ambassador.

In 1352, Ibn Battuta, a Moroccan scholar and traveler, visited the capital of Niani and gave a flavor of the griot's symbolic and literal power when he said "Dugha, the herald, stood at the door, wearing *zerdkhanan* clothes: on his head a fringed turban, typical of the country; he alone had the privilege of wearing boots on this day; he had a sword in a gold scabbard on his side; and he wore spurs, two gold and silver javelins with iron tips" (Diop, 1987, 84–85). As well as the obvious parallels that can be drawn to places where imperial messengers had both symbols of office and wore particular clothing, in a country with primarily an oral tradition, the griot is also the historian, institutional memory and check on those who might seek to re-write the past. Not only a musician and poet, the griot is imbued with *nyama*, a Mande term meaning the intangible power of words that is believed to live inside a griot making them the vessel of truth and clarity. As pointed out in Sundiata's epic (one of the first Mali rulers) "...whoever knows the history of a country can read its future" (Niane, 1965).

This quality also gives the griot a bond with the ruler and a "habitual place near the Mansa," a position made necessary by the fact that mansas never spoke aloud/directly to their people and their words had to be "repeat[ed] and embellish[ed]" by the griot in order to rally the audience (Hale, 1998, 31). Ibn Battuta goes on to explain, the herald/griot "served as a mouthpiece, transmitting orders, recovering the grievance and submitting them to the sovereign, who gave his decisions" (Diop, 1987, 85). Thus he becomes not only an "instrument of power, but [he] also influences the way it is exercised" (Kesteloot, 1991, 20). When acting as a diplomat, griots would perform whatever inter-regional tasks their leader needed them to do, "whatever diplomatic mission is required be it to see a local trouble maker, to carry a message of approval, or to visit a distant ruler to negotiate peace ... or war" (Poulton, nd).

(continues)

(continued)

In terms of specific sources of power, military seems less significant than economic and cultural. Natural resources produced a wealthy empire with economic power while the political balance of the confederation and constitution supported a stable system. Perhaps the most interesting element however, is the significance of 'magic' and the cultural power and position of the griot as interpreter and voice of the mansa both at 'home' and 'abroad.'

Sources and Further Reading

Diop, Chiekh Anta, *Precolonial Black Africa.* (Brooklyn: Lawrence Hill Books, 1987).

Kesteloot, Lilyan. "Power and Its Portrayal in Royal Mande Narratives" in *Research in African Literatures,* vol. 22, no. 1, pp 17-26. Trans. Thomas Hale, Richard Bjornson, 1991.

Ki-Zerbo, Joseph, *UNESCO General History of Africa, Vol. IV, Abridged Edition: Africa from the Twelfth to the Sixteenth Century.* eds. Joseph Ki-Zerbo, Djibril Tamsir Niane (University of California Press, 1998).

Niane, D.T. *Sundiata: An Epic of Old Mali.* Trans. G.D. Pickett. (Essex: Longman Limited, 1965).

Poulton, Robin Edward, "What Made Sunjata, The Lion King, 'Great'?" *Virginia Friends of Mali.* n.d. vafriendsofmali.org.

Yu, Ying-shih, *Trade and Expansion in Han China,* (Berkeley and Los Angeles, California: University of California Press, 1967).

terms of understanding current trends. Such thinkers have been trying to create a more coherent theory of diplomacy which, they suggest, has been largely left to one side in the discipline as a result of the theory/practice divide discussed earlier. These newer approaches have also been gaining attention as the debate around the effects of globalization and shifts in global power structures and the state itself become more pronounced in the practice of international affairs. By drawing on the insights and observations of more traditional theorists, and combining those with emerging critiques and key ideas from outside the traditional boundaries of international relations, the aim is to create a way to examine diplomacy as an institution in its own right that will help inform our understanding not only of the pre-Westphalian past, but our current situation and the stage of the global state we are now entering.

The first approach offers perhaps a slight, but still significant variation in the traditional history of diplomacy. A group of scholars in the United Kingdom formed the **British Committee on the Theory of International Politics** (though most were not British). Started in the 1960s by Cambridge historian *Herbert Butterfield* (Butterfield, 1981), this group was essentially linked to and also known as the 'English School,' with recognition given to the importance of the work of Charles Manning (Manning, 1962) *of the London School of Economics*. In any event, a core group loosely based and affiliated with the LSE remained stoutly state-centric—but with a difference, and this effectively forms the taproot of the approach taken here.

They suggested the idea, as distinct from the classical realists, that there was something they could identify as the 'European states-system,' by which they meant simply a group of states or entities that "recognize the same claim to independence by all the others" (Watson, 1992, quoting Martin Wight, 3). They made no claim that the European states-system was unique or singular, but one of many identifiable states-systems throughout history. However, their primary interest remained the European system or 'society'—effectively a more evolved form of system—and they treated the case studies of past civilizations effectively as stepping stones in the development of their 'real' focus: Western European states (and diplomacy) (Watson, 1992).

The English School also provided the inspiration for a second group represented by two authors who have been combined here in a kind of 'Revised English School.' This group includes James Der Derian (Der Derian, 1987), who developed six 'types' of diplomacy, and Paul Sharp (Sharp, 2009), who is less concerned with the historical and more engaged with the theoretical, in the pursuit of a diplomatic theory of international relations.

Finally, the work of Michael Mann (Mann, 1986, 1993, 2012), already mentioned as a scholar who examines past societies in great depth, will be examined, not with a view to explaining diplomacy as an institution, or even the state per se, but with an overview of all the entities and structures that people create. His goal was to identify different sources of power (well beyond simple ideas of 'hard' vs 'soft') and the process of their interaction from the perspective of the discipline of sociology. Almost inevitably, he also offers insights that are useful to this investigation of diplomacy along the way.

As indicated, this is not an exhaustive list of approaches to the study of diplomacy, but the identification of some emerging and important distinctions in the thinking about the purpose, role, and function of diplomacy and the systems in which it operates. The discussion will focus on three groups: the English School, the 'Revised English School,' and a 'Sources of Power' approach in the hope these related but distinct lines of thought can shed light not only on the story of the state as an entity, but also on the parallel and multilevel story of diplomacy.

English School

Hedley Bull (an Australian and member of the Committee), along with Martin Wight (another core member of the group who had a major influence on Bull), are generally considered to be the primary thinkers in what became known as the English School. Bull's contribution was the basic assertion that, despite the fact that states accept no higher authority and thus operate effectively in anarchy, that did not necessitate a complete adherence to the realist idea that conflict was inevitable and continuous. He argued that systems could develop and refine themselves into something he called the **international society**, which "*exists when a group of States, conscious of certain common interest and common values, forms a society in the sense that they conceive themselves to be bound by a common set of rules in their relations with one another, and share in the work of common institutions*" (Bull, 1977, 13). These 'societies,' Bull has suggested, must have commonalities in terms of culture, language, and religion so as to provide the necessary foundation for common rules and norms and the basis of a sense of identity and 'state'-hood.

The importance of this formulation of the international realm was twofold. First, it offered an explanation and justification for Europe to lead the world effectively. The European system was, after all, in their view, the most advanced system and had been able largely to overcome its differences to create a framework for global cooperation and governance in the post-WWII world. Second, it explained the tendency of the English School to privilege the European system both in its view of the past and the projection of European power into the future. Europe writ large was accustomed to being at the helm of international affairs and the English School reflected that default position with diplomacy as one of the four 'organizing institutions' (Watson, 1983, 17) of the European society of states. The other three are: international law, legitimacy, and the use of force (Watson, 2002, 202–206).

Within the English School, and specifically Adam Watson (a former diplomat and later a scholar), there was an interest in the process of the evolution of international society as part of the wider development of different states-systems through time. This was originally a project of the entire committee, but Watson eventually developed it further and, using papers from the Committee as well as his own work, offered a framework that suggested three broad chronological categories of states systems: the ancient states system, the European international society, and the global international society.

1. Ancient states system—this was defined by the English School simply as any system prior to the European and included ten different systems that were located around the world and across huge time frames. They had little in common with each other, except in the sense that they had developed forms of self-governance, established rules for their relations with others, and also had an identifiable, if shifting and not well 'bounded,' sense of territory—to be discussed further. These were: Sumer, Assyria, Persia, Classical Greece, Macedonia, India, China, Rome, the Byzantine system, and the Islamic system.

2. European international society—this category was the main focus of the English School and covered a much more focused time frame in comparison to the ancients, but also included key themes in the development of a society as the real purpose was to explain the shift away from what was only a system to what evolved into a more 'advanced' form or sense of society. The nine subjects Watson felt belonged in this area included: Medieval Europe, Renaissance in Italy, Renaissance in Europe, the Habsburgs, Westphalia, The Age of Reason, European Expansion, Napoleon, and Collective Hegemony.

3. Global international society—this final frame was recognized as early as the 1980s by Watson as the current period of development for international society. He did not explore the category in much depth, but merely indicated that the world had undergone a change that he felt was not dissimilar to the Westphalian settlement in that it would fundamentally alter the way in which entities interacted with each other. Indeed, Watson even suggested that ideas would need to be accepted from outside the Western tradition and drew particular attention to what he called the "high civilizations of Asia" (Watson, 2009, 308).

Challenges and Contributions of the English School

The important point to note is the shift from 'state-systems' to 'societies.' Following Watson's line of thought, while early state-like entities were able to create *systems* of operations, they were arguably not capable of creating societies per se, at least not as delineated by the English School. Or, in Watson's words, "Where a group of states are so involved with each other that without their losing their independence what one state does directly or indirectly affects all the others, it is useful to talk of a states-system, in the sense that we talk about the solar system for instance... There is room for discussion as to whether there have been a number of states systems in the past, or whether the only fully developed states system, conscious of itself as such, was the European one which grew up after the Renaissance" (Watson, 1983, 15–16).

This immediately highlights two things. The first is the importance that the English School placed on the state as understood in its 'pure' form, or at least in its more modern incarnation. The second point is a direct corollary of the first in that such a formulation clearly leaves out a great deal of time and material and is linked to the difference of opinion on the question of whether early civilizations are merely states-systems or whether they could have formed societies as well. Yet, the issue at the heart of this question is whether, without the idea of sovereign equality (and the anarchy this concept requires) it is possible to distinguish the importance of the move from necessary interactions that are bound to take place in any system, to the creation of norms and rules of cooperation that make up a real 'society.' In other words, how important are the features of Westphalia: clarity of territory and separation of entities or polities into something called states, to the process of norms and rules to the development of 'international society'? The English School answer is, by default, focused on the European approach to 'society, ' leaving ancient systems open for discussion, a point that will be returned to later.

Given Watson's interest in history, it is not surprising that he spent a great deal of time discussing different groups and cultures and the 'systems' they developed. However, his ultimate goal was not to identify long-term patterns, but to pick out those elements that led 'inevitably' to the development of the European society of states. To explain the shift from the ancient world to the European in terms of his three broad groupings, he points out, "Other systems of States such as the Hellenic, early Chinese and Indian, also developed highly sophisticated diplomacy. But all of these were, after many centuries, finally absorbed into a conquering empire like Rome or China without expanding to encompass other comparable states which remained outside their civilization" (Watson, 1983, 17). Watson seems to ignore the fact that while Rome and Greece "absorbed" many European cultures (and China and India also expanded to become regional empires), neither China nor India were ever entirely taken into a western empire, though the diffusion of state ideas did significantly change their respective behavior on the international stage. Thus, many in the English School were able to conclude that the value of previous systems to the modern or contemporary world was essentially as evidence of the movement from a European states system to the full glory of the European international society.

The 'directionality' in this narrative towards western states as the 'ultimate form' of governance is a common critique of the English School and international relations as a whole, as fundamentally (and often unashamedly) Euro-centric, privileging a Western/Christian/capitalist model of what constitutes 'civilization' and progress. For these purposes, the importance of the English School is that, in stark contrast to the standard narrative, which often simply leaves out ancient, or prior state-like entities, there is at least some recognition of these early state forms and of the place of the institution of diplomacy in those systems, even if it does not give these previous systems 'equal' weight or pursue them as potential candidates for societies of the future. (See Box 3.2) The English School also helps focus attention on the inherent problem in ideas of 'new' diplomacy given its general failure to examine systematically the practices of these ancient states-systems and choose, instead, to ignore their distinct approach and to assume that the power of the west would ensure that these alternatives would eventually disappear. Clearly, given its European and state bias, the English School cannot connect these historical precedents, such as the diplomatic practices of China and India, to current practice in a single narrative that would explain the shifts in the institution of diplomacy as the result of changes in the governing entity or ruling structure.

However, and despite what appears to be a significant blind spot in the English School approach, Watson was aware of the fact that important features of the European system were in flux and that these changes would affect diplomacy in terms of what he called the "dialogue between states." As early as 1983, Watson discussed the idea of a third category or a "global" world and its implications for the theory of the state as well as the practice of diplomacy. He asks, "Only in this century has a state system become for the first time truly global, encompassing a variety of civilizations and beliefs. What are the consequences of this expansion for the rules and practices of diplomacy?" (Watson, 1983, 18). This question will now be pursued from other perspectives.

Revised English School

Given the importance of the idea of rules, norms, and cooperation to the concept of an international society, the English School has provided both foundation and inspiration for a number of thinkers in diplomacy. Two in particular stand out as offering useful interpretations that are germane here, James Der Derian and Paul Sharp.

James Der Derian: Alienation and Estrangement

In the late 1980s, James Der Derian proposed a very different approach. As a poststructuralist, albeit one who studied with, and dedicated his influential book, *On Diplomacy* (1987), to Hedley Bull, Der Derian argues that his approach to diplomacy is a "genealogy of western estrangement." With the English School, he remains focused on the development of specifically European diplomacy, but sets up the directionality of his narrative as one not of states, but what could be considered a much more 'human' level. He seeks to explain the

BOX 3.2

The Persian Empire (550–331 BCE)

The Persian Empire is important in this context, not only because it is another complex system of governance and sophisticated communication system that spread ideas across the ancient world, but also because the Persians are often held up as an example of a very different type of rule, built on a form of tolerance (though generally after defeat) for differences in culture and localized rule.

'Persia' and 'Iran' have often been used interchangeably. However, while Iran is the legal name of the country today, the name 'Persia' comes from 'Pers,' which is, in turn, the European version of 'Pars'—today a province of Iran, but 2,500 years ago one of many small kingdoms in the region. Pars or Parsa was the dominant kingdom among the Iranian or Aryan kingdoms and began to spread their power and control in 550 BCE when Cyrus the Great conquered the Medes and the small Persian kingdom. He then went on to conquer the Lydians and the Babylonians.

Under later kings, the empire expanded to include Mesopotamia, Egypt, Israel, and Turkey, eventually stretching over 3,000 miles from east to west and lasting for more than 200 years and known in the West as the Persian Empire—the largest empire in the world to that point.

Cyrus's strategy (markedly different from that of the Assyrians who had ruled much of this area in the past) involved choosing both Median and Persian nobles to be civilian officials as he continued to expand the empire through throughout Anatolia (Asia Minor), finally taking all the lands to the east known as the Fertile Crescent where he again differentiated himself by freeing the Hebrew people from Babylonian rule.

This policy of toleration was not reserved for the Hebrews as he granted many conquered peoples the right to speak their own languages and practice their own religion and culture. He also created what has been called by some the first 'Charter of Human Rights' (though many historians disagree on the extent this claim is entirely accurate). Etched on a clay, the cylinder is typical of many similar artefacts in that it accuses the deposed ruler, in this case Nabonidus, of cruel treatment of his people while extoling the new king's virtues and those of his son for freeing the people and restoring their temples.

After Cyrus' death, there was a period of unrest until Darius I, who ruled from 522 – 486 BCE. Building on what Cyrus had achieved, Darius divided the Persian Empire into 20 *satrapies* or provinces in an effort to make the vast territory easier to govern and appointed a governor for each called a *satrap.*

(continues)

(continued)

IMAGE 3.2.1
The Great Cylinder
(Source: © The Trustees of the British Museum.)

These satraps, appointed by the king, were normally members of the royal family or of Persian nobility, and they held office indefinitely to carry out his orders in each province and to collect taxes.

Darius also reorganized and rebuilt the Royal Road that stretched around 1,700 miles from Sardis in Turkey to Suza in Elam allowing for news of the kingdom, goods and soldiers to be sent quickly across the empire. This facilitated not only trade and business through a new code of law, but also enabled the center to quickly reach (and put down) suspected rebellions from the empire's center of gravity.

Darius was also concerned, rightly, about the Greeks who he felt were creating instability in the empire. He therefore attacked Greece in 490 BCE and while he captured some city-states, he failed to capture Athens. In 480 BCE Darius' son, Xerxes I, attempted to finish what his father started and conquer all of Greece by amassing one of the largest armies of ancient times with hundreds of thousands of warriors. He initially won the Battle of Thermopylae against a much smaller army from Sparta, but the Greek fleet defeated his navy at the Battle of Salamis and he was eventually forced to retreat. The Persian Empire was finally defeated by the Greeks under Alexander the Great who conquered the Persians from Egypt all the way to the borders of India.

Persians and the Persian Empire are often used as a contrast to 'European' or 'Western' thought and a demonstration of a different approach to governance and power. As well as a use of strong force and military might, Persia supported its central and centered position in the system through the localization of economic, cultural and political power to maintain the balance of the empire as a whole.

fundamental purpose of diplomacy as not only a way to breach the alienation between entities, but also as the structure that reproduces that alienation by maintaining the sense of 'other.' Taking issue from the outset with the idea of a "supposed crisis in which diplomacy finds itself" (Der Derian, 1987, 1), he suggests the "circularity" of a genealogy as the best way to identify patterns of influence and to call into question aspects of the "classical approach" (Der Derian, 1987, 4). To do this, he develops what he calls "six interpenetrating paradigms" or theories which he uses... "to analyse the origins and transformations of diplomacy" (Der Derian, 1987, 5). They are not crucial to the argument here, but as Der Derian's overall approach and critique of the traditional narrative is unique, it is useful to briefly discuss his six categories: mytho-diplomacy, proto-diplomacy, diplomacy, anti-diplomacy, neo-diplomacy, and techno-diplomacy.

Mytho-diplomacy

In line with the notion of alternative narratives proposed here, Der Derian also recognizes that scholars have arguably avoided the distant past of diplomatic practice and been overly focused on the seventeenth and eighteenth centuries. Der Derian begins at a deeper/cultural level with what he calls mytho-diplomacy, or the basic structures of identity and social values that shape the way a society governs itself and how it interacts with others. He uses this first type of diplomacy to explain the idea that to use this "genealogical approach," one must first step back and "alienate the past itself" by asking the questions traditional diplomatic theory has, thus far, failed to pursue (Der Derian, 1987, 67), especially given its propensity to accept the status quo and a fundamentally western approach. Mytho-diplomacy, for Der Derian, and arguably in much the same way it is seen by Iver Neumann, reflects the fundamental values of a society and the ways in which those pre-national identities shape outlook and behavior. From that foundation, Der Derian sets up the rest of the book along essentially thematic lines, and while the remaining paradigms have connections to a historical timeline, chronological development is not the focus of the work. Der Derian presents a sociological concept of diplomacy as interaction and alienation which means that various aspects of each paradigm overlap or influence the next, but they are neither concurrent nor serial in the traditional narrative sense.

Proto-diplomacy

For example, the next paradigm, proto-diplomacy, ostensibly covers the period of conflict between the Holy Roman Empire and Islam. Der Derian's point, however, is not purely the geopolitical struggle of that time, but the importance of the clash of these cultures and the growth of one identity at the cost of the other. He argues that the point of this period, which covers a significant period of time and overlaps therefore with other 'paradigms,' is as the foundation of what became our 'prototypes,' or templates, for our modern understanding of the role of the warrior, the trader, and the cleric in diplomacy (or military, economics, and culture). For Der Derian, these roles are shaped in this way because they are the sites of the contestation of power and therefore provide the basis for his understanding of diplomacy as the estrangement of relations. The struggles in this period between the throne and the church, the West and the East in the form of battles between Christianity and Islam as well as the creation of what became international law and *raison d'état,* or reason of state/survival interests of the state as the driving defense for action, all support Der Derian's analysis that diplomacy acts at the point of alienation.

Diplomacy and Anti-Diplomacy

Diplomacy, used by Der Derian as the title of the third paradigm, is located in the heart of the more traditional diplomatic narrative and follows the development in the seventeenth and eighteenth century of the nation-state as traditionally understood. However, from Der Derian's point of view, if the most basic alienation was man from god on the mytho level, and their mutual estrangement created the basis of the state, this paradigm of diplomacy recognizes that the creation of states also creates a new society of equals or a 'club' of states with the power to control its own membership and interaction. This, Der Derian argues, creates a new "horizontal" perspective of "mutual estrangement" of one entity from another rather than between god and man.

However, he goes on to separate this paradigmatic time frame from the later "age of revolution" as the new form of state moved towards a different relationship with their own people, creating "intra-national estrangement," in turn giving rise to what he calls the "revolutionary inter-national estrangement of anti-diplomacy" or the sense that nationalist sentiments created a different kind of communication or interaction between states. Der Derian argues that the debates, current at the time, within the sciences and the stress increasingly being placed on the importance of reason, represent the desire for utopian thought in his genealogy of diplomacy (and if we assume that at least part of the role of diplomacy is that of peacemaker), suggesting something beyond the states themselves. Der Derian's point is that whereas diplomacy was focused on mediation between states, the goal of anti-diplomacy was "vertical" so as to "transcend all estranged relations" (Der Derian, 1987, 136).

Neo-Diplomacy and Techno Diplomacy

Revolution was also at the heart of neo-diplomacy in the nineteenth century as it "emerged as a revolutionary mediation for continuing a revolutionary war by other means" (Der Derian, 1987, 182). Neo-diplomacy, Der Derian explains, falling back on the 'new' vs 'old' dichotomy, is based on internationalism and the "power of reason" whereas the old diplomacy was founded on dynastic legitimacy and the "reasons of power" (Der Derian, 1987, 182). The outcome, he concludes, was not "progressive." Similarly, Der Derian's final term, techno-diplomacy, "refers to the global communication processes by which scientific or other organized knowledge is being systematically applied to, and inscribed by, power politics" and that dominate our attempts to mediate estrangement or create dialogue between states (Der Derian, 1987, 202). He concludes that techno- and the other "parallel" forms of diplomacy created by this new techno- world are set to drive diplomacy for the foreseeable future.

Alienation, Estrangement, and a Break from the Traditional

Der Derian covers much of the same ground in terms of time frames and historical storytelling as the 'traditional' narrative. If anything, his in-depth grasp of the historical events surrounding his ideas and the other philosophical, political, and sociological theory adds a great deal of context to more typical presentations of diplomacy. However, his purpose in using these broader examples and ideas is to "devalue" the idea that diplomacy is based on a notion of common sense or that its beginnings can be located in a specific time or place. His argument is, instead, that "the origins of diplomacy and of diplomatic culture, and their discontinuous history outside the domain of state sovereignty, could not be fully understood unless one investigated the multiple strategies and sites of power which produce and are sustained by the diplomatic discourse. We were, to repeat, out to discover the variety of interdependent relations between power and culture which made diplomacy necessary and possible" (Der Derian, 1987, 200). In other words, Der Derian's critique of the classic story is not simply that it privileges the state or even that it focuses unduly on the Westphalian/Western form of diplomacy. The main thrust is to expose the idea of power and the ways in which diplomacy not only serves a given entity, but also produces and sustains the entity by engaging power in many different ways.

Der Derian's approach is useful because it contrasts starkly with the interpretation of events offered by the traditional narrative, while not entirely abandoning the frame of distinct historical periods or events. His use of the concept of alienation and the estrangement of states highlights very different aspects of the development of diplomacy in terms of state pre-history and, more importantly, explains the development of different practices in light of deeper sociological forces at work in the international arena. The struggle of empires or monarchs are not simply struggles for power or domination, but at the same time part of a process of the alienation of peoples and societies from each other and from god. Rather than viewing diplomacy from the disciplines of political science, history, or even international relations, he uses a broad social theory, locating power in the system as a key part of the narrative and identifying the importance of culture and change in the face of modernity. He fights against the idea that he is offering a "history" by suggesting his work is, instead, a "genealogy"; but even as he downgrades the role of the state, he sets his exploration of social power and human isolation in a narrative bounded by time, both concepts to be explored later.

Paul Sharp: The Diplomatic Corps and Separateness

Paul Sharp is both less linked to the specifics of historical narrative and ultimately less stark than Der Derian, but also bases his work on the outlines of the English School in an exploration of the "separateness" of the diplomat. His goal is not a narrow form of diplomatic theory, nor is it a discussion of international relations and the role of the diplomat within them. His purpose is the creation of a diplomatic theory of international relations which he bases on Martin Wight's "three traditions" and is thus closely connected to the traditional narrative and the paradigms of international relations. The traditions are: Machiavellian/realist, based on power and interest with a view to survival and the ideas of Niccolò Machiavelli; Grotian/rationalist, based on interests and rights and the application of reason espoused by Hugo Grotius, an international lawyer often aligned with the liberal/pluralist paradigm; and Kantian/revolutionary based on the ideas of Immanuel Kant in terms of power and sense of justice or 'right' with the possibility of change and even transformation. Sharp, with other scholars, does not set these traditions in strict opposition, but as characterizations that coexist, creating permanent tensions in the international system. This tension, Sharp argues, is responsible for creating the space in which diplomatic actors can operate, given that the world is both "plural" and "separate" as people form distinct groups and societies yet still seek to interact with each other.

Here, Sharp's ideas on the importance of diplomatic "separate-ness" can be clearly distinguished from Der Derian, whose ideas, as we have seen, include the sense that diplomacy essentially supports and even recreates estrangement or alienation. For Der Derian, where diplomacy is a bridge connecting one side to the other, its main goal is to create a buffer or division that actually sharpens the boundary and holds the territories apart. Sharp, on the other hand, sees this bridge as a connector and the quality of separateness found among diplomats a necessary component of their ability to understand both the self and the other (even if the cost is the creation of a third identity that Sharp identifies as the "between world" of the diplomatic corps). In Sharp's view, it is precisely this neither-one-nor-the-other identity or sense of self that enables diplomats to understand their host while explaining and defending their government and creates not estrangement, but a middle ground of mediation. Arguably, other actors in the international arena may also find themselves in this position, but without the shelter offered by the particular role of diplomat as part of the state, they are less able to articulate or understand the implications of their ambiguous standing.

Sharp is not enamored with the English School and what he sees as the overly discussed distinctions between international "system" vs "society" vs "community." However, he does seem to concede there are a number of international societies, if only through his regular use of the plural when using the term "society" and the way he "maps" societal differences along the "three dimensional continua" of: integration-disintegration, or the social forces that bring people together, though in constant tension with those that pull people apart; expansion-contraction, the idea that power has a natural desire to expand and explore while at the same time such expansion cannot be sustained permanently and other forces are constantly challenging and pushing back on such expansion; and finally, concentration-diffusion, the concept that recognizes that there is both a drive towards bringing things together or allowing them to be more spread out (Sharp, 2009, 115).

Sharp uses these tensions to identify the drivers of interaction between entities, which he then places in three categories through time: **encounter**, **discovery**, and **re-encounter relations**. These terms are largely self-explanatory in that "encounter" simply means the initial meeting between one society and another, such as Marco Polo's first visit to China; "discovery" as the process of learning and knowing more through regular engagement which might be found after the creation of the permanent mission and the role of an ambassador communicating on a regular basis to his host and his home government; while "re-encounter" is a kind of arm's-length engagement that implies a sense of having the initial contact over and over again. This might occur in situations in which there is no regular contact or mission, but the contact continues through other venues in cases such as Iran or Taiwan who are not consistently recognized by all states as 'equals,' but who participate in important international venues and therefore come into regular, but not consistent contact with others.

Sharp proposes this frame, not for detailed analysis of different relationships, but to describe the way societies understand and think 'diplomatically' to reach beyond their inherent separateness. Using the terms "encounter," "discovery," and "re-encounter," he tries to explain and describe the way that actual diplomats must manage their relations with other cultures as they either work with, or against, the tide of events, in all of the dimensions in which they operate in this condition of separateness. The diplomat's role is one of constant connection and reconnection in the hope estrangement can be overcome, rather than Der Derian's more pessimistic idea of diplomats being responsible for the creation and recreation of separation.

The detail of Sharp's work is less important here than his narrative as to the purpose of diplomacy and the process of its evolution. In line with the English School, Wight and Watson in particular, Sharp's idea is that the purpose of diplomacy is to cope with the "plural" condition in which we live. Without laying out a chronology, he suggests that the historical record supports the idea that there will always be those considered "within" a group and those who are "outside." The importance of this fact, in the present day, is the possibility Sharp sees for multiple international societies to exist both on what he calls the "vertical" as well as the "horizontal" plane, which for Sharp means that states can be at very different points in their own individual development, but the plurality of modern life requires the interaction of such states despite these disparities.

Sources of Power

The final approach is perhaps the furthest away from the traditional narrative, but in some ways it reconciles aspects of the previous two by overtly drawing out the specific and distinct sources of social power through time that seem to be at the root of Der Derian's concern (though not overtly named by him), and essentially plotting the course of the three dimensions or tensions of integration-disintegration, expansion-contraction, and concentration-diffusion outlined by Sharp while not unraveling the basic line of the traditional narrative.

Michael Mann, a sociologist, is interested in what he proposes are the sources of social power and tracks them through the birth, rise and demise of the 'state' (in its broadest sense) in a narrative that runs roughly along the same lines as the English School idea of states-systems—including the identification of similar or nearly the same groups as are key in the development of human societies. At the same time, his long periodization over three volumes describes events starting literally at the beginning of time and working through to the end of WWII. This interest in power development provides context to the 'Revised School's' thematic deconstruction of estrangement and the notion of both horizontal and vertical planes of interaction. When applied to the narrative of diplomacy, Mann provides an interesting way to understand the development of the separate, but interlocked, networks of power that manifest themselves as different power structures or entities over time, but are much broader than simply the state or other kind of polity. This approach offers significant insight to the traditional narrative, which is primarily interested in 'hard' power or military might. Economic power is sometimes granted consideration, but it is only very recently that the dimensions of 'soft' power have been deemed as significant in international/political thinking whereas Mann begins with questions about these sources of power and identifies them specifically as the real drivers of change.

In 1986, Mann published the first of three volumes entitled *The Sources of Social Power*. Each volume is designed to cover a significant period of time on a global scale through what he sees as the four areas that constitute these sources: Ideology, Economics, Military, and Politics or what he calls 'IEMP.' From the series title, it is clear that his project is much broader than diplomacy, but rather an attempt to explain how we organize ourselves on a grand scale. He firmly argues that society is not a hierarchy of systems with one being the most important or influential driver of change, but that these sources of power combine to form a complex web. This view is in contrast to many previous thinkers, but he argues that society is made up of a series of networks that overlap and shift over time thereby opening up the possibility that both hierarchy and heterarchy can coexist even in a system that is anarchical by nature. Each area, in turn, changes as a result of things like technology or what becomes socially acceptable in one era vs another, but each of these changes also has an effect on the other areas—at the same time. It is such a complicated process that Mann himself suggests it is not possible to examine it in its entirety without doing at least some harm to our understanding of the significance of various connections because pulling one area out for examination means we must ignore other aspects and connections within the web.

Having identified these sources of power, Mann traces their connections as well as their ebb and flow over time while acknowledging ideas of both power and influence—territory and tribute as the basis for governance. Volume 1 begins literally at the beginning of time, at least in terms of the history of humankind, and outlines six pristine civilizations: Mesopotamia, Egypt, Indus Valley, China Yellow River, Meso-America, and Andean America, defending each one as significant to global development. He observes that many people have stopped asking why these civilizations came to be precisely in the places they arose and goes on to offer a fascinating rationale for the way in which the combination of the specific sources of power interacted in each of these geographic areas to create what he calls a "caged" or enclosed area. This, in turn, affected the different ways in which the peoples of that time and place operated and how development came to be so intense in these specific locations. The point that Mann makes is that civilizations need specific conditions to develop and to thrive as a coherent whole. These conditions were relatively rare, and spread over considerable time frames and distances, making their basic features all the more interesting given there was little or no scope for collaboration, diffusion of ideas, or shared technology. Thus, Mann is suggesting that the resulting structures or social entities should not be the primary focus, but the sources of social power that combine to create such entities because they are the consistent features across time and distance.

Mann goes on in his other books to outline the processes by which civilizations or societies came to be more engaged with other entities. However, while he is taking a long trek across the ages in a very broad frame, the story is more complex than usually found in 'mainstream history' as it seeks to talk not only about chronology, but the interactions of all of the different dimensions of society. By not creating a simple listing of events, but exploring each source of power and the changes in its flow, his account becomes more fluid as their separate, but linked evolution, interacts and responds to each of the other sources of power. Mann's approach is particularly important in this discussion because the four 'types' of diplomacy used here, overlap directly with the sources of power he identifies as IEMP: Ideology (is used here to mean Cultural), Economic, Military, and Political.

Ideology

The first letter in his acronym IEMP stands for ideology and it is a useful place to start so as to consider the deliberate conflation of this term with 'culture.' The basis for this decision lies with Mann's own definition of ideology as "derived from three interrelated arguments in the sociological tradition," and that includes "...meaning imposed upon sense perceptions...norms, [a] shared understanding of how people should act morally in their relations with each other...aesthetical practices..." and the "distinctive power... conveyed through song, dance, visual art forms and rituals" (Mann 1986, 22–23).

Understood in this broad way, and considering that Mann's definition encompasses many of the activities and ideas generally associated with culture, no significant harm seems to be done to his intention by considering it as such in terms of diplomacy. Whereas the term 'ideological' could be interpreted as overtly political and therefore unhelpful in this context, while recognizing that this adaptation of Mann may not be accepted by others, or indeed by Mann himself.

Economic, Military, and Political

Mann's use of the other terms are much more straightforward. In terms of the connections to diplomacy, the most 'traditional' source of power is military and considered by both realists and Mann to be a fairly direct correlation of might and power. Economic sources of power involve both trade and exchange of all kinds and the flows of ideas and technology that follow such exchange. However, as indicated in various ways above, this type of activity is often not considered as 'important' in the diplomatic arena or certainly as a source of power that ebbs and flows at different times and at different moments in the development of a society. Political power is both obvious and more subtle as it is about relationships in their entirety, not only among elites, but between the elite and the rest of society. At its most basic level, the political source of power relies on the ability to know when to count on allies and when they will prove inconsistent in their support. At a higher level, political power lies with the elite of an entity who govern through coercion or agreement. As the most pervasive form of diplomacy it is the backbone of all activities, while as a source of power it is both direct and indirect with outcomes that are often more visible than its processes. This is evidenced even in daily conversation in the way we talk about politics as both an undercurrent and an outcome.

Not 'New' but 'Alternative'

In the Introduction to the text, the term 'entity' was presented as an inelegant but practical way to discuss polities that existed prior to the modern form of the 'state.' The need for such a term becomes even more apparent as we look at these alternative ways to examine the institution of diplomacy free of the specific and time-limited concepts of statehood and sovereignty of the traditional narrative. The obvious point being that, if Westphalian state attributes did not extend into the distant past, surely, recognizing the fact that globalization has put pressure on this state form to the point it may be coming to an end, it is important to review the progress in the way entities have developed and the practices of the past that may be useful to the creation of a global state.

For example, despite the fact that Watson recognizes that the ancient states-systems were created by absorbing kingdoms, tribes, and bands and all the various polities that could be described as precursors to the state, he dismisses their potential to become 'societies.' These systems, used by many non-Western groups, were based on tribute or protection and known as **suzerainty,** *in which the powerful controlled their vassals*, or **tributary states** *in terms of their external relations, but that did not seek to control their internal activities.* This kind of governance is but one example of an international system that did not rely on hierarchy or bounded territories, but on heterarchy and a sense of a center of gravity. More importantly, this kind of system was widespread in the non-Western world and allowed rulers to have a huge influence over wide expanses of territory and to spread cultural values and norms (i.e., form a kind of society), without the responsibility or requirement for total control or the same notions of 'internal' and 'external' that Westphalian states hold so dear and defend so fiercely.

This alternative theory of global diplomacy recognizes the four sources of social power—politics, economics, culture, and the military—as the real drivers of change as they have been clearly identified and reflected in diplomatic activity over time. The use of these types as the real engine of the system, not only exposes the weakness of the 'new' vs 'old' diplomacy debate, but it also reveals the flaw of the theory vs practice divide as it enables a theory of diplomacy that is entirely grounded in practice. Further, this approach challenges notions embedded in the traditional or Westphalian approach such as linear Time, and a definition of power that is based almost exclusively on hierarchy and strength, by reintroducing the concept of a tributary state based in a heterarchical system with the possibility of different ways to structure these sources of power. Further that, as such different types of 'state' have coexisted through time, they are likely to continue into a more global future. Perhaps the biggest mistake of the classical or traditional approach is not the dominance of the idea of the state, or even the prejudice that non-European state-systems could not become societies. The biggest flaw of the 'old' diplomacy may simply be that it ignores the idea that, as we all become more interdependent, a 'global' state must recognize many different entities—official/state, informal/private, collective/social—simultaneously.

Conclusion

In this chapter, three alternatives have been offered as to where to focus in terms of the development of diplomacy as an institution. The English School offers the basic idea of states-system and takes issue with the realist paradigm of 'all against all' by suggesting there is such a thing as an 'international society' where states are primary, but governed by identifiable and perfectible norms. Yet the English School persisted in the notion that Europe is the most advanced example of such a society rather than pursuing the exploration of other states-systems or potential societies elsewhere in the world.

The 'Revised English School' approach presents two very different ideas as to the separateness required by states and by their diplomats on the way to creating a channel of communication and cooperation, but both effectively identify the crucial and inevitable nature of diplomacy as a horizontal institution (entity to entity) as well as a vertical one (between those who govern and the ruled within societies or the hierarchy among and between the different entities in the system) axes along which entities and their representatives operate and learn to interact. Der Derian and Sharp both identify the power of different perspectives of power and the dimension and tensions that operate across time, yet what neither author argues, but a point that logically follows, is that this revised line of thought reinforces the idea that diplomacy itself becomes a social constant. Diplomacy as a practice is affected by, and reflects the shape of the state or ruling entity, while diplomacy as an institution has a parallel, but distinct, history.

The final alternative was a glimpse at the international system using a sociological, or 'Sources of Power,' approach that highlights the development of society through a set of interlocking structures and the idea that governing entities or polities both shape, and are shaped by, these networks. Mann clearly sees the slow evolution of all entities as they have moved from ancient bands, tribes, and chiefdoms on to city-states or states, and finally from modern states to empires, and the resulting diplomacy of such shifts. He reiterates the idea that these sources of social power have no hierarchy, but rather create a backdrop for diplomatic action and development.

The combination of these three different approaches offers a useful hybrid and a more direct route to building a theory of global diplomacy that is less about states per se (as in the past) and more about communication and relations. This also helps to highlight diplomacy as a separate, but parallel institution with a key role in the systems of organization and mechanisms for communication, dialogue, negotiation, and representation between social entities. This idea of types of diplomacy and alternative forms of state over time will be the focus of Part II as the history of each type will be explored alongside examples of diplomacies of place so as to explore the 'global state' and the global diplomacy it creates.

CHAPTER REVIEW QUESTIONS

1. Define anarchy and explain its importance in these different approaches?
2. What are the main features of the English School?
3. What issues in the English School did the 'Revised English School' try to address?
4. How is the European state system important to the English School?
5. What are the main 'Sources of Power' according to Michael Mann?

SEMINAR/ESSAY QUESTIONS

1. What is the significance of the difference between a states-system and an international society?
2. How are the English School, 'Revised English School' and Michael Mann's 'Sources of Power' approach different from the 'classic' narrative?
3. Why is it useful to think of entities vs states in terms of diplomacy?
4. Why are Mann's 'Sources of Power' relevant to a longer term story of diplomacy?
5. By combining these three alternative approaches, we have a more 'global' perspective on the state and on diplomacy. Discuss.

References and Further Reading

Arte, Scholte. "From Government to Governance: Transition to a New Diplomacy" in *Global Governance and Diplomacy: Worlds Apart?* Andrew Cooper, Brian Hocking, and William Maley (eds). Basingstoke: Palgrave Macmillan, Jan 2008.

Barston, R.P. *Modern Diplomacy.* London: Longman, 1988.

Berridge, G.R. *Diplomacy: Theory and Practice* 4th Edition. Basingstoke: Palgrave, 2010.

Berridge, G.R., Maurice Keens-Soper and T.G. Otte. *Diplomatic Theory from Machiavelli to Kissinger.* Basingstoke: Palgrave, 2001.

Bull, Hedley. *The Anarchical Society: A Study of Order in World Politics.* Basingstoke: Macmillan, 1977.

Butterfield, Herbert. *The Origins of History.* New York: Basic Books, 1981.

Cohen, Raymond. *Theatre of Power: The Art of Diplomatic Signaling.* London and New York: Longman, 1997.

Cooper, Andrew, Brian Hocking, and William Maley (eds). *Global Governance and Diplomacy: Worlds Apart?* Basingstoke: Palgrave Macmillan, 2008.

Costantinou, Costas. *On the Way to Diplomacy.* Minneapolis: Minnesota University Press, 1996.

Craig, Gordon and Alexander George. *Force & Statecraft: Diplomatic Problems of our Times.* Oxford: Oxford University Press, 1995.

Crumley, Carole L. "Heterarchy and the analysis of complex societies" in *Heterarchy and the analysis of complex societies.* R. Ehrehreich, C. Crumley, and J. Levy (eds). American Anthropological Association Archeological papers, 6 (1995): 1–6.

Der Derian, James. *On Diplomacy: A Genealogy of Western Estrangement*. Oxford: Basil Blackwell, 1987.

Duffey, Joseph. "How globalization became US Public Diplomacy at the end of the Cold War" in *Routledge Handbook of Public Diplomacy*. Nancy Snow and Philip Taylor (eds). New York and London: Routledge, 2009.

Eban. Abba. *The New Diplomacy: International Affairs in the Modern Age*. New York: Random House, 1983.

Ellis, L. Ethan. *A Short History of American Diplomacy*. New York: Harper and Brothers, 1951.

Feltham, R.G. *Diplomatic Handbook*. London and New York: Longman, 1988.

Freeman, Chas. *Arts of Power: Statecraft and Diplomacy*. Washington, D.C.: United States Institute of Peace, 1997.

Hamilton, Keith and Richard Langhorne. *The Practice of Diplomacy: Its Evolution, Theory & Administration*. London and New York: Routledge, 1995.

Hoffman, John. "Reconstructing Diplomacy." *British Journal of Politics and International Relations*, Vol. 5, No. 4 (2003): 525–542.

Kennan, George. *American Diplomacy*. Chicago and London: University of Chicago Press, 1984, 1995.

Kerr, Pauline and Geoffrey Wiseman. *Diplomacy in a Globalizing World*. Oxford: Oxford University Press, 2013.

Leguey-Feilleux, Jean-Robert. *The Dynamics of Diplomacy*. London and Boulder: Lynne Reinner, 2009.

Mann, Michael. *The Sources of Social Power: A history of power from the beginning to A.D. 1760. Volume 1.* Cambridge: Cambridge University Press, 1986.

Mann, Michael. *The Sources of Social Power: The rise of classes and nation-states, 1760–1914. Volume 2.* Cambridge: Cambridge University Press, 1993.

Mann, Michael. *The Sources of Social Power: Global Empires and revolution, 1890–1945. Volume 3.* Cambridge: Cambridge University Press, 2012.

Manning, Charles. *The Nature of International Society*. London: G. Bell and Sons, 1962.

McGrew, Anthony. "Making Sense of Globalization" in *The Globalization of World Politics: Introduction to International Relations*. John Baylis and Steve Smith (eds). Oxford: Oxford University Press.

Muldoon, James, JoAnn Aviel, Richard Reitano, and Earl Sullivan (eds). *The New Dynamics of Multilateralism: Diplomacy, International Organizations and Global Governance*. Boulder: Westview Press, 2011.

Nicolson, Harold. *The Evolution of Diplomacy*. New York: Collier Books, 1966.

Nicolson, Harold. *Diplomacy*. New York: Oxford University Press, 1964.

Nye, Joseph. *Soft Power: The Means to Success in World Politics*. New York: Public Affairs, 2004.

Pigman, Geoffrey. *Contemporary Diplomacy*. London: Polity, 2010.

Riordan, Shaun. *The New Diplomacy*. London: Polity, 2003.

Sharp, Paul. *Diplomatic Theory of International Relations*. Cambridge: Cambridge University Press, 2009.

Sharp, Paul and Geoffrey Wiseman. *The Diplomatic Corps as an Institution of International Society*. Basingstoke: Palgrave Macmillan, 2007.

Snow, Nancy. "Re-thinking Public Diplomacy' in *Routledge Handbook of Public Diplomacy*. Nancy Snow and Philip Taylor (eds). New York and London: Routledge, 2009.

Stearns, Monteagle. *Talking to Strangers: Improving American Diplomacy at Home and Abroad.* Princeton: Princeton University Press, 1996.

Watson, Adam. *The Evolution of International Society: A Comparative Historical Analysis.* London: Routledge, 1993, 2002.

Watson, Adam. *Diplomacy: the Dialogue between States.* New York: McGraw-Hill, 1983.

Weisbrode, Kenneth. *Old Diplomacy Revisited.* London: Palgrave, 2014.

White, Brian. "Diplomacy" in John Baylis & Steve Smith, *The Globalization of World Politics: An Introduction to International Relations.* Oxford: Oxford University Press, 2001.

Wiseman, Geoffrey. "Distinctive Characteristics of American Diplomacy." *The Hague Journal of Diplomacy.* Vol. 6 Issue 3–4 (2011): 235–259.

Websites

Machiavelli, Niccolò. 1532 *The Prince.* http://site.ebrary.com.ezproxy.humboldt.edu/lib/hsulib/docDetail.action?do

de Callieres, Francois. 1716. *The Practice of Diplomacy.* http://archive.org/stream/practiceof-diplom00callrich#page/n7/mode/2upblic Diplomacy'

Wilson, Peter. The English School and its Critics http://www.youtube.com/watch?v=942nUl-C0KIM

CROSS SECTION 3.1

Diplomacy Timeline

DATE: 3000 BCE **END DATE:** 2370 BCE **PLACE/CIVILIZATION/PERIOD:** Sumer	**DESCRIPTION:** Sumer was made up of city-states in what is modern day Iraq. Each was ruled by a king in the name of a different god or goddess. A powerful city-state would be chosen to oversee the diplomatic relations, and while much is unknown due to the lack of documentation, there are records of missions being sent to neighbors to negotiate.
DATE: 2550 BCE **EVENT:** Treaty of Mesilim **PLACE/CIVILIZATION/PERIOD:** Mesopotamia	**DESCRIPTION:** World's oldest known treaty between two warring parties, Lagash and Umma, negotiated by Mesilim, which set a boundary for their territories that was marked by a stele or stone marker.
DATE: 2370 BCE **END DATE**: 2200 BCE **EMPIRE/DYNASTY**: Akkad	**DESCRIPTION**: Akkad is considered the first military empire in central Mesopotamia. Evidence shows that the Akkadian language became a diplomatic language.
DATE: 1900 BCE **END DATE**: 1600 BCE **EMPIRE/DYNASTY**: Babylon, First Dynasty	**DESCRIPTION**: The height of the Babylonian Empire was a period of intense diplomacy. No single state was clearly more powerful so rulers tried to attain power through often unreliable alliances.

DATE: 1754 BCE
EVENT: Hammurabi's Code
EMPIRE/DYNASTY: Babylon

DESCRIPTION: Hammurabi, the sixth king (1792–1750 BCE), developed and enacted one of the first recorded sets of laws or a 'code' credited as origin of "an eye for an eye" but included 282 laws with scaled punishments with the aim of protecting the weak from the strong.

DATE: 1550 BCE
END DATE: 1075 BCE
EMPIRE/DYNASTY: Egypt

DESCRIPTION: The Pharaohs of the New Kingdom were inclined towards militarism and imperialism. This, along with trade, brought Egypt into contact with others, though, when power was not successful, they relied on diplomacy, and a complex diplomatic relationship developed with the Hittites, including an institutional system for trade, boundaries, alliances, etc.

DATE: 1456 BCE
END DATE: 256 BCE
EMPIRE/DYNASTY: Zhou Dynasty

DESCRIPTION: The roughly 200 different 'states' that existed in China kept in contact with each other by messengers and official representatives. Nobles were used when it came to important negotiations. Diplomatic representatives were given safe passage and harming them was considered a serious offense. The customs of asylum and mediation were well-established.

DATE: 1250 BCE
END DATE: 600 BCE
EMPIRE/DYNASTY: Assyria

DESCRIPTION: The Assyrians had limited resources and relied on diplomacy to gather information on intentions, politics, and military of neighbors while negotiating alliances. At its height, Assyria wielded loose power over a large empire using local governments, which contributed to its downfall as locals retained authority to conduct diplomacy, forming coalitions that finally destroyed the empire.

DATE: 550 BCE
END DATE: 331 BCE
EMPIRE/DYNASTY: First Persian

DESCRIPTION: The Persian Empire was large and diverse, which required a decentralized system of government. Persia maintained diplomatic relations with city-states both in India and Greece, often lending support to weaker Greek city-states in order to protect them against the more powerful Greeks and also acted as mediator.

DATE: 500 BCE **END DATE:** 100 BCE **EVENT:** city-state diplomacy **PLACE/CIVILIZATION/PERIOD:** Classical and Hellenistic Greece	**DESCRIPTION:** Arguably played a more important role in the evolution of diplomacy than any previous system. Intense diplomatic interaction. Envoys chosen for oratorical skills because they had to plead their case in front of other city-state assemblies. As many as ten representatives were sent to present different parties/points of view. Rarely given full powers, instructions were detailed and restrictive. Often resorted to international arbitration to settle disputes. Resident consuls were created, local citizens representing interests of a foreign state.
DATE: c. 300 BCE **PERSON:** Chanakya (aka Kautilya) **EVENT:** *Arthaśāstra* **EMPIRE/DYNASTY:** Mauryan (322–185 BCE)	**DESCRIPTION:** Kautilya, advisor to Chandragupta (b. 371, d. 283 BCE), wrote *Arthaśāstra*, setting out complex guidelines for establishing an empire and the use of political power. He saw that there was natural conflict in the relations between states and argued importance of diplomacy in international relations.
DATE: 27 BCE **END DATE:** 395 CE **EMPIRE/DYNASTY:** Roman (before the divide in East and West)	**DESCRIPTION:** Used temporary envoys appointed by the Senate. Took pride in 'good faith.' Treaties were carved into bronze or stone and put on display and given political or religious importance. Heavy use of alliances and treaties. Immunity expanded to the staff of envoys. Those who committed a crime were sent home to be tried. Innovated arbitration by creating commissions made up of one person from each party and a neutral. Exchanged hostages as treaty guarantee.
DATE: 330 CE **END DATE:** 1453 CE **EMPIRE/DYNASTY:** Byzantine Empire (aka Eastern Roman Empire)	**DESCRIPTION:** Diplomacy regarded as one of their foremost skills. Used it more continuously than any government before. First to create a branch of government dedicated to diplomacy and training diplomats. Missions remained temporary. Used duplicity, opportunism, dishonesty, bribery, subversion, stealing, and intelligence to turn enemies against each other.

DATE: 400 CE
END DATE: 1400 CE
PLACE/CIVILIZATION/PERIOD: Medieval Europe

DESCRIPTION: Diplomatic contacts infrequent. Political marriages, alliances, truces, and peace treaties were negotiated. Reliant on the church. Envoys primarily just messengers. Terms 'orator,' 'nuncios,' 'procurator,' and 'ambassador' used interchangeably. Ceremony highly valued.

DATE: 1230 CE
END DATE: 1600 CE
EMPIRE/DYNASTY: Mali

DESCRIPTION: Mandinka/Bambara Empire in W. Africa spread along the Niger River built on a confederation of tribes with a constitution. The primary diplomatic envoy was the griot who was literally the 'voice' of the sovereign (who didn't speak directly to people) and primary negotiator and historian and considered to have 'magic' powers.

DATE: 1293 CE
END DATE: 1922
EMPIRE/DYNASTY: Ottoman

DESCRIPTION: Developed in contrast to European Diplomacy with foreign affairs conducted by the Reis ül-Küttab (Chief Clerk or Secretary of State), who also had other duties. Created a Foreign Ministry in 1836, though ambassadors appointed with temporary remits and not residential (unlike Europe). Trade based on 'capitulations' adopted from Muslims as a unilateral and temporary agreement made by the sultan to a nation's merchants. Also played a crucial role in balancing European powers as a powerful ally with strong military power.

DATE: 1300 CE
END DATE: 1600
EVENT: Italian city-state diplomacy
PLACE/CIVILIZATION/PERIOD: Renaissance (Europe)

DESCRIPTION: First permanent missions in capitals created by the 'great powers.' Ciphers and codes used to protect secrecy. Venetians began systematic archiving of diplomatic documents. Ceremony and symbol important. Meetings between sovereigns increased. Interests of state more important than ethics. Papal Court critical. First sign of diplomatic corps. No common language.

DATE: c. 1530 CE
PERSON: Francisco de Vitoria (b. 1480, d. 1546)
EVENT: International law and Theory of Just War
EMPIRE/DYNASTY: Europe (Spain)

DESCRIPTION: Focused on the question of what makes a war just. Argued that imperial claims were invalid and that all men were free under the law of nature. First western writings to separate war into offensive and defensive wars.

DATE: 1554 **EVENT:** Luso-Chinese Agreement **EMPIRE/DYNASTY:** Ming and Portugese	**DESCRIPTION:** A trade agreement between the Portuguese, headed by Leonel de Sousa, and the authorities of Guangzhou that allowed for the legalization of Portuguese trade in China by paying taxes, which expanded economic diplomacy and opened European-Chinese trade.
DATE: C. 1620-1640s **PERSON:** Cardinal Richelieu (b. 1585, d. 1642) **PLACE/CIVILIZATION/PERIOD:** Europe (France)	**DESCRIPTION:** The age of French diplomacy developed under Louis XIII and considered 'classical.' Restored integrity to diplomacy. Thought diplomacy should be used continuously and systematically. Encouraged professional diplomats. French became the language of diplomacy.
DATE: 1600 **END DATE:** 1919 **EVENT:** French Method	**DESCRIPTION:** Deemed diplomacy as the best way to conduct relations between civilized states. Courteous, dignified, gradual and attached importance to knowledge and experience and understanding of 'realities' of existing power. Europe considered crucial and established professional diplomatic service. Negotiation must be continuous and confidential. Centralized authority.
DATE: 1606 **EVENT:** Peace of Žitava **PLACE/CIVILIZATION/PERIOD:** Middle East and Western Europe	**DESCRIPTION:** Ends the Long War between Ottoman Turkey and the Habsburg Monarchy, which brings peace to Middle Eastern and European powers—for a time.
DATE: 1606 **EVENT:** Treaty of Vienna **PLACE/CIVILIZATION/PERIOD:** Western Europe	**DESCRIPTION:** Restores all constitutional and religious rights/privileges to the Hungarians in both Transylvania and Royal Hungary, though long before Westphalia.
DATE: 1612 **EVENT:** Treaty Nasuh Pasha **PLACE/CIVILIZATION/PERIOD:** Middle East	**DESCRIPTION:** Treaty between Ottoman Turkey and Persia in which Persia regained some of its losses in 1590, but indicative of the chaotic conditions not only in Europe but in many other regions as well.

DATE: 1648
EVENT: Peace of Westphalia
PLACE/CIVILIZATION/PERIOD: Western Europe

DESCRIPTION: Ended Thirty Years War between Catholics and Protestants. Known as the transition between feudalism and modern independent states. Classic balance of power and established twin ideas of independence and equality of states. Recognized separation of the Church and nations. France, Sweden, Netherlands recognized as big powers. Collective security and conflict resolution provisions never implemented.

DATE: 1689
EVENT: Treaty of Nerchinsk
PLACE/CIVILIZATION/PERIOD: Asia and Eastern Europe

DESCRIPTION: The first treaty between Russia and China. The Russians gave up the area north of the Amur River as far as the Stanovoy Mountains and kept the area between the Argun River and Lake Baikal. This border along the Argun River and Stanovoy Mountains lasted until the Amur Annexation in 1860.

DATE: 1701
EVENT: Great Peace of Montreal
PLACE/CIVILIZATION/PERIOD: Western Europe and 'New World'

DESCRIPTION: Establishes peace between New France and the 39 First Nations of North America.

DATE: 1727
EVENT: Treaty of Kyakta (Kiakta)
PLACE/CIVILIZATION/PERIOD: Europe and China

DESCRIPTION: Along with the Treaty of Nerchinsk (1689), regulated the relations between Imperial Russia and the Qing Dynasty until the mid-nineteenth century.

DATE: c. 1810s
PERSON: Lord Castlereagh (British) (b. 1769, d. 1822)
EVENT: European Congress Era Diplomacy

DESCRIPTION: Contemplated the creation of 'a sort of permanent European Congress' that would have permanent committees and a secretariat.

DATE: 1789
EVENT: French Revolution
PLACE/CIVILIZATION/PERIOD: Europe

DESCRIPTION: First modern idea of the citizen with rights and duties.

DATE: 1794
EVENT: Jay Treaty of Amity, Commerce, and Navigation
PLACE/CIVILIZATION/PERIOD: Europe and 'New World' United States and United Kingdom

DESCRIPTION: Beginning of modern history of arbitration. Set up arbitration to settle claims of property.

DATE: 1800 **END DATE:** 1900 **EVENT:** 19th Century Diplomacy—Concert of Europe	**DESCRIPTION:** European powers expanded the number of missions. Japan forced to end isolation in 1853 and accept foreign consuls. China forced to do the same in 1860. Multilateral diplomacy grew. Communication sped the process. Concert of Europe meetings designed to try and stabilize Europe.
DATE: 1814 **EVENT:** Treaty of Paris—Balance of Power between Great Powers **PLACE/CIVILIZATION/PERIOD:** Western Europe	**DESCRIPTION:** Austria, Russia, Great Britain, Prussia, Spain, Sweden, & Portugal signed the treaty with defeated France. Created the Balance of Power idea. ``Powers of the first order" briefly after defined as Austria, Great Britain, Russia, Prussia, France, and Spain.
DATE: 1815 **EVENT:** Holy Alliance Treaty —Balance of Power **PLACE/CIVILIZATION/PERIOD:** Western and Eastern Europe	**DESCRIPTION:** Bound Russia, Austria, and Prussian monarchs into an alliance, which brought some form of order to the entire continent.
DATE: 1815 **END DATE:** Start of WWI **PLACE/CIVILIZATION/PERIOD:** European Era of Congress (or Conference) Diplomacy **PLACE/CIVILIZATION/PERIOD:** Western and Eastern Europe	**DESCRIPTION:** Based on several treaties after Napoleon's defeat, royal rulers of Europe and/or their ministers gathered "for the purpose of consulting upon their common interests, and for the consideration of the measures which at each of these periods shall be considered the most salutary for the repose and prosperity of Nations, and for the maintenance of the Peace of Europe." Relied heavily on individual relationships. Conservative autocracies (Austria, Russia, Prussia) differed from more liberal constitutional monarchies (Great Britain & France).
DATE: 1815 **EVENT:** Congress of Vienna **PLACE/CIVILIZATION/PERIOD:** Europe	**DESCRIPTION:** Created common ranks of diplomats: 1) ambassadors, nuncios, legates; 2) envoys, ministers; 3) charges d'affaires. Seniority among the same rank depended on how long they were in a particular capital.
DATE: 1851 **EVENT:** The Treaty of Kulja (also Kuldja) **EMPIRE/DYNASTY:** Qing and Russia **PLACE/CIVILIZATION/PERIOD:** Europe and Asia	**DESCRIPTION:** Treaty between Qing Dynasty and the Russian Empire, opening Kulja and Chuguchak to Sino-Russian trade. Prepared by the first Russian consul to China, Ivan Zakharov, the treaty was preceded by a gradual Russian advance throughout the nineteenth century into Kazakhstan in direct competition with British efforts to open China.

DATE: 1863 **EVENT:** Founding of International Red Cross **PLACE/CIVILIZATION/PERIOD:** Global	**DESCRIPTION:** One of many global organizations founded in the late 1800s that were designed to operate specifically at the international level.
DATE: 1889 **EVENT:** Founding of Organization of American States **PLACE/CIVILIZATION/PERIOD:** Central and South America	**DESCRIPTION:** First International Conference of American States where 18 states resolved to create the International Union of American Republics (renamed International Commercial Bureau at Second International in 1901–1902, and finally, Organization of American States in 1948).
DATE: 1890 **EVENT:** Personal Diplomacy **PLACE/CIVILIZATION/PERIOD:** Global	**DESCRIPTION:** Official visits by crowned heads and heads of governments became important, though usually symbolic.
DATE: 1895 **EVENT:** The Treaty of Shimonoseki **PLACE/CIVILIZATION/PERIOD:** Global	**DESCRIPTION:** Treaty between the Empire of Japan and the Qing Empire, ending the First Sino-Japanese War. This treaty followed and superseded the Sino-Japanese Friendship and Trade Treaty of 1871 and brought order to what had been a chaotic region.
DATE: 1899 **EVENT:** First Hague Convention (26 countriesparticipating) **PLACE/CIVILIZATION/PERIOD:** Global	**DESCRIPTION:** Goal was to avert the upcoming war through a series of international treaties and declarations negotiated at two international peace conferences at The Hague in the Netherlands. These were some of the first formal statements of the laws of war and war crimes including the use of weapons of war.
DATE: 1907 **EVENT:** Second Hague Convention (44 countries participating) **PLACE/CIVILIZATION/PERIOD:** Global	**DESCRIPTION:** A third conference was planned for 1914 and later rescheduled for 1915, but it did not take place due to the start of World War I.
DATE: 1918 **EVENT:** Fourteen Points and New Diplomacy **PLACE/CIVILIZATION/PERIOD:** United States and Europe	**DESCRIPTION:** Woodrow Wilson's fourteen points marked a step change from 'old' diplomacy epitomized in the first point, "Open covenants openly arrived at, after which there should be no private international understandings of any kind, but diplomacy shall proceed always frankly and in public view."
DATE: 1919 **EVENT:** Treaty of Versailles **PLACE/CIVILIZATION/PERIOD:** Europe and Global	**DESCRIPTION:** Established the League of Nations. Collective security designed to promote cooperation and arbitration. No enforcement mechanism. Tried to abolish secret treaties.

DATE: 1919 **END DATE:** 1939 **EVENT:** Interwar Period Diplomacy **PLACE/CIVILIZATION/PERIOD:** Global	**DESCRIPTION:** League of Nations created. Collective security. International Labour Organization created. League did not end the use of resident diplomats in capitals.
DATE: 1928 **EVENT:** Paris Pact of 1928 Banning of War (Kellogg-Briand Pact) **PLACE/CIVILIZATION/PERIOD:** Global	**DESCRIPTION:** Attempted to broaden the prohibition on war but with no enforcement mechanism. British exempted actions to defend the empire and US still held on to Monroe Doctrine.
DATE: 1939 **END:** 1945 **EVENT:** WWII, Postwar Diplomacy, Bretton Woods **PLACE/CIVILIZATION/PERIOD:** Global	**DESCRIPTION:** Diplomatic priorities broad. First global civil aviation organization created. International structures multiplied. Conference diplomacy increased. Transgovernmental relations: government departments conduct foreign relations in their field without using the countries' diplomatic organization. Instant comm. NGOs have place at the table. **DESCRIPTION:** In 1944 the first global banking institutions were created at Bretton Woods.
DATE: 1945 **EVENT:** United Nations Charter **PLACE/CIVILIZATION/PERIOD:** Global	**DESCRIPTION:** Designed to introduce collective security and law and order into the international system. Preservation of peace was the goal. Has enforcement mechanism through the Security Council.
DATE: 1945 **EVENT:** International Court of Justice **PLACE/CIVILIZATION/PERIOD:** Global	**DESCRIPTION:** The primary judicial branch of the United Nations and based in the Peace Palace in The Hague, Netherlands. Main functions: settle legal disputes submitted to it by states and to provide advisory opinions on legal questions submitted to it by duly authorized international branches, agencies, and the UN General Assembly.
DATE: 1948 **EVENT:** Universal Declaration of Human Rights **PLACE/CIVILIZATION/PERIOD:** Global	**DESCRIPTION:** Codification of human rights.
DATE: 1949 **EVENT:** Vienna Convention **PLACE/CIVILIZATION/PERIOD:** Great Powers	**DESCRIPTION:** Negotiated in the aftermath of the Second World War and updated the terms of the first three treaties (1864, 1906, 1929), and added a fourth.

DATE: 1952 **END DATE:** 2002 **EVENT:** European Coal and Steel Community (ECSC) **PLACE/CIVILIZATION/PERIOD:** Western Europe	**DESCRIPTION:** Treaty of Paris (1951) created the European Coal and Steel Community signed by Belgium, France, West Germany, Italy, the Netherlands, and Luxembourg. It was the first organization built on ideas of supranationalism, joint authority, or 'pooled sovereignty.'
DATE: 1955 **EVENT:** Bandung Conference (29 countries participating) **PLACE/CIVILIZATION/PERIOD:** Asia and Africa	**DESCRIPTION:** First large conference between emerging/newly independent Asian and African countries with aim to promote economic and cultural cooperation and oppose colonialism. An important step toward the Non-Aligned Movement.
DATE: 1961 **EVENT:** Vienna Convention on Diplomatic Relations **PLACE/CIVILIZATION/PERIOD:** Global	**DESCRIPTION:** The establishment of diplomatic relations between states, and of permanent diplomatic missions, takes place by mutual consent.
DATE: 1963 **EVENT:** Founding of Organization of African Unity **PLACE/CIVILIZATION/PERIOD:** Africa	**DESCRIPTION:** Organization of African Unity founded (1999 became African Union).
DATE: 1967 **EVENT:** Founding of Association of Southeast Asian Nations **PLACE/CIVILIZATION/PERIOD:** Asia	**DESCRIPTION:** Association of Southeast Asian Nations founded.
DATE: 1993 **EVENT:** European Union **PLACE/CIVILIZATION/PERIOD:** Western Europe	**DESCRIPTION:** The regional body based on the ECSC, which evolved into the European Economic Community, the European Community, and finally, the European Union with the negotiation of the Maastricht Treaty in 1992 (which came into force in 1993).
DATE: 1998 (came into force in 2002) **EVENT:** International Criminal Court **PLACE/CIVILIZATION/PERIOD:** Global	**DESCRIPTION:** Governed by the Rome Statute, the ICC is the first permanent, treaty-based international criminal court established to help end impunity for the perpetrators of the most serious crimes of concern to the international community.

II

Types of Diplomacy and Diplomacies of Place

[A diplomat must]...regard himself as an economist, a commercial traveler, an advertising agent for his country; he wields the weapon of culture for political ends; he promotes scientific and technical exchanges and administers development aid... He must concern himself not only with the relations of governments, but also of politicians, scientists, musicians, dancers, actors, authors, footballers, trade unionists, and even women and youth...

—LORD TREVELYAN
(British diplomat, reformer of the diplomatic system, and administrator in India in the 1800s) (Rana, 2014, 30)

Part II: Introduction

BY ALISON HOLMES

In the first section, a number of ways to look at diplomacy were presented, along with an alternative frame to explore the idea of global diplomacy. The first approach was the classical or traditional narrative that centers primarily on the institution of diplomacy after the creation, in the mid-seventeenth century, of what is commonly called the 'state.' In many respects, this version recognizes earlier entities as nascent states with various diplomatic practices. However, it also tends to focus almost exclusively on official activities that are more accurately defined as taking place between 'modern' or, more specifically, 'Westphalian' states without taking into account the wider communication and interaction styles of older/other entities. This is not to suggest that the general narrative, and the paradigms of realism and liberalism/pluralism it is based on, are not useful, as these lenses continue to be utilized in many fields and can be very instructive when analyzing specific issues. The argument is simply that, by concentrating on the European states-system approach, other worldviews get ignored, which can lead to assumptions and conclusions about diplomacy (and states as a whole) that are too narrow in an increasingly global world. As states become more porous, and as non-European states become more powerful, and more actors—both state and non-state—become more visible and active in the international/diplomatic arena, both the frame and the lenses of theory need to be reviewed, as the traditional ideas of sovereignty and power, based on much later manifestations of the state, cannot fully explain the undercurrents of contemporary global affairs.

To balance this traditional view, three alternatives were examined: the English School, a Revised English School, and the Sources of Power approach. Various elements of these approaches were drawn out to help deal with specific issues or problems in the traditional understanding. However, it was suggested that, by combining aspects of these alternative views, there is the possibility of a new theory of diplomacy that incorporates a more global approach, capable not only of helping us come to a better understanding of the past, but also prepare for the future by incorporating concepts from the past that may prove to be more continuous than first thought. The goal of this combined/global approach was threefold. First, by building on the English School's identification of a range of historical states-systems there is the possibility of more diversity in the analysis by including other periods of time and cultural interpretations of statecraft. Crucially, in many respects, this diversity also opens space for alternatives to the default hierarchical and linear assumptions of Western ideas.

Second, looking at more thematic perspectives as offered by the Revised English School (and opposed to a classic chronological history) cleared the way for a different approach to the story of diplomacy as an institution. All of which led to the use of Mann's sociological separation of the Sources of Social Power to draw out the types of diplomacy, their congruence with the practical work of diplomacy, and their relative rise and fall in importance at different times. Combined with first two, Mann helps connect theory more directly to practice as types of diplomacy become the constant pillars that provide a more stable base for diplomacy as a separate and distinct institution rather than a mere shadow of the state or ruling entity.

Technology and the processes of globalization have produced shifts in the nature of the state (as opposed to the purpose or nature of diplomacy). These forces did not create a new diplomacy, but only highlighted these sources of power as separate and combined networks and made them more visible to the casual observer of international politics.

The purpose of Part II is to investigate the assertion that diplomacy is more accurately viewed in a longer time frame by doing two things. First, to examine the concept of 'type' proposed in Part I in more depth and over time through five guest chapters that will explore the history of the four sources of social power or 'types' of diplomacy: political, economic, cultural, and military. These were defined in Part I and largely correspond to the daily activities undertaken by diplomats as illustrated by Kishan Rana, an ambassador for India for over thirty years and who, like Trevelyan two centuries before, recognized the impact of globalization on diplomacy and argues that economic diplomacy is "at the center-stage" (Rana, 2014, 449) while "Culture is a weapon for international projection…to produce understanding that goes beyond stereotype images and to mold perceptions in a favorable way…this makes cultural diplomacy integral to the larger task for furthering a nation's interests in foreign countries" (Rana, 2014, 144). The position here is simply that diplomacy is not some elusive creature that stays in the shadows of a shifting, fickle state, but a solid institution in its own right that has always sought to engage in a dialogue that can represent, negotiate, and, above all, communicate the needs of all people in any society to the rest of their world.

This part of the text has the following structure: six guests, authorities in their respective fields, will effectively seek to 'track' each type of diplomacy through time, highlighting what was called in the Introduction the 'theory vs. practice' debate. For some obvious reasons (and some not so obvious), each type of diplomacy tends to employ different tactics and, as suggested at the outset, these theories or strategies of statecraft have real-world implications. The lenses of theory used to understand the world drive policy in both the domestic and the foreign arenas with dramatically different outcomes. However, practice also bridges strategy and tactic because it is the connector or translator of the world of ideas into the world of implementation, and it is in this area that diplomats spend most, if not all, of their time. Thus, using these four types of diplomacy effectively frees our thinking about diplomacy not only from time, space, and issue-specific questions, but also from strict ideas of sovereignty and territory, leading us directly to the ways in which diplomats of all stripes—both state and non-state—actually operate in the world.

However, even as our guests try to disentangle the specific threads of 'type,' and help draw a longer line of analysis across different time frames, it is important not to ignore the more place- and time-specific aspects of both type and tactic. Therefore, these 'histories of type' will be interwoven with case studies of three non-Western states-systems: Byzantium, China, and India. These are also places that were agreed on by both the English School and Michael Mann as key points of development, but from the point of view presented here, they are also places where diplomacy was not only operating effectively for centuries, but had developed along different worldviews. This gives important insight in that they reflect the varying value and weight to the diplomatic types which, in turn, resulted in different practices and 'diplomacies of place' particularly before the existence of the Westphalian state. Obvious differences aside, they also offer connections not only to each other, but also to the modern world in terms of practice as well as highlighting aspects ignored by the prevailing European/Western narrative. By using a process of alternating the longitudinal perspective with the case study, the hope is to effectively create 'cross sections' of diplomacy at different points in time so as to better understand the institution of diplomacy when unattached to the entity it represents and the efficacy of both practice and tactics at different times (Frey and Frey, 1999).

Time and Its Impact on Views of History

When reading the guest chapters together with the Diplomatic Cross Sections, it is important to recognize the "historical process that evolved the ideology or institution, and the contemporary reasoning process that explains its operation" (Bozeman, 1960, 143). In other words, there is a need to bear in mind the idea that current views are effectively biased by the present. Biased, not in a necessarily negative sense, but in the sense that the knowledge, perspective, and reference points used to discuss world affairs are ingrained and inseparable from a present-day perspective and, more importantly, entirely unknowable by the people and civilizations of the past. Thus, any interpretation of past motives should always be critically examined for the presumptions of omnipotence that permeate our thinking about the past. Or, more simply put, it is difficult for us to see the world without the knowledge that has become commonplace since the period of time under examination and thus almost impossible to appreciate what would have been the everyday and 'obvious' constraints for leaders and decision makers in the past. In turn, our 'reality' will be unrecognizable to people in the future and actions seen as 'inevitable' or 'unavoidable' today will look strange, if not ignorant and foolhardy, to those who come later.

As we look at types over time and prepare to look at the diplomacies of place, we need both information about and a consciousness of the context for what Bozeman calls the "junctions" or the "countless historical situations in which separate chronologies interlock through the diffusion of ideas" (Bozeman, 1960, 18). Whatever we may think of past systems and what we understand to be the ideas underpinning them, we must try to see them through the eyes of those living in that moment, despite the fact we effectively know 'what happened next.' In other words, we should approach history with humility and respect.

Herbert Butterfield, mentioned previously as a member of the English School, discusses this problem explicitly, not only in the context of his concern with the points in time or the events that caused the breaks in diplomacy from 'old' to 'new,' but also in terms of a concern that lies close to the heart of this text: the cultural roots of 'Time' itself (Butterfield, 1981). The English School recognized different states-systems and their conduct as diplomacy, but it was Butterfield, in his role as historian, who concerned himself specifically with two additional questions. First, who tells the story of history? The question of whether the author was the voice of political power, i.e., the 'palace' or the priests and religious leaders in the 'temple.' Second, who do we tell the story of history for? Is the audience those here in the present moment (and told for factual exchange or power and influence) or a story told for future generations (with accuracy perhaps taking second place to concerns of reputation or legacy)? His concern is particularly relevant here as he goes on to argue that the way the story is told in the "west" is almost unique. Further, that it is the "sense of destiny" ingrained in European history-telling that helps set that system apart (and above according to the English School) China and India, two of the states-systems we will discuss in this section, which, he argues, have "underdeveloped" or "unhistorical" approaches. As part of a concept he calls "scientific history," Butterfield offers the visualization of time as a contrast between cyclical and linear and goes on to defend the idea that the linearity of time is not only the basis of western thought, but 'progress' itself—the heart of the Western tradition and the Westphalian state (Butterfield, 1981).

On the other hand, two other scholars, Carol Greenhouse and Mary Dudziak, point to the dangers of Butterfield's 'scientific' understanding given the effect that time-as-worldview can have on our perceived reality. Dudziak, a legal historian, demonstrates that wars are effectively used to break time into 'pieces' and thus as 'markers' for the beginning or end of an era. Yet, as she goes on to explain, this essentially takes time for granted and overlooks deeper social aspects and longer-term patterns (Dudziak, 2010, 1677). Dudziak, who leans heavily on Greenhouse, is a contemporary sociocultural anthropologist and explains in great detail the ways in which linearity allows time to control both purpose and direction not only to the lives of individuals, but crucially for this discussion, the basic purpose of the modern nation-state. She contrasts the ubiquity of linearity with what she calls "cyclical" or "social time"—based on daylight and seasons, birth and death (Dudziak, 2010). While perhaps not practical for consistency and efficiency of power across distance or the purposes of industrial capitalism, cyclical time is more rooted in cultures that are relational and often based on heterarchical rather than hierarchical structures, and therefore useful to bear in mind.

Greenhouse goes on to demonstrate that "scientific time" was actually imported to Europe along with Christianity. However, far from being adopted immediately, cyclical and linear time continued to compete until approximately the thirteenth century (Greenhouse, 1996); a date worth noting as this was also a common 'milestone' in diplomatic history marking the beginning of the establishment of permanent missions in capitals. Further, she argues, it was not until World War I that linear time finally became dominant, and another classic breakpoint in the classic story of diplomacy.

Diplomatic Practice

In other words, the classic narrative has many embedded concepts, but by opening up alternative interpretations of time and hierarchy it may be possible to create more possibilities for the narrative of diplomacy as an institution designed to mediate the social sources of power. The classic narrative outlined in Part I insists that the types of diplomacy—military, politics, economics, and culture—are stacked (in that order) in a hierarchy of usefulness to statecraft. However, this view positions diplomacy as the awkward actor who refuses to stay in one place in the hierarchy as it works from grand strategy to tactics. Yet diplomacy, to exist at all, must operate in all these areas of theory and practice simultaneously.

Iver Neumann helps capture part of this idea through a more 'cultural' look at diplomacy. By using the observations of anthropologist Clifford Geertz, Neumann offers levels or other "layers" and identifies the importance of the "myth system" to the way a people operate and perceive the world. He also discusses the "narrative sociabilities" that are based on those myths, and finally arrives at diplomatic "practice." Neumann argues that this is important because diplomacy functions on all of these deeper levels as well as at the more visible layers simultaneously. As societies seek to interact and exchange ideas, they need to be aware of these myths and narrative sociabilities before they can really understand 'practice.' By this, he means that cultures have abiding systems of belief (which could be seen as a worldview), but making a crucial distinction from a strictly hierarchical view, points out that myths work from the level of the people, their history, and culture and move both up and out. These, in turn, form the bases of narrative sociabilities, which constitute the way a society interacts with others. Neumann offers the example of a stranger arriving in a community. In some cultures, the stranger is seen as an intruder, a potential enemy, or a threat. In others, strangers are automatically deemed to be guests who should be treated with care and respect. His point is that both kinds of welcome are culturally based and become the foundation for what we know and see in the behaviors of diplomatic practice (Neumann, 2012), enabling us to see that diplomacy is a "hybridized phenomenon" at both the level of "myth and practice." The first being the myth of "kinship and religion," while the level of practice includes gift exchange and the sharing of food (Neumann, 2011, 315).

The point here is simply that the classic approach does not explore its own embedded concepts, these deeper layers of interaction or the alternative frame created by the recognition of type, to the detriment to the study of diplomacy as a whole.

Types over Time

Types were discussed and defined in Part I, but it is worth recapping their respective roles as sources of social power. Political diplomacy is the term used for much of the work done by diplomats, although it can be used so broadly as to mean very little. However, most people have at least some understanding of what we mean by political work or the political arena and how it could be applied to much of the work of a diplomat. Economic diplomacy is more specific and relatively clear, thus why it is perhaps the area that has been regularly 'institutionalized' in terms of diplomacy. By that is simply meant that trade and investment between entities has been an area of regulation through negotiation for centuries and therefore economic diplomacy (whether carried out by diplomats or other kinds of envoys) has long been a part of the intercommunication of societies. Many would consider military diplomacy as the oldest form of diplomacy—though others would seek to divide the military from many forms of diplomacy; at least to the extent that diplomacy is designed to promote or repair relations before or after conflict, while the military is fundamental to the survival of the entity and thus arguably a linchpin of diplomacy. Finally, and often overlooked, is cultural diplomacy, the overall importance of which, in terms of intercultural understanding, demonstrates the most obvious reason that the idea of types can be useful, in that any attempt to place one area 'on top,' 'before,' or as 'more important' than any other is futile if we are to understand diplomacy in a more holistic or global way.

The guest chapters begin with politics as the most pervasive type of diplomacy, in that it is difficult to discern a real difference between the regular tasks of representation, negotiation, and communication and the bigger moments of what one might call strategic statecraft. Here, it also creates a frame for all the other types of diplomacy. The daily work of the ambassador or diplomat can, in fact, be quite dull, but as Kenneth Weisbrode begins with the more traditional narrative and examines the relationship between diplomacy and politics, there is a clear relation between diplomatic aspirations and political reality through the ongoing process of give and take, monitoring and acting, and watching and speaking just below the surface. Weisbrode puts the 'old' vs 'new' diplomacy debate into context, while suggesting there has not been 'new' diplomacy for a century. Some may disagree with that assertion, but certainly political diplomacy is a nuanced process that has been, and remains closely linked to, the center of power.

The next guest, Geoffrey Pigman, goes back to the 'beginning' in the sense that he asserts the role of economic diplomacy as the codification and structuring of our most basic impulse and intercultural practice: exchange and trade. He spans a huge time frame, but breaks the narrative into three 'transformations' which form four distinct phases in economic history writ large, but more specifically, the story of economic diplomacy. Pigman highlights China as a particular example of the complex notions of power as he brings out the importance of trade and weaves it around and through other narratives of politics, war, and cultural exchange.

If trade and economics are the natural extension of contact between entities, Giles Scott-Smith steps further into the nature of their communication as he discusses culture and its role in mutual understanding or projection of identity. From his chapter, the points of contact between a notion of culture and what Michael Mann called 'ideology' through the different ways states understand and implement cultural diplomacy are clear. Scott-Smith begins by distinguishing cultural diplomacy not only from other types, but also other disciplines. A contested area, Scott-Smith sets out the traditional narrative and, in an effort to set culture into context, he offers six 'signposts.' These become both map and chronology for a journey through the cultural diplomatic strategies and the variety of tactics different countries have used in support of their national statecraft. From these examples, it seems that cultural diplomacy, like politics, is diffuse, but this also makes it an effective way for countries to engage with others in what could be deemed a more natural and often non-threatening way.

Andrew Dorman and Mathew Uttley bring us back to 'reality' with a bump in their exposition of defense and intelligence in the diplomatic world. However, as they point out in their explanation of the evolution of different strategies and tactics, even the most fundamental of state objectives (and essential aspect of realist narratives)—survival—has been affected by the increasing interconnectedness of the world. If the long-term strategy is single-minded security, the tactics deployed are constantly changing.

Having covered the four types, it may seem excessive to return to politics, but it is important for two reasons. First, as political diplomacy as a 'type' writ large is the most constant aspect of diplomatic life, it was important to ensure that it was covered thoroughly and from different perspectives. Second, diplomacy is also writ small and therefore the connection from the daily business or role or institution of diplomacy is different from the way it is approached by a diplomat employed. How that is bridged in the person of a former diplomat was an angle of politics not to miss, and therefore Shaun Riordan offers a perspective as both insider and academic on issues such as the increasing interest in what is becoming more widely known as regional diplomacy (again using China) and linking this back not to the new/old debate, but directly to security and national interest.

Diplomac*ies* of Place

Both the Sources of Power approach and the English School identified specific civilizations and systems as being of particular importance in terms of the development of governance. While Mann outlined six 'pristine civilizations,' the English School broadened this to include ten 'states-systems' of the ancient world. Others have focused on groupings by "idea" (Bozeman, 1960) or culturally specific "purposes of state" (Reus-Smit, 1999) to make particular points. Yet, perhaps the most interesting observation is that while the list is not large in terms of numbers, the locations are global in scope. In other words, despite the number of cultures and systems that have existed through time, patterns in terms of the entities they create emerge. Further, given the relatively small number of societies, they are not concentrated in a single region or even time frame so that we might explain their development as part of a process of influence and interaction with each other. They cover vastly different times and locations, but a distinct form comes through and the value they consistently place on communicating with others, are the basis of strongly similar practices to support that aim.

In terms of the choice of case studies or more place-based investigations of type, a number of 'pristine civilizations' (to use Mann's terms) or 'states-systems' (the English School phrase) are available. However, any choice begs a prior question as to what constitutes a 'civilization' in this context and whether diplomacy is a function of some specific 'level' of development or form of entity. Bozeman, looking at the diffusion of ideas and culture, lists three inventions as key to civilization: iron, writing, and coined money (Bozeman, 1960, 39). Mann follows scholars such as Colin Renfrew and Gordon Childe by assessing civilization by the human-made artifacts that change the relationship between humans and nature. Renfrew, in particular, defines this as "insulation from nature": "namely ceremonial centres (insulators against the unknown), writing (an insulation against time), and the city (the great container, spatially defined, the insulator against the outside)" (Mann quoting Renfrew, 1986, 74).

Using such definitions as a base, other authors have pointed to significant milestones in the development of civilizations or state-systems as they evolved towards this notion of a 'society.' For example, Barry Buzan and Richard Little, often associated with the English School, argue that "pre-international systems" lasted until approximately 3500 BCE, when an "interlinked international system" developed, and then, in 1500 BCE, there was a move to what are called "global international systems" (Buzan and Little, 2000). William McNeill, using a broadly similar timeline, denotes entities as "pre-civilizations" until 3500 BCE, "civilizations" until 1700 BCE, then "inter-linked civilizations" until 1500 CE, when they finally move into "global civilization" (McNeill, 1963). (See Figure II.1)

Bearing these definitions and timelines in mind—and noting the fascinating coincidence of various key dates among diverse authors and disciplines—

the three states systems chosen here are Byzantium, China, and India. Under McNeill's system they would all be considered civilizations and inter-linked civilizations, or simply inter-linked international systems by Buzan and Little. However, it is important to recall the example of the griot of Mali and therefore there is no assertion that such indicators of 'civility' determine diplomatic capacity.

	60,000-40,000 BCE	10,000-6,000 BCE	3500 BCE	1700 BCE	800 BCE	1500 CE	1750 CE	1900 CE	2000 CE
Buzan & Little 2000	Pre-international System ------------------- ||-- Interlinked International Systems --- ||---- Global International Systems								
McNeill 1963	Pre-Civilizations-- || Civilizations|| Interlinked Civilizations|| Global Civilization								

FIGURE II.1 Civilizations Timeline

The overarching idea of this section is that diplomacy has more continuities than discontinuities when viewed over time. The use of 'type' is a way to see that constancy while the case studies highlight features of diplomacy, particularly before the state as the entity we know it, and allow for the examination of the impact of worldview on the manifestation of diplomatic practice through their interpretation of type in that place. This creates a sense of both weft and warp for global diplomacy as we pull out certain ideas by type, then weave them back into the fabric of specific times and places. The goal is for a better understanding of what statecraft without the state (or at least the state as we understand it today) looked like in the past and perhaps how global states may create a tapestry of diplomacy for today's interconnected world in the future.

References and Further Reading

Bozeman, Adda. *Politics and Culture in International History*. Princeton: Princeton University Press, 1960.

Butterfield, Herbert. *The Origins of History*. New York: Basic Books, 1981.

Buzan, Barry and Richard Little. *International Systems in World History*. Oxford: Oxford University Press, 2000.

Dudziak, Mary. "Law War and the History of Time. Legal Studies Research Paper Series." Legal Research Paper No. 09–6, (2010): 1668–1712.

Frey, Linda and Marsha Frey. *The History of Diplomatic Immunity*. Columbus: Ohio University Press, 1999.

Greenhouse, Carol. *A Moment's Notice: Time Politics Across Cultures*. Ithaca and London: Cornell University Press, 1996.

Mann, Michael. *Volume 1. The Sources of Social Power: A History of Power from the Beginning to A.D. 1760.* Cambridge: Cambridge University Press, 1986.

McNeill, William. *The Rise of the West: A History of the Human Community*. Chicago: Chicago University Press, 1963.

Neumann, Iver. "Euro-Centric diplomacy: Challenging but manageable." *European Journal of International Relations*. 18 (2) (2011): 299–321.

Rana, Kishan. *Inside Diplomacy*. New Delhi: Manas Publications, 2014.

Reus-Smit, Christian. *The Moral Purpose of the State: Culture, Social Identity, and Institutional Rationality in International Relations*. Princeton: Princeton University Press, 1999.

4 Diplomacy and Politics

BY KENNETH WEISBRODE

Introduction

For much of history the terms 'diplomacy' and 'politics' have been intimate, as diplomacy regulates and mediates politics between sovereign entities, which have principally meant nation-states and their governments. The diplomatic record includes episodes of rupture, namely wars. Military history, strictly speaking, is a subcategory of diplomatic history, which was once among the most prestigious of fields for professional historians.

This is no longer the case and has not been for some time. Diplomacy has not really recovered its prestige since the cataclysm of 1914. Some scholars, reacting to Woodrow Wilson's promotion during and after the war of what he called the "New Diplomacy," invented something 'new' of their own called the discipline of international relations. That some of these scholars sought to repudiate Wilsonianism—the ideology of the New Diplomacy—was beside the point. Its basis was not historical in the traditional sense outlined by Leopold von Ranke, in that it did not seek to uncover and reconstruct the past for its own sake, but rather to draw lessons about the ways statesmen *ought* to act. In this respect, international relations was not that much different from Wilsonianism: that is, it was a normative, programmatic discipline that derived from general laws of human behavior.

This trend continued into and well beyond the Second World War, and was buoyed by the popularity around the world of Anglo-American social science, where international relations resided. As late as the 2000s, students in introductory "IR" courses were assigned E.H. Carr's *The Twenty Years' Crisis* and Kenneth Waltz's *Man, the State, and War,* first published in 1939 and 1959 respectively, as the foundational texts of their discipline. The first was a bitter critique of Wilson and Wilsonianism; the latter a theoretical exercise in the behavioral interplay of individuals, states, and societies. Although the first was an historical essay and the second a work of political science, both were didactic, and both equated a counter-ideology with an empirical analysis of interstate relations. This analysis held many historical 'variables' constant, relying on a synchronic elaboration of the "international system." International relations has since blossomed into many schools and approaches—too numerous to recount here—but much of its underlying basis remains true to its quasi-scientific origin.

However, politics is an art not a science; so too is diplomacy. Thus, both may also be treated as a craft. This traditional, almost quaint, view is not extinct in the twenty-first century, if only because many, perhaps even a majority, of diplomats still subscribe to it. Yet the lines between politics and diplomacy have blurred considerably. Today, in the most general sense, diplomacy has a mainly functional definition. Americans, for example, like to call it 'just one tool in the toolbox,' the toolbox being something larger called 'foreign policy.' There are also military tools, cultural tools, economic tools, and so on. The diplomatic tool is associated with negotiations, usually after a war has broken out or ended, or, in rarer cases, before it has broken out. This is a departure from the classic definition of diplomacy, which, in its combination of the means and ends of power, was closer to statecraft, with diplomats serving, according to one of their promoters, the historian Sasson Sofer, as "... the courtiers of civilization. They are the counselors and priests of peaceful relations; they hover above the conclusion of truces, cease-fires, and peace treaties. It is platitudinous to suggest that diplomats represent the best that is found in human nature. They are, however, the custodians of the idea of international society, and the guardians of international virtues" (Sofer, 2013, 67).

Since the advent of the academic discipline of international relations, diplomacy's definition has narrowed. This has, in effect, divorced diplomacy from politics. Some other chapters in this volume show this definition, which corresponds in caricature to official communications between foreign ministries, to be unsuitable to the contemporary world. Many organizations besides foreign ministries are engaged in the business of diplomacy; many people besides official envoys and bureaucrats participate in it.

If the contemporary definition of diplomacy is to return to being more or less synonymous with international relations rather than understood as a mere procedural component of it, what effect would this have on politics? That is, where do politics fit in a broader definition of diplomacy and of the diplomatic craft, in the twenty-first century?

A Broader Definition

Diplomacy encompasses the entirety of relationships between sovereign entities, their representatives, and their inhabitants in the sovereign interest, and in the general cause of peace. Diplomatic activity may also take place between sovereign entities and transnational groups or private entities that do not have 'official' status, or among such groups themselves, although they ought to have a measure of cohesion and a collective identity to qualify as diplomatic actors. Diplomacy, then, is the act of one actor relating to the other in order to devise a workable relationship across a border; or, in the case of a failure, to do so, and in the event of a rupture of the peace, to maneuver and manipulate one another's political assets and relationships in order to gain a strategic or tactical advantage. It encompasses both policy and practice, that is to say, negotiations as well as the axioms and decisions taken that produce and accompany the negotiations.

In truth, the divergence of definitions between a narrow and broad concept of diplomacy is longstanding. Both in theory and in practice, diplomacy and policy have been treated distinctively as well as with more fluid gradations (Nicolson, 1977, 3–5). Before the advent of the telegraph, there may have been more of the latter than the former, with ambassadors in far-flung posts interpreting their instructions loosely, if not making them up outright. Later—certainly by the beginning of the twentieth century with the popularity of conference diplomacy—policy-making became almost coterminous with negotiation. Incidentally, this diplomatic vehicle, in the later incarnation of the 'summit,' has proved too popular to discard, although most professional diplomats regard it as less than an ideal forum for negotiation. Not only do they expose leaders to the whims of personality, but they also are nearly impossible to conduct with discretion; and therefore are usually less likely to succeed than quiet talks among diplomatic professionals, that is, unless the latter have already taken place with the summit or conference results 'cooked.' Here, superficiality is the price states pay for effectiveness. This counts politics as an intrusion, which now include efforts by amateurs of an even lower rank: for example, legislators, mayors, or private citizens, such as celebrities, acting in the name of the public will.

Because there is not, and probably will never be, a perfectly equal or just world, there will be, for the foreseeable future, nation-states of varying size and power; there will be alliances of the same; there will be jealousies, rivalries, and ruptures; and there will be some manner of hierarchy in the ordering of international relationships. Someday, perhaps, there may be a viable body like a more powerful United Nations that replaces 'international' politics with something else akin to a world parliament. Nations could remain sovereign, but would come to resemble constituencies more than autonomous political agents. If such a body ever succeeds, it will not have done away with traditional politics, or with diplomacy in the service of politics. It would merely offer an alternative setting and language for negotiating interests among its members. Put another way, it is not the structure of political systems that dictates the role for diplomacy; structures condition, but do not directly determine, let alone predetermine, it.

This is the starting point for understanding the inter-relationship of politics and diplomacy today. They have their root in the quantity and the quality of power in the world. The first relates how power rises and falls, who wields it, and how; the second relates how the powerful deal with one another and with the less powerful, and, occasionally, with the least powerful. Each has a normative aspect. Politics, by its association with government, is, on occasion, occupied with dispensing justice. Diplomacy, by its contraposition to war, is occupied with preserving peace. Good politics tend to be perceived as being just. Good diplomacy tends to be peaceful and, we could add, to the mutual advantage of the parties involved, however powerful they may be. That is to say, both good politics and good diplomacy extend beyond *raison d'etat* or 'reason of state,' even though the latter remains an important element of world order.

Diplomats are subservient to the state. Where politicians obstruct the interests of the state, diplomats are called in to show a way ahead. Where politics compel an aggressive policy, diplomats are charged with softening its edges. Where politicians suggest a reactive, or passive, policy, diplomats are meant to explore alternatives, usually indirect ones, to achieve the aims that a more direct, but impractical policy, would not achieve. All this is not to say that diplomacy is entirely auxiliary to politics. Wise diplomats learn how to determine the 'facts on the ground' through the purveyance of information, advice, and authority. Nevertheless, without a direct role in politics, diplomacy is weak given that its value and strength derive primarily from its capacity to enhance political leverage in the interests of the state, however indirect and intricate some of its methods can appear. There is rarely a use for diplomacy conducted for its own sake, divorced from politics. Yet, at the same time, politics without diplomacy would not always be viable. "As long as the state remains at the center of international relations," Sofer has written, "diplomacy will be anchored in the political domain, aspiring to relations without resorting to force. There is no adequate alternative for diplomatic practice as the most prudent method for reconciling contradictory interests, or for other parties to agree to an accepted resolution" (Sofer, 2013, 14). The claim is emphatic, but also true.

It has been said that diplomacy is useless without the latent (or sometimes blatant) threat of force. That underscores the above claim that neither diplomacy nor politics are ever isolated or separate. To borrow the famous line of Carl von Clausewitz, if war is politics (or policy) by other means, then diplomacy is war by other means, as well as its occasional ally or its antidote. All really are inseparable from power, a point associated not only with Clausewitz, but more commonly with a founder of modern politics, Niccolò Machiavelli. This may be ironic, for, as Sofer has noted,

> Diplomats are particularly vulnerable in their clash with sovereigns, where the aura of privilege and proximity to power often prove to be a double-edged sword. In the extreme case of a struggle between a virtuous prince and an ideal diplomat, the latter is merely a hunter with feeble arrows, or in Machiavellian terms, a fox of the second order. The diplomat is almost inevitably the civil servant chosen, by his manners, image, and practices, to serve as a scapegoat (Sofer, 2013, 58–59).

Not all diplomats are 'scapegoats,' and those who are so cast may not be as weak as they appear, for scapegoats, among other things, serve a necessary political function in preserving the appearance of public virtue. Put another way, although the ends of diplomacy may be public, the means are, by necessity, private, even if that means on occasion sacrificing a public reputation.

Transformations

The relationship between diplomacy and politics is essential, but it has also evolved unevenly. Its evolution, Harold Nicolson has written, is not uniform or necessarily progressive: "international intercourse has always been subject to strange retrogressions" (Nicolson, 1954, 1–2). Today, this is a minority view.

The adjective 'transformational' is now popular in many fields, including diplomacy. What does it mean? There are actually two meanings, one directed outward, the other inward. The first refers to statecraft: the ways by which diplomacy transforms particular places, problems, and relationships from one condition to another. The second refers to diplomacy itself and its methods.

The best-known example of the latter is the aforementioned 'New Diplomacy.' As a term of art it refers to the diplomacy made popular by Woodrow Wilson a century ago, but it has been used at other times as well, including today (for example, by Shaun Riordan) to describe the role of social networks, digital media, and their effects on the diplomatic profession. Wilson's New

Diplomacy was inspired similarly, for its most basic premise—open covenants openly arrived at—was, at root, a change in diplomatic method. However, the New Diplomacy then went much further because its aim was to govern a new world of imperial successor states that all adhered to the same liberal principles. The New Diplomacy took the Westphalian order a step further: no longer was state sovereignty enough; public opinion now counted, or was said to count, a great deal more than it had before, for the general public was much more interested, it was also said, in foreign affairs. The citizens of these states also had to be sovereign; they had to select and determine their own governments; they had to combine together to govern the world in a way that set their mutual interest over particular interests; and they had to choose and enforce a just world order.

None of this was new. Rules of conduct, including principles of universal character, date back, at least in the Western tradition, to the ancient Greeks and Romans. Among other things, the Greeks developed the concept of the collective will, and the cultivation of it through negotiation, cooperation, precedent, rules, and norms. So were certain familiar impediments to sound diplomacy, as Nicolson has noted them: a tendency to prize the clever over the reliable; the interference of legislatures in external affairs; and the proliferation of political quarrels (Nicolson, 1954, 10–11). Yet the Greeks also employed the basic article of diplomacy—the treaty—to settle disputes and preserve peace; they established the viability of leagues and alliances; the 'Amphictyony,' or ancient league of Greek tribes, for all its faults, was a worthy institution that was among the first successful attempts to stabilize and civilize the exercise of politics across borders; indeed, this early diplomatic institution became almost a spiritual buttress to politics by enshrining the league as a sacred body. The effect was to combine politics and culture—or, to be more precise, to couch a divisive politics within a common culture—so as to regulate the former and promote the latter. As such institutions later formed the basis of empires, they would see the subordination of power to law, or rather, the exercise of power through law, which diplomacy served.

This was the political tradition to which Wilson and his New Diplomacy adhered. By Wilson's time, there had begun "a shift in the centre of power" from monarchies and aristocracies to cabinets to citizenries (Nicolson, 1977, 30). Yet Wilson's proposed vehicle for collective security—the multilateral congress to be known as the League of Nations—was not too different, at least in spirit, from the many congresses and conferences that had come before. Even what we now call public opinion, so championed by Wilson, had had an important influence on diplomacy going back at least to the time of

Cardinal Richelieu. Diplomacy adapted from being the handmaiden of politics to its operative, engineer, and moral judge.

Perhaps this was the reason that the aforementioned 'realist' critics took so violently to Wilson's self-willed transformation. Diplomacy, they claimed, could not do or be all these things at once. Diplomats are servants, not masters, of the State, let alone of universal morality; they are not equally the enforcers and revelatory agents of just and desirable universal norms. Hence, the principled stand against the subordination of power to justice. For all that the latter may have been (and still may be) a desired end in the world, there are those who claim that pursuing it at all costs goes against human nature. The pursuit of justice first requires peace. Ignoring this particular natural law, realists say, results in the spread of neither peace nor justice.

Wilson's defenders have also claimed that national interests are served better in combination than in competition. He and his ideology were not idealist in the philosophical sense, they wrote, but rather a form of "higher realism" in the political sense. The New Diplomacy, and collective security, especially—described by Wilson as a community of power—are alternative sources of international order that he renewed with a more democratic form of politics for the twentieth century. His critics make a good point in highlighting their shortcomings, but fail to explain how a destroyed world was otherwise meant to rebuild and govern itself when so many traditional structures and ways had gone. It had been Wilson's view that a New Diplomacy and a new politics would offer a different, better future. It was also his view that the world did not really have a fair choice: it could embrace modernity—including a modern diplomacy—and survive, or it could resist, and die. In the event it embraced the new diplomacy, Wilson probably assumed the modern world would be more peaceful because human institutions had progressed to the point where they were better matched to the democratic will of the people, who, if properly taught, would choose peace and justice over rivalry and oppression.

To dwell upon Wilson is not to suggest that he was solely responsible for the transformation of diplomacy at the turn of the previous century, but instead to emphasize the durability of his concept of international relations, in spite of its having been followed by some terrible wars. He typified an understanding of both the theory and the practice of diplomacy which granted it an organic association with the specific nature of the international political system—and with the distinct political systems and forms of government in each nation-state. So a politically attenuated manner of diplomacy could both bring about and sustain such a system. Whether or not this belief represented a lower or a higher form of realism is beside the point. Wilson and his supporters regarded it as a more pragmatic response to the world's ills than the only other popular alternative then on offer: 'Bolshevism.' History would appear to have worked in their favor. One of Wilson's bitterest critics—his fellow American, the diplomat George Kennan—admitted many decades later, just before the Berlin Wall had fallen, that Wilson had been far ahead of his time. In other words, the international system had reached a point where the world itself had become too small for interstate rivalry to flourish. The world's politics was on the path to becoming, to use a phrase known to political scientists, fully 'interdependent.' Politics were transformed; so too was diplomacy. The choice facing statesmen and diplomats was not whether or not such transformations could be halted or perhaps hijacked; rather, it was how best to adapt official structures and both official and unofficial relationships to the 'new' circumstances; that is, to master rather than fight a political transformation as it was widely understood.

Order and Governance

To the diplomat, 'order,' however durable, is negotiable and temporary and requires frequent tending and cultivation, as would a garden. Since the late Renaissance, order has been measured by standards of external behavior irrespective, in principle, of internal politics. That is to say, states ought to be judged by their actions toward other states, less by how they treat their own people or how they otherwise govern their own affairs. The peak of this separation in practice was the period of "Old Diplomacy," during the seventeenth, eighteenth, and nineteenth centuries. In general, according to Nicolson, it was the

> ...method... that best adapted to the conduct of relations between civilised States. It was courteous and dignified; it was continuous and gradual; it attached importance to knowledge and experience; it took account of the realities of existing power; and it defined good faith, lucidity and precision as the qualities essential to any sound negotiation. The mistakes, the follies and the crimes that during those three hundred years accumulated to the discredit of the old diplomacy can, when examined at their sources, be traced to evil foreign policy rather than to faulty methods of negotiation. It is regrettable that the bad things they did should have dishonoured the excellent manner in which they did them (Nicolson, 1954, 72–73).

This division of official action—between internal and external—was eroded by the failures leading up to the First World War and by Wilson's innovation that followed it. The tone, character, and dimensions of domestic politics all have become difficult to separate from their international effects, and vice versa. The domestic and the foreign realms in many countries today are interpenetrated and even interdependent. They are also rather disordered. When politicians and diplomats speak of order, the term carries a whiff of reaction. Old Diplomacy did rely on a hierarchy of powers; the more powerful—which fashioned themselves as the Great Powers—certainly held sway over weaker ones. However, the Great Powers also bore the greatest responsibility for maintaining peace, or what they liked to call 'equilibrium.' This demanded as much, or even more, restraint and good sense than more overt forms of political interference meant to impress or compel obedience.

The popular word today for the ways of responsibility is 'governance.' How does it differ from order? Less than we might think. Both terms connote stability, peace, and regularity, or at least some insulation from drastic political and social change. But they differ in their relation to politics. Order rests on the line drawn between the domestic and the foreign. Governance erodes this line by promoting a normative measurement of political rule both within and among states. Whereas, in theory, order is more or less stable, governance is rated as more or less 'good.' Good governance is judged, in other words, less by its political viability or longevity at particular junctures than by its adherence to certain standards and values in perpetuity.

These differences may blur in practice. A stable order may cloak forces of instability, many deriving from bad governance. A good system of governance may cloak resentments that lead to social and political disorder. Yet with both conditions there is a dependency similar to the one between peace and justice. It is hard to imagine the promotion of good governance in the absence of a peaceful order. Put more prosaically, one must survive in order to thrive. For all that the proponents of good governance tout its superiority on moral and political grounds, it may be that they take the latter too often for granted. Few states at war find it easy to be well governed.

Nevertheless, there is no desirable alternative to good governance, just as there is none for justice. Few responsible societies would advocate one. Nevertheless, for diplomats, many of whom have not disavowed the pursuit of order, the diplomacy of governance can pose difficulties. Such diplomacy can degenerate to what former British Prime Minister Benjamin Disraeli once dismissed as a "policy of scold." There are other names for it: the "diplomacy of insult" or "megaphone diplomacy." Most are variations on one of the more ineffective modes of politics, that of name-calling. The diplomat in such cases is converted into a cheerleader or taskmaster, passing and pushing judgments on the actions of foreign governments. Too often this merges with accusations of hypocrisy, and with blind interference. The diplomatic task is thereby inverted: diplomats are meant to persuade others to do what is, ideally, in their mutual interest—or, as it has been said by cynics, to do what is in the diplomat's interest while thinking it is in their own. Now, diplomats are meant to persuade others that they are acting against their own interests, and what ought to be their own values, because they do not comply with particular standards.

It would be difficult not to apportion some of the blame to Wilson. Politics, in his progressive tradition, ought to be overtaken by superior administration. Interests and passions were no longer political subjects, but rather technocratic objects. Diplomacy, accordingly, has become the exercise of 'ensuring compliance,' to use another popular Americanism. In such a world, diplomats are again mere political auxiliaries.

This depiction of governance is not meant as a caricature. The ideology of good governance is a fact. So too have been many positive results. However, what role is there for diplomats in a world ruled by legal regimes, norms, and institutions? Diplomats do not eliminate politics from human affairs, but their political methods resemble bureaucratic or legislative logrolling more than diplomacy. The most familiar case of this is the European Union, whose origins were in a diplomatic agreement between France and Germany over their respective steel and coal industries. The development of the European Communities, and eventually the European Union, became an exercise in multilateral diplomacy of the first order, featuring a series of negotiations, summits, and treaties. Yet now that the EU and its many institutions exist, where do the diplomats fit? One place is in the new European External Action Service, a de facto EU foreign ministry. Most of its officers come from national foreign ministries. Yet within the EU itself, there is little for national diplomats to do; most decisions are left to politicians and bureaucrats.

This again is consistent with the Wilsonian vision. Its governing body was meant to be the League of Nations, which would not have been so much a league or an alliance, but rather a supranational organ that would have eliminated the need for traditional diplomacy. So much for the theory. Yet even the broadest sketch of contemporary international relations would show that they have much more in common with the Wilsonian legal-moral-institutional tradition than with any alternative, the persistence of realpolitik notwithstanding. Today's diplomats find themselves less occupied in resisting the obsolescence of their profession than, at least in principle, in devising more adaptations to an ever more complicated world. The intricate inter-state negotiations of the past now join other negotiations among states and other entities, and even among parties within states. Diplomacy has not seen so much a blurring as a multiplication of political lines during the past few generations. If the defeat and dismantling of the European empires in the twentieth century and the emergence of new nations as well as supranational institutions in their place has led to anything, it has been to the further convergence of politics and diplomacy. As more states grow more disinclined to wage war, diplomacy has also grown more coterminous with statecraft. The diplomat's traditional assets of adaptability to circumstances, empathy, and intuition are needed as much as they ever have been.

The Shape of Diplomacy

Knowing how adaptable and innovative diplomacy has been historically, it is striking that no 'new' diplomacy has emerged in nearly a century. It may be possible, as the aforementioned remarks by George Kennan suggest, that Wilson was so far ahead of his time, politics have merely caught up with the theory, ideology, and principles he espoused. Indeed, it is hard to contemplate a greater standard for statecraft than universal virtue; there is, by definition, no larger canvas on which to paint a desirable world order. Yet, this is a relative judgment. A verdict on the Old Diplomacy—and here we speak, again, narrowly of only European diplomacy during that period—may have been roughly equivalent in novelty. Just as we cannot know the precise future evolution of global politics, we cannot know how precisely diplomats will adapt to it. We may insist, however, that adaptation shall happen somehow or, if not, politics and diplomacy will just cease to progress.

One of the advantages of diplomatic tradition comes from this paradox: it is always adjusting to the world around it, yet it does so slowly, almost imperceptibly. Aspects of diplomacy that are now taken for granted—the summit, for example—have evolved accordingly. Whereas, during the Cold War they scaled up, as the name suggests, to the level of heads of state, in the past couple of decades they have scaled back down, so that it is not uncommon to see 'summits' of interior or environmental ministers, or even without any ministers at all, as the large number of non-governmental organization conferences, nearly all professing to influence or even make policy, probably would attest.

Whether or not such activity rises to the level of statecraft, or even produces the political change it seeks, is open to question. What is less in doubt is the disorder that has accompanied it. Disorder is not just the result of greater numbers of people trying to do more things at once; it is also the result of another paradox. Popular summits in lieu of traditional diplomacy are, on the surface, apolitical, or sometimes proto-political. Their organizers seek to supplant the roles of diplomats and other state actors in the name of transcending politics as usual. So far the record has been mixed—for example, in the declining utility of the summits of developed nations (G-7, etc.), which began in the 1970s as a small, informal collective meeting of finance ministers, have since devolved into a global circus at which neither state nor non-state actors achieve much of a concrete nature besides their own self-promotion. Some theorists of governance would call this evidence of 'empowerment,' but from the traditional diplomatic point of view, it is the opposite. Diplomacy is measured by its tangible results, however continuous the process of reaching them may be. Yet, at the same time, who can say that global governance does not require regular public affirmation? Diplomacy, after all, is both representative and representational. Diplomats represent their leaders and fellow citizens; they also represent an idea or concept of international society, and, again, of civilization. If the standards of representation change alongside society, so too should the shape of their expression, whether they come in summits (G-7, G-20, and the like) or some other forum yet to be invented.

Geopolitics has not stood still either. In the middle-twentieth century, Woodrow Wilson's concept of the universal community of power was replaced, partially, by a narrower concept: the regional security community. The most familiar example is the North Atlantic, later called the Euro-Atlantic. On the one hand, such a community was based on the rule of law and all the norms that Wilson espoused, with the partial exception of free trade, which took some time to negotiate. Wilson imagined that his international community would supplant forever the concept of the balance of power. In fact, such regional communities did the opposite: they supplanted Wilson's universalism with smaller entities that took into account the realities—that is to say, the balances and imbalances—of power, including military power. A North Atlantic regional community probably never would have succeeded without NATO, for example; although, to be fair, the formal definition of NATO was never exclusively military.

Such communities are nevertheless diplomatic inventions. They formed around treaties, understandings, and arrangements in the classic, Old Diplomatic fashion, but with the aim of furthering, piece by piece, a world order that was more Wilsonian than not.

The final point is instructive for understanding today's relationship between politics and diplomacy. Postwar regional communities were not fixed. They were, as the saying went, 'organic.' There had been a few diplomats and statesmen—notably the American diplomat Sumner Welles and the British Prime Minister, Winston Churchill, who each imagined a world of sovereign regions in concert as larger versions of nineteenth-century European nation-states. This vision did not prevail because it was not consistent with the politics of the time. Both the Soviet Union and the United States would proceed to create spheres of influence, some of which had a regional character, and others which did not. Regional spheres in both Europe and Asia were expansive vis-à-vis one another. Borders were drawn but many proved to be temporary. After the end of the Cold War, the borders were even more expansive, and even more temporary. Even an entity as rule-bound and complex as the European Union has invited new members, based not on ethnicity or any other historically fixed criteria, but on a nation's willingness to abide by various norms and standards, and, secondarily, on other factors like geography and demography. This may change, of course, but, until now, regional integration on a functional basis has been the dominant, or at least the most promising, guide to contemporary diplomacy, and geopolitics.

This is the legacy that twentieth-century diplomats, politicians, and statesmen have left their successors in the twenty-first century. Regionalism has so far been well-suited to an interdependent world. Yet, regional bodies also may prove easier to destroy than to build, just as empires once were. The facility of destruction was a lesson of August 1914 as countries began to declare war in what became World War I; and the diplomats, by most accounts, were just as culpable as the politicians in bringing that about. Perhaps, in addition to all the other familiar failures of decision and action they committed, each had taken the stability of several generations for granted. If so, their example reminds us that diplomacy is as much the art of the possible as is politics, to include possible disaster when their agents work at cross-purposes.

CHAPTER REVIEW QUESTIONS

1. How does Weisbrode define diplomacy?
2. What was the Wilsonian view of Old Diplomacy?
3. How does Weisbrode distinguish 'governance' from 'order'?
4. What is 'transformational diplomacy'?
5. What is the relationship between power and diplomacy?

SEMINAR/ESSAY QUESTIONS

1. Why does Weisbrode suggest the evolution of diplomacy is a paradox?
2. Can diplomacy exist without the state?
3. Regional and functional diplomacy are the trends of the future for diplomacy. Discuss.
4. Explain what Weisbrode means when he says diplomacy is both representational and representative?
5. What is the relationship between diplomacy and politics for Weisbrode?

References and Further Reading

Berridge, G. R. *Diplomacy: Theory and Practice*. London: Prentice Hall, 1995.

Bull, Hedley. *The Anarchical Society: A Study of World Order in Politics*. New York: Columbia University Press, 1977.

Carr, E. H. *The Twenty Years Crisis 1919–1939: An Introduction to the Study of International Relations*. London: Macmillan, 1940.

Cooper, Andrew F. *Celebrity Diplomacy*. Boulder: Paradigm Publishers, 2008.

Craig, Gordon A. and Alexander L. George. *Force and Statecraft: Diplomatic Problems of Our Time*. Oxford: Oxford University Press, 1983.

Duchêne, François. *Jean Monnet: The First Statesman of Interdependence*. New York: Norton, 1994.

Freeman, Chas. W., Jr. *The Arts of Power: Statecraft and Diplomacy*. Washington, D.C.: United States Institute of Peace, 1997.

Goodby, James E. *Europe Undivided: The New Logic of Peace in U.S.-Russian Relations*. Washington, D.C.: United States Institute of Peace, 1997.

Hamilton, Keith and Richard Langhorne. *The Practice of Diplomacy: Its Evolution, Theory and Administration*. London: Routledge, 1995.

Hinsley, F. H. *Power and the Pursuit of Peace: Theory and Practice in the History of Relations Between States*. Cambridge: Cambridge University Press. 1963.

Kaufmann, Johan. *Conference Diplomacy: an Introductory Analysis*. New York: Oceana Publications, 1968.

Kennan, George F. *American Diplomacy 1900–1950*. Chicago: University of Chicago Press, 1951.

Kennan, George F. 1989. "The Future of U.S. Soviet Relations," testimony to the United States Senate Committee on Foreign Relations, April 4, 1989, available at cspan.org.

Link, Arthur S. *Wilson the Diplomatist: A Look at His Major Foreign Policies*. Baltimore: The Johns Hopkins University Press, 1957.

Mazower, Mark. *Governing the World: The History of an Idea*. New York: Penguin, 2012.

Nicolson, Harold. *Diplomacy*, 3rd Edition, Oxford: Oxford University Press, 1977.

Nicolson, Harold. *The Evolution of Diplomatic Method*, London: Cassell, 1954.

Ninkovich, Frank. *Modernity and Power: A History of the Domino Theory in the Twentieth Century*. Chicago: University of Chicago Press, 1994.

Nowotny, Thomas. *Diplomacy and Global Governance*. New Brunswick: Transaction, 2011.

Reynolds, David. *Summits: Six Meetings that Shaped the Twentieth Century*. London: Allen Lane, 2007.

Riordan, Shaun. *The New Diplomacy*. London: Polity, 2002.

Schweitzer, Karl and Paul Sharp (eds). *The International Thought of Herbert Butterfield*. New York: Palgrave, 2007.

Sharp, Paul. *A Diplomatic Theory of International Relations*. Cambridge: Cambridge University Press, 2009.

Sofer, Sasson. *The Courtiers of Civilization: A Study of Diplomacy*. Albany: SUNY Press, 2013.

Waltz, Kenneth. *Man, the State, and War: A Theoretical Analysis*. New York: Columbia University Press, 1954.

CROSS SECTION 4.1

The Mandala, Politics, and Territory

BY ALISON HOLMES

As Weisbrode's chapter suggests, the worlds of politics and diplomacy remain inextricably linked. He also clearly demonstrates the continuing debates around the old vs. the new diplomacy and theory vs. practice. Clearly, governance, regionalism, and the willingness to abide by rules and norms form the basis of contemporary diplomatic interaction. Yet the chapter also demonstrates other aspects of the classic, Western/European narrative, which is the embedded nature of hierarchy, linear time, and power as strength. In a more global narrative, an alternative perspective of power is illustrated in the concept of the **mandala** and heterarchy and lends itself to an alternative form of state, often tributary in nature, and in stark contrast to the Westphalian state of the classic narrative.

Mandala as the base of tributary states and heterarchy

If the Westphalian state comes weighed down with these concepts of hierarchy, linear time, power and territory, a vivid way to visualize the alternative perspective of a tributary state and heterarchy, with all the difference in terms of power that implies, is to briefly examine the concept of the mandala. The mandala is particularly relevant because it operates in the case studies of both India, where it was developed, and in China, where it was also used, but some background is useful in terms of what a mandala involves before discussing

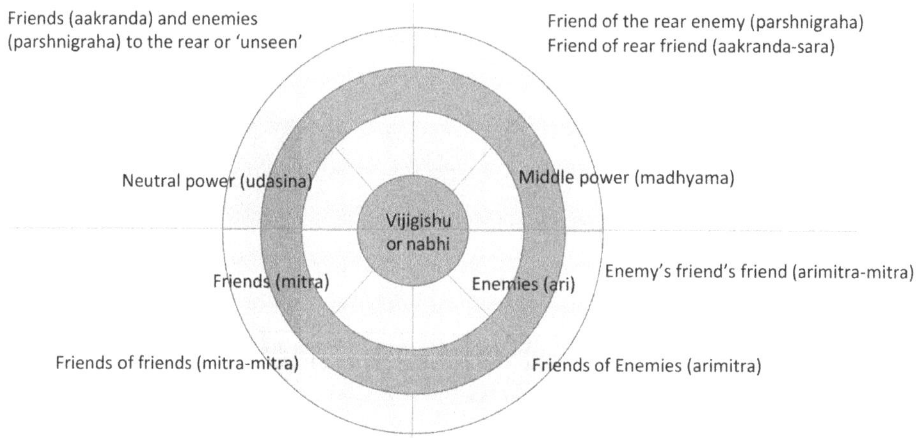

FIGURE 4.1.1 Mandala: Basic Circle of States

specific locations. Mandala is the Sanskrit term for 'sacred circle' (Dellios, 2003) or, more specifically, the rajamandala 'circle of kings.'

Visually depicted as concentric circles the mandala "represented a particular and often unstable political situation in a vaguely definable geographical area without fixed boundaries and where smaller centers tended to look in all directions for security" (Wolters, 1999, 28-29) and is made up of three basic principles: center, symmetry, and cardinal points (Dellios, 2003). Together, they represent the wheel of power or, as Sarkar suggestively argues, the wheel of the chariot of state that represents not only the crucial balance of power, but also the need and aspiration to expand, *vijigeesoo* (Sarkar, 1919)—also or *vijigisu* (Dellios, 2003) or *vijigishu* (Kumar, 2014). The king is at the center as the point of gravity (*nabhi*)—unlike western systems that focus on the boundaries to the wheel while the other four players are laid out in a kind of constant push/pull or "tug of war" primarily between enemies (*ari*) and friends (*mitra*), as well as two others with specific roles, to form an inner 'quartet': the medium power (*madhyama),* who is close to both the king and his enemy, and the neutral (*udasina*) power who may be more powerful than the madhyama, but more distant though able to help any of the players (Sarkar, 1919; Kumar, 2014). However, the system also fully recognizes there are friends of enemies (*ari-mitra*) and friends of friends (*mitra-mitra*), and even the enemy's friend's friend *(arimitra-mitra)* as well as the 'unseen' enemies and friends to the rear—*parshnigraha* (enemy in the rear) and *aakranda* (friend in the rear), *parshnigraha-sara* (friend of rear enemy), *aakranda-sara* (friend of rear friend) (Kumar, 2014) for a total of twelve states each with their own balance to maintain. Thus, a primary point in the analysis is that any player can change its role at any time. Some may be enduring enemies or friends, but the possibility of a shift should be considered as part of the geometry of alliance and power. (See Figure 4.1.1.)

It should be noted that there are various ways to describe these 'zones' of the ruler's circle (and many use slightly different spellings or even different terms—see Dellios, 2003 for a detailed description), but the important concepts remain the same. There is a constant need to adjust and readjust to circumstance, guided by six principles: 1) the king shall develop his state; 2) the enemy shall be eliminated; 3) those who help are friends; 4) the best course is the prudent course; 5) peace is preferable to war; and 6) the king's behavior in victory and in defeat must be just (Kautilya, Rangarajan translation, 1992, 546).

The idea of the mandala and its diffused/relational power spread throughout Southeast Asia during the Han dynasty in China (206 BCE–220 CE), who used the concept of concentric circles of power and alliance to explain, and even to predict, relations between entities in their sphere of influence. The Chinese version created a kind of "Sinic" or inner Asian zone where the center of gravity was reserved for those deemed to be Chinese, although this often included contiguous neighbors and tributary states and even nomadic and semi-nomadic peoples. The point was that this inner circle did not need to be culturally Chinese, though many may have been close in various ways, but those who recognized the power base and were willing to 'be Chinese' for these purposes. As with the Indian mandala, the power waned the further one moved out across the zones until one reached the outermost zone, reserved for 'barbarians.'

The hierarchy and power of the relationship was generally judged by distance from the imperial center, but could be shifted and reorganized as the Han Chinese even had a system by which they could grant a people or group the "official seals" if the non-Chinese group they were negotiating with participated in and observed the correct ceremonies and rituals (Frey and Frey, 1999, 24).

Unfortunately, we do not have time to consider the overlapping and contrasting aspects of the mandala systems used in Southeast Asia, India, and China (see Wolters, 1999 for specific information on this part of the world and the use of mandalas), but the importance of their similarities in terms of their relational/non-hierarchical approach will be outlined further in the case studies later in Part II.

Unfortunately, our present-day bias often leads us to conflate the concept of 'Greek city-states' or 'Chinese dynasties' with our views of present-day Greece or China despite the fact that these 'states'—as we understand them today—did not exist. Even the use of the term 'state' when discussing such time frames, can be misleading in that we tend to forget that we mean something very different from the Westphalian state or modern state, but a suzerain power controlling tributary states through heterarchical structures. Thus, the issues faced by historical leaders in terms of security or trade, politics or representation, were all potentially compounded by the fact that there was little sense of 'internal' or 'external.' In many, if not most, of the ancient world societies, there was effectively no divide between the 'domestic' and the 'foreign.' 'Territory' could be associated with a realm of influence, but there were no agreed points of demarcation that separated neighbor from neighbor or imagined lines as borders. Instead, there were many centers of gravity with power that extended their influence to the 'edges' of their 'territory' through relationships and communication channels that combined to create bounded realities, but not the kind of boundary that needs the same types of protection as those that came to be the norm in Europe and, eventually, much of the world.

The notion of a territory as a distinct and well-defined area only comes much later and, as we shall see, is much more highly regarded in the West than elsewhere. As Black points out, the need for rulers to "define their position towards the Holy Roman Emperor" meant that the distinctions between foreign and domestic in terms of territoriality became the foundation of their "independent political legitimacy and thus foreign policy" (Black, 2010, 25), and of European statehood as a concept. Whereas, territory as a space of shared power was operating in many places around the world for centuries and developing different diplomacies.

Essentially, historical leaders had very little structural power to implement policies towards their own people, let alone the ability to create a consistent 'foreign policy.' To most, those outside their own 'people' (a definition that varied widely between cultures) were 'barbarians,' a term often used more in a descriptive than a pejorative sense. All those outside one's own circle essentially had to be considered at least a potential threat until ways were found to create the 'liberal international societies' with the rules and structures associated with a more normative agenda. One could even wonder if this pervasive lack of information regarding the intentions of one's neighbors in a non-territorial, relational context might be at the root of what is arguably a different kind of 'realism' and a contrast to the traditional 'realist' approach of the Western system.

System and Society

This raises a final point before continuing on to explore types and diplomacies, and that is the difference between what is known as a 'system' of states and an international 'society' and a suggestion as to how the European or

Westphalian system became dominant in world affairs. Adam Watson, already mentioned as a member of the English School, uses the definitions for these terms set out by his colleague, Hedley Bull, in that a 'system' is the "impersonal network of pressure and interests that binds states together closely enough 'to make the behaviour of each a necessary element in the calculation of others'" (Watson, 2009, 4). On the other hand, a 'society' is more evolved or developed and has an enmeshed nature that includes "a set of common rules, institutions, codes of conduct and values which some of all states agree to be bound by" (Watson, 2009, 4). Again, from the perspective of what could reasonably be described as a society, the lack of structure within a system bears repeating. The alliances or partnerships of a system are not based on any normative set of rules or overarching expectations of behavior and even less on the ability to enforce a decision. This distinction is a main tenet of the English School and the basis of its view that Europe is the only place we see an international 'society' emerge. The reason, they argue, is that previous states systems fell, were merged, or assimilated by other cultures before they were able to attain the more 'advanced' stage of a society. It is this assumption that may well prove to have been the major stumbling block to a more global approach, as it sets up an inbuilt bias towards hierarchy and ignores the possibility that more flexible or fluid structures of power such as heterarchy might be able to maintain order and/or create a society of states.

Building on this systems/society dichotomy, Watson's examination of historical states-systems offers the visual of a pendulum of states to describe these relationships (Watson, 1992, 2009). (See Figure 4.1.2) Spanning this continuum, Watson suggests that the 'natural' resting place in the swing of inter-state relations lies in the area of competing hegemons, with empire at one end of the spectrum and anarchy among independent states at the other. The argument being that, while states may seek to expand their power, they must also ensure their security. Thus, empire is a difficult position to sustain as it requires great effort and resources. Similarly, at the other end, anarchy between independent states is also difficult to maintain given the lack of allies and resources. The default position of this pendulum becomes a world in which states are reasonably content to be in different groups or strata, with a regional or even global hegemon holding the actors in check (Watson 1992, 2007, 2009). A particular challenge inherent in this idea is that the presence of many different states seeking, or able to fulfill, different roles in the system creates a layering or even a fragmenting of the international stage. This concept will return, but in the meantime, the idea brings attention to Robert Cooper's idea about states operating in 'real time' from the position of very different stages of development, or places, along Watson's pendulum.

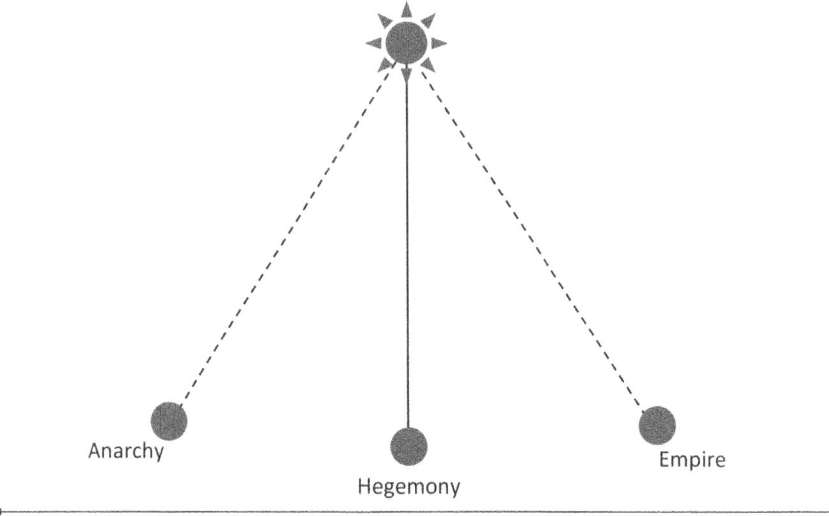

FIGURE 4.1.2 Basic version of Watson's Pendulum

This recognition of an entity's development, as well as a location in time and space vis-a-vis others in their own system, is particularly useful when looking at the development of historical states-systems. Their relations along these different dimensions will help us go outside the traditional hierarchy/anarchy dichotomy and open the possibility of heterarchy and the willingness of many entities to engage as tributaries in a suzerainty, or satellites of a much larger, regional, or even global hegemon. It also opens the possibility of systems of hierarchy coexisting with heterarchy.

Much has been written about these distinctions and their importance to the English School and to international relations theory generally, but the crucial point here is very simple: the identities of states are persistent, but they do change. Further, as they change, their role and potential for leadership in the international arena also evolves. In some respects, the specifics of their leadership or governance may have some impact on that process, but states are altered by the actions and fates of other actors, even of those with whom they have no direct interaction. In other words, a state's development is not entirely in the hands of any given leader or leadership and can be shaped by forces beyond style or form of government. There is a deeper process at work and one which warrants further exploration in terms of guidance as to how the global interactions, including the diplomacy of the future, may develop as we continue to explore both types and the diplomacies of place, beginning with economic diplomacy and the importance of trade as a type of diplomacy over time.

References and Further Reading

Black, Jeremy. *A History of Diplomacy.* London: Reaktion Books, 2010.

Bozeman, Adda. *Politics and Culture in International History.* Princeton: Princeton University Press, 1960.

Butterfield, Herbert. "The Historical States-Systems." The British Committee on the Theory of International Politics. Chatham House Papers. January 8–11, 1965.

Butterfield, Herbert. *The Origins of History.* New York: Basic Books, 1981.

Dellios, Rosita. "Mandala: from sacred origins to sovereign affairs in traditional Southeast Asia." *Centre for East-West Cultural and Economic Studies.* Paper 8, 2003.

Dudziak, Mary. "Law War and the History of Time. Legal Studies Research Paper Series." Legal Research Paper No. 09-6 (2010): 1668-1712.

Frey, Linda and Marsha Frey. *The History of Diplomatic Immunity.* Columbus: Ohio University Press, 1999.

Greenhouse, Carol. *A Moment's Notice: Time Politics Across Cultures.* Ithaca and London: Cornell University Press, 1996.

Kumar, Niraj. "Building Grand Strategy within Indian Characteristics for Rebounding India." *Journal of Indian Research.* Vol 2., No. 1 (January-March, 2014): 4-34.

Neumann, Iver. "Euro-Centric diplomacy: Challenging but manageable." *European Journal of International Relations.* 18 (2) (2011): 299-321.

Rangarajan, L.N. (translation). *Kautilya—The Arthashastra. Edited, Rearranged, Translated and Introduced.* New Delhi: Penguin Books, 1992.

Rues-Smit, Christian. *The Moral Purpose of the State: Culture, Social Identity, and Institutional Rationality in International Relations.* Princeton: Princeton University Press, 1999.

Rues-Smit, Christian. *The Moral Purpose of the State: Culture, Social Identity, and Institutional Rationality in International Relations.* Princeton: Princeton University Press, 1999.

Sarkar, Benoy Kumar. "Hindu Theory of International Relations." *The American Political Science Review.* Vol. 13, No. 3, (1919): 400-414.

Watson, Adam. "The Indian States System." Paper to the British Committee on the theory of International Politics. Chatham House Papers, April 21-24, 1967.

Watson, Adam. *The Evolution of International Society.* London and New York: Routledge, 1992/2009.

Watson, Adam. *Hegemony and History.* London: Routledge, 2007.

Wolters, O.W. *History, Culture, and Region in Southeast Asian Perspectives.* Ithaca: Cornell Southeast Asia Program Publications, 1999.

5 Trade, Diplomacy, and the Evolving Global Economy

BY GEOFFREY ALLEN PIGMAN

Introduction: Millennia of International Trade as Diplomacy

International trade, as it has evolved through history, has served as a metaphor for how we engage with the other, the unfamiliar. Diplomacy is a means of communicating, establishing, and maintaining relationships with strangers. Trade describes the movement of goods, services, labor, and capital. Hence, international trade and diplomacy originated, in effect, from the same motivating force. Over time, diplomacy facilitated the evolution of relationships between states to a point at which one of diplomacy's distinct purposes could be said to be to facilitate trade. Once this transformation had occurred, trade could take place independently of the diplomacy itself. In order to facilitate trade for its own sake, governments have had to negotiate over monetary relations and eventually about facilitating cross-border flows of investment capital. Hence, what we think of today more broadly as economic diplomacy sprang from the needs of international trade. What follows here traces how the evolving diplomacy surrounding trade and other cross-border economic activity affects the international (and eventually global) economy, and how the evolving international economic system, in turn, affects that diplomacy. In particular, the effects of three significant transformations in the diplomacy of international trade upon the international economic system, and the reciprocal impact of the international economy upon diplomacy thereafter, are highlighted. Tracing the history of the relationship between these transformations in diplomacy and the evolving international economic system generates an account of the strengths and weaknesses in economic diplomacy and the international economic system today and stimulates prescriptions for reforms going forward.

Despite the focus of diplomacy on issues of *haute politique,* or 'high politics,' or strategic questions and security issues since the founding of the modern diplomatic system of nation-states, generally pegged at the 1648 Peace of Westphalia and particularly during the Cold War, trade since ancient times has been at the core of the agenda of diplomats (Lee and Hudson, 2004, 343–360). However, trade has not only been a primary object of diplomatic representation and communication. In an important sense trade itself 'is' a key form of diplomacy. Trade by its nature reconstitutes, redefines, and changes the subjectivities and the identities of the persons and polities that engage in it. Trade, or exchange, is an ongoing process. The 'we' who are trading become different by trading. Even as trade creates value by realizing economic efficiencies through specialization of production, trade also redistributes wealth, assets, and power both within and between polities. This process invariably brings social change, which can redress or aggravate inequality and distribution of wealth between economic sectors, regions, and social groups. What we now understand as trade in services often involves the movement of persons across borders either to deliver or to consume a service. A new diplomatic studies paradigm, which frames diplomacy more broadly than earlier understandings of the field, illuminates these processes by focusing not only on the negotiation and politics of trade agreements, but also on the ongoing diplomatic representation and communication required to manage trading relationships (Pigman and Vickers, 2012, 19–41).

Thinking about international trade from the perspective of diplomacy poses important questions: How do the ways that diplomatic representation and communication are undertaken affect diplomacy involving international trade, finance, banking, and monetary relations? What effects do the changing factors that qualify something to be considered a diplomatic actor and the emergence of new venues and institutions for diplomacy have on economic diplomacy? How does the rising importance of public diplomacy affect diplomacy addressing trade and other economic issues? How does diplomacy facilitate or hinder political trade-offs between trade issues and other major social and economic issues on the global agenda, such as monetary cooperation, environment, intellectual property, etc.? How have diplomats negotiated and re-negotiated what trade means, in the sense of what issues count as international trade issues for purposes of negotiation and governance? The European Union, which originated as a customs union in 1957 and went on to become the world's greatest supranational economic integration body, and the *World Trade Organization (WTO),* which originated in 1947 as an agreement without an institution to manage it, can be seen as some of the world's greatest diplomatic achievements. Yet the challenges facing the WTO in terms of the stalemate of the multilateral trade negotiations known as the Doha Development Agenda designed to deal with a long list of complex tariffs that arguably affected poorer countries adversely after over thirteen years of relatively little fruit, and the recent financial and monetary crises besetting the Eurozone represent some of the greatest-ever tests for diplomacy. A fuller understanding of international trade from a diplomacy perspective will equip decision makers better to analyze and contribute to solving these crucial global problems.

Using diplomacy to facilitate international trade today seems paradoxical. International trade flourishes: trade is a driving force behind the explosive growth in emerging economies from Asia to Africa to Latin America. Yet at the same time much of the diplomacy that takes place within the institutional structures established to facilitate trade expansion, such as the WTO, gives the impression of such efforts having run aground. Prospects for successful completion of the Doha Development Agenda are more uncertain than ever. Preferential trade agreements (PTAs), which, many argue, thwart the progress of multilateral trade liberalization, continue to be signed. Ongoing regional integration around the world threatens to change the nature and standing of the nation-state actors that have hitherto negotiated trade agreements. As the balance of global power shifts towards large emerging economies such as China, monetary policy clashes again pose increasing risks to trade relations, as they did between the two world wars. Trade and financial diplomacy today serve as a vehicle for how actors talk to one another about how globalization works or fails to work, and how it should work. Domestic political battles between winners and losers from globalization within states result in positions taken that diplomats must represent to their counterparts and for which they must negotiate.

Just as diplomacy in the broadest sense has continued to evolve, diplomacy surrounding economic issues has changed quite dramatically over the past three and a half centuries. Diplomacy relating to international trade in particular has undergone three significant transformations in the era since nation-states and their governments emerged as major actors in the international system in the mid-seventeenth century. Each transformation has changed in fundamental ways how and why trade diplomacy is undertaken. Each successive transformation has foregrounded particular processes, mechanisms, and objectives of trade diplomacy: the purposes of trade missions, the types of treaties that structure trade relations, the use of institutions as venues for trade diplomacy, the processes by which trade disputes are resolved, and the goals themselves of international trade agreements and organizations.

These transformations have, in turn, been driven by changes in the nature of the actors in the international system and by changes in the processes of diplomatic representation, communication, and negotiation. The nature of states as actors has changed. How interests are represented in the politics of states has evolved. Multilateral organizations, global firms, and global civil society organizations (CSOs) have emerged as major players alongside states in the international system. Hence, states first became the dominant actors, but then they became somewhat less so, notwithstanding the emergence of multilateral institutions such as the World Trade Organization that are organized primarily upon state representation. The transformations in trade diplomacy have played a central part in governing how diplomacy concerned with all the related aspects of economic relations has evolved: monetary, banking, and investment issues. In some cases, similar and parallel transformations in these areas of diplomacy have taken place. In others, the process of change has been more gradual. Not only structural factors, but agency has also played a key part in driving transformations in economic diplomacy. Agency can be manifested through the ideas and actions of individuals at particular times and places, such as the advocacy of free traders Richard Cobden and Michel Chevalier. Agency is also evident in the popularity of ideologies, such as free trade, in mid-nineteenth century Britain and northwestern Europe, or anti-imperialism, in the form of demands for special and differential treatment for developing countries since World War II.

The three transformations in trade diplomacy effectively divide the international trading system into four historical phases: trade-as-diplomacy; liberalization (from the early nineteenth century); institutionalization (from the early twentieth century); and judicialization (from the late twentieth century). However, the processes of transformation reveal more than the attributes of the phases that extend between and during the transformations. During each phase, particular modes of diplomatic representation and communication were dominant. For example, during the earliest phase, trade-as-diplomacy, the sending and receiving of bilateral diplomatic missions in which trade was central to, and inseparable from, other core issues to be negotiated, tended to be most common. However, the transformations have not been tidy, clean, step changes: each has appeared initially in traces before reaching a tipping point, and it is difficult to pinpoint an exact time at which a transformation began or could be said to be complete. Each transformation has tended to layer on new ways of, and purposes for, undertaking trade diplomacy alongside and on top of existing ways. As different means of, and reasons for, trade diplomacy emerged, it did not mean older approaches and processes were superseded uniformly by newer, better methods and justifications. A shifting jumble of, approaches to, and rationales for, economic diplomacy characterizes contemporary international politics. Hence, the transformations, the processes of adding to and changing methods of and reasons for trade diplomacy, reveal the most about why economic diplomacy has come to operate as it does today (Pigman, 2015).

Trade began as one of the earliest forms of interaction between human societies (Sharp, 2009, 93–96). Trade negotiations, the essential and original form of human negotiation, resolve political disputes over who-gets-what (Strange, 1996, 68). Trade missions, expeditions to faraway places to exchange goods, were one of the oldest forms of diplomatic mission. Trade diplomacy is as old as diplomacy itself, which history suggests is nearly as old as the coexistence of distinct human civilizations geographically and culturally divided from one another. Trading achieves the core diplomatic objective of overcoming alienation and mediating estrangement, as Der Derian put it (Der Derian, 1987, 5–7). From a classical economic perspective, trade takes place because it leaves each party better off. After trading, a relationship exists between the counterparties that did not previously exist. The establishment of relationships within which trade can occur is the essence of diplomacy. In order for trade to take place, parties must first communicate about what is to be exchanged for what. Communication and negotiation are both core functions of diplomacy. The parties need to understand each other, and what is being offered for exchange, enough to negotiate terms for trade.

The oldest 'diplomatic' missions identified by historians involved trade at least as a major, if not a sole, objective. Historical documentation from the Amarna period, during the fourteenth century B.C.E., chronicles a rich record of intensive diplomatic interaction between the governments of states in the Eastern Mediterranean, the Levant, and West Asia: Egypt, Babylonia, Assyria, Mittani, Hatti, Alashiya, Arzawa, and numerous vassal states thereof (Cohen and Westbrook, 2000, 1–12). One of the primary forms of diplomatic interaction between the kings was the exchange of gifts such as gold and silver, and services provided by professionals such as physicians and exorcists, often of significant value. These gifts served ritual diplomatic functions of symbolizing respect and affection.

Perhaps the most comprehensive manifestation of trade-as-diplomacy was the silk trade that developed between China and Europe over two millennia. The desire of Chinese silk producers to export thread, and that of European consumers to acquire silk fabric, created a link between two distant and unfamiliar parts of the world that required successful diplomacy to be developed and maintained. Evidence exists of a trade route used for shipping silk from China to Europe as early as the second century B.C.E. (Zhang 2005,

12–17). At that time, the leaders of Han Dynasty China sought to establish diplomatic relations and develop military alliances with states that lay to the west of China and through which silk bound for Europe traveled (Zhang, 2005, 19–25). Zhang's diplomatic missions on behalf of Emperor Wudi at the same time served as trade missions, indicating that the imperial court viewed trade and diplomacy as compatible and related functions (Zhang, 2005, 24). East-west trade on the Silk Road over subsequent centuries oscillated between periods of flourishing, facilitated by diplomacy between the dominant states of the day, and periods of disruption, punctuated by wars between the states and domestic political disorder (Zhang, 2005, 67–68). The silk trade flourished under the Tang Dynasty in China (C.E. 618–907). China's government, which then sat at Chang'an (present day Xi'an) instituted the use of passports for traders and a system of taxation for use of the roads. Traders were also used by the Tang government periodically as diplomatic envoys (Zhang, 2005, 77–80).

The first successful recorded overland journeys between Western Europe and China once again combined trade and diplomacy (Zhang, 2005, 139–144). Marco Polo and his father and uncle, also Venetian merchants, traveled extensively through the Levant to Central and East Asia and the subcontinent for over two decades beginning in C.E. 1260. *La Serenissima*, the Venetian Republic, was already known as a trading state, sending missions to Asia and Africa to exchange goods. The Polos' journey was originally conceived as a 'market opening' mission to convince Barka Khan, the ruler of the Western Tartars, to trade with Venice. (Polo, 1958, xii) On what became an epic journey, Marco Polo and his family members also carried out many functions common to contemporary diplomats: carrying messages and gifts between leaders of different states, going on missions abroad to gather information for a head of state, representing a government to foreign courts at ceremonial functions such as royal weddings. Polo kept a detailed chronicle of the lands he visited, focusing in particular on the variety of goods that each land produced and traded. Owing to the Polos' evidently agreeable diplomatic manners, rulers ranging from Barka Khan in the Levant to Kublai Khan in China were moved to seek greater interaction and exchange with the Christian polities of Europe. In the first diplomatic exchange between Europeans and Kublai Khan, the Polos carried communications and gifts of value for exchange between Kublai Khan and the newly elected Roman Catholic Pope, Gregory of Piacenza (Polo, 1958, vii–xxxix, 1–14).

The emergence of markets for raising capital in the Netherlands to finance long-distance seagoing trade missions in the fifteenth century, and the securitization of those missions and the profits flowing therefrom, permitted trade to rise in economic importance alongside the rise of nation-states in Europe. Long-distance trading voyages were too costly for individuals to undertake without financial backing, either from governments or private sources of capital or both. Monarchs and other European nobility saw trade missions as an opportunity to increase their power by acquiring precious metals and other luxury goods from overseas. The subsequent development of popular tastes for exotic goods, both a product and a driver of the development of capitalism, motivated the desire to trade across long distances. The need of traders, sometimes with military backing, to engage with those with whom they traded in distant lands was coupled with curiosity about distant peoples and societies. Meanwhile, at home in Europe, rulers of nation-states growing accustomed to governing the spiritual, as well as the temporal affairs of their territories and peoples, established a system for diplomatic relations that is still recognizable today (Hamilton and Langhorne, 2010, 29–85).

However, the practices of this emerging Europe-centered diplomatic system did not extend to the still vast parts of the world that were distant from Europe. The opportunity for trade-as-diplomacy between Europeans and non-Europeans was still great. The different processes by which European states established colonies in the Americas, Africa, Asia, and Oceania can be viewed in many cases as examples of trade-as-diplomacy, even if, before long, colonial expansion on numerous occasions was undertaken for geopolitical objectives such as preventing a rival from gaining or expanding a foothold in a particular region. By the late seventeenth and early eighteenth centuries, rivalries between the nation-states in Europe were being projected across the rest of the world through a competitive drive to develop exclusive trading relationships with distant sources of precious metals and tropical produce, in what became known as an age of mercantilism. From the Caribbean and the Americas, to the Indian subcontinent and Southeast Asia, European traders, backed by their home governments, had established trading posts, trade routes, production facilities, and agricultural plantations to serve the growing demands of European populations. In the mercantilist version of trade-as-diplomacy, European governments used their control over trade, and primarily their ability to limit or prohibit trade, as an instrument of war in a struggle for dominance over European rivals. Military rivalry between England and France dominated the eighteenth century, during which a primary strategy of each was to attempt to deny the other access to goods transported from distant colonies and other trading partners by sea. On occasion, treaties that facilitated trade were signed, but in those cases diplomacy was conducted in service of broader military objectives. The Methuen Treaty, signed by England and Portugal in 1703, was negotiated by John Methuen, English ambassador to Portugal, as part of a strategy to entice Portugal to abandon their French allies and join England's side in the Anglo-French War of the Spanish Succession. The treaty gave Portuguese wines at least as favorable tariff treatment entering England as French wines and granted English textiles duty-free entry into Portugal. Although the treaty liberalized bilateral trade between the two countries in goods in which each possessed a comparative advantage, the English government used trade concessions explicitly to strengthen their military position relative to France in a classic example of mercantilist diplomacy.

International trade missions that served simultaneously as diplomatic missions, trading posts that also served as stations for consular relations, and messages exchanged between sovereigns by traders traveling long distances between continents and capitals played a central role in the establishment of inter-'national' relations and the creation of a modern international system of nation-states marked by King Henry VIII's 1536 Act of Supremacy, the 1648 Peace of Westphalia, and events that followed. As governments of nation-states got to know one another, trade-as-diplomacy as defined by its original objective of getting to know the unknown, had outlived its usefulness, as governments subordinated international trade entirely to objectives of state politics. Trade was not recognized by most leaders of states as having value, economically or politically, for its own sake. Before the Industrial Revolution, trade was too small a part of overall economic activity for governments or the public to recognize and rate its benefits. Yet, and before governments realized it, the rise of capitalism meant that trade had already become important for its own sake. One of the primary roles of the state had become the management of trade relations with other states.

As modern nation-states evolved in Europe, trade-as-diplomacy increasingly took the form of military forces securing political control of distant lands with which their traders wished to do business. By the eighteenth century, trade was one amongst many tools used by leaders and their diplomats, and was more often used as a hostile instrument. Governments used trade prohibitions and embargoes as useful diplomatic weapons with few associated costs. The Napoleonic Wars, effectively a world war lasting nearly two decades in the late eighteenth and early nineteenth centuries, arrayed the allies of what were, by then, the two major seafaring nations of the world, England and France, against one another. The conflicts of the Napoleonic Wars had the effect of systematically disrupting or suspending the seaborne trade in goods that had begun to grow appreciably even amidst government-imposed trade barriers. By the end of the conflict, the shortcomings of mercantilism and the growing importance of international trade for the economic well-being of nations were becoming apparent both to governments and to their constituents. However, a different approach to diplomacy would be required to bring about a different framework of diplomatic relations within which increased international trade could take place.

The Diplomacy of Trade Liberalization

Only occurring after trade-as-diplomacy had been practiced for several millennia, the first significant transformation in trade diplomacy took place in the nineteenth century as widespread liberalization of trade policies became the norm in Europe. For the first time, trade diplomacy became distinct from, and often different from, the rest of diplomacy. Trade issues began to be debated on their own intellectual and ideological merits, focusing on the benefits liberalization would—or would not—bring. Specific diplomatic missions were sent to negotiate and sign trade liberalization treaties. The linkage between trade policy objectives and other diplomatic objectives was not severed, as Richard Cobden's championing of free trade as a means of promoting peace indicates. Yet trade interests came to be understood separately from other foreign policy interests, sometimes congruent and sometimes in competition therewith. International trade began to be seen as advantageous both for its own sake and for state treasuries, following the end of the Napoleonic Wars, as the Industrial Revolution's transformation of production and consumption of goods and services accelerated. Mechanized production generated surpluses of goods that could be exported abroad, and tariffs on increased imports could serve as important sources of government revenue. Hence, debate began in earnest within governments and amongst interest groups in Britain and in other countries about how best to facilitate trade. Using diplomacy to facilitate trade in ways that had not been employed previously became an option. The 'most favored nation' (MFN) treaty became a common early form of trade liberalizing agreement, under which signatories agreed to extend to each other the lowest trade barriers that they offered to any other state.

However, just because diplomacy to promote international trade for its own sake became possible did not mean that its practice was a foregone conclusion. A serious debate arose within states as to whether trade liberalization should be undertaken unilaterally or whether it should be done using diplomacy: through the negotiation of treaties regulating bilateral trade, e.g., by setting tariff rates. This debate still echoes in contemporary times under various guises. Proponents of unilateral trade policy argue that trade should be managed domestically by legislation and regulation, so that the government of a state can alter or restore a tariff or trade barrier whenever they deem it necessary, or in response to pressure from constituents. Advocates of negotiated trade policy argue that binding international agreements are needed to lock in gains from trade liberalization for a fixed period of time in order to entrench support from beneficiaries of trade, such as consumers and exporters. As Britain industrialized first and dominated international trade for much of the nineteenth century, the debate in Britain over unilateral vs. negotiated trade liberalization had an inordinate impact upon the development of trade diplomacy and of the nineteenth century international trading system overall. Whilst Britain began signing trade agreements regularly with France, Prussia, and other states in the quarter century that followed the 1815 Congress of Vienna, Britain's first phase of major trade liberalization in the decade following their repeal of the Corn Laws (tariffs on imports of grain) in 1846 was predominantly unilateral. Indeed, Britain's primary trade diplomacy undertaking in this period was a public diplomacy thrust led by Cobden designed to win over hearts and minds of opinion leaders and the educated public in continental Europe to the cause of free trade by drawing attention to the advantages accruing to Britain from unilateral tariff cuts (Edsal 1986, 174–188).

The brief dominance of negotiated trade liberalization as British trade policy lasted little more than ten years, but was nonetheless long enough to unleash a torrent of trade diplomacy that drastically reduced tariffs across Europe. In so doing, the international trading system was permanently changed. The Anglo-French Commercial Treaty of 1860, which Cobden negotiated with his French pro-free trade counterpart, Michel Chevalier, had national security objectives for both countries, bringing the 'peace through commerce' argument to the fore. The treaty also addressed what was needed to increase trade flows between the UK and France. The *Cobden-Chevalier treaty* was an innovative engine of trade liberalization, in that it combined the exchange of unconditional MFN status with bilateral tariff reductions on particular goods sought by each country, such as coal, steel, wine, and spirits. For Britain, the Cobden-Chevalier treaty and those that followed were different from the earlier generation of commercial treaties in that Britain unilaterally granted the concessions granted to France in the Cobden-Chevalier treaty to all other states (Illiasu, 1971, 71). Britain and France's bilateral tariff cuts, combined with Britain's unilateral extension of benefits to third countries and France's extension of tariff cuts to MFN treaty partners, generalized the tariff reductions to most European states (Dunham, 1930, 8–100). British diplomat Sir Louis Mallet calculated that, after the Cobden-Chevalier Treaty was signed, between fifty and sixty treaties were concluded in Europe that, between them, reduced overall European tariffs by fifty percent (Mallet, 1905, 60).

In many ways, the transformation in trade diplomacy that the Cobden-Chevalier treaty embodied was a victim of its own success in the decades leading up to the Great War, as trade liberalization diplomacy facilitated German political unification under Prussian leadership by 1870. Germany's growing continental power after the Franco-Prussian War and the lengthy agricultural depression in Europe further conspired to constrain the possibilities for continuation of a diplomacy of trade liberalization using the diplomatic instruments that had evolved thus far. Many states in Europe signed bilateral trade liberalization treaties, and Britain also practiced the public diplomacy of unilateral free trade policy (leadership by example) and promotion of free trade abroad. The agricultural depression, which caused world commodity prices to fall by about a third between 1873 and 1896 and slowed world economic growth significantly, was caused, in part, by lower transport costs, which allowed a surge of American grain and cotton into British and European markets in the 1870s (Landes, 1969, 231 and Pollard, 1981, 254). Britain's response to rising protectionism in its continental European trading partners was largely to retreat more and more toward unilateral free trade, not negotiating vigorously as trade treaties came up for renewal to maintain and extend low treaty-based tariffs. Whilst European governments generally did not return to the early nineteenth century policies of trade prohibitions, tariffs outside Britain were higher than they had been in the 1860s (Foreman-Peck, 1973, 118–119). Average duties on manufactures doubled between 1875 and 1895 (Pollard, 1981, 259). The international trading system built around bilateral MFN treaties, some embodying specified tariff cuts, ultimately ran out of steam as a diplomatic engine for ongoing trade liberalization. Such treaties, usually either of fixed duration or easily denounceable by either side after a fixed period, were often difficult to renegotiate or extend in domestic political climates that had often changed. Moreover, in an international system where the benefits of bilateral tariff cutting were spread wide through the MFN mechanism, countries that waited to negotiate tariff treaties often found themselves forced to extend their lowest tariffs to other countries through MFN without having any leverage to extract equivalent concessions from trading partners. When tariff treaties expired, MFN could work as a powerful engine in reverse to raise tariff levels between large numbers of trading partners.

In the second half of the nineteenth century, diplomacy intended to facilitate international banking cooperation and financial and investment flows also developed, initially in support of trade liberalization. From modest beginnings in the early stages of capitalism, cross-border flows of investment capital would grow to dwarf flows of goods and services many times over by the late twentieth century. Governments tended to favor setting monetary policy unilaterally over negotiation, at least until the early twentieth century, when governments devaluing their currencies against gold in a retaliatory fashion resulted in trade flows becoming so unstable that leaders were forced to seek an alternative, more diplomatic approach to monetary relations. Early monetary policy, dating from the mercantilist era in the late seventeenth and eighteenth centuries, arose as governments of states consolidated power and undertook responsibility for defense. Monetary policy was employed to maintain and grow reserves of precious metals, which could be used to make purchases needed in times of war. The liberalizing transformation in trade diplomacy that began in the nineteenth century changed the objectives of states' monetary policies, however, and opened the way for a new sort of liberalizing monetary diplomacy. The first significant international monetary agreements were the Latin Monetary Union and the Scandinavian Monetary Union. Negotiated initially between France, Belgium, Switzerland, and Italy in 1865, the Latin Monetary Union standardized the issue of coinage amongst members, set the fineness of coins' gold and silver content, and thereby allowed the coinage to be accepted across borders by making coins' value readily apparent to users in member countries. Additional countries joined, and the union functioned until the political turmoil unleashed by the Great War made its continued operation unviable. The Scandinavian Monetary Union, signed between Denmark and Sweden in 1873, and subsequently joined by Norway, functioned similarly and for a similar duration. In an economic environment of relative peace, falling tariffs and other barriers, and rapidly growing trade flows, it was attractive for governments to negotiate this sort of agreement, as it facilitated the movement of gold and silver across borders to settle accounts. However, monetary cooperation rested on a substrate of stable diplomatic relations in a broader sense and has remained vulnerable whenever that foundation has been eroded. The last significant attempt at treaty-based monetary diplomacy was the Tripartite Monetary Agreement signed between the United States, France, and the United Kingdom in 1936. The agreement was intended to re-establish currency stability between these three countries in the wake of the collapse of the international gold standard in the early 1930s and the destabilizing 'competitive' currency devaluations, with the attendant collapse in international trade that followed. The agreement largely achieved its aims, but was soon rendered moot by the outbreak of the Second World War in 1939.

Banking and financial diplomacy began to evolve at the end of the nineteenth century as a response to international financial crises, such as the first collapse of London-based Barings Bank in 1895. As trade increased in an age of liberalizing tariff treaties and regional monetary unions, private financial institutions increasingly financed overseas business ventures and thus became exposed to foreign firms, financial institutions, and currencies. Central banks began to work together and with large private banks to stabilize international financial flows and exchange rates during periods of instability. The Bank of England and its counterparts in France and Germany developed an effective working relationship, but they faced difficulties in engaging diplomatically with the United States, the economic importance of which was increasing rapidly in the decades prior to the Great War. Before the creation of the Federal Reserve System in the USA in 1913, there was no permanent central bank to act as a diplomatic interlocutor on behalf of the United States. Hence J.P. Morgan, head of the eponymous American merchant bank, tended to play the part unofficially, coordinating the actions of other US banks and talking to overseas counterparts in crisis situations, as he did in the crisis following the collapse of the New York-based Knickerbocker Trust Company in 1907. As the value of foreign investments increased, governments were increasingly pressed politically to support the interests of investors based in their territories when investment-related conflicts arose abroad. Diplomacy over private investment issues in the early years tended to be confrontational, as in the well-known boundary dispute between the United Kingdom and Venezuela in 1896 in which the US and UK governments took strong positions in the interest of investors in their respective countries.

The Institutionalization of Economic Diplomacy

Multilateral trade diplomacy ultimately proved difficult to conduct effectively ad hoc on an ongoing basis. Hence, as the second major transformation in trade diplomacy began in earnest at the beginning of the twentieth century with the signing of the Brussels Sugar Convention of 1902, diplomats began to create multilateral institutions to serve as venues for, and implementers of, trade diplomacy. The creation of such institutions fundamentally changed the way trade diplomacy was conducted, in part because the institutions themselves gradually became new diplomatic actors. Institutions were granted powers, limited at first, to engender compliance with the rules to which their members agreed upon joining. The process of institutionalization is also significant for creating venues in which diplomats have debated a broadening sphere of economic, social, and cultural issues under the rubric of trade relations. Whereas the prior transformation had the effect of distinguishing and separating trade issues from other subjects of diplomatic negotiation, such as security, post-World War II institutions such as the General Agreement on Tariffs and Trade (GATT), the United Nations Conference on Trade and Development (UNCTAD), and the WTO have facilitated the broadening of the definition of what constitutes 'trade,' both in terms of what is traded (to include services and investment capital) and in terms of trade-related issues. Particular 'behind the border' policy domains of national governments, such as environmental and labor regulation, intellectual property protection, competition policy, and industrial policy became subjects for negotiation in trade diplomacy institutions owing to the institutions' assessment of their ability to affect trade relations between states.

The earliest multilateral agreements established institutions that facilitated the least contested and most mechanical elements of international trade. For example, the International Telegraph Convention, signed in 1865, established the International Telegraph Union (ITU), an organization to administer the creation and maintenance of international telecommunications standards. The ITU, which later became the International Telecommunications Union, a specialized agency of the United Nations with 193 nation-state members and over seven hundred private organizations, still facilitates international commerce: cross-border telegraph services, telephony, and more contemporary telecommunications services such as radio transmission and the Internet (ITU website). However, the Brussels Sugar Convention stands out as the first multilateral agreement to institutionalize trade diplomacy over a major traded good—sugar. Global demand for sugar and for foodstuffs containing sugar had increased dramatically over the course of the nineteenth century owing to industrialization. Increased competition between tropical sugar producers, predominantly British colonies, and continental European sugar beet farmers had resulted in European governments paying export subsidies, or bounties, to help their producers capture a greater share of the international sugar market, which was particularly large in Britain. After several decades of unsuccessful bilateral and multilateral negotiations, delegates of nine European nations, including Britain, finally signed a multilateral agreement at Brussels in 1902 that contained many of the elements that would become standard in the GATT and WTO and other later twentieth-century trade institutions. The treaty prohibited payment of all export bounties on sugar and created a multilateral Permanent Sugar Commission to supervise and enforce implementation of the convention. The Permanent Sugar Commission, the first such institution in trade diplomacy, had the authority to impose sanctions against states not complying with the convention's ban on trade-distorting export subsidies on sugar, whether those states were signatories to the convention or not. The Commission, which was effective at facilitating ongoing diplomacy between signatories aimed at meeting the agreement's objectives, operated successfully up until the outbreak of the Great War in 1914 (Pigman, 1997, 185–210).

Attempts to re-organize the international trading system diplomatically between the two world wars was unsuccessful, in part because the growing United States had not yet been willing to fill the global economic leadership gap left by Britain. Although the quantitative trade barriers of the Great War were dismantled by 1920, many countries, including the United States, retreated largely to the practice of unilateral trade policy. Although the United States had become the world's largest creditor nation by the end of the Great War, and could have used that surplus to promote revival of the international trading system, the US Congress instead passed bills in 1921 and 1922 raising tariffs dramatically (Curzon, 1965, 21–24). A multilateral attempt in 1927 to establish an international regime to regulate quantitative trade restrictions and prohibitions, the World Economic Conference and Conference on Import and Export Prohibitions and Restrictions, narrowly failed because not enough countries ratified the treaty and because of plans by the US administration of President Herbert Hoover to raise tariffs further on agricultural imports (Winham, 1986, 34–37). Following the stock market crash in 1929 and the onset of a global depression, world trade declined over four years to 35 percent of its 1929 value (Lake, 1988, 185–186). During World War II, intensive negotiations began principally between the United States and the United Kingdom, over the future shape of the postwar international economy. The war would leave the United States as the only substantially undamaged major economy and military power, with over half of world manufacturing, one-third of total world production, and, in 1947, one-third of world exports (Scammell, 1983, 19–22). Yet notwithstanding the USA's dominant position in a postwar global economy, the United States itself needed the trade expansion that a liberal economic order would bring, so as to maintain US peacetime employment levels, promote private enterprise, and safeguard international security (Gardner, 1980, 101-102). In order for the United States to be able to lead a postwar international economic system successfully, the Americans would first have to reach agreement with the other major powers in the postwar global economy on the rules of the system and on mechanisms for enforcing the rules. As Arthur Stein has argued, if a state is to be a leader of the international economy, it needs willing followers (Stein, 1984, 358, 366–67).

The Americans envisioned the UK as a 'junior partner' in the new postwar system, given Britain's history as a former leader of a liberal international trading system and an ongoing center of global finance (Stein, 1984, 377). Out of extensive US-UK bilateral wartime diplomacy, which mediated strong differences over the form and priorities of the postwar international economy, emerged most of the core principles and diplomatic bargains that would define and, critically, the new institutions that would administer, such a system. The allied governments advanced their plans for international monetary and financial cooperation at a multilateral economic conference held in July 1944 at a resort hotel at 'Bretton Woods,' New Hampshire, in the United States. Over seven hundred delegates representing forty-four countries attended. Bretton Woods was a signal achievement in economic diplomacy, as negotiators were able to reach agreement not only on the need for rules to govern the international economy, but also, crucially, on the need for multilateral institutions to administer the rules. Conferees recognized three separate, but interlocking, sets of economic objectives: cooperation in managing and regulating exchange rates, liberalizing and maintaining liberal international trade, and assisting war-torn countries to rebuild their economies and underdeveloped regions of the world to pursue development. A structure of three international organizations was envisaged: an International Monetary Fund (IMF), an International Bank for Reconstruction and Development (IBRD, or World Bank), and an International Trade Organization (ITO).

In the original Bretton Woods vision, flows of goods, services, capital, and labor were all understood as closely interlinked. The delegates' objectives for the international trading system, which included non-discrimination, tariff reductions, and economic development, were to be underpinned by an international monetary system of freely convertible currencies based on gold and a system of international financing of reconstruction of war-damaged economies and development of the less industrialized parts of the world. Each of the respective institutions was designed to support and underpin the work of the others. However, the respective priorities of the major components in the new system held by each of the participating countries differed widely. In particular, the priorities of the United Kingdom and United States diverged sharply. Foreshadowing the key cleavage in global economic diplomacy from that time until the present, developing countries' desire to use trade, finance, and monetary policies to promote development stood at variance with the interests of most industrialized countries. In 1947, the year that the IMF and World Bank became fully operational, diplomats faced huge economic and geopolitical challenges to the process of negotiating a new institution and rulebook for international trade. Nonetheless, in that year negotiators representing twenty-three countries signed the General Agreement on Tariffs and Trade. The GATT reduced tariffs on manufactured goods substantially and limited tariff preferences modestly. The following year, conferees agreed on the Havana Charter to establish an International Trade Organization. However, substantial opposition in the United States and United Kingdom to different provisions in the Charter prevented either government from submitting the Charter for ratification and resulted in the ITO not coming into operation. But unwilling to abandon the gains of the GATT, diplomats adapted the GATT's provisional operating arrangements pending the launch of the ITO into an ad hoc secretariat not requiring formal treaty approval. This provisional institution facilitated the diplomacy required to enable GATT signatories to meet their obligations under the 1947 agreement.

As an institutional venue for trade diplomacy, the GATT addressed many of the problems that had plagued the pre-war trading system. Contracting parties to the GATT, as countries that signed up were known, agreed to follow a rulebook for international trade that included the expectation to participate in multilateral trade liberalization. The multilateral trade liberalization round, of which the 1947 Geneva Conference that led to the signing of the GATT was the first, became the standard GATT format for trade liberalization. The 'offer-request' system of parallel, simultaneous bilateral tariff negotiations between principal suppliers of goods limited the risk of a country having to make tariff concessions without receiving concessions in return. As tariff schedules became more complex in the 1960s, the offer-request system was supplemented by use of 'across the board' formulas for tariff cutting. Participation was expected to be permanent: few countries ever withdrew from the GATT, and GATT and WTO membership have steadily increased to the point that today only a small number of countries are not yet WTO members. The GATT contained a dispute settlement mechanism enabling states to withdraw trade concessions, under limited conditions, from fellow GATT signatories found to have violated their GATT obligations.

Once up and running as a provisional institution, the GATT served as a venue for diplomacy that facilitated the evolution of an international trading system that advanced most of the major objectives of the wartime planners with considerable success, even if at different speeds. As decolonization proceeded in the 1950s and 1960s, non-discrimination became the norm amongst GATT members. Tariff reductions were accomplished through successive multilateral trade negotiating rounds, which became the GATT's primary vehicle for negotiating trade liberalization multilaterally. By the 1970s, average tariffs on trade in manufactured goods between GATT members had been reduced to such a low level that the negotiating focus for many GATT members began to shift to the more challenging task of lowering of non-tariff barriers (NTBs) to liberal trade, such as government subsidies, dumping, and discriminatory government procurement codes. Other GATT objectives also advanced, although more slowly and not without considerable difficulties: liberalizing trade in agricultural goods, expanding the membership, using the international trading system to promote economic development, and transforming the provisional institution into the fully-fledged international trade organization that diplomats at Bretton Woods had envisaged. The Uruguay Round, which began in 1986 and concluded with the signing of the Treaty of Marrakesh in 1994, increased the participation of developing countries in the system significantly and was the most ambitious GATT multilateral round ever. The Uruguay Round, the eighth multilateral GATT round liberalized trade in services for the first time, achieved significant reductions in agricultural trade barriers, and mandated the creation of the World Trade Organization, an international trade organization that would incorporate the GATT as part of its rulebook. Addressing concerns about the weakness and slow speed of the GATT dispute settlement process, the treaty established in the WTO contained a much more robust dispute resolution system, backed by the threat of penalties.

The institutionalization of monetary, banking, financial, and investment diplomacy began between the two world wars and evolved alongside that of trade diplomacy, but the way that international financial institutions evolved was somewhat different. These institutions have remained rather more limited in scope than the GATT and WTO. The same growth in international economic activity that drove the need to institutionalize trade diplomacy created a need for institutions to facilitate diplomacy involving monetary, financial, and business relations. The first such institution, the International Chamber of Commerce (ICC), was founded in 1924 with a membership of private firms, which also made the ICC the first institution to facilitate diplomacy between non-state actors. The ICC established the International Court of Arbitration to assist in resolution of disputes between businesses that extended across borders and were thus more difficult to resolve either through domestic legal systems or using conventional diplomacy (Kelly, 2005, 259–271). The Bank for International Settlements, founded in 1930 as part of the Young Plan to fund Germany's Great War reparations payments, became the primary venue for diplomacy and cooperation between the world's central banks. In this way, the institutionalization of investment and banking diplomacy got a head start on trade diplomacy. Yet after the Second World War, neither the IMF nor the World Bank became the sort of encompassing institutional venues for monetary and development finance diplomacy that the GATT and WTO did for trade. A run on sterling and a currency shortage in the UK in 1947 following Britain's ill-timed restoration of currency convertibility, which was mandated by the December 1945 Anglo-American Financial Agreement, resulted in temporary suspension of many of the functions of the IMF and World Bank envisaged at Bretton Woods. The US and Canadian governments substituted the Marshall Plan as a more aggressive short-term foreign assistance strategy to reconstruct Europe and restart Europe's economic growth in the face of a rise in US-Soviet geopolitical tensions resulting from crises in Greece and Turkey (Curzon, 1965, 32).

International monetary relations remained enmeshed with trade relations, as governments can use currency devaluations and depreciations as trade barriers in lieu of tariffs. Yet the IMF and GATT never worked as closely together as envisaged at Bretton Woods. For a start, different diplomats with differing areas of expertise and priorities did the negotiating in each institution. Had the more ambitious UK-backed Keynes Plan rather than the US-backed White Plan been approved at Bretton Woods, a much better capitalized IMF with greater powers over creditor nations as well as debtors, might have evolved into a highly institutionalized monetary diplomacy. In an international system in which currency values were pegged to gold, the IMF's intended power to facilitate exchange rate adjustments by reining in the monetary policies of governments running both persistent deficits and surpluses, did not materialize owing to US unwillingness to cooperate (either when running surpluses or deficits). This limitation, alongside diverging economic and monetary objectives of the major Western allies in the 1960s, led to the collapse of the Bretton Woods gold standard and its replacement, by 1973, with a system of managed floating exchange rates. Thereafter, the IMF became more specialized, as its main focus shifted to providing balance of payments and exchange rate stability to developing countries.

Monetary diplomacy since the 1970s has been conducted analogously to the nineteenth-century Concert of Europe system, in which the Great Powers met as often as required to keep the system functioning and to coordinate responses to crises. What became the Group of Seven (G7) was conceived of as a more informal replacement for IMF management of fixed rates. Heads of government of the Great Powers meet informally to get to know one another better. Their finance ministers 'manage' floating exchange rates through agreements that would involve finance ministries and central banks taking positions in international currency markets. Managing floating rates has become progressively more difficult for financial diplomats, at least in times of crisis, as currency swings in the 2007 financial crisis made clear. With the advent of electronic funds transfer at the end of the 1960s, financial flows became increasingly decoupled from, and much vaster than, trade flows of goods, services, and labor. At the same time, shifting exchange rates have had a progressively greater impact upon trade flows and have thus made monetary diplomacy more high profile in domestic politics. Prominent examples have been Japan-US negotiations over the yen-dollar rate in the 1980s and China-US negotiations over the *renminbi*-dollar rate in the 2000s and 2010s. The European Union, as a regional institution, has proven effective as a venue for monetary, financial, and development diplomacy in the face of major negotiating challenges, including the 1:1 *ostmark/deutschmark* exchange rate for German reunification in 1991, the convergence criteria for eligibility to join the Euro preceding monetary integration in 1999, and a stabilization plan for troubled countries in the Eurozone's first major financial crisis in 2010.

Judicialization and Future Transformations

The process of institutionalization of the global economy had lost its momentum by the 2000s, as the expanding membership of the WTO, the increasing divergence of interests of its members, and the shifting distribution of power toward large middle-income countries (Brazil, India, China) made successful negotiation within the multilateral trade negotiating round format increasingly difficult. The Doha Development Agenda, launched in 2001, remained unfinished in 2015, with prospects for completion highly uncertain. Hence, the most recent and, as yet, far from complete transformation in trade diplomacy has seen the primary focus of trade diplomacy shift gradually away from more traditional bilateral and multilateral diplomatic representation, communication, and negotiation. This latest transformation, which began with the commencement of operations of the World Trade Organization and its stepped-up mechanism for resolving trade disputes in 1995, is shifting the dominant method of trade diplomacy toward the legal, judicialized Dispute Settlement Understanding (DSU) established under the WTO and in regional trade agreements such as the North American Free Trade Agreement (NAFTA). Whereas in the first forty-seven years of operation of the GATT, fewer than three hundred complaints were brought under the GATT 1947's dispute settlement procedure, in the first fifteen years of the WTO DSU alone, over four hundred complaints were lodged (Evans and Shaffer, 2010, 2 and Shahin, 2010, 277). *Stare decisis*, the principle of judicial precedent under which judicial decisions become part of the law considered in making future judgments, and by which jurists effectively become policy makers, though not a formal principle of WTO dispute settlement, has, in effect, become the norm. WTO dispute settlement panels and Appellate Body hearings are becoming the leading venues for trade diplomacy. Judicialized trade diplomacy is coming to resemble domestic political procedures for resolving disagreements more than traditional forms of diplomacy. Such procedures replace direct diplomatic negotiations over contested issues with specialized consideration of, and rulings on, particular cases, which then must be generalized through subsequent rulings on future disputes (Matsushita, 2012, 507–534).

This judicialized form of trade diplomacy has a range of implications, not only in terms of the impact of its results on trade diplomacy and policy. Conducting trade diplomacy primarily by means of adjudicating disputes marginalizes processes of direct diplomatic negotiation of contested issues. Dispute settlement is less effective when different interests wish to negotiate changes to the rules than when they wish simply to apply them. Judicial systems, by their nature, appear depoliticized, as the process by which views are contested is less transparent to the global public. This undermines perceptions of procedural legitimacy that have become so important in an age of increasingly public diplomacy. Wealthier and larger states are able to take advantage of the system in ways that smaller and developing countries are not: devoting substantial institutional resources and diplomatic personnel to WTO dispute settlement and using the services of law firms well-versed in international trade disputes, to name a few. Some large emerging powers, such as Brazil and China, have benefited already by emulating the strategies of the actors that have used the dispute settlement system most effectively: the USA and EU. However, and notwithstanding the continued dominance of nation-state actors, judicialization also permits a more systematic articulation of the interests of non-state actors such as transnational firms and civil society organizations through mechanisms such as the filing of *amicus curiae* (friend of the court) briefs in dispute settlement cases (Matsushita, 2012, 513–525). CSOs such as the Advisory Centre on WTO Law (www.acwl.ch) have already proved important in assisting least developed countries (LDCs) in learning to use the dispute settlement system to advance their interests. ACWL assistance enabled Bangladesh to win an antidumping case against India over lead-acid batteries in 2005, in the first WTO dispute won by an LDC (Taslim, 2010, 230–247). The judicialization of trade diplomacy under the aegis of formal dispute settlement mechanisms extends considerably beyond WTO, as regional trade institutions like the EU, NAFTA, and MERCOSUR, and even bilateral PTAs have established analogous procedures for their members.

Since judicialization has begun to transform trade diplomacy, there has been a measure of divergence between trade diplomacy and monetary diplomacy, which, by its nature, would not lend itself to case-by-case dispute resolution. Monetary diplomacy remains managed by a club of Great Powers and is not fully institutionalized even to the extent that the Bretton Woods conferees had imagined as they crafted the IMF. Monetary diplomacy has changed to the extent that the G7 has increasingly been supplanted by the G20 (Group of 20) as its primary venue—particularly since the 2007 financial crisis. By including prominent emerging markets as members, as well as the EU and Australia alongside the old G7, the G20 bids for greater global legitimacy by claiming to represent 90 percent of global GDP and 80 percent of world trade directly. As might be expected, the G20's increased legitimacy over that of the old G7 comes at a cost of greater divergence of views and difficulty in reaching and implementing decisions. In practice, G20 monetary diplomacy can be viewed as more a success of communication and coordination than of substantive policy cooperation.

Financial and investment diplomacy have evolved more in parallel with trade diplomacy than monetary diplomacy has done. As many financial and investment issues increasingly fall under the remit of the WTO, financial and investment diplomacy have begun to be transformed by judicialization alongside other trade issues. Agreements negotiated as part of the 1994 Treaty of Marrakesh, such as those on TRIMs (Trade-Related Investment Measures) and TRIPs (Trade-Related Intellectual Property Rights), and the Agreement on Subsidies and Countervailing Measures, which regulate government subventions to industry such as trade finance, became part of the 'single undertaking' that countries joining the WTO from 1995 had to accept in full as a condition of membership. This has resulted in numerous potential investment and finance-related conflicts between states becoming eligible for adjudication by the WTO's Dispute Settlement Body. Judicialization of investment diplomacy has also taken place through bilateral investment treaties (BITs), now a common mechanism through which governments exchange national treatment, intellectual property protection, and other investment-friendly guarantees, as BITs often include their own dispute resolution mechanisms.

Whilst international trade in goods, services, and capital continues to grow, public perceptions are increasing that opportunities for greater economic growth through trade are being missed, and that benefits from trade continue to be spread unevenly. The institutions and processes for economic diplomacy are regularly identified by journalists and politicians as responsible for these shortcomings. One possible resolution of the lack of transparency and legitimacy that trade diplomacy by dispute resolution engenders is to build a better deliberative mechanism for diplomatic negotiation between sovereign actors than the current model of GATT/WTO multilateral rounds afford, and which have resulted in their overshadowing by judicialized trade diplomacy. The first supranational organization to craft such a mechanism for making and enforcing economic policies and conducting economic relations amongst its member states, however imperfectly, is the European Union. Crucially, it remains diplomatic, in the sense that it mediates effectively between member states that retain their sovereignty and choose to continue to do so. In the numerous treaties that European Union members have signed and implemented since the 1950s, however, member governments and their publics decided to pool aspects of their sovereignty and to participate in supranational legislative and judicial mechanisms that would collectively make and enforce trade policy. Some EU member states have subsequently pooled sovereignty over monetary policy through creating the single currency in 1999, and more recently over financial and banking policies as well. The process is better balanced between legislation and judicial review. EU policy is negotiated and approved through the EU's deliberative and administrative organs, the Commission, the Council, and the Parliament. Weighted majority voting in the European Council reflects differences in size and power of the EU's sovereign member states. Legal challenges by member state as well as by non-state actors, including firms, CSOs, and individuals, are heard by the European Court of Justice. The EU's legislative process, and the trade and other economic policies that it produces and implements, is often fiercely contested, both inside and outside of the process. For example, there has been disagreement for decades over funding the EU's Common Agricultural Policy, which subsidizes often uncompetitive European farm production, yet the process has continued to work, notwithstanding the EU's steady enlargement over more than a half century to embrace an economically increasingly diverse group of member states. The EU may be able to continue to develop better tools for trade negotiation, as it has done with regulatory competition, as an approach to services and technical barriers to trade (TBT), because it has a better designed and balanced legislative-judicial apparatus than the WTO (Messerlin, 2012). The EU, flawed though it be, may serve as a better, if still not ideal, model for reforming the institutions of global economic diplomacy in the future, in that it serves as a set of mechanisms for sovereign member states to negotiate differences and reach agreements on policies, for implementing those policies, and for resolving the disputes that will inevitably arise.

CHAPTER REVIEW QUESTIONS

1. Define diplomacy in relation to trade.
2. Define trade in relation to diplomacy.
3. What are the four historical phases of trade diplomacy?

4. What are the main issues of the trade liberalization debate?
5. What was the significance of the Cobden-Chevalier Treaty?

SEMINAR/ESSAY QUESTIONS

1. Why was the Silk Road so important to early diplomacy?
2. What does Pigman mean by the broadening of the definition of 'trade' in more modern times?
3. What are the three transformations in the development of international trade and diplomacy?
4. What were the two achievements of Bretton Woods and the three economic objectives achieved there?
5. Why is judicialization important in trade diplomacy today?

References and Further Reading

Cohen, Raymond and Raymond Westbrook (eds). *Amarna Diplomacy: The Beginnings of International Relations*. Baltimore: The Johns Hopkins University Press, 2000.

Curzon, Gerard. *Multilateral Commercial Diplomacy*. London: Michael Joseph, 1965.

Der Derian, James. *On Diplomacy; a Genealogy of Western Estrangement*. Oxford: Basil Blackwell, 1987.

Dunham, A.L. *The Anglo-French Treaty of Commerce of 1860 and the Progress of the Industrial Revolution in France*. Ann Arbor: University of Michigan Press, 1930.

Edsall, Nicholas. *Richard Cobden, Independent Radical*. Cambridge: Harvard University Press, 1986.

Evans, David and Gregory C. Shaffer, 'Introduction' in *Dispute Settlement at the WTO: The Developing Country Experience*. Gregory C. Shaffer and Ricardo Melendez-Ortiz, (eds). Cambridge: Cambridge University Press, 2010.

Foreman-Peck, James. *A History of the World Economy*, Brighton: Wheatsheaf Books, Ltd., 1972.

Gardner, Richard N. *Sterling-Dollar Diplomacy in Current Perspective*, 2nd ed. New York: Columbia University Press, 1980.

Hamilton, Keith and Richard Langhorne. *The Practice of Diplomacy*, 2nd ed. London: Routledge, 2010.

Iliasu, A.A. "The Cobden-Chevalier Commercial Treaty of 1860." *Historical Journal*, 14: 67–98. 1971.

Kelly, Dominic. "Global Monitor: The International Chamber of Commerce." *New Political Economy*. Vol. 10, No. 2 (2005): 259–271.

Lake, David A. *Power, Protection and Free Trade*. Ithaca, NY: Cornell University Press, 1988.

Landes, David. *The Unbound Prometheus*. Cambridge: Cambridge University Press, 1969.

Lee, Donna and David Hudson. "The old and new significance of political economy in diplomacy." *Review of International Studies*. Vol. 30 (June, 2004): 343–360.

Mallet, Sir Bernard Mallet. *Sir Louis Mallet*. London: James Nisbet & Co., Ltd., 1905.

Matsushita, Mitsuko. "The Dispute Settlement Mechanism at the WTO: The Appellate Body—Assessment and Problems," in *Oxford Handbook on the World Trade Organization*,

Amrita Narlikar, Martin Daunton, and Robert M. Stern (eds). Oxford: Oxford University Press, 2012, 507–534.

Messerlin, Patrick A. "The Influence of the EU in the World Trade System." in *The Oxford Handbook on the World Trade Organization*. Amrita Narlikar, Martin Daunton, and Robert M. Stern (eds). Oxford: Oxford University Press, 2012, 505–549.

Pigman, Geoffrey Allen and Brendan Vickers. "Old Habits Die Hard? Diplomacy at the World Trade Organisation and the 'New Diplomatic Studies Paradigm.'" *International Journal of Diplomacy and Economy*. Vol. 1, No. 1 (2012): 19–41.

Pigman, Geoffrey Allen. "Hegemony and Trade Liberalization Policy: Britain and the Brussels Sugar Convention of 1902," *Review of International Studies*. Vol. 23 (April, 1997): 185–210.

Pigman, Geoffrey Allen. *Trade Diplomacy Transformed; Why Trade Matters for Global Prosperity*. London: Palgrave Macmillan, 2015.

Pollard, Sidney. *Peaceful Conquest*. Oxford: Oxford University Press, 1981.

Polo, Marco. *The Travels of Marco Polo*. R.E. Latham, tr. Harmondsworth: Penguin Books, Ltd., 1958.

Scammell, W.M. *The International Economy Since 1945*, 2nd ed. New York: St. Martin's Press, 1983.

Shahin, Magda. "WTO dispute settlement for a middle-income developing country: the situation of Egypt," in *Dispute Settlement at the WTO. The Developing Country Experience*. Shaffer and Melendez-Ortiz (eds). Cambridge: Cambridge University Press, 275–297.

Sharp, Paul. *Diplomatic Theory of International Relations*. Cambridge: Cambridge University Press, 2009.

Stein, Arthur A. "The Hegemon's Dilemma: Great Britain, the United States, and the International Economic Order," *International Organization* 38 (2) (Spring 1984): 358–67.

Strange, Susan. *The Retreat of the State: The Diffusion of Power in the World Economy*. Cambridge: Cambridge University Press, 1996.

Taslim, Mohammad Ali. "How the DSU worked for Bangladesh: the first least developed country to bring a WTO claim," in *Dispute Settlement at the WTO. The Developing Country Experience*. Gregory C. Shaffer and Ricardo Melendez-Ortiz (eds). Cambridge: Cambridge University Press, 2010, 230–247.

Winham, Gilbert R. *International Trade and the Tokyo Round Negotiations*. Princeton: Princeton University Press, 1986.

Zhang, Yiping. *Story of the Silk Road*. Jia Zongyi, tr. Beijing: China Intercontinental Press, 2005.

Websites

International Telecommunications Union, About ITU, http://www.itu.int/en/about/Pages/default.aspx

Advisory Centre on WTO Law, http://www.acwl.ch/e/index.html, accessed November 18, 2013; Agreement Establishing the Advisory Centre on WTO Law, http://www.acwl.ch/e/documents/agreement_estab_e.pdf

CROSS SECTION 5.1

Byzantium: Trade and Culture

BY ALISON HOLMES

Chronologically, Byzantium is the most recent of the three investigations into the diplomacies of place, but it is a useful place to start because this system incorporated many previous practices, and passed down many more to succeeding 'European' empires. Utilizing both trade and culture as the 'coin of the realm,' the Byzantine Empire existed for one thousand years, approximately 330 CE to 1453 CE, as both a trading giant and cultural expansionist. Constantinople—built on the former Greek city of Byzantium, and then later became Istanbul—was the capital of one of the longest lasting, as well as one of the more clearly structured, 'empires.' The vast territory extended west to east from what is modern-day India to China and south to north from inner Africa to northern Europe, encompassing a huge range of languages, cultures, and forms of governance, but all organized from an explicitly Christian perspective. As Bozeman points out, Byzantine history has often been regarded as an "appendix to ancient Rome" or a "prelude to the history of modern Greece," as well as being important as perhaps the first real exchange between Christian and Islamic cultures (Bozeman, 1960, 307). Byzantium is useful because it demonstrates the importance of diplomacy as well as the spread of diplomatic practices across this ancient world and into the modern day through both trade and the explicit use of culture.

The Byzantine Empire was originally part of the greater Roman Empire (or Western Roman Empire), which lasted from 27 BCE–476 CE. However, as the Roman Empire grew, so too did the divisions and tensions, until there was a permanent rift between east and west and the Byzantine Empire split from the Western Roman Empire in 395 CE when Rome could no longer maintain control. The ultimate struggle was essentially part of a much larger issue between religious and temporal sources of power. This was particularly true of the Western Empire as it was forced to fight on many fronts simultaneously before finally losing the eastern part of the empire and falling into total collapse by 500 CE.

Once free, the capital of Constantinople came into its own in terms of building a structure under a single authority that was able to encompass both politics and religion. This idea of a 'priest-king' or **basileus** (the *title Greeks had used for the Persian 'king of kings'*) was very hierarchical and centralized, a synthesis of the Roman, Persian, and Hellenistic traditions with interlocking government institutions to help balance and direct that power (Bozeman, 1960). As Christianity and the Greek language became the dominant cultural features of the empire, so too its leaders became increasingly convinced of its power and superiority in terms of its ability and even its right to rule (Watson, 2009, 107).

A keystone in this foundation was the Hellenistic tradition of education, which the Byzantines believed should be put into the service of the state—unlike Western Europe where the main political struggle was in terms of the rights of the individual (Bozeman, 1960, 322). This produced a very different concept of society that was applied not only at home, but also abroad. Given the expanse of the empire, a basic observation is the presence of many cultures, both literate and non-literate, created a necessity for both alliance building and the monitoring of enemies—real and imagined. The size of their territory, as well as their geopolitical position, also meant they were literally unable to isolate themselves from potential enemies, a fact the Byzantines made both a point of pride and a part of the routine of extensive emphasis on business as they sought to be sensitive yet vigilant in terms of the cultures under their rule and to take education wherever they went. As the empire expanded, it followed both a 'Persian' policy as well as that found in the *Arthaśāstra* discussed below, by recognizing that a principle of 'loyalty not conformity' would be a more stable policy (Watson, 2009, 108).

The diplomatic process inevitably followed this social structure and held that the emperor was effectively the 'diplomat-in-chief.' However, given the size of the empire, this was not practical and therefore a special department of external affairs, as well as an organized foreign service, was created, along with specific grades and types of training for its diplomats after passing an examination. Once admitted, these negotiators were given detailed instructions—clearly important given their regard for their sovereign—but they were also tasked with collecting as much practical information as possible about the customs and habits of their hosts and contacts. Indeed, Byzantine diplomats were known for detailed reports on "personal tastes and suitable gifts" (Watson, 2009, 109) as crucial aspects of the intelligence necessary to a political strategy based on exchange, incentive, and often bribes. The Byzantines were also known for effectively co-opting citizen diplomats from amongst a huge network of traders and others who had regular contact with outsiders. The mission of these non-professional diplomats was essentially information gathering that was then fed into the process of relationship and alliance building—as well as enemy baiting and outright treachery. However, to be effective, these diplomatic efforts had to be coordinated and, by most accounts, were seen as an organic part of the machinery of the empire, designed to protect the state. All institutions—including and especially the institution of diplomacy—were deemed vital in that pursuit.

Today, many people would suggest that the Byzantines were experts in what we call public diplomacy. However, while many of the activities might be classified this way now, at that time, it is more accurate to argue they were classic examples of the use of economic and cultural diplomacy as the core of their strategy, supported by political and military diplomacy—though only as a last resort. As Bozeman suggests, the Byzantines focused on ways to garner and enforce influence through the use of 'soft' as well as 'hard' power was perhaps their most "original contribution to the art of international politics" (Bozeman, 1960, 339). They not only engaged all levels of society, but they also regularly invited those they wanted to keep an eye on to Constantinople, where guests were treated extravagantly, observed constantly, and even subjected to forms of psychological pressure in that they were not allowed to leave this gilded cage until their hosts had deemed them sufficiently impressed (and intimidated) by the wealth and the power of the empire to return home. The assumption was these guests would report the best strategy was to remain subservient to the Empire. The use of symbol in this process deserves particular mention in that the Byzantines became known for the trappings, ceremonies, and rituals associated with diplomacy and functions of state. For literate and non-literate peoples alike, this kind of grand presence should not be underestimated as it meant that force was not the main tool of the empire, but that influence and diffusion were used extensively. Thus the crown, scepter, rich vestments, coinage, titles, and rules of etiquette were all put to use in terms of swaying the opinion of friend and foe alike.

Byzantine diplomacy helped maintain this power by controlling the political development of those under its rule, contributing to active exchanges through commerce and trade and supporting the spread of religion and

BOX 5.1.1

Byzantine Symbolism – robes and staff

When the Byzantine emperor received visitors he was covered in an imperial robe covered in emblems testifying to his universal authority and power. Covered in stars and celestial constellations it connected the emperor with heaven itself. It also showed the hemispheres and continents of Europe, Asia and Africa reflecting vast earthly territory as well. The robe was introduced to Europe in the early eleventh century when the Duke of Apulia presented such a robe to Henry II of Saxony. From here it spread to Germany and other European kingdoms (Bozeman, 1960).

For the diplomat, the staff or caduceus was a symbol or insignia of office and symbolized both his position and immunity. Also part of the Mali/griot regalia, in Byzantium, it was modelled on the staff of Hermes and was made up of twisted serpents staring at each other. Both the diplomat's wand and the king's sceptre were symbols of a power conferred by heaven (Frey and Frey, 1999).

education across this huge space. Interestingly, while they doubtless believed that they were spreading their own style of rule, they also consciously and unconsciously assimilated various ideas and adopted aspects of the diplomatic practices of those with whom they came into contact. For example, the family of kings, dynastic marriage, protocol and hospitality, as well as the use of merchant ambassadors were all present in Mesopotamia before becoming part of the Byzantine approach. Neither Greece nor Rome are particularly known for their diplomacy, but the Byzantines also adopted and combined various aspects of these cultures and empires to skillful effect. For example, the Greek language became that of the Empire and the notion of rhetoric and negotiation, as well as the use of soft power over local and foreign clients, were incorporated. From Rome, a logical influence on the empire, the Byzantines learned divide and rule, the buying of mercenaries and allies, bribing their way out of trouble, impressing visitors, and providing aid to allies in practical forms such as engineering projects. All this, combined with the adoption of Christianity, set the Byzantines up as both superior at home and with a mission to convert the world.

However, the resulting complicated system of balances, intelligence, and relationship building could be interpreted in a negative, as well as a positive light. As both the finances and the military strength of the empire waned, so too did its ability to play the interests of others off each other and maintain a central position. The capital's role as connector, even if not as ruler, of the world, eventually became too much, particularly as the neighboring areas began to shape their own identities and governance structures. Yet the practices of the Byzantine Empire were not lost. As part of its expansion and effort to spread both religion and education, many of its ideas had already spread to various trading partners and been taken up by powerful players such as Venice, who, in turn, spread this regard for ceremony and ritual throughout the Italian city-state system. These concepts then found their way into the courts of Western Europe and took on new and glamorous manifestations as monarchs adopted many Byzantine symbols and ceremonies—as well as habits of intrigue and propaganda (Neumann, 2011). The Byzantine Empire is an example of Bozeman's somewhat more blunt argument that "the international history of diplomacy is indivisible" (Bozeman, 1960, 327), as both trade and culture enabled them to expand and solidify its position of power. This relationship between trade and culture is as intimate as it is complex, as we shall see in the next chapter, looking specifically at culture and its role in diplomacy over time.

References and Further Reading

Bozeman, Adda. *Politics and Culture in International History*. Princeton: Princeton University Press, 1960.

Neumann, Iver. "Euro-Centric diplomacy: Challenging but manageable." *European Journal of International Relations*. 18 (2) (2011): 299–321.

Watson, Adam. *The Evolution of International Society*. London and New York: Routledge, 1992/2009.

6 Cultural Diplomacy

BY GILES SCOTT-SMITH

Definitions

In 1989, Joseph Nye popularized the term 'soft power' to denote the power of attraction expressed through norms, values, services, and opportunities that appeal to others (Nye, 1990, 2004). Since then, the term has become ubiquitous as a useful way to sum up all manner of material and non-material means that a state may possess that favorably influence the opinion of (usually foreign) publics. What Nye did not do, to any great degree, is look at the mechanisms, both public and private (and often in combination), which are used to actually utilize soft power in an international setting. This is the domain of cultural diplomacy.

Before examining cultural diplomacy, culture itself needs to be defined. The distinction made by Raymond Williams is useful here. The sociologist differentiated between culture as process—the cultivation of something—and culture as "a thing in itself." Williams delved into the genealogy of this distinction, marking the shift from one to the other around the late eighteenth and early nineteenth centuries. Moving from the cultivation of natural life to the training of the human mind, it became closely related with "the idea of human perfection" and "the general state of intellectual development in a society as a whole," within which cultural production through the arts was of central importance (Williams, 1966, 16). This essentially Western Enlightenment definition secured the association of culture with progress, and thus became part of a hierarchical (and fixed) system of judgment on cultural development among different peoples. Williams later took this further, distinguishing between what he called the idealist and materialist interpretations of culture: the former, focusing on the "informing spirit of a whole way of life, which is manifest over the whole range of social activities, but is most evident in 'specifically cultural' activities"; and the latter, with its emphasis "on 'a whole social order' within which a specifiable culture, in styles of art and kinds of intellectual work" is produced (Williams, 1981, 11–12).

Williams's contribution to the topic at hand comes from his emphasis on the historical development of understandings and meanings of the word 'culture,' and how, at a certain point, it became invested with a great deal of social and political importance. A similar approach can be applied to the use of cultural diplomacy. The phrase points to a given actor, the diplomat, using culture within a recognizable diplomatic environment, for purposes that exceed the mere edification of the culture in question. An orthodox interpretation will insist that the diplomat must be in the employ of a national government or inter-governmental organization, restricting cultural diplomacy to the realm of inter-state interactions. There is nothing wrong with this interpretation; it merely fixes this activity essentially in the era of the modern nation-state. This does not exclude non-state actors; it only determines that the tasks they carry out are, at some level, in the service of the 'national interest,' as defined by the government of the time. Paradoxically, advocates of cultural diplomacy will often draw on the fact that it is a centuries-old activity in order to justify a higher status in the modern era, where it is regularly faced with budgetary cutbacks and accusations of superfluousness (Arndt, 2005).

Broadly speaking, many of these definitions of cultural diplomacy tend to refer to the employment of cultural products, heritage, transactions, and (educational and cultural) exchanges by a state as a way to improve understanding and appreciation of its qualities and identity, in support of its political and economic objectives abroad. J.M. Mitchell, who refers to seeking "to impress, to present a favourable image, so that diplomatic operations as a whole are facilitated," identifies two layers at work: the negotiation and signing by states of official treaties and conventions that promote international cultural exchange, is cultural diplomacy of the first order; the second involves the actual carrying out of these agreements by appropriate public and private actors (Mitchell, 1986, 5).

Cultural diplomacy is generally separated from public diplomacy, which covers a whole set of other activities related to promoting state interests abroad. For example, Nicholas Cull has identified five principal areas of activity: listening (which includes research and analysis); advocacy (promoting a set of political and/or economic interests); exchange diplomacy; international broadcasting; and cultural diplomacy, described as "the dissemination of cultural practices as a mechanism to promote the interests of the actor, which could include an international tour by a prominent musician" (Cull 2008, xv). A further distinction—at the center of the following discussion—can be made between cultural diplomacy and cultural relations. Diplomacy in its traditional sense necessarily involves the state as the decisive actor, steering contacts and discussions in relation to other foreign policy interests and goals. Cultural relations, on the other hand, refers to those cross-border contacts and transactions that occur outside of any state involvement. These interactions—involving tourism, study abroad, cultural artefacts, book and media circulation, migration and intermarriage, the transfer of ideas by whatever medium—"grow naturally and organically," according to Mitchell (Arndt 2005, xvii). For some, cultural relations, covering all cross-border interactions, therefore encompasses cultural diplomacy as no more than a subset of activities. The task of the cultural diplomat is partly to identify and latch on to those trends and movements already occurring in order to optimize the impact of their own particular set of activities. For others, an expanded interpretation of 'diplomats' and 'ambassadors' is required that effectively removes the cultural relations / cultural diplomacy dichotomy entirely. As diplomacy is taken in this text to be an institutionalized form of dialogue between entities of social organization through time, the relations/diplomacy distinction has already been considerably weakened.

Signposts

When was cultural diplomacy first applied? As stated above, most interpretations of diplomacy assume the involvement of a state as the legitimate political unit, seeking to interact (politically, economically, culturally) with similar units. An orthodox periodization of this phenomenon would therefore logically point to the era of the nation-state as the most appropriate context for analyzing its evolution and charateristics. States have, after all, invested a great deal in culture for their own purposes. Yet the period before the establishment of the (European) state system should not be discounted, and neither should the era of the state system—the Westphalian system of lore—be considered static. The state, as some kind of a fixed political-territorial institution, should not dominate the interpretation of cultural diplomacy, as other actors have been involved, and continue to be involved. To facilitate this investigation, therefore, six signposts are used to indicate different understandings of cultural diplomacy over time.

Importance of the Gift

The first is the gift. Building on Marcel Mauss, Richard Arndt notes the centuries-long importance of gift-making between cultures (Mauss, 1990

[1954]). Gifts served several purposes, but all of them involved communication in some form. They were "the diplomat's opening, a form of socio-political currency and a pledge of honor" (Arndt, 2005, 2). Obviously, prestige was at the center of this, the most valuable gifts having the most impact. Aiming to impress the other is one part of the gift, often with an added undertone of intimidation. Yet the reference to a pledge of honor also highlights how this involved a two-way transaction. By giving a valuable gift, the expectation was being made overt that this would be reciprocated, if not in kind, then certainly in behavior. The link here with offerings to the gods is clear. A gift was an opening, not only for immediate contact, but also, potentially, to a new form of relations in the longer term. Hence, the importance of people as gifts, e.g., family members destined for marriage, but also slaves. Gifts were vital as a means to overcome the linguistic and cultural divides—not to mention knee-jerk friend-enemy distinctions—when different peoples encountered each other for the first time. The items taken by the Jesuit Matteo Ricci to China in the late sixteenth century, among them an intricate clock and a clavichord (or type of piano), gave him an entrance, and the respect, of the emperor (Spence, 1985). However, this already indicates a shift in the thinking on the gift that goes back to Williams's historical understanding. Ricci's generosity was also designed, in true Jesuit fashion, to emphasize the superiority of the messenger over the receiver. This was no longer splendor and wealth, it was also knowledge and intellect—the determination that a learned culture would recognize a superior culture when confronted by it.

Learning

The second signpost is learning itself. From the Alexandria in Egypt of the third century BCE onwards, libraries were a prime means to gather not only the products of knowledge, but also the most learned minds. Libraries became the principal nodes of what we would now refer to as educational exchange (Casson, 2001). Centers of learning were widely recognized as sites of symbolic power, and with the rise of Christianity and Islam they formed an integrated network of non-state (or pre-state) cultural diplomacy in their own right. Prestige is again at work, but it is the missionary element that gives this signpost additional importance. The drive not only to attract the best minds, but to go out and proselytize, links this phenomenon with the gradual determination of rulers to express their national characteristics elsewhere as edifying and unique.

Nationalism

The third signpost is, inevitably, nationalism. France was first to adopt learning as a means to national greatness in the modern era. Under the Renaissance rule of Francis I (1496–1547), the classical model was revived and merged with a Christian belief system and a sense of national superiority. Here, learning became embroiled in not only communication, but also competition. One might argue this was always present, and it would be a mistake to assume that nationalism from the sixteenth century onwards somehow corrupted the use of the arts and knowledge for political gain over rivals. Yet the extra ingredient of inter-state interaction in Europe undoubtedly changed the environment for cultural diplomacy. This was a gradual transition that, for some time, involved the cultural proselytizers occupying a prime position. Poets and artists as diplomats were a commonplace in Renaissance Europe, their erudition and insight being valued as the perfect ambassadorial qualities to represent national 'greatness.' Education was also for export, and the verve and self-belief of the Jesuits fed directly into the passion and chauvinism of the French cultural diplomats. The church was gradually sidelined, but not before its missionaries had established new centers of learning in places such as Beirut, Lebanon and, later, when the Americans became involved, in Cairo, Egypt, and places in China. Francis had already established the Collège de France in Paris in 1530 to break the church's monopoly on education.

An unexpected but vital agent in this nationalist era was the military. Usually regarded as no more than the tool of conquest, military forces also took with them artifacts, scientific knowledge, and cultural norms, all of which influenced the recipient populations. The ultimate test for military prowess may have been demonstrated on the battlefield, but the ramifications of demonstrations and displays of hard power went far beyond the simple dictum of 'power out of the barrel of a gun.' President Theodore Roosevelt's use of the Great White Fleet in 1907–1908 was more than a simple expression of US military might. Its fourteen-month, forty-five-thousand-mile world tour was as much "diplomacy, as preventive strategy, as technical training, and as a sheer pageant of power" (Morris, 2001 and Hodge, 2008). The tour announced that the United States had arrived as a world power and that it was prepared to use that power as the foremost agent of (Western) civilization.

Cultural expression as power came into its own during the age of nationalism in the nineteenth century; its foremost exponents were Britain and France. Both were united by a sense of mission to civilize the non-European world, but, beyond that, they differed considerably. Britain concentrated on its industrial prowess and imperial reach, amply demonstrated at the Great

Exhibition held in the Crystal Palace in Hyde Park during 1851. This approach was effectively culture as civilization, as progress, and as prestige (Auerbach, 1999). Aside from this, culture in the sense of the arts did not feature much in the British worldview. France, on the other hand, pioneered and perfected the use of culture as a means to disseminate its influence around the world, and, in a quote from 1941 that is still apposite today, "they clung with astonishing tenacity to their position as the leading influence in civilisation" (Routh, 1941, 7). Behind this lay an unshakeable self-belief in the superiority of the French intellect and the arts, dating back through the Enlightenment and the humanism of *les philosophes* to the time of Francis I. Investment in education, both domestically and abroad, was therefore a priority, so that the instruction of others incorporated the spread of the French language and knowledge of French cultural achievements. Prestige and power went together, but in a different form from that of Britain. Concentrating on the lands around the Mediterranean, the French tools of cultural diplomacy in the late nineteenth century were educational, philanthropic (orphanages and hospitals), and tuitional (agricultural development). Private organizations such as *Alliance Française*, established in 1883 to promote the teaching of the French language abroad, also occupied a key role (Gosnell, 2008, 227–243). Again in contrast to Britain, the value of this cultural approach for foreign policy was recognized very early on, and the Ministry of Foreign Affairs soon decided to take a coordinating role. In 1910, the Ministry formed the *Office des Ecoles et des Universités françaises à l'étranger* to be the central point both within government and for public-private liaison. In 1920, the French Budget Commission could openly declare that "our universities and schools abroad are real focal points of pro-French propaganda; they constitute a weapon in the hands of our public officials" (Mitchell, 1986, 36). All cultural relations—therefore including the private sector— were now considered the ultimate responsibility of the Ministry. Britain, in contrast, created a public-private arrangement whereby the British Council received its funding from the Foreign Office, and still functions as an independently-run institution. It was not considered a matter of governmental responsibility to promote British culture abroad—but neither was it deemed wise to abandon the field of activity entirely to the private sector.

For its part, the British Council was established in 1935 in response to the rising challenge of Italian fascist designs on the Mediterranean as *Mare Nostrum* ('our sea'), thus exposing the potential weakness of British imperial lines of communication (McMurry and Lee, 1947, 137–181). It is worth reflecting on how the French determination to pursue dominance through cultural diplomacy also partly came from a position of relative military weakness vis-à-vis other powers. The post-Napoleonic era resulted in France losing European superiority to Germany and imperial superiority to Britain. In an age of increasing inter-state competition, France would invest the most heavily in cultural diplomacy as both tactic and practice in pursuit of their strategy.

Ideology

The fourth signpost is ideology. In the early twentieth century, the rise of new forms of socio-political and economic organization—fascism, Nazism, communism—created an environment where mass media, information, and propaganda took on a new, combative meaning. The advent of radio gave instant access to mass publics, and this, in turn, greatly influenced political strategizing. Following unification in 1870, Germany began to take note of its diaspora population abroad as a means to strengthen and spread 'Germanism' through educational institutions and cultural relations. This continued through the Weimar Republic, with a focus on German minorities around Europe and further afield in North and Latin America in an effort to maintain German citizenship, identity, and allegiance. Yet already before the coming to power of the National Socialist German Workers' Party (NSDAP) in 1933, the Weimar government was being challenged abroad by the NSDAP's Foreign Division that, from 1931, was actively gathering new supporters around its mantra of a revived, racially distinct 'Greater Germany.' This meant that the Nazis already had an active international network of cultural propaganda two years before taking power which they solidified institutionally by creating the Auslands-Organization based in Stuttgart. In contrast to the utilitarian British and the assimilatory French, the Germans pursued a cultural diplomacy that was based entirely on identity politics, racial hierarchies, and dutiful allegiance to the NSDAP ideology and mission. As one report put it in the wake of World War II, every German citizen abroad, "whether they liked it or not they became a dynamic part of the German concept of total global war" (Bradford, 1946).

The ideological counterpart to the Nazi organizations was the Soviet All Union Society for Cultural Relations with Foreign Countries (referred to by its Russian acronym, VOKS). An interesting detail here is that it was established in October 1925 after the abandonment of hope for world revolution. In other words, Soviet cultural diplomacy was always pursued as much to support the Soviet state as it was to promote communist ideology per se. By 1927, there were twenty ties with pro-Soviet friendship organizations across Europe, North America, and Asia. Much of this activity was based on displaying the building of the new Soviet state and society to the rest of the world and how it could achieve the highest forms of artistic expression, particularly in new fields such as photography and cinema (Fayet, 2010, 33–49). Throughout the Soviet period, individuals of undoubted cultural eminence were vital to the state's program as totems of cultural prestige, with key roles given to the likes of writer **Maxim Gorky** and composer/pianist **Dmitri Shostakovich.** Inviting such prominent figures to tour the major sites of Soviet industrialization and urbanization was a key aspect to this, and many returned home to produce favorable publications. Interesting examples include early Socialist groups such as the **Fabians** (and founders of the London School of Economics), Sidney and Beatrice Webb, whose *Soviet Union: A New Civilisation?* appeared in 1935, although others used their trips to express disillusionment with the Soviet experiment (Gide, 1936). The ideological phase of cultural diplomacy also emphasized the power of spectacle. Present from the very beginning of inter-cultural contacts and manifested in slightly different ways through the ages, what links these efforts is the deliberate aim to impress large numbers of people as a single mass. The Nazi Nürnburg rallies illustrate this most strongly, but similar approaches were evident in the Soviet, Italian, and Japanese campaigns of the 1930s, all aimed at submerging the individual into a mass movement moving forward collectively to determine the future. The high point of this competition was probably the World's Fair of 1937, held in Paris, where the rival pavilions of Nazi Germany and the Soviet Union confronted each other under the shadow of the Eiffel Tower, both of them claiming universal dominance for their message of superiority. In the wake of Francis Fukuyama and his well-known thesis on the "End of History," some might question the continuing relevance of ideology as a motivational factor in twenty-first-century cultural diplomacy, but if it is stretched to include religion, the argument ends (Fukuyama, 1989). Actors ranging from the Vatican, to private Christian, Islamic, and Hindu organizations, to the Islamic State of Iran and the state of Israel which conduct large-scale campaigns that emphasize cultural difference and uniqueness as much as togetherness, and incorporate an unmistakable utopian element, have made them very effective amongst publics searching for 'answers.'

Subterfuge

The fifth signpost is, perhaps surprisingly, subterfuge. The Soviet cultural diplomacy campaign was aimed at gathering support abroad for the homeland, which meant overcoming widespread suspicion and mistrust of Bolshevik methods and motives. As a result, organizations were formed that hid their pro-Soviet position, but which nevertheless acted in Moscow's interests. The master behind many of these 'fronts' in the 1920s and 1930s was the German communist **Willi Münzenberg**, who established a global network of publishers, newspapers, theaters, film studios, and cinemas, all operating as independent entities, but nonetheless connected via his Berlin headquarters. Through his high-profile connections with some of the most well-known intellectuals of the period (Albert Einstein, Bertolt Brecht, Upton Sinclair), Münzenberg used the anti-fascist and anti-Nazi cause as a means to gather support, generate publicity, and raise funds for his communist superiors (McKeekin, 2003). Although Münzenberg became a victim of Stalin's purges in 1940, his approach, which involved establishing a spectrum of fronts to mobilize activity across civil society, from sports to women's organizations, journalism to law, became standard for Soviet information and culture campaigns after World War II. Münzenberg's techniques were also the inspiration for the Central Intelligence Agency's covert counter-campaign to mobilize civil society in favor of democratic freedoms (Wilford, 2008 and Lucas, 1999). The question is whether these covert activities can still be categorized as cultural diplomacy. The latter's success in influencing individuals and publics relies on the perceived integrity, credibility, and legitimacy of the programs that are run, requiring, in the first place, full disclosure of who is in charge, where the funding is coming from, and what the goals are. Since use of front organizations is a deliberate way to obfuscate control, funding, and goals, even though cultural messages and means are being applied, it is contested whether this still merits the label cultural diplomacy (Kennedy and Lucas, 2005 and Scott-Smith, 2005).

Liberalism

The sixth signpost is Liberalism. There is a solid assumption among cultural diplomacy advocates, drawing on some of the fundamental principles of Liberal thought, that greater contact between cultures and peoples leads to an undermining of stereotypes, a lessening of tensions, and the building of inter-cultural bridges that can then be used to solidify more lasting economic and political relationships. As a result, there is a close connection between this approach and *the promotion of democracy as a means to secure peace* (the **Democratic Peace Theory**). This could also be placed under ideology, yet Liberalism's distinct influence across (US-based) theory and practice in cultural diplomacy means that it deserves separate consideration. The cultural diplomacy of the United States stems firmly from this belief system and relies heavily on the positive effects of personal contact with the United States, its people, and achievements. 'Mutual understanding' is its catch-phrase, and it is true that this model seems to have amassed enough evidence, in both anecdotal and statistical form, to justify the claims made on its behalf. Well-known counterfactuals do exist, the most notable being the experience of Sayyed Qutb, the Egyptian civil servant who made use of a State Department grant to study in Colorado in 1948–49, but returned so antagonized by American morals and social behavior that it contributed to his radicalization as an Islamic fundamentalist (von Drehle, 2006). The psychological dimensions of inter-cultural contact and communication has been an important sub-field of research (Rhoads, 2009, 166–186). As Frank Ninkovich once remarked, the universalist pretensions of the Liberal approach mean that those on the receiving end of US cultural diplomacy are effectively being asked to trade in their cultural identities and traditions in favor of a 'better' version—a process that does have underlying imperial tendencies (Ninkovich, 1996). Recent scholarship on the formative years of US cultural diplomacy during World War II has gone further to refer explicitly to the imperial-type thinking that was wired into the otherwise progressive Liberal mindset (Hart, 2013).

In the twenty-first century, the major test is whether this American Liberal openness can match the counter-narrative of the rise of China and Chinese cultural achievement. One cultural 'battleground' concerns the rising numbers of Chinese students studying at US universities. In the 2012–2013 academic year, 235,000 Chinese students studied in the United States, about 35 percent of the total number of foreign students. The attraction of US schools and universities is still very high and this is often trumpeted—particularly by Joseph Nye—as a continuing sign of the dominance of US soft power. However, does this mean that the majority of foreign students are 'taken in' by the American way of life and views on the rest of the world? Some earlier research on the Fulbright exchange program suggests they might, but the scale of this inter-cultural interchange means any conclusions are still premature (Xu, 1999, 139–157).

A final overarching factor is globalization, with the additional rubric, the 'digital global.' While the Cold War infosphere was dominated by the superpowers and the ideological contest between Left and Right, communism and capitalism, collectivism and individualism, other players have now entered the field. Principal among them is the People's Republic of China, a former power that in the second half of the twentieth century began its gradual (re-)ascent to superpower status by positioning itself as the champion of the underdeveloped Third World. Since the 1990s, Beijing has instituted a multilayered cultural diplomacy strategy that draws on spectacle (the 2008

Olympics), prestige (the 2010 Shanghai World Expo), and cultural achievement, with the main outposts being the Confucius Centers established around the world to promote the Chinese language and develop interpersonal and inter-institutional contacts (Dale, 2010). Chinese cultural spectacle has impressed the world before, but the combination of this with a new economic power and political status, makes it a more effective demonstration this time around. Yet there is more here than the mere promotion of a nation, as China is using its cultural outreach as part of a wider foreign policy campaign that promotes "Beijing's transformative, leading role in the rise of a Chinese brand of capitalism and a Chinese conception of the international community, both opposed to and substantially different from their Western version" (Halper, 2010, 11). This is meant to be a 'peaceful rise,' and cultural diplomacy is an ideal—and unthreatening—way to emphasize this strategy.

Other states lack Beijing's ambition and resources, but the advent of a new means for information dissemination via the World Wide Web, and the concomitant exponential possibilities for exposure and accessibility, have evened out the playing field between the different actors. On the one hand, this has improved the ability of non-state actors to influence global publics faster and more cheaply with campaigns that undermine the controlling position of the nation-state in affairs of public policy. Think here of the campaigns of Greenpeace against the oil industry in Nigeria starting in the 1990s or in the last decade in Russia, and Amnesty International's longstanding efforts on behalf of political prisoners worldwide. On the other hand, nation-states have themselves adapted to the radically changing environment by taking on board corporate mass marketing techniques, foremost among them being the notion of branding. The concept of '*nation-branding*' as a means to improve reputation has seen an explosive growth in the last decade, it now being a million-dollar consultancy industry, a fixture on the agenda of many foreign affairs ministries, and a sub-field of public diplomacy research that has threatened to outgrow its sub-field status. Examples of this trend might be seen in the journal, *Place Branding and Public Diplomacy*, begun in 2004, and the Nation Brands Index run by consultant Simon Anholt. In 2014, Anholt also launched a 'Good Country Index' (available at www.goodcountry.org). In such guides, Spain and South Korea are often put forward as prime examples of successful (re-)branding, and these processes can also interact closely with so-called 'niche diplomacy,' whereby a nation-state positions itself as possessing particular status and skills in a particular field. Examples include Norway with conflict resolution, Canada with peacekeeping, and the Netherlands with water management (Henrikson, 2004). To be successful, the nation-brand needs to highlight those positive characteristics of a people and the intellectual and cultural contribution that make their nation attractive to others. The difference between branding and cultural diplomacy, then, is that the brand does not allow for much space for self-criticism. Brands are defined largely by the sense of belonging to a community peopled by those who consume them, whereas cultural diplomacy implies more of a process of negotiation and learning, whereby openess about the negative aspects of a nation-state's general welfare or foreign policy outlook can ultimately generate more goodwill. Cultural diplomacy has not entirely become a digital exercise, but much of its communicative and outreach activity is now being played out in the digital arena.

Purposes and Application

How can we sum up these six signposts for understanding cultural diplomacy through history? Overall, eight factors regarding the purposes of cultural diplomacy can be identified:

1. Establish a dialogue and build trust with other nations;
2. Seek cultural (and political) recognition;
3. Pursue economic benefits;
4. Improve the image and reputation of the national culture;
5. Undermine prejudices and antagonisms;
6. Contest competing (negative) interpretations of the national culture;
7. Lay the groundwork for future partnership in other activities;
8. Promote a worldview based on a particular narrative, belief system, or ideology.

So how does this all add up in terms of activity? It is worth concluding with the important relations that lie behind every cultural diplomacy campaign. Unlike traditional diplomacy which, strictly speaking, can be carried out only by the professionals of the respective diplomatic services, cultural diplomacy necessarily requires the involvement of the private sector as a partner to produce and provide the products, services, contacts, and expertise required for international cultural outreach. State-private cooperation, whether contract-based or structural, theme- or regionally-focused, is therefore fundamental. In practice, this means that a typical state's cultural diplomacy may involve a host of collaborators, from organizations (museums and NGOs) to individuals (entrepreneurs), pursuing a range of diverse objectives with different partners abroad. Critics regard the involvement of the state as, at best, the subordination of cultural interests to the dominant political, economic, and security interests of foreign policy, and, at worst, the collapse of cultural expression into propaganda. Whereas this may well fit the cultural diplomacy of states determined to micro-manage the entire apparatus and output of cultural diplomacy for ideological or religious reasons, it does not fit the reality of most existing programs. Certainly, states often aim to utilize and mobilize cultural producers, and the framework for the cooperation is set out according to a perceived 'national interest.' However, this does not mean that the interests of the private sector are sidelined or undermined, and the public-private cooperation at the center of cultural diplomacy must involve a certain negotiation between the parties to ensure that different interests and goals are taken into account.

There is no standard model of cultural diplomacy that can be applied in all situations. Since it aims at communication across cultures, cultural difference has to be taken into account in each context as a basic requirement. The same message with the same delivery will not fit all audiences. Any suggestion that there might be 'a "science" of cultural diplomacy'—even with the additional quotation marks—is therefore wide of the mark (Gienow-Hecht, et al., 2010, 21). The application of techniques and approaches must not be driven according to simplistic goals, but to the needs of the partners and the context in which they will be received and assessed. All cultural diplomacy also depends heavily on credibility. A message can be delivered, but if the form of the message or the way it is delivered cause doubt in the receiver's mind, the message will not achieve its goal. This applies to all forms of cultural diplomacy covered above. By focusing on the structure (Who is involved? Who is in charge?) and concept (What are the motivations? What are the chosen tools? Which are the most effective and why?) of respective cultural diplomacy programs, it is certainly possible to build up an understanding of 'best practices' as to what works and what doesn't. Yet this can still provide no more than a guide for what to apply in other situations.

CHAPTER REVIEW QUESTIONS

1. Why is culture such a difficult term to define? How is it specified here?
2. What six signposts does Scott-Smith outline in the development of cultural diplomacy?
3. Give three examples of events used as opportunities for cultural diplomacy?
4. What is nation branding and why has it become central to diplomatic communications?
5. Define propaganda and explain how it is different from cultural diplomacy.

SEMINAR/ESSAY QUESTIONS

1. Why does the practice of cultural diplomacy differ among nations?
2. Identify two examples of cultural diplomacy being used to support another type of diplomacy and what those countries hope to achieve with this approach.
3. Scott-Smith argues that the European or Westphalian system is not static. Can you think of ways that cultural diplomacy has changed recently?
4. Cultural diplomacy is always propaganda and misrepresents and misuses the art/music/literature it claims to promote. Discuss.
5. Does cultural diplomacy create and help maintain stereotypes that are unhelpful in the long term?

References and Further Reading

Arndt, Richard. *The First Resort of Kings.* Dulles: Potomac Books, 2005.

Auerbach, Jeffrey. *The Great Exhibition of 1851: A Nation on Display.* New Haven: Yale University Press, 1999.

Bradford, Saxton. "Deutsche Auslandspropaganda," *Department of State Bulletin*, February 24, 1946.

Casson, Lionel Casson. *Libraries in the Ancient World.* New Haven: Yale University Press, 2001.

Cull, Nicholas J. *The Cold War and the United States Information Agency.* Cambridge: Cambridge University Press, 2008.

Dale, Helen. "All Out: China turns on the Charm," *World Affairs.* 174/1, July-August, 2010. available online at <http://www.worldaffairsjournal.org/article/all-out-china-turns-charm> (accessed July 17, 2015)

Fayet, Jean-Francois. "VOKS: The Third Dimension of Soviet Foreign Policy," in *Searching for a Cultural Diplomacy,* Jessica Gienow-Hecht and Mark Donfried (eds). New York: Berghahn Books, 2010.

Fukuyama, Francis. "The End of History," *National Interest.* 4 (1989): 1–18.

Gide, Andre. *Retour de l'U.R.S.S.* Paris: Gallimard, 1936.

Gienow-Hecht, Jessica and Mark Donfried (eds). *Searching for a Cultural Diplomacy.* New York: Berghahn Books, 2010.

Gosnell, J. "The Alliance Francaise, Empire and America." *French Cultural Studies.* 19/2 (2008): 227–243.

Halper, Stefan. *The Beijing Consensus.* New York: Basic Books, 2010.

Hart, Justin. *Empire of Ideas: The Origins of Public Diplomacy and the Transformation of US Foreign Policy.* Oxford: Oxford University Press, 2013.

Henrikson, Alan. "Niche Public Diplomacy in the World Public Arena: The Global 'Corners' of Canada and Norway," in *The New Public Diplomacy: Soft Power in International Relations,* Jan Melissen (ed). Basingstoke: Palgrave MacMillan, 2004.

Hodge, Carl Cavanagh. "A Whiff of Cordite: Theodore Roosevelt and the Transoceanic Naval Arms Race, 1897–1909." *Diplomacy and Statecraft.* 19/4 (2008): 712–731.

Kennedy, Liam and Scott Lucas. "Enduring Freedom: Public Diplomacy and US Foreign Policy." *American Quarterly*. 57/2 (June, 2005) 309-331; and the response by Giles Scott-Smith, "Enduring Freedom—A Critique." https://www.americanquarterly.org/interact/archives.html

Lucas, Scott. *Freedom's War*. Manchester: Manchester University Press, 1999.

Mauss, Marcel. *The Gift: Forms and Functions of Exchange in Achaic Cultures*. London: Routledge, 1990 [1954].

McKeekin, Sean McMeekin. *The Red Millionaire: A Political Biography of Willi Münzenberg*. New Haven: Yale University Press, 2003.

McMurry, Ruth and Mona Lee. *The Cultural Approach*. Chapel Hill: University of North Carolina Press, 1947.

Mitchell, J.M. *International Cultural Relations*. London: Allen & Unwin, 1986.

Morris, Edmund. *Theodore Rex*, New York: Random House, 2001.

Ninkovich, Frank. US Information Policy and Cultural Diplomacy. *Foreign Policy Association Headline Series*, No. 308, 1996.

Nye, Joseph Nye. 1990 and 2004. "Soft Power," *Foreign Policy* (Fall 1990), later expanded into *Soft Power: The Means to Success in World Politics*. New York: PublicAffairs, 2004.

Rhoads, Kelton Rhoads. "The Cultural Variable in the Influence Equation," in *Routledge Handbook of Public Diplomacy*, Nancy Snow and Phuilip Taylor (eds). New York: Routledge, 2009.

Routh, H. V. *The Diffusion of English Culture Outside England: A Problem of Post-War Reconstruction*. Cambridge: Cambridge University Press, 1941.

Spence, Jonathan Spence. *The Memory Palace of Matteo Ricci*. Harmondsworth: Penguin, 1985.

von Drehle, David. "A Lesson in Hate: How an Egyptian student came to study in 1950s America and left determined to wage holy war." *Smithsonian Magazine*, February, 2006. Online at http://www.smithsonianmag.com/history/a-lesson-in-hate-109822568/?no-ist=&page=1 18 December 2015

Wilford, Hugh. *The Mighty Wurlitzer*. Cambridge MA: Harvard University Press, 2008.

Williams, Raymond. *Culture and Society 1780–1950*. Harmondsworth: Penguin, 1966 [1958].

Williams, Raymond. *Culture*. Glasgow: William Collins, 1981.

Xu, Guangqiu. "The Ideological and Political Impact of U.S. Fulbrighters on Chinese Students 1979–1989," *Asian Affairs* 26/3 (1999): 139–157.

Websites

Nation Brands Index website, available at <http://www.simonanholt.com/Research/research-introduction.aspx> (accessed July 17, 2015)

Good Country Index, available at <http://www.goodcountry.org/> (accessed August 21, 2014).

Digital Diplomacy Bibliography compiled by the Clingendael Institute and the USC Annenberg Center and issued in July 2014, available at

<http://www.clingendael.nl/sites/default/files/Digital_Diplomacy_Bibliography_2014_CLI-CPD.pdf > (accessed August 21, 2014).

CROSS SECTION 6.1

China: Zhou Dynasty—Culture and Confucius Meet Military Might

BY ALISON HOLMES

If Byzantium was a great connector of peoples and cultures by virtue of plan and position, the Chinese states-system was nearly the opposite, with long periods of warfare and consolidation while remaining relatively isolated from the diffusion going on in other parts of the world. The most 'shared' aspect with the ideas of the Byzantines is perhaps the very clear Chinese sense that everyone outside their reach—i.e., their non-Chinese neighbors—were barbarians (Bozeman, 1960; Watson 2009), although both economics and culture were points of access with China, as seen in the discussions of economic and cultural diplomacy.

The Yellow River, one of Mann's pristine civilizations, was developing throughout the Xia (Hsia) dynasty (2205–1755 BCE), and by 1500 BCE, the middle of the Shang Dynasty (1600–1050 BCE), China bore all the hallmarks of civilization listed above, including a system of writing, urban areas, a ceremonial center, a monarchy with divine connections and human sacrifice, walled cities and forts, bronze technology, and horse-drawn chariots (Mann, 1986). It is interesting to note that there is a pervasive sense that China had been ruled by a single power in the deep past. While not true, Bozeman suggests this may be the basis for the consistent desire to find the natural harmony between heaven and earth, which was fundamental to Chinese culture, even before Confucius, who did not develop his

FIGURE 6.1.1 Confucius (Source: sewebel/iStock)

philosophy until the third or Zhou (Chou) dynasty (Bozeman, 1960, 135). Like the Roman Empire, the Zhou dynasty was also made up of an east and west—Western Zhou (1046–771 BCE) and Eastern Zhou (771–256 BCE)—and both had a highly developed and steeply hierarchical political and social system based on the ancestral beliefs of Confucianism. The royal house was at the apex of this system as part of a cult of heaven (*tian*) which conferred a mandate to rule (*tian ming*) on the emperor (Watson, 2009).

All men, including the emperor, and all communities, from the smallest village to what they saw as a kind of a world state, were subject to the 'will of heaven'—a structure that effectively protected this preordained order. This hierarchy was core to a natural order or harmony and could be demonstrated through respect for the five fundamental human relationships: man and woman (husband and wife); father and son; older and younger brother; friend and friend; sovereign and minister (or subject). The goal of such a system was to create an environment in which there was a sense of timelessness in these patterns with the view that peace would flow from respecting their order and importance (Bozeman, 1960).

However, by the second half of this dynasty, or the Eastern Zhou period starting in 770 BCE, there were as many as two hundred separate 'states' held in suzerain authority. As mentioned above, this meant there was no overt attempt to run the internal affairs of these smaller units from the center, but the subject or vassal peoples were part of a tribute system that involved trade and protection from the constant danger posed from other, outside powers. This slowly began to break down until it became what is called the 'Warring period,' and ended completely when Zhou's once-strong center was sacked and overrun in 256 BCE by outlying tribes.

In this period, it is interesting to note various initiatives or attempts at order and organization that could easily be identified as the diplomatic practices of today. For example, in 589 BCE, a covenant was agreed among the larger units to establish a kind of 'balance of power.' This agreement meant they would not attack smaller places or take water from them—a particularly salient point given that environmental/water politics are considered very recent in world politics. Similarly, in 546 BCE, the central, smaller, more organized (and usually more traditional) entities gathered in a kind of summit and sought to build a mutual protection group (Bozeman, 1960).

Practices were discussed in Part I, but here the important issue remains that these alliances and agreements could not be sustained and the center fell to the attacks of the more peripheral 'barbarians'—essentially anyone further outside the circle of protection or tribute. In an attempt to call attention to these other styles, it may also be useful to go one step further to note that the barbarians (from the Chinese point of view) were winning because they had also recognized the need to become more organized. They had gained a technological advantage through the professionalization and training of their military forces. They had received horses and cavalry training from nomadic tribes and began to use a form of crossbow such that, by 500 BCE, they had become a formidable force and were able to take down the core of this system (Watson, 2009).

In terms of diplomacy, it is perhaps not surprising, in a system that believed the emperor to be the 'son of heaven,' that envoys from other places were not generally held in high regard, but seen instead (and in parallel to the treatment given to envoys who went to India) as lowly messengers—though ones who may also consider themselves as 'son[s] of heaven' (Frey and Frey, 1999, 23). That said, the messengers had a specific role, particularly between warring states on an ad hoc basis, as laid out in classical Confucian texts such as the *Yili* from the Zhou dynasty. The *Yili* set out three types of mission and detailed elaborate ceremonies for the reception of envoys and rules governing their privileges. Confucius even suggested that the ability to be successful in a foreign mission should be regarded above filial piety, a particularly important point given the value and respect associated with different levels of relationship outlined above (Frey and Frey 1999, 21).

The gradual dissolution of what was, in effect, a useful fiction of equality between lords and minor powers—had important consequences for diplomacy in this system. The chaotic end of the Zhou period, the ongoing competition for power between rival semi-autonomous units in what became known as the 'Spring and Autumn period' (770–475 BCE), the period of the Warring States (475–221 BCE), and finally, the shift to the repressive and centralized administration of the Qin (Ch'in) Dynasty (221–206 BCE) meant there was effectively less need for communication and negotiation. As a result, the status of diplomats was similarly diminished and, while they remained largely protected, this was more at the choice, or even whim, of any specific ruler at any moment in time (Frey and Frey 1999, 22).

Despite China's relative isolation, it is important to note the parallels between 'European' or Byzantine diplomacy and China in terms of the development of rules of etiquette, symbols, and the immunities and privileges granted to those who were essentially the representatives of one group to another. These agents of various kinds were often sent by the ruler, or at least with the ruler's consent, but others were conducting their own business yet 'used' by the ruler for their own ends. Thus, what became the 'agreed' mode as well as the process of deciding who was an 'official' representative vs. those working a 'private' capacity became more significant, regardless of origin or system. These developments are also interesting in that while there are claims as to the connection between religious philosophies and political statecraft (and therefore reflective of their morality and honorable intention) in different places, the reality of behavior is often more shared than the virtuous intentions from which it springs. For example, many of 'normal/accepted' tactics used by the Byzantines (such as treachery and deceit) were condemned by Chinese philosophers who held persuasion, courtesy, and good faith in high esteem—even if they were not always implemented in real life (Bozeman, 1960).

In terms of types of diplomacy, we can conclude that China used political, economic, and military diplomacy in its maintenance of the tribute system. While difficult for the center to militarily control to the furthest reaches of what Chinese rulers considered to be their circle of power (an important consideration in heterarchy and a visualization that will be discussed particularly in relation to the Indian system, but also a key contrast with the hierarchical western/European system), they did not hesitate long in terms of taking up arms rather than negotiating or talking their way out of difficulty. Yet the fact the Chinese were able to absorb other cultures while still insisting on its own superiority suggests they were not trying to encourage cultural exchange as much as they were willing to incorporate other groups—as long as those groups understood and accepted and performed their role in the system. The Chinese were also willing to assimilate even people they considered to be barbarians (much like the Romans) if they learned the language and accepted the appropriate rules of behavior. The goal was to preserve the sanctity of the center as a long as possible. The creative, if unsuccessful, use of diplomatic practices even as war began to undermine this social structure also seems to support the idea that political diplomacy was a first line of strategic approach while the decline in diplomacy as such cultural structures finally collapsed reminds us that diplomacy is indeed a reflection of the entity it seeks to represent. In a situation of fragmentation and breakdown it is not surprising that the representatives of the old system also lost their power as the connecters of systems. This issue will now be discussed more directly by turning to military and intelligence concerns as a type of diplomacy.

References and Further Reading

Bozeman, Adda. *Politics and Culture in International History.* Princeton: Princeton University Press, 1960.

Frey, Linda and Marsha Frey. *The History of Diplomatic Immunity.* Columbus: Ohio University Press, 1999.

Mann, Michael. *Volume 1. The Sources of Social Power: A History of Power from the Beginning to A.D. 1760.* Cambridge: Cambridge University Press, 1986.

Watson, Adam. *The Evolution of International Society.* London and New York: Routledge, 1992/2009.

7 Defense and Intelligence Diplomacy

BY ANDREW M. DORMAN &
MATTHEW R. H. UTTLEY

Introduction

Adolf Hitler famously remarked that "when diplomacy ends, war begins." It is certainly the case that a longstanding and normative ontological distinction has been drawn between diplomacy as a tool of statecraft, and the moral and practical aspects of military power as a "crude instrument" with an attendant capacity to kill, maim, coerce, and destroy in the pursuit of national interests (Garnett, 1987, 3). Perhaps the clearest manifestation of this distinction can be found in the "last resort" tenet of "Just War Theory," which decrees that military force may be employed only after all peaceful and viable alternatives to resolve disputes between states have been tried and exhausted (Childress, 1978).

Correspondingly, Adam Watson contends that to place diplomacy and the possession by states of military power in "polar opposition" is, at best, simplistic, because:

> War and diplomacy are inseparably joined under the common heading of means by which States, in pursuit of their interests, bring their power to bear on one another as actual or prospective allies and enemies, and indeed as partners of rivals in trade and commerce. Just as war, the concentrated and disciplined use of armed force to achieve political ends, has been and still is one instrument by which states seek to persuade one

> another, so that in such cases compulsion is the means of persuasion, so diplomacy also is a general means of persuasion, which takes account of and reflects the pressures of all the relevant influences including the existence of armed forces and the willingness and capacity of governments to use them (Watson, 1982, 59).

Watson's contentions reflect the fundamental assumption shared through time by **Sun Tzu**, **Thucydides**, **Machiavelli**, **Clausewitz**, **Jomini**, and all subsequent generations of strategic theorists that the possession and application of military force is inherently subordinate to the interests of policy (Ayson, 2008). Under this construct, what unites non-military forms of diplomacy, the possession and potential application of military force, and national intelligence capabilities are that they all constitute *means* available to states in the pursuit of their political *ends*. 'Strategy-making' has emerged as an overarching term for the processes by which states seek to convert these 'levers' of national power into the achievement of policy goals in their interactions with actual or potential adversaries or allies.

These central assumptions about national levers of power and strategy-making underpin Strategic Studies: a distinct sub-field of international relations that focuses on the study of strategy and the role of armed force in international politics. This chapter draws on concepts and issues in Strategic Studies to focus on three aspects of the nexus between defense, intelligence, and diplomacy. David Lonsdale notes that "... despite the seeming novelty of warfare in the modern period, the very *essence of warfare has remained the same*. Across time and place, although the *character* of war has altered, its *nature* has remained constant" (Lonsdale, 2008, 16). The first section provides an introduction to issues and debates surrounding the enduring nature and changing character of the relationship between defense, intelligence, and diplomacy. In order to understand the variation and complexity of defense and intelligence diplomacy, the second section examines the interaction of each in turn in three broad contexts—peacetime, periods of crisis, and during war or conflict. National defense, intelligence, and diplomatic functions within states are typically located within separate agencies and institutions, which raises conceptual and practical challenges for inter-organization coordination. The third section considers these challenges in the context of the perennial quest by states to develop either explicit or implicit 'grand' or 'national security' strategies that harmonize these instruments of state power in pursuit of national policy goals.

The Nature and Character of Defense and Intelligence Diplomacy: Simplicity and Complexity

Theorizing about defense and intelligence as tools of diplomacy is far from new and readers with an interest in strategic history are recommended to consult Colin Gray's 2007 edition of *War, Peace and International Relations*. Rather than engaging in detailed periodization, this section introduces perspectives on the enduring nature and changing character of defense and intelligence as diplomatic tools. In doing so, it seeks to distinguish between the relative simplicity of enduring assumptions regarding the nature of defense and intelligence as diplomatic tools, and the immense complexity and contestation surrounding their contextual application in strategy-making.

Assumptions about the enduring 'nature' of defense and intelligence diplomacy are grounded primarily in the realist tradition and its four foundational assumptions concerning the nature of international relations (Wohlforth, 2010, 131-149). The first assumption is that politics takes place within and between groups and the most important groups in the international system are nation-states. The second is that when states act politically they are ultimately driven by self-interested considerations and will seek to establish clear goals, actions predicated on rational cost-benefit calculations. The third is that states interact in an anarchic system of self-help which imposes constraints on the ability of states to achieve their objectives. The final assumption is that the intersection of self-interested states in an environment of anarchy means that international relations is largely a politics of power and security. As Wohlforth suggests, the consequences are that:

> When no authority exists that can enforce agreement—"anarchy"—then any State can resort to force to get what it wants. Even if a State can be fairly sure that no other State will take up arms today, there is no guarantee against the possibility that one might do so tomorrow. Because no State can rule out this prospect, States tend to arm themselves against this contingency. With all States thus armed, politics takes on a different cast... The signature realist argument is therefore that anarchy renders States' security problematic and potentially conflictual, and is an underlying cause of war (Wohlforth, 2010, 135).

By inference, states are inherently preoccupied by questions of power and security reflected in cost-benefit calculations about options concerning the generation of military power and the potential application of military force, either independently or in conjunction with allies. These questions form central elements of 'grand strategy' making, or "the process that converts forms of state power into policy effect" (Kane and Lonsdale, 2012, 13). Key calculations concern the actual or potential defensive or offensive employment of military force either to defend or extend what are assessed by a state to be its vital national interests. However, as Garnett points out:

> Military power may depend to a large extent on the availability of military force, but conceptually it is quite different; it emphasises a political relationship between potential adversaries rather than a catalog of military capabilities. In a nutshell, the difference between the exercise of military force and military power is the difference between taking what you want and persuading someone to give it to you. In a sense, therefore, the use of military force represents the breakdown of military power (Garnett, 1987, 84).

Consequently, states confront the scenario of initiating or responding to two discrete forms of "coercive diplomacy" or "organized coercion" that fall short of the actual employment of military force. One form is "compellence": the threat to use force to induce an adversary to behave differently than it otherwise would (Byman and Waxman, 2008, 158). Conceptually, successful compellence occurs where party B ceases what party A wants it to cease doing because it believes that party A would harm B if it does not comply. The second form is "deterrence," characterized by a situation where Party A attempts to "prevent party B from undertaking a course of action which A regards as undesirable, by threatening to inflict unacceptable costs upon B in the event that the action is taken" (Baylis et al., 1987, 69). Core prerequisites for both forms of coercive diplomacy are the credibility, capability, and communication of threats and potential punishments. Intelligence gathering and analysis is a key source of "enabling information" for strategists to evaluate the validity of each of these prerequisites. The possession of military power also provides opportunities for states to pursue non-violent and non-coercive strategies of 'defense diplomacy' in support of national interests. Defense diplomacy forms a component of what Joseph Nye refers to as "soft power" and relies on a strategy of co-opting the leaders of another state by convincing them to change an aspect of their behavior because it is in their interest (Nye, 2004).

The tenets forming the nature of defense and intelligence diplomacy suggest a degree of analytical simplicity in terms of both the international context in which states find themselves and the strategic options open to them in developing, deploying, and responding to military power. Correspondingly, the constantly changing 'character' of defense and intelligence diplomacy, and the role of strategy-making within in it, impose substantial challenges for policy-makers and practitioners that arise from a complex interplay of variables. The essence of this complexity is encapsulated by David Lonsdale's synthesises of key factors that explain why strategy-making is perennially difficult. One factor is the potential for difficulties in aligning the policy aspirations of a state's political leadership with what the military instrument of state power can deliver. A second factor stems from complex "multidimensional" considerations that confront practical strategy-making. A myriad of societal, cultural, economic, and industrial elements can impinge on how and where military power is employed, and whether it ultimately achieves national political goals. A third factor is encapsulated in the maxim that "the enemy has a vote." Strategies are employed against intelligent, reflexive, and adaptive adversaries who will seek to offset and undermine any such strategy. For example, to counter the conventional advantages of the US-led missions in Iraq and Afghanistan, the opposition resorted to a variety of so-called asymmetric tactics including improvised explosive devices (IEDs). A fourth factor is "friction," or unforeseen events that undermine the efficiency of armed forces in meeting their objectives. For example, the entry of the Chinese into the Korean War changed the dynamics of the whole conflict and ultimately ensured that a form of stalemate would ensue. A related factor reflects inherent practical challenges in harmonizing the grand strategy elements of national power (economic, industrial, political, and military components) with subordinated levels of decision-making and action at the "military strategic," "operational," and "tactical" levels. A final factor is the "polymorphous character" of warfare, which means that each context in which military force is either threatened or applied will have unique characteristics, which militates against a situation where a strategist can plan with certainty about the outcomes. The consequence of these factors is encapsulated in Michael Handel's observation that "that war is an art, not a science—that each military problem has many potentially correct solutions (not just a single, optimal solution) which are arrived at through the military leader's imagination, creativity and intuition" (Handel, 2005, 24-25). The art of grand strategy is further complicated by the different contexts in which a state and its armed forces may find themselves. In the next section, these have been roughly divided into peacetime, crisis, and war. This implies some form of clear distinction between them. This is not always true, and some have started to refer to a form of 'ambiguous warfare' where states and non-state actors engage in various forms of competition and conflict over time but never in an overt conflict. An example here might be NATO and Russia at the present time.

Defense and Intelligence Diplomacy in Peacetime

Role of Defense and Intelligence in developing understanding

Within the international system there is a basic requirement for states to be able to interact with one another and with other organizations and groups. To do this, states need to have some form of understanding of others and the likely implications of their actions. This is particularly true when it comes to issues of defense and security. Both the armed forces and the intelligence communities of a state provide mechanisms for developing this understanding and conveying or signalling concerns and intentions. The problem is that there are also capabilities and activities which they wish to hide from other states and groups. For example, the international community continues to remain concerned about the alleged Iranian nuclear program and North Korea's known nuclear program. At a more mundane level, individual nations are interested in the size, composition, and capabilities of each other's militaries. For example, one of the reasons states let their military aircraft fly near to, or even over each other's territories is to establish the capabilities of the air defense networks in terms of their ability to detect and then organize a response.

In peacetime, there are activities that both comply with international law and convention and activities that are deemed to be illegal. For example, in defining a state's boundaries there are a series of different demarcation lines when it comes to the waters around a state. Thus, a nation will have economic rights over the waters that stretched up to two hundred miles from its shores (unless the water between two nations is less than four hundred miles, in which case the mid-point is taken). However, this economic right does not apply to the idea of freedom of the seas and the right of passage. In this case, the accepted convention is that one state's warships, including submarines, should not approach to within less than twelve nautical miles of another nation without permission (UNCLOS—United Nations Convention on the Law Of the Sea). Similar conventions apply to airspace and its management (see International Civil Aviation Organization). Yet, in reality, nations do transgress each other's waters and airspace and this can cause friction. For example, in 2001 a Chinese fighter aircraft collided with a US Navy surveillance aircraft forcing the latter to divert to a Chinese airbase (*USA Today*, 2001). This incident was not unique. In 2014, the US complained to the Chinese government about "dangerous flying" by a Chinese aircraft near to a US Navy aircraft more than a hundred miles east of China's Hainan Island (Sky News, 2014). In both cases, the US aircraft was engaged in gathering intelligence about the Chinese, which is a perfectly legal activity when it is conducted in international airspace.

At the other end of the peacetime spectrum, there are far less legal forms of intelligence gathering, which include the infringement of another nation's air and sea space. For example, in probably the most famous incident, a US U-2 spy plane was shot down over the Soviet Union in 1960 and the American pilot taken prisoner. The mission of the aircraft was to gather photographic information on Soviet military facilities for the US and her allies. More recently, the Swedish Navy hunted for a Russian submarine that was believed to be in its waters near Stockholm (Crouch, 2014).

In a similar way, the type of actor involved will help determine the difference between legal and illegal activities in peacetime. Thus, diplomats, including defense attachés, have immunity from arrest and have the ability to observe the activities occurring within a state whilst those without diplomatic immunity can be arrested for the same activities.

Signalling

Linked to a nations diplomacy is how its armed forces are constructed and deployed. The problem for any state or collection of states lies in the interpretation over how a particular weapon system may or may not be used. The reality is that few weapons systems can be seen to be purely defensive in nature. For example, the members of NATO have been debating for some years about whether to deploy an anti-ballistic missile system (ABM) on the territories of a number of the eastern members (see NATO, 2015a). The stated goal is to provide a limited defense capability geared towards the Middle East and, in particular, Iran. From a NATO point of view, this is a purely defensive matter aimed at providing reassurance to their populations. However, the Russian view is somewhat different (European Parliament, 2012). For Russia, such a system is part of NATO's attempt to develop a nuclear first-strike capability aimed at Russia. The argument made here is that the majority of Russia's nuclear capabilities are based on land in the form of its intercontinental ballistic missile (ICBM) force. A significant number of these could be destroyed in the event of a NATO first strike against Russia, and any surviving missiles, if launched in a counter-strike, would then be intercepted by NATO's ABM system. Thus, a NATO decision to deploy an ABM system would undermine the current condition of mutual vulnerability and encourage NATO into a nuclear war. In other words, the development, acquisition, and potential deployment of any weapons system and/or military force can serve to send diplomatic signals in peacetime.

Similarly, the location of armed forces, who they train with, the nature of that training, and the degree to which any of this is permanent also sends an important signal. For example, as a result of Russian action towards the Ukraine and the absorption of the Crimea into Russia in 2014, NATO sent additional aircraft to support its air policing mission over the Baltic States (Ministry of Defence, 2014). This sent a signal to Russia that the airspace of the Baltic States remained sovereign. Moreover, since the initial reinforcements were from the major military powers within NATO—from France, the United States, and United Kingdom—the message was reinforced. Subsequently, in the wake of the shooting down of the Malaysian airliner over Ukraine by Ukrainian separatists, and further steps by Russia to support the rebels (BBC, 2015), the NATO members agreed at their meeting in Wales in September 2014 to undertake a series of training exercises on the territories of its Eastern members to provide them with reassurance about Russia. The aim was to reinforce the message to Russia that NATO's Article V mutual defense pledge remains applicable to all members (see NATO, 2015b). In essence, NATO has drawn a line in the sand about any further Russian expansionism westwards. How NATO will react to any further moves in the Caucasus remains open to debate.

More generally, nations use military deployments and exercises to send important signals to allies, potential opponents, and neutrals alike. Such deployments can be both overt and covert. Thus, the United Kingdom in recent years has permanently maintained a force of mine-countermeasures vessels to the Persian Gulf. "Operation Kipion," as it is named, aims to signal the UK's intent to keep the waterway from the Persian Gulf to the Indian Ocean open in the face of any state's desire to close the waterway through the use of mines (Royal Navy, 2015). Similarly, if the United States wishes to send a diplomatic signal linked to hard power, there is the announcement of the deployment of one of its aircraft carriers (Cohen, 1981). The advantage of such maritime commitments is that they can take place in international waters, and ships and submarines are far easier to withdraw. The deployment, whether temporary or permanent, of ground forces and, to a degree, air forces, sends a far stronger signal because of their permanence and the fact it means that one state has accepted another state's armed forces into its territory. Thus, the announcement that a small force of US Marines would deploy to Australia sent a significant political signal from both the United States and Australian governments to China (Stewart, 2014). In the case of Australia, this was particularly important because whilst the United States remains Australia's principal military ally, China represents Australia's principal trading partner. In this case, the small size of the deployment sent the signal that whilst Australia was looking to limit China's expansionism by increasing its military links with the United

States, it was also not looking to directly threaten China's interests and that this shouldn't interfere with trade.

The problem with such signalling can frequently be about what is not said. For example, when the US National Security Council produced a document called **NSC-68** in 1950, it was drawn up in the context of perceived Soviet moves towards Western Europe and the fall of China to the communists (NSC-68). The outlined policy of containment included the idea of preventing further communist expansion, particularly in the Asia-Pacific region, by drawing a line in the sand. The subsequent Korean War (the invasion of the South by the North occurred between the secret production of NSC-68 and its approval by the Truman Administration) proved problematic because Korea lay to the west of the line in the sand and the United States and its allies then had to decide what to do. In other words, to include some states and/or issues is to exclude others.

Partnering and Alliances

There are a number of reasons for states to engage in partnerships and alliances, whether formal or informal, in peacetime. For smaller and/or weaker states there can be the perception that there is greater safety either by coming together or by obtaining the protection of a large, more powerful state. A good example here is NATO, which now comprises some twenty-eight nations based on the principle of collective defense (see NATO, 2014). For many of its members the reality is that NATO membership brings with it the protection of the United States. Interestingly, the European Union also has a defense and security element, despite the fact that a number of its members have historically been neutrals, and it is not clear how this might work.

A second reason for entering such partnerships is to help improve capabilities, ensure that armed forces can work together, or simply to share the cost of providing capabilities. For example, the ABCA program (American, British, Canadian, and New Zealand Armies' Program) is supposed to optimize the inter-operability (ABCA, 2015). In a similar way, the UKNL Amphibious Force brings together United Kingdom and Netherlands marines into an amphibious force capable of supporting both NATO and EU missions (Brinkman, 2006). Taking this a step further, the Netherlands and Belgium governments agreed to the pooling of their naval capabilities as a means of saving money (Benelux Declaration, 2012) whilst the US Navy and British Royal Navy share a common pool of Trident ballistic missiles.

Third, states often provide training, support, and bases for others as a means of influence. This can occur in a variety of forms ranging from the training and education of individuals at host military academies and colleges to the granting of access to facilities such as training ranges or the deployment of military assets to a particular region. For example, most military staff colleges have some foreign students included within the student cohort. Taking this a step further can include the permanent exchange of military staff. In support of the United Kingdom's 'International Defence Engagement Strategy,' the British Army have tasked each of its Adaptable Force Brigades with engaging with a specific part of the world with the express aim "to promote the interests of the UK and contributing to a more stable world" (British Army, 2013, 21). The training option can also be the source of significant revenue and encourage states to offer facilities to others.

Economic

The final aspect of defense and intelligence diplomacy in peacetime directly links to the economic dimension. According to the Stockholm International Peace Research Institute (SIPRI), global military expenditure for 2012 amounted to $1.75 trillion (SIPRI, 2013). Many states lack the ability to provide for all or even part of their defense requirements. Thus, defense sales provide a potential source of revenue and a means of maintaining employment, particularly in terms of high-end skills. Thus, the world's major arms exporters—the United States, Russia, France, Germany, China, and the United Kingdom—compete for market share and diplomacy plays a major factor. This process becomes more complicated at the higher end of the complexity spectrum where major defense programs can involve several nations.

For example, the Eurofighter Typhoon project involves the United Kingdom, Germany, Spain, and Italy. It has been successfully exported to Austria, Oman, and Saudi Arabia and the consortium continues to compete for further sales. Throughout the program there have been disputes and delays as the different nations have sought to maintain or increase their relative work share. This has become more heated as individual nation's defense spending has continued to fall in relative terms.

Defense and Intelligence Diplomacy in Crises

In times of crisis, at least in theory, the diplomatic and defense elements of the machinery of government should be brought into far greater alignment. Yet, there is no set or agreed on mechanism for undertaking this process. Partly, this is because where the executive power lies and who is head of the armed forces varies between states. For example, in the United

States, the president is commander-in-chief whilst in the United Kingdom this position rests with the queen acting under the guidance of the prime minister. Similarly, there is no standard process for coordinating all the levers of state power. In the case of both the United States and the United Kingdom, this is now undertaken by a National Security Council. In the case of the former, its members include the heads of various government departments (State, Defense, etc.) who have been appointed by the president with the approval of Congress. In the case of the United Kingdom, the National Security Council is a relatively new thing, having been created in 2010, and is a subcommittee of Cabinet comprising ministers (i.e., members of Parliament) responsible for specific Departments of State and their officials. Even within armed forces, there are differences in how crises are managed. Some have a form of centralized or joint organization, while others rely on a more coordinated response between the three services. There is also variation in the level to which a nation's parliament is involved. For example, the German Bundestag has to approve the Rules of Engagement for every deployment of the German armed forces and this is reviewed annually. In contrast, in the United Kingdom this decision still legally remains part of the royal prerogative and therefore in the hands of the executive branch.

Bargaining

Whilst it might be assumed that only the strong would be prepared to risk crises as a mechanism for resolving issues and getting their own way, the reality is somewhat different. Crises can be used by relatively weaker states as mechanisms to gain attention and encourage stronger states and groups of states to negotiate over particular issues. For example, the North Korean regime has frequently sought to draw the United States into direct negotiation by developing some form of crisis related to its nuclear program or, alternatively, by heightening tension with South Korea. The goal of such action seems to be to obtain some form of concession from the United States in return for the promise of conformity in the future.

In a similar way, it emerged in 1997 that the Greek Cypriot government intended to acquire long-range surface-to-air missiles from Russia. Their range would have given the Cypriot government the ability to threaten Turkish airspace, and the Turkish government, perhaps unsurprisingly, responded with threats to destroy the proposed bases by air strikes and possibly re-invade Cyprus. In the end, after some posturing and negotiation, the missiles were sold to Greece in return for other military hardware. Thus, there are a number of ways in which even a weaker state or group of states can force others to respond, and at the very least, return to some form of negotiation to bring the crisis to an end.

Compellence

Conversely, a state or group of states may choose to resort to the threat of military action in order to force another state or organization to take a particular course of action. The US-led coalitions have attempted to do this with Iraq in both 1990–1 and 2002–3. In the former case, the aim was to get Iraq to leave Kuwait (Freedman and Karsh, 1993). Unfortunately, the Iraq government chose not to listen to the demands of the international community and ultimately Kuwait was freed by the use of force. In 2002–03, a US-led coalition attempted to get Iraq to comply with various UN Security Council resolutions, particularly those pertaining to weapons of mass destruction. Again, the decision of the Iraqi regime not to comply led to the use of force.

The challenge in trying to compel a state or organization to undertake a particular course of action is threefold. First, it needs to be in a position to successfully communicate the intention to undertake a particular course of action if the party concerned does not do as it is told. Second, it should convince the party concerned that the threat is meant. Finally, the party concerned needs to be in a position to calculate that it is better for them to comply than to fail to comply with the threat.

Evacuations and other operations

Instability in states can also lead to the use of armed forces by other states in their territory without any intent to engage or become embroiled in a war. State collapse, coups, and other forms of instability can lead to the need for other nations to evacuate their citizens or become embroiled in the situation.

For example, in December 2013, in South Sudan internal differences between different factions led to the United States and the United Kingdom sending military aircraft to evacuate foreign nationals (FCO & MOD, 2011). The same was true in 2011 in the initial stages of conflict in Libya. On this occasion, a far greater number of states took action to evacuate their citizens by air and sea without the permission of the Libyan government (BBC, 2011).

The requirement for such operations can occur at relatively short notice, and the reality is that there are relatively few nations with the ability to project military power rapidly over a distance. The vast majority are dependent at best on sending a chartered civilian or military transport aircraft or ship and not facing any opposition to their evacuation. The situation will be further complicated by the order in which individual citizens are evacuated. For example, the United Kingdom's first priority is to evacuate its citizens, dual citizens, citizens of European Union members who are not represented by embassy staff in-country, and citizens of those countries which the United Kingdom has agreed in advance to be responsible for (nations can divide up responsibility for different states). It will then evacuate remaining European Union and Commonwealth citizens where they, or their country, indicate they are prepared to cover the costs. Finally, the remaining foreign nationals will be evacuated if there is the capacity available.

A good example of such an operation was the May 2000 deployment of British military personnel to Sierra Leone (Dorman, 2009). The initial reason for what became known as *Operation Palliser* was the seizing of a number of United Nations peacekeepers and military observers by the Revolutionary United Front (RUF) and the fear that the RUF would move to overthrow the Sierra Leone government. In response, the UN Security Council publicly condemned the actions of the RUF and called on them to lay down their arms and free their hostages. In private, the UN Secretary-General and the French and US ambassadors to the United Nations indicated that the British government had a responsibility to Sierra Leone and the international community inside the country. In response, and with the full support of the Sierra Leone government, the British deployed a force of helicopters, Special Forces, and 1st Battalion of the Parachute Regiment to undertake a services-assisted evacuation of all entitled personnel. To get the helicopters to Sierra Leone, the Foreign and Commonwealth Office had arranged transit rights for the inbound helicopters and aircraft whilst they were in flight from the various countries along the route. Moreover, the French and Senegal governments gave permission for the British to use a French airfield in Senegal as a base to support the operation. Some five hundred entitled personnel were evacuated in the space of two days. The British forces in Sierra Leone then helped the Sierra Leone government and United Nations peacekeeping forces mobilize and organize themselves to counter the RUF. The mission required the British government to coordinate its diplomatic and military mechanisms with the United Nations based in New York, the government of Sierra Leone in-country, various other nations providing support, such as Senegal, and its own armed forces.

Foreign militaries can also be called in by a recipient state where there has been a catastrophic disaster. The 2004 Indian Ocean earthquake and resultant tsunami devastated the coastal areas of a number of states and the international community deployed a significant amount of aid including military forces to help in the recovery operation. Here the military has significant capabilities to support the civilian authorities including manpower, engineering and medical capabilities, and command-and-control systems, which have frequently been lost in such a situation. More recently, the United Kingdom and United States have deployed military medical personnel, engineers, and helicopters to West Africa to help in trying to combat the Ebola breakout. An important point worth noting here is the expectation that former colonial powers still retain a responsibility. In this case, the US has focused on Liberia given its historical association with that country, whilst the United Kingdom has focused on Sierra Leone.

Defense and Intelligence Diplomacy in Times of War and Conflict

The fact that a war or conflict has started does not mean that diplomacy is put to one side whilst the fighting occurs. Ultimately, the war or conflict will have to end in some form of resolution, be that a temporary cease-fire, such as that which has been in place between North Korea and South Korea since 1953, or something more substantial such as a resolution of the causes of the war or conflict. Moreover, in most conflicts, the adversaries invariably keep some back channel of communication open or use intermediary parties to pass on messages. For example, throughout much of the 'Troubles' in Northern Ireland the British government was in communication with the leadership of the Provisional IRA and ultimately a peace agreement was negotiated. There are a number of reasons for this, and they will be examined in turn.

Managing and/or limiting the conflict

In a war between two or more parties there are invariably a set of tacit rules which the parties choose to abide by. These can vary between conflicts but they will emerge in different forms. Some of these relate to the laws of wars. For example, there may be information exchanged relating to prisoners and or the dead so that relatives can be informed. In more traditional wars, this may involve organizations such as the International Committee of the Red Cross visiting prisoner of war camps and hospitals to confirm a party is abiding by the Geneva Convention and so forth. Similarly, information may be exchanged where safe passage is sought for a hospital ship.

Alliances and Coalitions and Third Parties

Many of the wars and conflicts that have occurred since the end of the Cold War have involved formal and informal coalitions of groups and states. For example, in 1999, it was NATO that took action in Kosovo to bring to an end the ethnic cleansing that was occurring. This war highlighted many of the challenges of conducting coalition warfare, with individual countries vetoing particular targets and placing limitations on how their own armed forces might be used (Dorman, 2008). Keeping a coalition together can frequently become the most challenging task and an area which the enemy will often seek to target.

Even once a war or conflict has commenced, the parties involved will continue to articulate the justification of their case for the war and the actions they are taking. This links to the whole concept of a 'Just War' involving both the reasons for war and the conduct of war itself. Moreover, participants will also seek to bring in other parties to provide forms of support or merely to prevent them from supporting the other side. Thus, in the 1982 Falklands Conflict, both the United Kingdom and Argentina sought to get the moral and practical support of the United States. After some debate within the US administration, the United States supported the United Kingdom and provided a good deal of material support ranging from runway matting to intelligence and air-to-air missiles (Freedman and Karsh, 1993). This support even went as far as offering to lend the Royal Navy an old US aircraft carrier should they lose one of theirs. Other nations were also engaged for support and the United Kingdom was able to use, for example, Freetown as a stopover for supplies for some of its ships heading towards the South Atlantic.

Ending the conflict

Any war and conflict needs to end in some form. Unless one party completely defeats the other and then occupies their territory, there will need to be, at the very least, some form of meeting where one side surrenders to the other. More often than not, a clear-cut victory is not achieved, but either one party has achieved a sufficient localized superiority, as in the Falklands, or there is more of a compromise agreement. This is particularly the case in civil wars where the conflict is between different factions. In this case, some form of political solution, albeit at times temporary, will have to be negotiated. For example, the fighting in Rhodesia was ultimately brought to an end when the government negotiated a deal with the two principal rebel groups. In this case, the United Kingdom, as the former colonial power, was asked to deploy military forces to oversee the disarmament of both sides and, in particular, facilitate the rebel groups safely leaving the bush to enter the disarmament process (Moorcraft and McLaughlin, 2008).

Defense and Intelligence Diplomacy in the Context of Domestic Politics

The chapter thus far has focused on issues concerning the nature, character, and application of defense intelligence and diplomacy as a tool of statecraft. As the first section highlighted, much of the discourse on national strategy-making is grounded in realist assumptions and has tended to assume that the actions of states in international relations are predicated on rational self-interested cost-benefit calculations intended to maximize the national political objectives. This is reflected in John Spanier's observation that:

> One model of decision making—the rational-actor model—has been central to first-level analysis, in which each State is viewed as a unitary actor, making foreign policy choices in four clearly separated steps: selecting objectives and values, considering alternative means of achieving them, calculating the likely consequences of each alternative, and selecting the one that is most promising. (Spanier, 1984, 410)

In this section we briefly introduced debates surrounding the utility of the rational-actor model and the contenting decision-making model in the analysis of "grand strategy-making," states' identification of "national interests," and the role and conduct of defense and intelligence diplomacy as an element of statecraft. The focus here is therefore on domestic determinants foreign and security policy-making and implementation.

Graham Allison's book, originally published in 1971, entitled *Essence of Decision,* interrogated the prevailing rational actor assumption in the case study of the Cuban Missile Crisis (Allison, 1971). Allison's approach sought to explain key decisions made by the United States and Soviet Union employing the rational actor model and two alternatives. The first alternative—the "organizational process" model—drew on existing studies that argued existing governmental bureaucracies place limits on national action, and posited that political leaders will respond to international crises by applying pre-existing organizational standard operating procedures (SOPs) and, because of time limitations, pursue the first acceptable proposal that adequately addresses the policy problem and is often called "satisficing." The second alternative—the "governmental politics" model—proposed that decision-making by the political leadership is influenced by the organizational perspectives and interests of those bureaucracies with official responsibilities in the formulation and execution of foreign policy. The significance of Allison's study, which identified shortcomings in rational actor assumptions, is that it has stimulated ongoing theoretical and empirical research and debates between advocates of rational expectation theories and alternative explanations (Stuart, 2010).

Of particular relevance to analysts of all forms of state diplomacy are the subsequent empirical and conceptual developments of what Allison termed the "governmental politics" model, which focuses on the proposition that "foreign policy decisions are often the product of deliberations among a small group of political insiders, many of whom are *ex officio* representatives of government agencies" (Stuart, 2010, 585–586). This "governmental model" is relevant because the "grand strategic" level of national strategy-making is the interface between the political leadership and the senior representatives of those organizations responsible for the provision of the state's non-military and military diplomatic capabilities and functional expertise. It is also the juncture at which political decisions are reached about relative national security priorities and the allocation of finite budget resources between those organizations, as well as decisions concerning the specific levers of state power (diplomatic, military, intelligence, economic) that are employed in response to specific risks and threats to national interests. It is therefore the locus of statecraft where potential bureaucratic politics is most likely to be played out.

Morton Halperin's successive editions of *Bureaucratic Politics and Foreign Policy* offer the most comprehensive empirical analysis of the interplay of organizational objectives and inter-organizational competition in the process by which decisions are made and actions are taken by the US government in the field of national security and foreign policy (Halperin, 1974). On the one hand, Halperin's work suggests that all institutional participants in the national security decision-making process profess to be pursuing the national interest, but often have differing notions about what these national security interests are depending on their organizational backgrounds and perspective:

> The participants, while sharing some images of the international scene, see the world in very different ways. Each wants the government to do different things, and each struggles to secure the decisions and actions that he or she thinks best. (Halperin et al., 2006, 4)

On the other hand, Halperin demonstrates that the bureaucracies, and the individuals that represent them, accord high priority to the protection and advancement of six institutional interests: budgets, roles, missions, capabilities, influence, and essence. These findings are also supported in a range of theoretical treatments of domestic determinants of states' foreign policies (Fearon, 1998).

CHAPTER REVIEW QUESTIONS

1. How does military strength relate to diplomacy?
2. What is signalling?
3. How does compellence work?
4. How do smaller states use alliances?
5. Is diplomacy as a form of intelligences gathering a way to spy?

ESSAY/SEMINAR QUESTIONS

1. What is the role of diplomacy in times of conflict?
2. Is 'coercive diplomacy' really diplomacy? Or just a threat by another name?
3. Can military diplomacy be anything other than 'realist' and how is modern realism different from the realism we saw in the three ancient world examples?
4. Summarize the debate around the use of the rational-actor model strategy.
5. Is it possible to keep the use of the military in humanitarian/evacuation operations separate from other military operations?

References and Further Reading

ABCA, 2015, http://www.abca-armies.org/

Allison, Graham. *Essence of Decision: Explaining the Cuban Missile Crisis.* Boston: Little, Brown, 1971.

Anderson, James H. & Phillips, James. "Defusing the Missile Crisis in the Aegean," *Executive Memorandum no.553,* Heritage Foundation, October 5, 1998. http://www.heritage.org/research/reports/1998/10/defusing-the-missile-crisis-in-the-aegean

Ayson, Robert. "Strategic Studies" in *The Oxford Handbook of International Relations,* C. Reus-Smit & D. Snidal (eds). Oxford: Oxford University Press, 2008.

Byman, Daniel L. & Matthew C. Waxman. "Kosovo and the Great Air Power Debate" in *Strategic Studies: A Reader,* Mahnken, T.G. & Maiolo, J.A. (eds). London: Routledge, 2008.

Baylis, J. K. Booth, K., J. Garnett, & P. Williams, P. *Contemporary Strategy I: Theories and Concepts.* London: Holmes & Meier, 1987.

BBC. "Libya protests: Evacuation of foreigners continues." *BBC Online,* February 25, 2011. http://www.bbc.co.uk/news/world-middle-east-12552374

BBC. "MH17 Malaysia plane crash: What we know." *BBC Online*, August 11, 2015, http://www.bbc.co.uk/news/world-europe-28357880

Benelux Declaration 2012. http://www.militarycooperation.eu/index.php?option=com_content&view=article&id=59&Itemid=63

Brinkman, Marc. "The Dutch Contribution to the UKNL Amphibious Force: Adapting to Changes in the Global Security Situation." *RUSI Defence Systems* (Summer 2006):70–1, https://www.rusi.org/downloads/assets/brinkman.pdf

British Army. "Transforming the British Army—An Update July 2013." http://www.army.mod.uk/documents/general/Army2020_Report.pdf

Cable, James. *Gunboat Diplomacy 1919–1991: Political Applications of Limited Naval Force*, Basingstoke: Macmillan Publishing Ltd, 1994.

Childress, James F. "Just-War Theories: The Bases, Interrelations, Priorities, and Functions of Their Criteria." *Theological Studies* 39 (1978): 427–45.

Cohen, R. "Where are the aircraft carriers?". *Review of International Studies*. Vol. 7, No. 2 (1981): 79–90.

Crouch, David. "Sweden calls off hunt for submarine." *Guardian Online*. October 24, 2012.

Dorman, Andrew. *Blair's Successful War: British Military Intervention in Sierra Leone*. Farnham: Ashgate, 2009.

Dorman, Andrew. "Kosovo" in *War and Diplomacy*, Andrew M. Dorman & Greg Kennedy (eds). New York, USA: Potomac Books, Inc., 2008.

European Parliament, 2012. http://www.europarl.europa.eu/meetdocs/2009_2014/documents/dnat/dv/dnat061112russianreactions_/dnat061112russianreactions_en.pdf

Fearon, James. "Domestic Politics, Foreign Policy, and Theories of International Relations." *Annual Review of Political Science*. 1 (1998): 289–313.

Foreign & Commonwealth Office & Ministry of Defence. "RAF evacuates Britons from South Sudan." December 20, 2013. https://www.gov.uk/government/news/raf-evacuates-britons-from-south-sudan

Freedman, Lawrence and Efraim Karsh. *The Gulf Conflict 1990–1991*. London: Faber and Faber Ltd., 1993.

Garnett, John.. "The Role of Military Power" in *Contemporary Strategy I: Theories and Concepts*. J. Baylis, K. Booth, J. Garnett and P. Williams (eds). London: Holmes & Meier, 1987.

Garnett, John. "Strategic Studies and its Assumptions" in *Contemporary Strategy I: Theories and Concepts*.

Gray, Colin S. *War, Peace and International Relations: An Introduction to Strategic History*. Abingdon: Routledge, 2007.

Halperin, Morton and Priscilla Clapp with Arnold Kanter. *Bureaucratic Politics and Foreign Policy*. Washington, D.C.: Brookings Institute Press, 2006.

Halerpin, Morton. *Bureaucratic Politics and Foreign Policy*. Washington D.C.: Brookings Institute, 1974.

Handel, Michael I. *Masters of War: Classical Strategic Thought*. London: Frank Cass, 2005.

Kane, Thomas M. and David J. Lonsdale. *Understanding Contemporary Strategy*. Abingdon: Routledge, 2012.

Lonsdale, David. "Strategy" in *Understanding Modern Warfare*. D. Jordan, D. Kiras, James, J. Lonsdale, David, I. Speller, C. Tuck, and C. Dale Walton (eds). Cambridge: Cambridge University Press, 2008.

Ministry of Defence. "RAF deploys Typhoon jets to bolster Nato air policing mission." April 28, 2014. https://www.gov.uk/government/news/raf-deploys-typhoon-jets-to-bolster-nato-air-policing-mission

Moorcraft, Paul and Peter McLaughlin. *The Rhodesian War: A Military History*. Barnsley: Pen and Sword, 2008.

NSC-68, https://www.trumanlibrary.org/whistlestop/study_collections/coldwar/documents/pdf/10-1.pdf

NATO 2014, http://www.nato.int/cps/en/natolive/nato_countries.htm

NATO 2015a, http://www.nato.int/cps/en/natolive/topics_49635.htm

NATO 2015b. http://www.nato.int/terrorism/five.htm

Nye, Joseph. *Soft Power: The Means of Success in World Politics*. New York: Public Affairs, 2004.

Royal Navy 2015, http://www.royalnavy.mod.uk/news-and-latest-activity/operations/red-sea-and-persian-gulf/kipion-mcmv

SIPRI. "World military spending falls, but China, Russia's spending rises, says SIPRI," Apr. 15, 2013: http://www.sipri.org/media/pressreleases/2013/milex_launch

Sky 2014, http://news.sky.com/story/1323932/china-defends-barrel-role-near-us-spy-plane

Spanier, John. *Games Nations Play*. London: Holt, Rinehart and Winston, 1984.

Stewart, Joshua. "U.S. and Australia to sign 25-year deal for Marines in Darwin." *Marine Corps Times*, August 11, 2014. http://www.marinecorpstimes.com/article/20140811/NEWS08/308110050/U-S-Australia-sign-25-year-deal-Marines-Darwin

Stuart, Douglas T. "Foreign-Policy Decision-Making" in *The Oxford Handbook of International Relations*. C. Reus-Smit, and D. Snidal, (eds). Oxford: Oxford University Press, 2010.

UNCLOS, http://www.un.org/depts/los/convention_agreements/texts/unclos/unclos_e.pdf

USA Today. 2001 http://usatoday30.usatoday.com/news/world/2001-04-01-collide.htm

Watson, Adam. *Diplomacy: The Dialogue Between States*. London: Methuen, 1982.

Wohlforth, William C. "Realism" in C. Reus-Smit and D. Snidal, D. (eds). *The Oxford Handbook of International Relations*. Oxford: Oxford University Press, 2010.

CROSS SECTION 7.1

India: Chandragupta and Chanakya, Military Strategy and Political Power

BY ALISON HOLMES

India, the final example of a diplomacy of place, was an ancient civilization based on local and regional trade in the Indus Valley (current-day Pakistan) and encompassed a large variety of peoples and cultures from as early as 2300 BCE. A society on the rise just as the Zhou dynasty in China was waning, the focus here will be on the Mauryan dynasty (323–185 BCE), particularly under Chandragupta (322–293 BCE), to create a frame that takes the narrative of states-systems and diplomacy beyond the end of the Zhou dynasty (256 BCE) and Warring States (221 BCE) essentially up to the point of the story of the first example of the Byzantines, which begins in 330 CE. In this discussion, it will be clear that this civilization operated with a theory of statecraft that could be considered deeply reminiscent of the concepts of signaling and compellence just discussed, through military might that was strategically placed in a political frame.

The Indus Valley at this time had no single authority, but was more of a patchwork of independent and dependent communities. Some were kingdoms, though there were also city republics and even elected rulers, while other groups followed a matrilineal line that went from mother to daughter while the husband governed (Watson, 2009). Around 1500 BCE, the Aryans, a nomadic tribe from the Asiatic plains, swept into the northern part of what is today India and continued to spread throughout the region until, by 700

BCE, there were sixteen clearly separate kingdoms. This multi-power system remained relatively stable until 530 BCE when the Persian Empire moved into the Indus Valley from the northwest, only later to be overrun by Alexander the Great, the Greek King of Macedon, in 327–325 BCE. The significance to note here is the change from a balance of power or multi-power system of different 'local' kingdoms to that of an invading empire, and finally to a ruler like Alexander the Great who controlled vast areas. These shifts are important because they reflect the interaction of hierarchy and heterarchy and will ultimately underpin the practices of diplomacy encountered in this part of the world and the potential for coexistence of different worldviews and their diplomacies.

At this point it is key to delve into the Indian approach to government and diplomacy in more depth as this marks the beginning of what became the Mauryan Empire under Chandragupta, advised and guided by his friend and Brahmin, Chanakya.

Chandragupta and Chanakya, also known as Kautilya, were exiles from the Nanda Kingdom of Magadha who, after Alexander's death in 323 BCE, began to take advantage of the relative chaos. They are credited with a series of military and propaganda campaigns and for sparking the native revolts that ousted not only the Macedonian garrisons, but also the Nanda rulers and put Chandragupta in charge. He ruled from 322–298 BCE, when he handed the throne to his son, Bindusara, who expanded to the south primarily through military conquest, ruling from 298–272 BCE. The throne then came into the hands of Chandragupta's grandson, Aśoka, who ruled from 269–231 BCE. While Chandragupta made major advances in terms of the area he controlled, it was Aśoka who, through a number of ruthless and bloody campaigns, managed to control nearly the entire subcontinent of India. There is, however, considerable debate as to the 'state-like' qualities of this entity with identifications such as "segmentary state," "regional state," or even "galactic polity," which is to say that there are different versions of how much control or centralized authority can be attributed to this entity (see Sunait Chutintaranond, 1990, for a fuller survey of this discussion). For these purposes, India was a major power that reached from the Caspian Sea to the Bay of Bengal and north to Kabul (Bozeman, 1960) not through a hierarchy, but through what will be identified as a more relational approach.

The focus here will be on the ideas of Chanakya, also known as Kautilya, and the ideas contained in his great Hindu work, the *Arthaśāstra,* outlining his theory of statehood. It has become the trademark of Indian statecraft, but even from the beginning it has been shrouded in mystery or controversy. The first and very basic question concerns his birthplace and his name. Some-sources claim he was from north India while others claim him in the south. Some suggest he was the son of Chanin while others argue his father was Chanak and hence his name Chanakya. Still others give him the name Vishnugupta. There are also interpretations as to whether it is more accurate as Kautalya or Kautilya, the difference being that the second derives from a Sanskrit word meaning 'crooked' or 'shrewd' (Frey and Frey, 1999, 20), while the first is more benign as the clan patronym (called a *gotra*), *kutila*. In learning about the work, it will become clear why some people wish to defend one version over another, though it seems that both could be deemed valid if we assume a simple difference over the use of vowels between Indic dialects (Scharfe, 1993, 73). Myth and legend continue in terms of his background with some suggesting that he was a poor boy from the south who came to the Nanda court to find his fortune, but was insulted and swore revenge on the king, while others suggest that he was from the north and studied at University; most concur that he was not a handsome man and may even have been disfigured or deformed in some way (Fabian, 2012, 39-40), which, some have suggested, influenced his carefully detailed, codified approach to statecraft.

Arthaśāstra: the law of the fish

The *Arthaśāstra* was developed in a time of uncertainty, a fact amply reflected in this manual on statecraft. Designed primarily for small states (rather than larger rulers or hegemons), it is more 'realistic' than 'realist' in that order and prosperity (and not coercion and power for its own sake) are at its core. The 'law of the fish' as it is known, is simply the recognition that the larger and stronger fish will always swallow the weaker (Frey and Frey, 1999, 20) but a fate that can be avoided through the stewardship of a worthy king. "In the presence of a king maintaining just law, the weak can resist the powerful" (Kautilya, Rangarajan translation, 1992, 108). Nevertheless, other influences can also be seen in India. As Watson points out, while Hinduism was a great source of unity and community between many different cultures, the ideas of the Greeks and Buddhists were arriving in India and offered Chandragupta the opportunity to create an empire "based on Indian practice, but Persian in scope" (Watson, 2009, 78).

The name *Arthaśāstra* comes from a division in types of power that K.P. Fabian lists as: the "intellectual arising from good counsel, the strength coming from prosperous treasury and a strong army and valor, the basis for moral and energetic action" (Fabian, 2012, 42). In this system, and unlike China (or Egypt and Japan, systems we will not go into here), the king does not derive his power from a divine source because divinity was only for Brahmins as the interpreters of 'eternal law' (*dharma*). The ruler's job was therefore to enforce the law through the 'rule of the rod' (*danda*). Practical politics (*artha)* on either the national or international level (and bearing in mind there was relatitvley little notion of any difference between these two at this point) is essentially "that science which treats of the means of acquiring and maintaining the earth." Thus, *dharmaśāstras* and *arthaśāstras* form the fundamental binary distinction of Indian political science (Bozeman, 1962, 120–21).

The effect of this lack of presumed divinity was that there was no preordained order and kings could be divided between those of equal, superior, and inferior power. Further, as there was no power above the king, it was only by 'being' powerful that a king could hope to keep and gain the power necessary to do their job. Using this worldview, Chanakya recognized the networked nature of the political world as well as its intrinsic instability. He could also see the importance, not only of allies, but also of the relations between enemies and allies and the continuous shifting of position that those relations involved. Benoy Kumar Sarkar argues that this was a key to this approach in that it was not about a single state or entity, but that "sovereignty is not complete unless it is external as well as internal" and that only "great misery...comes of dependence on others" (Sarkar, 1919, 400). Thus, the idea that those who had been defeated should be allowed to continue without interference (Watson, 2009, 78), as well as the acceptability of the breaking of an agreement with a rising power (Bozeman, 1960), was all part of the complex balancing of the shifting source of power—the primary object of all statecraft.

For Chanakya, the system of diplomacy flows directly from the seven basic elements of the state—though some scholars list only six (Kautilya Rangarajan translation, 1997). They are:

1- the king (*Svāmīn*);
2 - the higher bureaucracy or councillors (*amātya*);
3 - the territory along with the population (*janapada*);
4 - the fortified cities and towns (*durgas*);
5 - the treasury (*kosha*);
6 - the army or forces of defense / law and order (*danda* or *bala*); and,
7 - the allies (*mitra*)
(Fabian, 2012, 41 and Singh, 2005, 21).

These elements of the state area are all taken into account by calculating one's own power, that of others in the system, and whether they are allies, neutral states, or enemies before deciding on one of six policy options: war, peace, neutrality, invasion, alliance, and biformal relations. Campaigns are then planned based on the key factors of power, time, and place (Kautilya Rangarajan translation, 1997, 627). In this system, the role of diplomacy was to "progress a state from a condition of deterioration to stabilization and from stabilization to advancement" and to determine a policy, while fundamentally based on might and presuming both world conquest and world domination which could be "varied…[by] the environment calling for a particular type of diplomacy. A well consolidated state, Chanakya argues, can "evolve itself into a world power" (Ramaswamy, 1962, 34) and a wheel of state or chakravarti that "rolls everywhere without obstruction" as a world state or universal sovereign (Sarkar, 1919, 409)—though Chanakya did not ever seek to expand beyond the subcontinent of India (Kautilya Rangarajan translation, 1992).

The *Arthaśāstra* is often compared to other major strategic works such as Aristotle's *Politics*, Sun Tzu's *Art of War,* and Niccolò Machiavelli's guide, *The Prince,* but Max Weber suggests that, when compared to the *Arthaśāstra,* Machiavelli is harmless (Fabian, 2012, 39). The more important point in terms of comparison is that Chanakya is more detailed and prescriptive in his outlook both in terms of variables to consider and potential strategies to follow. A relatively small portion of the work is actually about foreign policy, but its hefty size is due to the fact that it also deals with morality (both within and outside marriage), weights and measures, rules of the road, fire prevention and firefighting, chemical warfare, law and justice, as well as the "art of making oneself invisible" (Fabian, 2012, 41)—a useful skill in any political situation.

The work's real aim is to create the infrastructure necessary at every level of society to support order and promote prosperity because, in Chanakya's view, every level of society is connected; from the rules concerning the maintenance and upkeep of the elephant forest (Kautilya, Rangarajan translation, 1992, 44) to the appointment of spies, often semi-permanent and located for long periods of time in a single location (a 'dark' version of the permanent mission but appearing much earlier than in Europe) (Kautilya, Rangarajan translation, 1992, 503). The mandala discussed earlier reflects this sense of interconnection as it lays out the relative power and political distance of both friend and foe from the center without forming a centralized structure or hierarchy (Dellios, 2003). In other words, each interaction is not merely a bilateral exchange without consequence to others, but each exchange, by definition, has the power to alter other relationships and loyalties. There is a constant assessing of space and distance between all those deemed to be in the wheel as well as the relation between one mandala group or another as there was a recognition of overlapping areas and power bases—a stark contrast to Western ideas of territory and sovereignty.

In terms of placement and interpretation of the circle, the king must assume that his enemies are closest to him—whatever their literal geographical position. Moving out, there are more remote enemies, but who may offer support to the closer enemies as well as allies who similarly offer support or play other roles in terms of the center of gravity. A group of ten entities (*decennium*) can constitute one mandala (Sarkar, 1919) though there are often twelve, with one deemed to be the *vijigisu* (Dellios, 2003). This can ultimately consist of approximately seventy-two variables to take into account the state of the kingdom and other factors, including existing and potential alliances (Watson, 2009, 79). A crucial point to remember is that it all works in a circle. In other words, there are always enemies and allies, etc., generally consisting of five states in five zones and enemies and allies to the rear made up of four more states in four zones (Dellios, 2003) both in front and behind the center, and all adding to the complexity of this relational system.

Following on, the king (and his circle) may adopt one of three specific "strategies of state" also laid out by Chanakya: the "snake charmer" who lulls his enemies (*saman*), "outright assault" (*danda*), or various practices of "deceit" (*maya*) (Bozeman, 1960, 123) while the qualities of the diplomats who would carry out these strategies were, according to Chanakya, the same as the *amatya* or a councillor, and required skill in both theory and practice:

> The king may appoint a childhood friend, so long as he is not allowed to overreach himself; or an associate in secret activities so long as he is not allowed to blackmail the King; or one of proved loyalty, provided he has also proved himself efficient in government; or one from a hereditary family so long as he does not become all-powerful; or bring in new blood, if he has both theoretical ability and practical experience. In any case, anyone who is appointed as a councillor must have the highest personal qualities. (Kautilya, Rangarajan translation, 1992, 197)

There is an interesting caveat in this system in that a person judged to have only three quarters of those skills could be appointed as an envoy to carry out limited missions, while those with only half of the appropriate skills could still be appointed, but only as messengers (Fabian, 2012, 45).

In return, the major works and guides of the time are mixed in terms of the treatment meted out to diplomats. The *Arthaśāstra* states that "even the lowest born (envoys) are immune from killing" and the Sanskrit classic, the *Ramayana*, written in the third century BCE and attributed to Valmiki, stresses that killing an envoy was "opposed to the general conduct of kings," while another classic, the *Mahābhārata*, composed between 20 BCE and 200

BCE and attributed to Vyasa, reminded statesmen with even more finality that "the king who slays an envoy will sink into hell with all his ministers." Unfortunately, there are riders to these exhortations in that the *Arthaśāstra* allows that diplomats or envoys may be punished and both the *Arthaśāstra* and the *Ramayana* allude to the possibility of punishment while the *Mahābhārata* specifically allows for the fact that envoys could be branded, maimed, disfigured, or detained—not pleasant options, but not death (Frey and Frey, 1999, 20).

The Indian state-system is perhaps the most elusive in terms of using the idea of types of diplomacy. While based on complex political reasoning and machinations (with its large and complex handbook on how to conduct such relations), it is clear that Chandragupta and his successors used a great deal of military positioning and force to at least establish control. Economic considerations and securing the population's prosperity are deemed by Chanakya as a key role of the ruler (and much of the *Arthaśāstra* is about trade, taxation, and the regulations of business), such that economics must be considered a mainstay of strategy. Culturally speaking, the *Arthaśāstra* has a religious tone on many domestic issues, but one that could just as easily be argued as on basic human rights given it discusses the employment of women, the need for the humane treatment of slaves and animals, and penalties for mistreating nuns and prostitutes. In foreign affairs, this tolerance may be less in evidence, but there seems to be an underlying desire for a 'sense of fairness' and a clear code of behavior even in a realist perspective. As outsiders, it is easy to be overly attracted to the exotic ideas of the mandala, but it continues to be useful to separate each of these strands of diplomatic practice as elucidated by Chanakya and implemented by Chandragupta and return to the politics of both theory and practice in the final guest chapter.

References and Further Reading

Bozeman, Adda. *Politics and Culture in International History*. Princeton: Princeton University Press, 1960.

Chutintaranond, Sunait. "Mandala, 'Segmentary State' and Politics of Centralization in Medieval Ayudhya." Journal of Siam Society. 78, No. 1 (1990): 89–100.

Dellios, Rosita. "Mandala: from sacred origins to sovereign affairs in traditional Southeast Asia." *Centre for East-West Cultural and Economic Studies*. Paper 8, 2003.

Fabian, KP. *Diplomacy: Indian Style*. New Delhi: Har-Anand Publications, 2012.

Frey, Linda and Marsha Frey. *The History of Diplomatic Immunity*. Columbus: Ohio University Press, 1999.

Mann, Michael. *Volume 1. The Sources of Social Power: A History of Power from the Beginning to A.D. 1760*. Cambridge: Cambridge University Press, 1986.

Ramaswamy, T.N. *Essentials of Indian Statecraft: Kautilya's Arthaśāstra for Contemporary Readers*. New Delhi: Munshiram Manoharlal Publishers, 2007.

Rangarajan, L.N. (translation). *Kautilya – The Arthaśāstra. Edited, Rearranged, Translated and Introduced.* New Delhi: Penguin Books, 1992.

Rues-Smit, Christian. *The Moral Purpose of the State: Culture, Social Identity, and Institutional Rationality in International Relations*. Princeton: Princeton University Press, 1999.

Sarkar, Benoy Kumar. "Hindu Theory of International Relations." *The American Political Science Review*. Vol. 13, No. 3 (1919): 400–14.

Scharfe, Hartmut. *Investigations in Kau⊠alya's Manual of Political Science*. Wiesbaden, Germany: Harrassowitz Verlag, 1993.

Singh, G.P. *Political Thought in Ancient India: Emergence of the State, Evolution of Kingship and Inter-State Relations based on the Saptā⊠ga Theory of State*. New Delhi: DK Printworld, 2005.

Watson, Adam. "The Indian States System." Paper to the British Committee on the theory of International Politics. Chatham House Papers. April 21-24, 1967.

Watson, Adam. *The Evolution of International Society*. London and New York: Routledge, 1992/2009.

Watson, Adam. *Hegemony and History*. London: Routledge, 2007.

8 The European Tradition of Diplomacy

Alliances, Coalitions, and Professional Diplomats

BY SHAUN RIORDAN

There is sometimes a temptation to trace the history of diplomacy back to ancient times. Diplomatic practices are discovered, or posited, in the interactions of Sumerians or Babylonians. Lawrence Freedman, in his masterpiece *Strategy*, even discusses strategic, or diplomatic, behavior between chimpanzees (Freedman, 2013). There is much value in this. Thucydides' *History of the Peloponnesian War* still lays down the basic principles of the Realist School of International Relations. Examination of the practice of diplomacy in Europe prior to the Treaty of Westphalia of 1648 can offer insights into a world where states are not the only diplomatic actors (Thucydides, 2000). However, this chapter will focus on a particular Western tradition of diplomatic thinking and practice based around the nation-state, and the relation of diplomacy and security in promoting national interests and objectives.

It can be argued that this tradition of diplomacy really begins with Cardinal Richelieu in the seventeenth century (Kissinger, 1994). Richelieu was the Chief Minister of Louis XIII, entrusted, among other things, with designing and implementing France's foreign policy. He was one of the first European statesmen to think in terms of national, rather than religious or dynastic, interests, seeing his objectives as being to curb the power of the Habsburgs and to develop France as Europe's dominant power. To these ends, he shocked his contemporaries by entering the Thirty Year's War on the side of the Protestant princes against the fellow Catholics of the Holy Roman Empire, thus enshrining the principle that 'my enemy's enemy is my friend.' More broadly, he conceived of France's foreign policy in terms of maintaining a balance of power in Europe. At home, he created the first Foreign Office to develop his diplomatic strategies and issue instructions to his ambassadors and ministers around Europe. This office was also tasked with explaining Richelieu's foreign policies both at home and abroad. In this sense, Richelieu can also be seen as the inventor of what today would be called 'public diplomacy.' The themes of Richelieu's foreign policy and diplomacy echo through European history until the end of the twentieth century.

Richelieu did not live to see the Treaty of Westphalia (1648), but together with the later Treaty of Utrecht (1713), it encapsulated the principles of diplomacy which Richelieu had practiced. Above all that, international relations existed between states of equal status, although not of an equal military or economic power, and it was understood that states do not interfere in the internal affairs of other states. This became known as the 'Westphalian system.' Another element was also crucial to the development of this 'diplomatic' system. European history since 1400 can be seen as a series of failed attempts to secure regional hegemony. Unlike other regions, where a particular ethnic or cultural grouping has been able to secure domination (for example, the Han in China), every time a would-be hegemon made his bid for domination, he was blocked by an alliance of other European states. Thus, the bid for hegemony by Spain in the sixteenth century was blocked by a coalition of England, France, and the Netherlands (Kennedy, 1989). For example, Austria in the seventeenth century was blocked by France allying with the German princes and Sweden. France in the eighteenth and nineteenth centuries was confounded by a series of alliances sponsored by England, but including Austria, Russia, and the rising Prussia. In the twentieth century, the United States had to be brought in as well to deny German aspirations. A key role was played by England, which, as an island, had no aspirations to regional domination, but was determined that no other European power should achieve such status either (Simms, 2014). Thus, England functioned as what John Mearsheimer has called an "off-shore balancer," supporting the second most powerful European state against the most powerful, creating continually changing coalitions and allegiances as the continental power balance changed (Mearsheimer, 2014). This consistent diplomatic strategy earned England the reputation of *perfidious Albion* among Europeans, but was encapsulated by nineteenth English Prime Minister Lord Palmerston in his famous pronouncement: "We have no eternal allies, and no perpetual interests. Our interests are eternal and perpetual, and those interests it is our duty to follow."

This perpetual struggle to gain and to block regional hegemony has had several consequences for the practice of diplomacy as it developed in Europe:

1. The basis of the entire concept of international relations (often called the Westphalian system), in which individual states are formally recognized by their peers. Recognition affords equal status between states, although not equal standing in the power relations. Protocols are developed to manage these relations which, in turn, evolve into a primitive form of international law.

2. The creation of a 'caste' of professional diplomats to manage the relations between the states. The diplomats likewise have to be accorded equal status, although not equal importance (with apologies to Orwell: all ambassadors are equal, but some ambassadors are more equal than others). Traditions and protocols also evolved around the behavior and treatment of diplomats, codified eventually in the *Vienna Conventions* and, less formally, in *Satow's Guide to Diplomatic Practice* (Roberts, 2011).

3. Paul Sharp has argued convincingly that the diplomatic corps has developed shared values and worldviews that crossed national borders to the extent that diplomats had more in common with each other than with their fellow citizens or the citizens of the countries where they were posted (Sharp, 2009). This shared "life form" meant that international relations increasingly became the exclusive preserve of the professionals.

4. Diplomacy focused on the creation and disruption of coalitions between states in pursuit of national interests, to promote or overthrow the balance of power. Diplomacy and security became bound together. Although governments undoubtedly pursued commercial as well as security interests, and commercial treaties were signed, professional diplomats regarded (and many still regard) 'trade' as secondary. It is no accident that the board (and now online) game *Diplomacy* reflects this focus on coalition creation and disruption.

This is not to say that professional diplomats were the only actors in Europe's international relations. Non-state actors such as companies were also influential, and the Anti-Slavery League can be seen as the first international campaigning NGO. However, within the Westphalian system, non-state actors were less influential, and secured less access, than either before or after. It is also important that its main features—inter-national relations between states of equal status, a professional cadre of diplomats, and a focus on coalition creation and disruption—arose from the specific contingencies of European history. They are not necessarily replicated elsewhere. In China, for example, the Han were able to prevail over the other ethnic groups living in the region. Although the successive empires periodically collapsed in chaos, China was generally ruled by a hegemonic state—even if not always an ethnically Chinese dynasty (as explored elsewhere in this collection in relation to the Zhou dynasty). This also had several consequences for China's interactions with the rest of the world, and because the Chinese region did not live in a perpetual state of competition between, theoretically, equal states, it never developed a concept of international relations (nor did it develop the constant drive for innovation and competitive advantage that made the Europeans so militarily and commercially effective). Rather than international relations, China developed the concept of tributary relations, in which all other rulers (Chinese thinking tended to focus on rulers rather than the states themselves—as European thinking also did in the Early Middle Ages) were clearly inferior to the Chinese emperor, and their precise status was decided by their tributary relationship (Kissinger, 2012). This also meant that rather than developing diplomats in the European sense, China had court officials focused on the precise interpretation and implementation of court protocol. The point is that European-style international relations and diplomacy are only one way of approaching the outside world, shaped by European experience. China has a different experience and accordingly, a different approach, to diplomacy, which is being explored by some Chinese scholars under the concept of "relational diplomacy" (Qin, 2011). Taking the consequences for European diplomacy of the continent's historical experience, I will focus on three aspects:

- the diplomatic corps as a professional diplomatic club;
- diplomacy centered on the creation and disruption of networks and coalitions; and
- diplomacy integrated within national security, as one of the tools to pursue national security and commercial objectives.

The Diplomatic Corps

I have already referred to Paul Sharp's conception of the diplomat, or the collective of diplomats, as a life form in the sense of Wittgenstein's *Lebensform* (Wittgenstein, 1953). Alienated from their home roots, yet not quite integrated while abroad, diplomats live in a halfway world where they have the most in common with their fellow diplomats. Even diplomats from belligerent nations are able to converse easily when on neutral territory, even as their fellow citizens are killing each other elsewhere (Lord Templewood recounts anecdotes of his encounters with Italian counterparts in Spain during WWII—Templewood, 1946). This tendency of diplomats to get on better with other diplomats than their fellow countrymen has been both mocked and criticized, whether for their membership of a cozy international elite or the perception they represent the foreigners' interests rather than those of their own country (many a British politician has quipped about the Foreign Ministry being the Ministry of Foreigners in London). Nevertheless, as Sharp argues, in the European tradition, this shared *Lebensform* has been essential to diplomats carrying out their functions, especially in a continent of continuous conflict and tensions and an equally continuous shifting of alliances and coalitions. They can talk and act in ways in which politicians cannot, allowing them to maintain dialogue even during times of heightened tension or conflict. This informal means of regulating and mitigating tensions and conflicts in international relations may be at risk as the number of different international actors increase and the influence of the diplomatic corps declines. Even within the diplomatic corps, many diplomats representing newer countries, or modernizing diplomatic services do not share the diplomatic *Lebensform* and are therefore less able to play the mediating role between states. This may become a factor in a more volatile international environment.

Network and Coalition Disruption

The nature of European geopolitics meant that for much of the modern period European diplomacy has focused on the creation and disruption of coalitions. As the modern nation-state consolidated following the treaties of Westphalia and Utrecht, rival coalitions came to incorporate ever-increasing percentages of the continent, so that by the time of the Napoleonic Wars in the early 1800s, virtually all European states belonged to one coalition or another. Coalitions were never stable, and smaller members, in particular, could be wooed away to rival coalitions. The need to maintain coalitions, and keep the smaller members on side, could give these members an influence over decision-making disproportionate to their size. Sometimes maintaining members of a coalition could be as venal as bribery (one of the original functions of the Rothschild banking families was to facilitate payments by the British government, officially called 'subsidies,' to various European states to persuade them to form successive coalitions against Napoleon; more recently, much of the wealth of the March family in Spain arose from the role of its patriarch, Juan March, in facilitating bribes from Churchill's government to keep Spain out of WWII). On other occasions, junior members of coalitions have insisted on having a real say in decision-making. This phenomenon of the diplomatic tail wagging the diplomatic dog is not new either: Thucydides complains of it during the Peloponnesian War. The creation and disruption of coalitions remains central to European diplomacy through the nineteenth century and First and Second World Wars and was carried through by both the United States and Russia into the Cold War. It differs from, for example, traditional Chinese diplomacy by having to persuade theoretically equal actors to join or leave coalitions. In Chinese diplomacy, international actors do not have equality of status and therefore cannot be incorporated into coalitions, but rather into tributary structures.

Diplomacy in Europe has also focused largely on, if not exclusively, in terms of security, a consequence of the constant conflict to achieve, or block, regional hegemony. Even when trade has been the prime aim of diplomacy, within Europe it has been set in a competitive framework (outside Europe, trade, particularly the slave trade, could be set in a more collaborative context; however, it is still interesting to note the more peaceful consequences of China's 'tributary' approach to contact with other countries as opposed to the Europeans' more competitive approach, for example, the respective impact of Zheng He's treasure fleet and the Portuguese in East Africa in the fifteenth century (Ferguson, 2013). In this sense, diplomacy should be seen as one of the tools, together with trade and military action, available for the pursuit of national security and economic objectives. It is not opposed to war, but forms part of the toolkit available to European statesman seeking to secure their ends. Clausewitz famously states that war is the continuation of policy by other means, but former Chinese premier Zhou Enlai (1949-1979) added that diplomacy is the continuation of war by other means. Both were correct, in the European context, as there is a dialectical relationship between them. European statesmen have alternatively deployed diplomatic, military, and economic tools in pursuit of their strategic goals, and have tended to be most successful when ensuring they are complementary.

National Security Strategy

This close relationship between diplomacy, war, and trade is captured in the concepts of Grand Strategy and National Security Strategy. 'Grand strategy' is essentially an American term, but useful in discussing how European statesmen have brought together the tools of their international relations (Brands, 2014). Grand Strategy provides a general narrative or framework in which a statesman deploys these tools. It is more flexible than national objectives, which may prove too rigid when confronted by the unpredictable non-cooperativeness of the real world (what Clausewitz called "friction"—von Clausewitz, 2008—or what former British Prime Minister Harold Macmillan more elegantly described as "Events, dear boy, events"). It prevents the statesman being blown off course by every reverse or unexpected event, but without tying him rigidly to unrealistic objectives. The capacity of diplomats, and diplomacy, to adapt to an ever-changing international environment clearly is essential to Grand Strategy. However, Grand Strategy, and the narrative or framework it provides, also protects diplomats from the accusations that they are 'too adaptable,' or that their flexibility leads them to promote the foreigner's rather than their own country's interests. Aside from unfair accusations, this can also be a temptation for diplomats attempting to flexibly understand the geopolitical environment in which they are operating—called 'going native' in the trade. Provided that diplomacy is operating within the framework of the grand strategy, the diplomats continue to work for their own national interests.

National Security Strategy is an alternative way to conceptualize the relationship between national objectives and military and diplomatic tools, more modest in terminology and possibly aims. Where grand strategy, by implication, has a broader reach, a National Security Strategy focuses more narrowly on maintaining the security of the state. Although not necessarily so, there is a strong implication that the strategy should be primarily defensive. This does not rule out pre-emptive actions, diplomatic or military, that might be interpreted as aggressive by other countries, but it does not aim at national aggrandizement. Diplomats play an important role in the development and implementation of a National Security Strategy as providers of intelligence, analysts of the intentions of others, and the chief interlocutors of other states. Diplomacy as the creation and disruption of coalitions is likewise central, both as complement to and preparation for military action. In this sense, war should not be seen as necessarily the failure of diplomacy (although it may be), but often the logical outcome of or complement to diplomacy in the implementation of the National Security Strategy—or indeed, grand strategy (Hocking et al., 2012).

As the diplomatic environment has changed, the term National Security Strategy begins to seem narrow. Foreign Policy and National Security are no longer the preserve of diplomats and the military, with occasional interventions from the Ministries of Finance and Trade. A plethora of new actors, governmental and non-governmental, have entered the stage. Career diplomats are increasingly a minority in embassies as a broad range of other ministries and government agencies have expanded their activities, and personnel, abroad. Governments frequently seek to draw NGOs and other non-governmental or semi-governmental agencies into the pursuit of foreign policies. This has led some scholars to posit the existence of a "national diplomatic system," in which diplomats and the military are only two parts (although key parts) of a broad array of governmental and non-governmental agencies and actors that governments bring together to promote and protect national interests abroad.

However conceptualized, the keys to European diplomacy have been its implementation by a club of professional diplomats, the focus on the creation and disruption of coalitions, and the close interrelationships between diplomacy, war, and trade pursuits of national strategies. We have already seen some of this at work with Richelieu in the seventeenth century. It can be followed through the eighteenth and nineteenth centuries up to the Cold War. To some extent it could even be argued that European diplomacy in its traditional sense dies with the end of WWII, its mantle being taken up in slightly different ways by the US and USSR. Yet returning to the end of the eighteenth Century, the key features of European diplomacy can be seen clearly in the approach of British leaders, especially Castlereagh to the defeat of Napoleon and the aftermath of the Napoleonic Wars (Bew, 2011).

Key Events in the Evolution of European Diplomacy

British Grand Strategy following the French Revolution was clear: to prevent Revolutionary, and then Napoleonic, France becoming the regional hegemon within Europe. In doing so, Britain played its traditional role as the "offshore balancer," constructing and reconstructing a series of continental coalitions against France. Britain's own military focus for most of this period lay in the Royal Navy, with the British army only becoming a significant factor towards the end of the Napoleonic Wars. For the earlier period, Britain's main activity in continental Europe was primarily diplomatic, persuading (often through bribery or, as indicated, 'subsidies') European allies to fight France on Britain's behalf. If, as Daniele Vare argued, diplomacy is the art of letting someone else have your way, then never was it more effective than during the French Revolutionary and Napoleonic Wars (Vare, 1938). Britain's control of the seas was important, not least in giving Britain 'Great Power' credibility (there are good reasons diplomats crave the credibility military power bestows, hence the eagerness of most British and French diplomats to cling onto their countries' nuclear weapons). However, in the continental conflict, British diplomacy, backed by the dispersal of British gold by the banks of the Rothschild's, may have been even more important.

Following Napoleon's defeat at Waterloo, British Foreign Minister Castlereagh was confronted by a new situation, but a similar problem. His objective at the Congress of Vienna was to ensure that France's collapse did not create a power vacuum that would be filled by a new would-be hegemon, whether Austria, Russia, or the newly rising Prussia, while at the same time keeping Britain out of European entanglements. The Congress of Vienna is, incidentally, an interesting case study in itself for students of multinational diplomacy. The vast majority of participants had little to do, and little influence on the outcome. They were left to drink, dance, and womanize in Vienna while the real business was carried out elsewhere by a small group of 'Big Powers,' in this case Britain, Prussia, Russia, and Austria, later joined by France. The parallels with later multinational diplomacy, from the Permanent Members of the Security Council to the various informal 'contact' groups created to deal with crises from Bosnia and Kosovo to the Iranian nuclear weapons program, are inevitable. The real business at Vienna was dominated by Castlereagh and the Austrian Foreign Minister Metternich, who sought to create European stability through a balance of power that would prevent any one state becoming too dominant. To ensure a balance between the more conservative and more liberal powers, Castlereagh ensured an early return to European leadership for France, in the form of its long-serving Foreign Minister Talleyrand. The new balance of power was formalized in the 'Concert of Vienna,' a system for bringing the major powers together to resolve disputes, although it rarely met.

The diplomatic system carefully constructed by Castlereagh and his colleagues in Vienna was blown apart by Prussian Chancellor Bismarck and the unification of Germany in 1870, even though the next Europe-wide war did not break out until 1914, a decade after Bismarck's death. Debate still rages among diplomatic historians about whether Bismarck was a great diplomatic strategist, or rather a brilliant tactical opportunist (Steinberg, 2014). The answer probably lies somewhere in the middle (and the debate itself may misunderstand the concept of 'strategy'). Nevertheless, Bismarck's approach to foreign policy demonstrates many of the features we have identified as central to the European concept of diplomacy, in particular the combination of military and diplomatic tools in the pursuit of national interest and the focus on the creation, and disruption, of coalitions and alliances. Prior to German reunification, Bismarck forged an alliance with Austria to fight Denmark in the War of Schleswig-Holstein in 1864, isolated Austria in the Austro-Prussian War of 1866, and isolated France in the Franco-Prussian War of 1870. Although the Prussian military and, above all, Chief of Staff von Moltke, delivered the victories on the battlefield, Bismarck's prewar diplomatic maneuvering was central in ensuring that Prussia's enemies were always isolated and ripe for military picking. However, once German reunification had been achieved on Prussian terms in 1870, Bismarck was perhaps first in recognizing the revolutionary implications. Through reunification, Germany was on the verge of achieving the hegemonic status in Europe that the Concert of Vienna had been designed to avert. This inevitably risked the other European powers 'balancing off' against Germany, creating a coalition to constrain German power and influence. Bismarck's foreign policy for the rest of his career, therefore, centered on preventing just such a counter-balancing coalition which he did by creating separate 'cross-cutting' coalitions to prevent any effective anti-German coalition. Crucial to this was the Reinsurance Treaty with Russia, Balkan rival to Germany's other ally, Austria, and the only effective potential ally for France. This single treaty with Russia in effect prevented an anti-German counter-balancing coalition. It was when Bismarck's successors failed to renew this treaty that they re-created the possibility of such a coalition, and the descent of Europe into the confrontational alliance system that ultimately fought WWI (Clark, 2014).

The violence and loss of life of WWI was blamed by many on the "Old Diplomacy" of secret treaties and networks of alliances. Whatever the responsibility of the Old Diplomacy for the outbreak and continuation of the war, the League of Nations was a deliberate attempt to replace the traditional European diplomacy of the promotion of national interest through the creation and disruption of coalitions with the concept of collective security (Bobbitt, 2003). With the benefit of hindsight we know that it failed, and was probably doomed to failure once the United States Congress voted not to join.

However, from the point of view of the European approach to diplomacy, the most interesting period was the 1930s when the collective security and traditional balancing-off approaches to prevent the emergence of a regional hegemon clashed and undermined each other. As Hitler rose to power, Britain and France had already contemplated balancing-off strategies to complement the collective security approach of the League of Nations. The key was the recruitment of the Italian Prime Minister Mussolini to a coalition to constrain the power and ambitions of Hitler's Germany. This was effective in 1934, when the mobilization of Italian forces in the Brenner Pass persuaded Hitler to back away from a Nazi-putsch in neighboring Austria. The crisis arose with the Italian invasion of Ethiopia in 1936. The provisions of collective security insisted that Italy withdraw or suffer sanctions. However, traditional European diplomacy prioritized the maintenance of Italy in a balancing coalition against Germany. The British and French initially sought to secure the latter through the *Hoare-Laval Pact*, but public outrage forced it to be abandoned in favor of sanctions against Italy. The upshot was that Britain and France secured neither collective security nor an effective balancing coalition against Germany. Indeed, despite hurried attempts to put together an anti-German coalition in 1939, following the guarantees to Poland and Romania, European powers were unable to put together one sufficient to prevent the outbreak of war in 1939. The coalition that would win only came into effect in 1939 with the entry of the US and Russia into the war. This example shows the difficulty for the European approach to diplomacy in running collective security and balancing-off strategies in parallel (Cowling, 1975).

After WWII, the advent of the Cold War meant that the European role in diplomacy was taken on by the USSR and the United States (Gaddis, 2007). To that extent, the Cold War was replete with the European foci in diplomacy we have been looking at: the combination of military and diplomatic means in pursuing national (alliance) interests, the creation and disruption of coalitions (and, in particular, the maintenance of those coalitions and the attempts to poach members of the opposing coalition, albeit mainly at the margins), and the use of professional diplomats, who, despite repeated tensions, were able to maintain cordial relations among themselves. Indeed, it can be argued that it was because of this caste of professional diplomats that, on several occasions and through the creation of back channels and deniable conversations, the Cold War was prevented from turning 'hot.'

The Europeans themselves, meanwhile, focused very largely on diplomacy among themselves. WWII, even more than WWI, had rendered warfare no longer acceptable as a policy tool. Apart from the colonial wars of dying empires, responsibility for security, and security decisions, was largely taken up by the Europeans' Cold War patrons, whether the US or the USSR. For the first time since the age of Richelieu, European diplomacy could be separated from European security. European diplomats increasingly focused on non-security aspects of national interests, particularly in the context of the growing European Common Market, and then European Union, in which the common agricultural policy (CAP) could be more important than the relative military strength of different members. This growing division between diplomacy and security had limited significance when security was guaranteed by the US and the USSR. However, within Western Europe it generated a theory that security no longer meant military power and that it would be possible to develop an approach to security built around a new diplomacy constructed on economic and social relationships. Thus, two planks of the traditional European approach to diplomacy would be abandoned: the tight relationship between security in the military sense and diplomacy; and the focus on the construction and disruption of coalitions. Insofar as diplomacy was also increasingly about domestic, as opposed to a specifically foreign, policy (e.g., agricultural, health, environmental policy, etc.), and to the extent that such issues needed to be dealt with by expert officials from home ministries (or the European Commission), the professional diplomats with their shared form of norms and values also began to be undermined.

This new understanding was given a more structured presentation after the end of the Cold War in the works of former diplomats like Jean-Marie

Guehenno (Guehenno, 1995) and Robert Cooper (Cooper, 2007). Cooper, in particular, has argued that European states should be seen as postmodern (as opposed to premodern—failed—states and modern—traditional Westphalian—states), eschewing military means to secure national objectives, but as sharing sovereignty to secure common benefits and public goods. Cooper's classification of premodern, modern, and postmodern states implies, although Cooper denies it, a historical progression in which the states of the European Union are, in some sense, the highest expression of political organization.

Cooper's thinking has been reflected in the European approach to diplomacy in the post-Cold War thinking, and in the differences between the European and US approaches (not to mention the Russian approach). The crises of the post-Cold War can to some extent be seen through the framework of the European approach to diplomacy: a combination of security (military means) and diplomacy in the pursuit of foreign policy objectives (national interests); the creation and disruption of coalitions and the existence of a professional caste of diplomats. It could be argued that the West has been most successful when keeping closest to these frameworks, and less successful when it abandons them. For example, in the first Gulf War, diplomacy and military means combined to secure the West's aims of expelling Iraqi forces from Kuwait and restoring Kuwaiti sovereignty. Diplomatic resources were deployed to secure the broadest possible coalition against Iraq, leaving Saddam's regime virtually isolated, both in the UN and more broadly. The role of the professional diplomats in securing this isolation of Iraq was significant. So is the contrast with the second Gulf War, where the diplomatic and military tools were to some extent split, with priority being given to the latter. Professional diplomats were relegated to a lesser role by the politicians and a plethora of political advisors and politicized officials. The US was far less successful in constructing a coalition either to support its own aims or to isolate Saddam. Indeed, it can be argued that Saddam was even able to construct a spoiling coalition. The US and its few allies were again successful militarily, but lacked support in the post-war, especially when the post-war turned sour. This is not to argue that the failure to keep diplomatic and military tools and strategies bound together, to create a broad coalition, or to make full use of the professional diplomats would have turned the Iraq War into a success. Indeed, sticking to these principles may have made the war itself impossible to wage, at least on the time frame the US sought. That, in itself, may be an interesting conclusion.

Perhaps the most interesting post-Cold War crisis in terms of the evolution of European diplomacy was the war in Bosnia following the collapse of Yugoslavia in the 1990s. The author must confess a personal interest in this, as he served as a policy officer in the British Foreign Office during the war. If the second Gulf War saw an excessive reliance on military tools over diplomatic tools, it can be argued that the Bosnia War illustrated what happens when the Europeans rely entirely on diplomatic tools, eschewing almost completely the military option. It is true that military forces were deployed to Bosnia, but as part of a United Nations Protection Force (UNPROFOR), which, far from serving as the military arm of a broader diplomatic strategy, effectively served to undermine any credible military threat throughout four years of slaughter. UNPROFOR, and the need not to put its personnel at risk, became the main justification for not deploying effective air strikes regardless of the provocation and atrocities committed by the Bosnian Serbs, and, to a lesser extent, the Bosnian Croats. Instead, the Europeans, who took the lead in negotiating a solution until the US took over following the Srebrenica massacre, sought a solution by diplomatic negotiation alone, backed up by the weaker threats of UN sanctions. Shuttle negotiations continued as negotiator succeeded negotiator while both Serbs and Croats were able to consolidate their positions. Within our framework, this can be seen as seeking to pursue international objectives through diplomacy alone, divorced from the military side. This fit well with the Europeans' self-conception as postmodern states, but did little to resolve the problems on the ground.

The Bosnia War also revealed an interesting aspect of the diplomatic corps (Simms, 2002). The majority of prewar Yugoslav diplomats had been Serb or Slovenian. With the dissolution of Yugoslavia, the Serbian rump inherited almost intact the old Yugoslavian diplomatic service, while the Slovenes were able to create a new professional service relatively simply. The Croats and Bosnians, on the other hand, had to cobble together diplomatic services from whatever resources they could find, often academics or businessmen who found it much harder to integrate with the professional European diplomats and were often seen as amateur and difficult. In the author's experience, this had a significant impact in attitudes towards the diplomats of the respective parts of the former Yugoslavia.

It is perhaps striking that once, following the Srebrenica massacre, the US insisted on re-wedding military and diplomatic means, a resolution of the Bosnian War was secured relatively quickly. The aim of this brief canter through European diplomatic history has been to show how key aspects of the European approach to diplomacy, especially the combination of military and diplomatic tools in broader strategies to secure national objectives and the focus on the creation and disruption of alliances and coalitions, have been recurring themes. To a lesser extent, it has also pointed up the importance of professional diplomats. The examples from after the end of the Cold War show the dangers of prioritizing the military at the expense of the diplomatic, or vice-versa. Looking towards the future, the revival of geopolitics and the challenges posed by the reviving powers, such as Russia, or emerging powers, such as China, are likely to reinforce the importance of these strains in European diplomacy, at a time when the European Union itself still seeks to rely on diplomacy alone. At the same time, the process of diplomacy has become much more complex with the entry of new governmental and non-governmental actors, enhanced by new Information Communications Technology (ICT). The alliances and coalitions that diplomats construct in the twenty-first century will no longer be primarily of states only, but will bring together subnational as well as national governments, companies, NGOs, and other non-state and civic society actors. This has already been seen in negotiations surrounding world trade and climate change.

Conclusion

There may be one more lesson for the future. This chapter has sought to argue that the European concept of diplomacy, indeed of diplomatic relations as a whole, arose from the specific historical contingencies of Europe's own development. In particular, they arose from European states' continual struggle to secure, or block, regional hegemony. Other countries, especially the major Asian powerhouses of India and China, do not have this history, and thus have very different traditions of interacting with the outside world. It will be interesting to see, as their international self-confidence grows, to what extent they will develop their own intellectual frameworks for diplomacy and international relations, and how that will affect diplomatic practice in the twenty-first century.

CHAPTER REVIEW QUESTIONS

1. What is a National Security Strategy?
2. How does Riordan define the relationship between trade and politics?
3. What is the importance of 'region' in this discussion?
4. What is the role of the diplomatic corps and how has it changed?
5. How is 'old' vs 'new' defined here?

SEMINAR/ESSAY QUESTIONS

1. How does Riordan compare Europe to China?

2. Which case study of European diplomacy do you find most interesting and why?
3. Does location determine the resulting diplomatic system or could something entirely different from the Westphalian system have been developed in Europe?
4. Richelieu is the 'father' of European diplomacy. Discuss.
5. 'Balance of Power' is seen as very important in the European/Westphalian system. Will it have this importance in the future? Discuss.

References and Further Reading

Bew, John. *Castlereagh.* London: Quercus, 2011.

Bobbitt, Philip. *The Shield of Achilles: War, Peace and the Course of History.* London: Penguin, 2003.

Brands, Hal. *What Good is Grand Strategy? Power and Purpose in American Statecraft from Harry S. Truman to George W. Bush.* Cornell University Press, 2014.

Clark, Christopher. *The Sleepwalkers: How Europe Went to War in 1914.* London: Penguin, 2014.

von Clausewitz, Carl. *On War.* Oxford: Oxford University Press, 2008.

Cooper, Robert.. *The Breaking of Nations: Order and Chaos in the Twenty First Century.* New York: Atlantic Monthly Press, 2007.

Cowling, Maurice. *The Impact of Hitler: British Policy and British Politics 1933-1940.* Cambridge: Cambridge University Press, 1975.

Ferguson, Niall. *Civilization: The 6 Killer Apps of Western Power.* London: Penguin, 2012.

Freedman, Laurence. *Strategy: A History.* Oxford: Oxford University Press, 2013.

Gaddis, John Lewis. *The Cold War.* London: Penguin, 2007.

Guehenno, Jean-Marie. *The End of the Nation State.* Minnesota: University of Minnesota Press, 1995.

Kennedy, Paul. *The Rise and Fall of Great Powers: Economic Change and Military Conflict from 1500 to 2000.* New York: Vintage, 1989.

Kissinger, Henry. *Diplomacy.* New York: Simon & Schuster, 1994.

Kissinger, Henry. *On China.* New York: Penguin, 2012.

Mearsheimer, John.. *The Tragedy of Great Power Politics.* New York: Norton and Company, 2014.

Qin Yaqing. *Development of International Relations Theory in China: Progress through Debates.* International Relations of the Asia Pacific. Vol. 11, No. 2 (2011): 231-253

Roberts, Ivor (ed). *Satow's Guide to Diplomatic Practice.* Oxford: Oxford University Press, 2011.

Sharp, Paul. *The Diplomatic Theory of International Relations.* Cambridge: Cambridge University Press, 2009.

Simms, Brendan. *Europe: The Struggle for Supremacy.* London: Penguin, 2014.

Simms, Brendan. *Unfinest Hour: Britain and the Destruction of Bosnia.* London: Penguin, 2002.

Steinberg, Jonathan. *Bismarck: A Life.* Oxford: Oxford University Press, 2012.

Templewood, Viscount. *Ambassador on Special Mission.* London: Collins, 1946.

Thucydides. *The History of the Peloponnesian War.* London: Penguin, 2000.

Vare, Daniele. *The Laughing Diplomat.* London: John Murray, 1953.

Wittgenstein, Ludwig. *Philosophical Investigations.* Oxford: Blackwell, 1953.

Part II: Conclusion

BY ALISON HOLMES

This section sought to explore the usefulness of 'type' in terms of diplomacy by posing a basic question to six experts, essentially asking them to apply the concept to their own area: What is the history of each type of diplomacy? The section also investigated the ways different worldviews affect the practices that become diplomacies of place. The guests answered, often in direct relation to the traditional narrative, but in a process that revealed the fact that diplomacy has different meanings that are often dependent on and contained by what has been identified as 'type.' When combined with the overviews of Byzantium, China, and India, it is also clear that types move through, in and around an entity's idea of itself, but also that each type interacts with other sources of power, alters the entities deploying them, and shapes the institution of diplomacy itself. Through this examination of types over time and diplomacies of place at specific points in history, it is possible to make at least four observations about diplomacy in the past that will help us craft a more global diplomacy for the future.

First, and perhaps most obvious, is the fact that the empires of the ancient world, be it the typically studied realms of Greece and Rome or those examined here—Byzantium, China, and India—all evolved practices that enabled them to connect across whatever entity, polity, or power that represented a given people, culture, or territory and they all operated through the types of diplomacy that have been identified as: culture, economics, military, and politics. Further, these connections were so fundamental to their approach that, despite the fact all three arguably have a strongly 'realist' approach to their own people and to those outside their spheres of influence, they all pursued strategies that reflected the even more 'realistic' understanding of the fact (and without the benefit of modern technology or a 'global' perspective) that every part of the system is connected and no actor can be truly isolated, and must therefore interact in a way that encourages and creates the shared norms of diplomatic behavior. Thus we are able to go beyond the traditional ideas of 'realist' approaches and demonstrate the idea suggested by Lee and Hudson that "other sources of social power are also significant to the study of world affairs rather than just (one particularly narrow definition of) political power" (Lee and Hudson, 2004, 351).

Second, the use of types demonstrated through the historical states-systems have enough in common with each other (and with our modern practices) to argue that the 'new' vs. 'old' dichotomy as commonly used is more than out of date, but positively misleading. We should therefore continue to direct attention to the types of diplomacy as a better way to identify the unchanging mission of diplomacy as communication, representation, and negotiation while also enabling a way to chart the interesting ebb and flow of difference practices and tactics and the development of the state as an entity—and potentially its demise in the future.

Third, while the 'Western European' states-system has evolved into a "society," according to the criteria of the English School, it also seems clear that other states-systems had deep associations and normative frameworks geared not only to the security and prosperity needs of their people, but that governed behavior towards outsiders, enemies as well as allies. Similarly, when the linearity of Western 'Time' is replaced with a more relational view of progress and an appreciation of the importance of space, distance, and a sense of belonging that exists from the center of the circle to the outer edge in terms of converting some and protecting the rest. This creates room to discuss a non-linear/non-Western normative form of order that could also be deemed to be an "international society."

Fourth, many institutions of power, and certainly diplomacy, seem to have a much broader reach and deeper history than suggested by the idea that it is purely 'Western European' or only possible in a society of states. This grants diplomacy a wider pedigree and potential applicability than acknowledged by those who might wish to discredit the study of diplomacy purely on the basis of a sense that it has an inbuilt or developed Western bias. This insight is particularly useful here, in looking for ideas on how to move towards a more global awareness.

The conclusion to draw from this tour of types and ancient state-systems is that all entities—tribe, kingdom, nascent state, regional power, and even vast empire—consistently create a space that is protected by rules and norms for one fundamental reason: intercultural communication demands at least basic interoperability. This observation also supports the main argument that diplomacy is not connected to the modern/post-Westphalian model of the state in any intrinsic or essential way, but was, is, and will remain an institution that adapts to reflect the societies as they seek to interact—indeed, diplomacy must interact to survive. As Kishan Rana points out in his discussion of the 'Twenty-first Century Ambassador': "The tools and techniques through which different countries implement their foreign policy are for the great part similar, almost identical. Thus, there exists a 'diplomatic process' that is shared between countries, with a methodology routinely practiced by the diplomatic services of different states. Of course there is potential in the system for change and innovation as well, but most of these are transportable, capable of emulation and adaptation" (Rana, 2005, 3).

The Introduction of this text discussed the way strategy can produce tactics, but also how tactics can change strategy or how tactics are led by strategy, but can become practice. The guests have ably demonstrated the way that theory cascades down, but also the reverse flow or feedback that creates an institution in constant motion that we see most often and most clearly from the outside. From peace accords and treaties to economic summits and arms negotiations, through to musical tours and study abroad programs—these are all types of diplomacy in action and, as Sending, Pouliot, and Neumann would argue, the products of the relations that create the "agents," "objects," and "structures" of diplomatic practice (Sending, Pouliot, Neumann, 2015).

In the closing chapter of this section, Riordan observes that 'grand strategy' is a particularly American phrase. Perhaps it is indicative to note that Chinese scholars have also been developing a concept they call Comprehensive National Power (CNP) which seems to encompass many of the same features: comprehensiveness, openness, dynamism, and a multilayered structure (Chan, 1999, 30). However, and in contrast to the more 'realist' or 'American'/traditional view of grand strategy, CNP has built in soft and intangible elements of power as well as overtly considering the linkages between each of these aspects and the balance between them at home and within the external environment (Chan, 1999) or what is argued here to be a more relational style.

This point is simply to illustrate the way states develop along their own historical and cultural trajectory, but in broadly parallel terms as entities seek to coexist and communicate in the international system. This thought is important because Part III will develop models for the interaction of different states-systems that help visualize the ways in which entities at different levels of development or different historical and cultural perspectives operate. The argument is essentially that, given this exploration of types and place, it is possible to consider the idea that previous states-systems have not entirely disappeared and that the truly global feature of current diplomatic practice involves the ability to see how these different entities, systems, and types operate in 'real time.' As more non-Western and non-state powers come to the fore in the international arena, there is mounting evidence as to the continuity in purpose of diplomacy that should also help to gain an understanding not only of the idea of the global state, but also global diplomacy as a whole.

CHAPTER REVIEW QUESTIONS:

1. What is a suzerain system and how does it differ from a 'state' in the Western system?
2. Name two 'European' diplomatic practices that originally came from somewhere else and discuss how that process worked.
3. List some 'Byzantine' diplomatic practices and explain how this term might have come to be used today to suggest that something is overly complicated.
4. What are the main characteristics of a mandala?
5. What is the importance of the 'law of the fish?'

SEMINAR/ESSAY QUESTIONS:

1. What do the three historical states-systems have in common and how important are those features?
2. In your view, why is a relational system different from a Western system and does it matter? Use China and India as your examples.
3. Linear time supports the Western/European system of states and erodes our sense of connection and more human relations in world affairs. Discuss.
4. Compare 'Grand Strategy' to 'Comprehensive National Power.'
5. Review the 'types' of diplomacy and the ways each of these three states-system used (or did not use) them in their rule.

References and Further Reading

Chan, Gerald. *Chinese Perspectives on International relations: A Framework for Analysis.* London: Palgrave, 1999.

Lee, Donna and David Hudson. "The old and new significance of political economy in diplomacy." Review of International Studies. Vol. 30,(June, 2004): 343–360.

Rana, Kishan. Inside Diplomacy. New Delhi: Manas Publications, 2014.

Sending, Ole Jacob and Vincent Pouliot and Iver Neumann. *Diplomacy and the Making of World Politics.* Cambridge. Cambridge University Press, 2015.

Stephen, Matthew. "The Concept and Role of Middle Powers during Global Rebalancing." Seton Hall Journal of Diplomacy and International Relations. (Summer/Fall, 2013): 36–52.

Watson, Adam. *The Evolution of International Society: A comparative historical analysis.* London: Routledge, 2002.

Models of Diplomacy and Global States

Part III: Introduction

BY ALISON HOLMES

Part I had four primary functions. First, to trace the classic narrative and traditional theory of diplomacy through the storyline of historical conflicts, 'big bang' events with consequent discontinuities in practice, and the developments in technology that produced breaks and a sense of 'new' vs 'old,' that ultimately become part of the fabric of the Westphalian state model. Second, to lay out the common strategies and tactics that make up what is commonly understood as statecraft through the 'practice' of diplomacy. Third, the section offered three theoretical alternatives that highlighted different perspectives on the idea of the 'state' writ large, the development of states-systems and societies, and the importance of fundamentally different understandings of structure, time, and power. Finally, Part I was designed to suggest that a combination or hybrid of these alternatives could be built on an understanding of four sources of social power (politics, economics, culture, and the military) as fundamental drivers of change and thus key to a more a 'global' theory of diplomacy. The focus on continuity challenged the traditional ideas of hierarchy and territory that underpin the classic narrative, while the use of 'types' of diplomatic activity and a clear identification of purpose, was used to propose diplomacy as the institution that mediates between these shifting ebbs and flows of power, regardless of entity or form of governance.

In Part II, a series of guest authors explored these four diplomatic 'types' in more depth, while cross sections of specific concepts and societies illustrated those types in different cultures, times, and places. Through that process, it was clear that different states-systems overlapped not only chronologically and physically (through trade and conquest), but also, and crucially, these types had a role in altering both the shape of the governing entity and the mode of diplomacy through the conscious or unconscious assimilation of ideas and symbols and the diffusion of culture. The authors helped connect the theory and purpose of diplomatic statecraft and strategy to the practices and the tactics of the four types as they evolved in relation to the development of both pre-state forms of governance and the more clearly identifiable states that make up the Western/European system or international society of today. It was also clear that, just as Mann predicted, these sources of power shift, not only across time, but also in relation to each other. He also warned that, by pulling them apart there is a risk of losing some of their complexity, but from the vantage point of diplomacy, there seems to be more at stake by not exploring those flows and linkages given that, without a longer term/deeper understanding, diplomacy would continue to be 'guilty' of the charge of Euro-/state-centrism. Whereas, by charting diplomacy's separate but parallel history from that of a specific form of 'state,' the critical communications role that diplomacy has in dialogue, representation, and negotiation becomes more visible. The charge of Eurocentrism cannot be denied, but it is accurate only insofar as those telling the story have been focused on one form of governance or polity. However, as states are currently and continuously in the process of fundamental change, there is also the possibility of a better understanding of the features of this global world—and of diplomacy as an institution that has always been, and remains, a bridge that, even as it holds societies apart, is fundamentally about communication and connection.

In Part III, the project is to link the classic story and its paradigms to the concept of diplomatic types. Recalling the warning that history is often seen as a journey with a single destination that arrives at today, the challenge will be to uncover layers of interpretation. The 'paradigm shifts' between realism and pluralism, or even between the 'old' and the 'new' diplomacy, are significant, but the fact that the previous interpretations do not simply disappear—however significant the shift in paradigm—is too often neglected. One view may become 'mainstream' or 'dominant' while others are considered 'critiques' or 'fringe' interpretations, but they are all part of the discourse and guide different flows of power.

As the Introduction to the text pointed out, theories help frame the world and that the lenses used, affect the ability to examine, interpret, and predict events in the world. Theory has a crucial role, not only in the thinking process, but in the outcomes and actions taken at the local, national, and global level. This is particularly relevant when turning to the international arena in the early twenty-first century as the goal is to try and understand the patterns in the way states act and react to each other. Past theory and diplomatic 'types' were the focus of Parts I and II and will now be brought together by exploring the way all these levels interact and further by proposing three 'models' that can be observed in actual behavior in Part III.

For these purposes, the assumption is that the English School was correct in its identification of a European states-system, and that this system even managed to create something 'larger' or 'deeper' in the form of an international society. However, while the English School may be right in this initial assessment, their particular view of the past, and the way they privileged specific features and activities, meant that they did not consider the continuing process of change, and almost completely ignored the ongoing development of other states-systems—even those they had already recognized. Ironically, and despite discussing the 'evolution of international society' explicitly, the English School rarely turned their attention to the future either in terms of how the European model might evolve or the possibility that other states-systems may not have disappeared and therefore still exist in some form and act in the international system. Using the past and looking at the ways states-systems operate in today's global society, the suggestion here is that there are three 'models' of practice in evidence.

What is meant by 'model'? Thus far, there have been a number of issues concerning terminology. The terms 'entity' or 'polity' have been used rather than 'state' so as to deal with the different names for governance structures over time. The concept of 'types' was suggested as a way to examine the institution of diplomacy in the long-term while the historical 'states-systems,' and particularly the way many different styles of communication and interaction from around the world influenced the shift from a European states-system to an international society, demonstrated the fact that many different cultures are woven into current diplomatic practice.

At this point, a distinction from the English School needs to be drawn in that, while there may have been a step change between a system and a society, the English School goes on to conclude that international society is—by default—European, without including any mechanism for continuing evolution in that system or the role of other systems in that process. In distinct contrast to this point, two ideas are central to a more global diplomacy: first, that the European states-system (or society) has not stopped evolving; and second, perhaps more controversially, far from the idea that other states-systems were entirely subsumed by the Western approach, the argument is that 'other' systems significantly influenced European development. As states become more 'global' in form, their modes of interaction are less Westphalian state-like and even less 'states-system-like.' If this fundamental difference has merit, a different perspective or level of analysis is required and called here a **model** of interaction.

Bear in mind that *models are not intended to be a detailed examination of the way in which things work, but an archetype or a representation of that process.* The argument here is that the continuing evolution of the European states-system has produced two models and that other factors have combined to create a third model that is becoming increasingly visible in contemporary world affairs.

It may helpful at this point to go back to Buzan and Little's timeline of state development/civilization and their suggestion that 'states' (and others) are operating within a 'global international system' as groups of actors through processes that are defined and enmeshed, but not always formal. In some respects this 'globality' was anticipated by Watson, but goes further here by proposing the idea that within a global system, and by virtue of the different stages of development in given states, different models have evolved that reflect the members of those groups. Logically, it follows that these different models will have different modes of operation or diploma*cies* based on these differences and, depending on the issue or the expertise of each actor. Following Buzan and Little's combination and naming of the ancient world as an 'interlinked international system,' the modern world, too, has different 'models' at work in what is now a 'global system.'

Essentially, as states themselves have continued to shift and evolve both in terms of economic structures of industrialization and political governance from what some have identified as premodern to modern, and finally, to 'postmodern' (Cooper, 2003), the diplomacy of the western/Westphalian/European states-system has also changed. This process has produced two models for interaction or practice (and diplomacy) for the Western European/Westphalian system: the Community and the Transatlantic models, which will be briefly examined in Chapter 9.

However, the argument thus far has been that the notion of 'postmodernity' does not accurately capture the sense that states are not merely postmodern, but are developing what could be identified as 'global' features and entering a new phase in their development. Further, that 'global' states interact in different ways than their premodern or modern predecessors precisely because of the growing awareness of the presence and increasing power of those entities or states that have developed along a different trajectory. Part of the global reality is a more level playing field between entire state-systems that have previously not been forced to recognize these deep undercurrents of history and culture. Whereas, and following the pattern of Part I, an alternative model operating in non-Western states-systems will be offered in Chapter 10. By returning to India and China, effectively 'left behind' by the English School and generally ignored by the traditional narrative of diplomacy, it is possible to address the increasing gap in our understanding of both states and diplomacy through the creation and exploration of what is identified as a Relational model of diplomacy.

Essentially, the three models developed here will endeavor to connect the theories of Part I, not only to the types and diplomacies of place in Part II, but, by identifying the features, strengths, and weaknesses of the different styles of interaction, also begin to chart the evolution and different outcomes of the states-systems and offer a view as to how they might develop in the future. The goal is to begin to move beyond the simple identification of the reality of a *post*-modern state and towards the beginnings of an understanding of the global state and the global society and diplomacy this society will inevitably generate.

References and Further Reading

Cooper, Robert. *The Breaking of Nations: Order and Chaos in the 21st Century*. London: Atlantic Press, 2003.

9 The European States-System

The Community and Transatlantic Models

BY ALISON HOLMES

May 1943. **Warsaw.** German forces returned to the ghetto on April 19, the eve of Passover, expecting to deport the remaining Jewish population within three days. The army was repelled and returned with reinforcements, but resistance fighters hid in attics, cellars, makeshift bunkers, and the sewer, harrying the troops in surprise attacks often with homemade weapons. Frustrated, Nazi troops moved house to house, throwing grenades into every potential hiding place and setting alight anything that would burn. Fellow soldiers were poised, ready to shoot anyone who ran out while the screams of those who burned inside filled the air. The resistance command center was finally captured on May 8 and there was only sporadic fighting until the Germans blew up the Great Synagogue on May 16 (US Holocaust Memorial Museum, ushm.org).

May 2003. Warsaw. Crowds throng the streets, not running or screaming, but enjoying the carnival atmosphere outside the Castle at an EU 'Yes' rally in anticipation of the upcoming referendum on whether Poland should join the European Union. People made speeches and young people in blue and yellow t-shirts sang, in Polish, the EU's official anthem drawn from the works of two famous Germans—Beethoven's Ninth symphony and poet Friedrich Schiller's "Ode to Joy" (Garton-Ash, 2012, 2). One month later, Poland did indeed vote 'yes.'

September 2001. London. Hundreds, if not thousands, of people stand in front of Buckingham Palace in a chilled hush, waiting for the Changing of the Guard. The Queen is on her way back to London, having cut short a break at Balmoral, while the US Ambassador to the United Kingdom of only six weeks, Ambassador William Farish, stood beside the Duke of York as he took the formal salute. The Ambassador raised his hand to his heart as the Queen's own Coldstream Guards struck up the "Star Spangled Banner" for the first time in history (Thomas, BBC News Online).

These anecdotes speak volumes about the history and trajectory, strengths and weaknesses, heroism and tragedy contained in 'western' notions of the 'European society of states.' However, the goal here is not to recount the human toll of European history, but to follow the argument that states are not stagnant, states-systems continue to evolve, and that change at both these levels is reflected in the institution of diplomacy. This chapter will look specifically at the 'original' states-system in Europe and lay out two models of interaction, 'Community' and 'Transatlantic,' as the modes of diplomacy that have grown out of change in Europe at both the state and the system levels.

Where Is 'the West'?

Before moving on, there is an inherent challenge regarding the conflation or compression between 'Western' and 'Western European,' phrases often used synonymously. 'Western Europe' is, strictly speaking, the region comprising the westerly countries of Europe. However, it has come to mean different things at different points in time. For example, during the Cold War (approximately 1945-1991) the phrase was used to describe the countries associated with the Western European Union. The WEU, in turn, was a military alliance established by seven European nations allied with the United States and tasked with implementing the Modified Treaty of Brussels (1954). As the formal European Union grew and gained strength, the WEU was deemed unnecessary and was wound up in 2011, and the WEU's functions brought into the EU itself.

In the post-colonial/Cold War world, the Western and Western European delineation is also used both as a way to describe the politics of former imperial powers towards their previous colonies and as a distinction often made between the 'first' and 'third' worlds. A related term might be considered to be the 'Anglo-sphere,' a phrase that also has a dual meaning. The first use is simply an indicator of the English-speaking world (as in Franco-, Russo-, or Sino-phone for French, Russian, and Chinese respectively), but the term has also been used to suggest a bias in the international system towards the more powerful players on the international stage.

It is particularly important here to recall that the English School only sought to apply their idea that the 'European states-system' had evolved into an 'international society' to the specific area of Western Europe. They did not focus either on the influences from other places on what became 'Europe' or the potential for what might be called the 'next stage' in the evolution of this specific states-system. Their view of Europe as the most 'advanced' system and society did not leave much room for the consideration of continuing change in that system or elsewhere, but that was never the intention.

Despite the English School reluctance, it is only logical to assert that their term 'society' should be used in relation to many other countries, states, and even entire regions. Perhaps the best example of a non-European member of the international 'society' is the United States, a former colony of the United Kingdom, but now a world power. Many other countries arguably fit into this 'advanced' group. However, this categorization is quickly complicated because it seems unlikely that international society, at least as defined by the English School, would be able to include all the former colonies of every European power or every commonwealth member—although the web of interconnections would be difficult to separate.

For these purposes, and sticking to this distinction between system and society, the argument is that the European states-system evolved and then effectively split into two 'societies.' Further, that these distinct societies have developed very differently and have, in turn, produced two different modes of diplomacy, or diploma*cies*—thus far. In other words, there is a need to re-inscribe the line that has become blurred between 'Western Europe' and 'the West' so as to identify two discrete contemporary models of diplomatic interaction. This approach is in distinct contrast with Westphalian thinking where all states are generally placed in a single category, 'equal' in sovereignty and territorially rigid, with the unspoken corollaries that all states operate on the basis of a linear, hierarchical structure. The result has been a relatively 'two-dimensional' position for diplomacy that remains dependent, even hobbled, by this particular form of states-system, whereas the goal here is to produce a more nuanced understanding of the 'Western' model by separating it into component parts.

The first model to be discussed accepts the traditional European states-system as the starting point, but suggests that the international society has continued to develop and produced a literal 'European Community' from which a Community model of diplomacy has grown. The creation of the European Union (as distinct from Europe as separate, ongoing states) is a clear example of the shared norms, values, and behavior found in a 'society,' but the institution has gone much further by linking key aspects of state agency and building a structure based on the 'pooling' of sovereignty with an expectation of joint, or at least agreed action, in all areas of statecraft—including military,

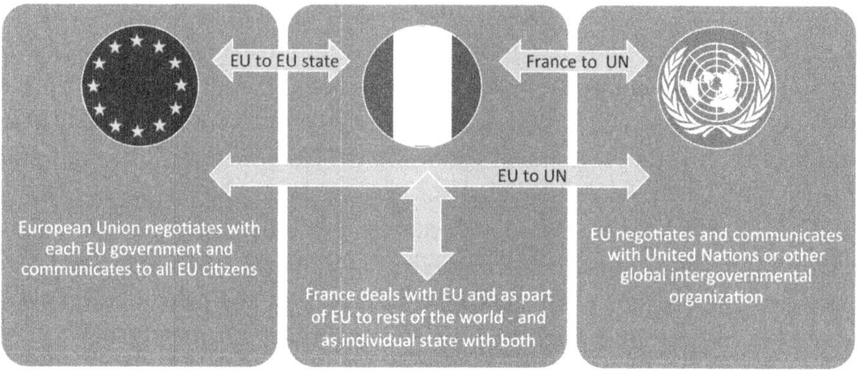

FIGURE 9.1 Community model

generally considered the most vital aspect of sovereignty. The European Union, for all its struggles and flaws, now offers such a powerful example that other regions of the world, particularly South America or Southeast Asia, have looked to, and even emulated aspects of this intricately structured regional society of states.

The second model is the Western or 'Transatlantic' model and also named for the relationship that best illustrates this approach, namely that between the United Kingdom and the United States. To many, this relationship is considered 'special,' but the position argued here is that this quality of 'specialness' ultimately has less to do with shared history and language (though these elements are clearly significant, as culture is a prime driver of institution building), but more to do with their common stage of development as states or entities which produce a shared approach to both domestic and global issues, separately and in combination. Thus positioned, it is possible to expand the concept of 'specialness' to help not only better understand UK/US relations, but also to explain the increasing number of perceived 'special' non-European, bilateral relations. Such pairs might include: Canada and the United States (Dumbrell and Schafer, 2009 among others), Ireland and the United States, Canada and Australia, and the United Kingdom and Australia. Other pairs, that don't include an obvious hegemon or former colonial power relationship, such as Cuba and Brazil, or countries recently free of the shadow of Soviet Russia, could all be possibly included on the basis of claims to 'specialness' in their own region, on particular issues, or through personal/ideological links.

The 'Community' model offers the story of interpenetrating states overcoming divisions to create a union of states that is both wide and deep, forging

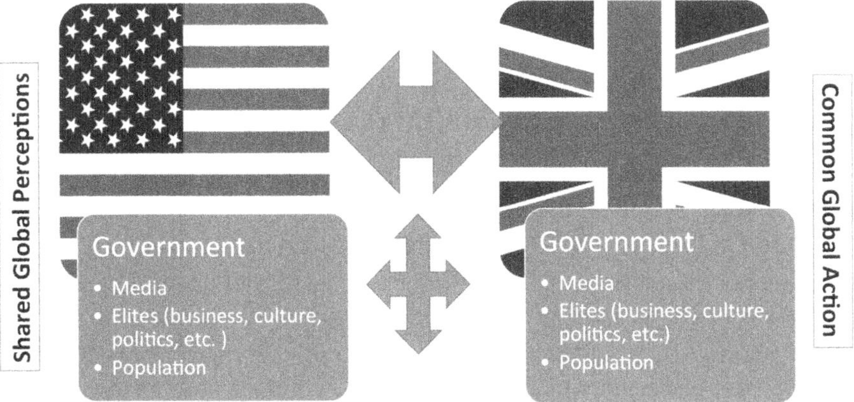

FIGURE 9.2 Transatlantic Model

habits of consensus and cooperation where once there was a regular pattern of war (Figure 9.1). The 'Transatlantic' model sets out the United Kingdom and the United States as strong, separate, sovereign, but intimately and mutually involved states acting in their own interests, but also acting in concert at the transatlantic and global level (Figure 9.2). On one level, these models reflect the paradigms of the classical narrative in that the Community model is clearly based on a positive view of human nature, the possibility of progress and shared norms and values from a more liberal or pluralist view, while the Transatlantic model is arguably focused on a less flattering view of human tendencies and more distinct ideas of sovereignty and the importance of power and territory, and potentially more 'realist' in approach. However, at another level, they both demonstrate the intricacies of theory as the paradigms of international relations are never entirely or solely 'responsible' for a specific event. Thus, it is impossible to jump from the idea of paradigm or model to the level of a particular practice or tactic. They are interwoven as both cause and effect in statecraft as different decision-makers and motivations are present in any single issue, with each actor or institution operating on the basis of different approaches or normative values. The purpose of a model is simply to identify broad patterns and directionality of process. Both models will now be presented while the question of paradigm and type will be returned to below.

The European Community and the Community of Europe

The Community model begins by accepting the English School notion that there is a European states-system. However, to understand diplomacy as expressed in this model, it is important to extend the original concept and

BOX 9.1

European Union (EU) and the European Coal and Steel Community (ECSC)

The modern European Union (EU) is a product of what originated as the European Coal and Steel Community. The Inner Six—Belgium, Italy, France, Netherlands, West Germany, and Luxembourg—created the European Coal and Steel Community (ECSC) as a means to foster political and economic cooperation through the creation of a common market between the key actors of World War II. Leaders from the Inner Six member states hoped that an economically and politically integrated region, with increased cooperation in achieving economic goals, would reduce the conditions for a climate that produced the Second World War. The ECSC Treaty was signed in Paris in 1951 and was enacted the following year with a 50-year expiration date. The ECSC Treaty's expiration in 2002 ushered in the current era of the European Union with 28 member states and 19 participating in the region's common currency or monetary union. The EU operates via several supranational and intergovernmental institutions, responsible for regulating and creating comprehensive policies that respond to the economy, justice and regional policy.

consider the fact that the international society 'founded' in Europe is not static. First, as a 'system' and then as a 'society,' the European Union in all its incarnations has evolved by adjusting even the most fundamental ideas of sovereignty in light of changes in perception of boundary, time, and space. This places 'the West,' or Europe writ large, as the cornerstone, and connects what became the Transatlantic model to the starting point of the European Union or Community model as the most recent evolution of that same states-system—though crucially not the basis of all systems currently used in the world.

Of course, it should be noted that the EU was also built with the benefit (or curse) of rapid technological development and constant mass communication in a post WWII era of relative peace. This may help explain why the European Union has effectively become a "hybrid" in terms of the more typical definitions of sovereignty (Smith, 2011) as well as a laboratory of a "post-national"/ "post-Westphalian" polity (Van Ham in Davis and Melissen, 2013), while the United States (and arguably the UK, as both 'Western' and 'Western European' in this context) retain aspects of the older 'warrior state' image in which both expend a great deal of 'blood and treasure' defending the traditional state features of sovereignty, state action, and an unfettered use of force.

FIGURE 9.3 ECSC to Modern Day EU

Politics, Culture, Economics, and the Military in the Community Model

Following the types of diplomacy discussed in Part II as a constant of diplomatic activity over time and as deployed by the diplomacies of place, it is possible to examine the Community model for similar evidence. For example, Martin Shaw discusses this difference in approach and identifies the split by arguing that the United States is at the center of a particular form of "globality" that is "centered on the complex of national and international state institutions that both constitute the political West (North America, Western Europe, Japan, and Australia) and frame its military, political, and economic dominance worldwide." He then offers the European Union as an "alternative model of international integration through institutionalization and law rather than alliance and bilateral lineages" (Shaw, 1997 and 2000) making it a "unique" if not the "extreme case" of state organization resulting from the processes of globalization. He goes on to suggest that this means that Europe has "several distinct levels of state organization at the national, European, Western (Transatlantic), and global levels (not to mention national and sub-national regional state forms)" (Shaw, 1997, 511).

In terms of European diplomacy, specifically that of the European Union, the suggestion is that it is "overlaid by a post-modern layer," which produces a form of international politics that moves the whole system or society away from the traditional issues of sovereignty and the domestic/foreign divide. The European model, he suggests, is instead "driven by the logic of mutual interference in each other's domestic affairs, pursuing security through transparency and transparency through interdependence" (Hocking, 2012, 75).

Jan Melissen also points to the importance of "economic interdependence," "interconnectedness," and "interpenetration" in the European model, not only at the governmental level, but also between the peoples and cultures of different national societies and regions. As he points out, the rest of the world is not yet as "permeable" as European states and thus it follows that other states have not developed the same kind of depth in their relations in which both ideas and practical politics move across boundaries in ways not seen in more traditional interactions (Melissen in Davis and Melissen, 2013). Given that he is speaking specifically about the European Union, he does not venture to speculate on whether such relations might be possible between other actors, nor does he comment on the already embedded nature of transatlantic relations as an arguably 'less developed' states-system, but still a society of sorts.

The European version of embedded relations is illustrated in the diagram of the Community model. (Figure 9.1) Using France, it is clear that there will be situations in which the interests of a specific European state do not overlap or even intersect with those of the intergovernmental organization of which they are a member. The conflict in Iraq in 2003 became a significant case in point as different policies and approaches were highlighted by then-United States Secretary of Defense Donald Rumsfeld who distinguished between 'old' and 'new' Europe. He felt that France and Germany resisted the

American foreign policy in the Middle East while the countries that had more recently joined the European Union were identifying more closely with the American view. Of course, military issues are a particularly sensitive area of sovereignty, and though the North Atlantic Treaty Organization (NATO) includes many, if not most, of the Western European powers of the EU, it does not include all, making the military diplomacy of the Union one of the more complicated areas in which to agree action. The important point, as indicated in the diagram, is that the European Union goes beyond the traditional concepts of domestic vs. foreign, or what international relations theory often calls the "great divide" (Hill 2003, Clark 1999, Halliday 1994, among others) by creating or rather formalizing two layers of interaction. These could, more accurately, be called the 'inner-national' world of relations between states within the European Union, but beyond the separate nation-states and including the Union's communications with its own members, and the 'outer-foreign' level of relations between the EU and other intergovernmental organizations (again, to distinguish EU relations from the 'foreign' relations of each individual member state to every other state outside its borders). Such issues have been explored by various scholars (e.g. Huijgh and Duke in Davis and Melissen, 2013) in an effort to understand this multilayered statecraft both in terms of strategy and tactic, and reflected in Community diplomacy.

The Transatlantic model, by way of comparison, remains more 'traditional' and more 'state-centric' even as the EU evolved 'beyond' these concepts. The EU has now become a 'post-national' actor conducting a diplomacy that is 'post-Westphalian' in its experiments with majority voting, and has been developing such an open model of decision-making that the type/number of identity of the actors in the process has become much broader (Van Ham in Davis and Melissen, 2013, 157-158). Interestingly, this may be another area where the idea of horizontal and vertical interaction discussed previously may be useful as the 'old' and 'new' methods of diplomacy continue to mingle in what Hocking suggests are "complex patterns" that "cut across time periods, producing patterns of change at three interrelated levels of the diplomatic environment: the global, national and regional" (Hocking et al., 2012, 12). Certainly, we can see the way that types intersect and affect each other both internally—or within the specific system—and other states in other 'systems.'

Features of the Community Model

To summarize, the European Union, understood as the archetype of a Community model, has four features:

1. Treaty-based, Community members are bound not only by shared culture, values, or sense of national interest of 'international society,' but by international law and creating a space into which even 'outside' those norms could still be brought in—if the members agree;

2. A new concept of sovereignty that not only creates transparency, but allows mutual 'interference' in domestic affairs—entirely against the Westphalian basics of anarchy and autonomy;

3. A formal and shared policy-making structure that has effectively replaced distinct and clear institutions based on 'national interest' and regularly override internal decision-making processes; and

4. A lack of territoriality that permits a free flow of money, people (and ideas) across state boundaries.

Some of these features are distinctly European, but there are other practices that have no particular geographic/spatial aspect. For example, one might argue that NATO, mentioned above, operates in parallel to the Community model—though only in the subject area of the military. Equally, as Geoff Wiseman suggests, the practices of diplomacy at the United Nations have become so specialized that there is an argument as to whether this intergovernmental organization is forming a separate Community (Wiseman, 2015) but one that could be considered as operating within this kind of structure in the future. While one could speculate on the importance of treaties to the Community model or ask if geography and subject area are necessary features of the Union or only supporting factors, the point is that the nearly exclusive focus on the features of equality and sovereignty and the Westphalian state has led us to conflate 'Europe' with the 'West' and 'society' with 'advanced and democratic.' This, in turn, can obscure the significance of the shift in a stage of development at the state level and the creation of a separate model at the systemic level.

The Community Model and 'Classic' Theories

In light of these features and habits, and based on the classic narrative of international relations and diplomacy, the Community model becomes an anomaly. If state sovereignty is intended to protect the right of each state to non-interference in their internal affairs by other similar entities, the concessions that have been made across the different types of state activity—politics, culture, economics, and the military—within the Union are not only remarkable, but a watershed moment for the Westphalian state as traditionally conceived. The 'realist' version of European history inevitably includes the struggle of monarchies and the wars of religion, economic advantage, and territory. The constant condition of anarchy requires self-help or the need to anticipate and protect against the actions of others on the part of each state while national interest demands action in relation to 'outsiders' that is both defensive and offensive. However, this approach has been steadily giving way to a more 'liberal' or 'pluralist' understanding of complex interdependence and embedded relations. Questions such as whether to have a 'core' of stronger states that help drive a Europe that has 'multi-speeds' and 'variable geometry' for those less able to bear the economic, political, or often the regulatory weight of the Union, have been debated by politicians and policy experts all the way back to 1989. The goal of a unified (and peaceful) Europe, particularly as the Union discussed the issue of continued expansion to the East, was put above the issues presented by the inclusion of countries at very different levels of development. Translated into international relations theory, such ideas readily confirm liberal ideas of progress, normative ideals, and institutional alliances designed to move Europe to a more open and 'advanced' form of engagement.

Strengths and Weaknesses of the Community Model

In its favor, the Community model as a postmodern, peace-driven ideal looks enticing and part of a wider trend identified as regionalization and that seems to be steadily increasing. On the other hand, it seems difficult, if not impossible, to replicate such a structure given that the incentive was two world wars that deeply scarred the region and arguably prepared people to pool aspects of sovereignty that were once deemed fundamental and indivisible. Thus, the Community model of state interaction and diplomatic structure is not without its own challenges.

For example, the ideas of 'inner-national' and 'outer-foreign' present endless diplomatic challenges in terms of coordination and control given the need to operate at every level simultaneously and in real time. The practical world of European politics is far more complex than any model could represent as the political, economic, and cultural outcomes are mixed, with both winners and losers regardless of the model by which they are negotiated. The daily triumphs and tragedies, from the falling Berlin Wall in 1989 and the opening ceremonies of the 2012 London Olympic Games, to austerity protests that began in Greece in 2010 and Syrian refugees literally dying to reach Europe to escape a civil war that began in their country in 2011, will be dealt with, not by the strong sovereign, territorially-bounded, state on its own, but by a group whose people consciously decided that a shared form of governance, beyond the form of state that was invented there, was more important.

This may go some way toward explaining why the Union has not, until relatively recently in its history, begun to seriously grapple with the question of creating a shared diplomatic corps. Yet, from the point of view of the arguments made here, the fact they have begun such a process supports the suggestion that this is a distinct stage in the evolution of the European states-system, and further, that it represents a form of diplomacy reflective of this model while remaining true to the purpose of diplomatic communication: representation, negotiation, and dialogue as evidenced by the activities of the Union across all the 'types' discussed.

Whatever the ongoing tensions in the Community model, the European states-system has clearly evolved from a fundamentally state-centric Westphalian 'society' to a Community model of interaction that is more inclusive, less bound by traditional definitions of statehood and statecraft. Arguably, this 'liberal'—but more important for this argument—'enmeshed' form of governance produces a diplomacy that continues the process of "communication and managing of relations between polities" that Iver Neumann suggests may be the real basis for the next layer of development in a "global diplomacy" (Neumann, 2012).

Transatlantic Diplomacy

Turning to the Transatlantic model, the relationship between the United Kingdom and the United States is currently the best example of the effects the traditional diplomatic narrative for an understanding of specific bilateral relations. At its core, the standard story of the UK/US 'special relationship' is one of shared enemies, military prowess, and intelligence-sharing among elites. If the Community model is a liberal/pluralist template, the Transatlantic model, and specifically the UK/US relationship, is essentially a realist interpretation of 'high' politics that asserts a linear history of 'progress.'

Thus, in many ways, the "post-Cold War narrative" (Shaw, 2000) or the 'shoulder-to-shoulder' view of UK/US relations commonly found in the popular press, follows the shape of the debates in international relations and diplomacy from Part I quite closely. First, as ministers, and later, as ambassadors, diplomats between the United States and the United Kingdom have been providing the official channel of communication between governments, presidents, and prime ministers from the moment envoys, John Adams of the United States and George Hammond of the United Kingdom, were sent across the Atlantic in 1785 and 1791 respectively to represent their governments to their transatlantic opposite numbers. There was an identifiable step-change in the diplomacy of the post-World War I era, another such shift at the end of World War II (led by changes demanded of Europe by the United States), and still another at the end of the Cold War (this time led, to a certain degree, by the United Kingdom, and Europe more broadly, as the European Union began to take real shape). Thus, the customary view that the evolution in diplomacy follows that of the state and is related to periods of conflict, remains intact.

The problem is that, by default, this timeline and the relatively narrow role this construct leaves for diplomacy has two damaging consequences. First, state-centricity leads to a focus on bilateral boundaries rather than seeing the transatlantic relationship as part of a wider community of states, and that is changed by the constant 'inter-*re*actions' between levels and actors on the horizontal or vertical plane.

This leads to a second problem in that, by holding to a 'divide' between internal and external, or foreign and domestic, other key structures such as the foreign ministry or the offices of the president and prime minister are not scrutinized in light of this analysis. Yet, in the case of Transatlantic diplomacy, even a cursory examination demonstrates a level of parallel development and a resulting entwined relationship throughout their history that is difficult to predict from the traditional literature. For example, the UK Foreign Office and the US State Department both made significant changes to their foreign affairs structures as early as 1782. They again made very similar changes in terms of professionalization in the 1850s, and in the 1870s they both reorganized again to take regional and departmental functions into account. During and after WWI and WWII, both sides made significant changes to their teams and their structures as a result of the conflicts, but perhaps the most obvious and most recent example occurred in 2006, when, within weeks of each other, Condoleezza Rice, then US Secretary of State, and Jack Straw, then UK Foreign Secretary, announced "Transformational" (www.state.gov) and "Active" Diplomacy (www.gov.uk), respectively. Without any overt reference to each other, these initiatives were designed to prepare their departments for the 'global' world and went about it in almost identical ways. Similarly, the offices of president and prime minister have steadily drawn power towards their respective centers in terms of their own system, while remaining more consistently open to each other at a personal level in ways not conceivable between any other pair of countries or leaders.

Politics, Culture, Economics, and the Military in the Transatlantic Model

Looking back, it is difficult to say whether these changes were deliberate, or whether, as powers with a clearly 'global' reach, the UK and the US were simply reacting similarly to the same external shifts in social power, be it

BOX 9.2

Timeline of UK/US Diplomacy

1782. Office of the Foreign Secretary was established in United States and the United Kingdom abolished the 'Northern' and 'Southern'—splitting the responsibility between foreign and domestic concerns.

1815. Congress of Vienna recognized the sending of envoys to other countries

1850s. Both the US and the UK began to professionalize their services by introducing an exam system (which initially failed in the US).

1870. Both US and UK reorganized departmental functions.

1881. UK emulated regional system.

1893. American Legations abroad became Embassies—with reciprocal recognition provided to representatives from other countries sent to Washington. Sir Julian Pauncefote, British Minister in Washington at the time, quickly announced himself as the first Ambassador to the United States, ensuring himself the position of **doyen** in the diplomatic corps.

1900s. Both services again underwent significant re-structuring as the services tried to elevate their role from 'clerical' to 'advisory' in the policy process.

WWI & WWII. Both countries underwent significant change due to war with WWII becoming a point of much closer transatlantic coordination

2006. Within weeks of each other, Condoleezza Rice, US Secretary of State, and Jack Straw, UK Foreign Secretary, announced Transformational and Active Diplomacy, respectively. Without any direct reference to each other, these initiatives were designed to prepare their departments for the 'global' age in almost identical ways.

political, cultural, economic, or military. The net result remains the same in that, not only have these two countries created an infrastructure that can operate jointly, in parallel or at tangents when the need arises, they are, on many levels 'friends' in a way that overcomes the private/public divide implied by the term to form horizontal and deeply reciprocal relations that are enmeshed (Devere and Smith, 2010).

As indicated in Figure 9.2, this version of 'friendship' is not merely among political, economic, or even the media elites, but also closely aligned from the top to the bottom of the social spectrum and across the full range of levels in terms of industry, civic groups, and individuals. Following the logic of types it therefore seems obvious that the bonds go well beyond the usual cultural affinities that are pointed out as 'special,' e.g., language or religion, and that the associations in politics and culture run similarly deep. Some may argue, however, that it is in the realm of the military that the UK and US have achieved a connection that is even more 'post-modern' than the European Union, in that the transatlantic relationship puts great store in the 'interoperability' of their military capacity and further in their joint/shared actions around the world.

An interesting question to ask, given that the European Union has a relatively difficult time with its external military operations, is whether the ability to go beyond sovereignty in the realm of state security might be considered the 'real' test of being able to overcome the constraints of sovereignty to be 'more' or 'less' advanced as a state, despite the fact it may also suggest a more 'realist' or militaristic approach to foreign relations as a whole.

Features of the Transatlantic Model

To summarize, the three main features of the Transatlantic model are:

1. The possibility of retaining a strong notion of sovereignty while still allowing for a mutual 'porous-ness' not only between diplomats abroad, but between all agencies and departments (political, economic, cultural, etc.) at home;
2. A policy process driven by heads-of-state and their entourages, supported by officials not separated by demarcations of foreign versus domestic, appointee versus civil servant, generalist versus specialist; and
3. The opportunity for a more stakeholder-oriented 'dialogue of states' or diplomacy that accepts there are different areas of expertise in different states, while recognizing the different cultures and levels of responsibility required of the different voices—including non-state actors.

For many of these features, and given the examples offered, it seems that this kind of 'special' or Transatlantic relationship is easier to achieve in small groups and perhaps only in pairs, as the level of trust required for such enmeshed behavior may be difficult to replicate. That said, it seems entirely possible that states can have more than one 'special' or linked relationship. Further, that the features traditionally identified as part of 'specialness' may be more accurately identified as functions of the state and thus reflected in its diplomacy,—and more importantly here, suggest the possibility of a different basis for a society in which norms and values are clearly present, making the 'pooling' of some features of sovereignty unnecessary.

The Transatlantic Model and 'Classic' Theory

The role that different countries play in the international arena—and the interpretations of those roles by others—have been changing rapidly in recent years. One underexplored effect of globalization on the state is the breaking down of characterizations or stereotypes of one state's behavior in relation to another. The change in the role of the United States is a particularly apt example of a state that is now, more than ever, seen as an overreaching hegemon not only in North America or the Western hemisphere, but in the world. Understood as a realist **superpower** *or a power that can project power (usually military) on a global scale without challenge* and thus little need or desire to listen to the needs of others, many are suspicious of American motives for action, even when the intention is humanitarian. However, the opposite line of attack from a more 'liberal' perspective is also common. The United States, as arguably the world's most powerful 'progressive' world leader, is expected to intervene with money, force, or both in far more situations than the United States could possibly take on.

The real conclusion that may be drawn from such observations is that there are many layers to the actions of each entity. A 'realist' or 'pluralist' analysis can be useful as a broad category, but only goes so far in terms of an interpretation of statecraft. Moreover, if we can so clearly see these differences in the current day, we should be careful to ensure we don't assume a monolithic character of states or entities as they conducted diplomacy in the past.

Strengths and Weaknesses of the Transatlantic Model

The strength of the Transatlantic model is perhaps best demonstrated by the longevity of its quintessential example: UK/US relations. There is a common perception in both places that the world's issues are also of national/domestic concern and an existing pattern of collaboration across every level of government that regularly leads to joint action as well as parallel, but individual action in a variety of international fora. They hold, and often share the burden for a military might that can be brought to bear in any part of the world and remains nearly unmatched, while their domestic situations remain stable. However, great strength can sometimes hide great weakness. Looking around the world, the power of such a friendship or partnership of 'equals' is clearly sought by others as evidenced in the way new states enter the international arena—in the post-colonial/post-Soviet context or those seeking to take advantage of their rising economic status. Such states, and even non-states or other kinds of entity, are tremendously anxious to protect the more 'traditional' features of statehood, rather than engage in this more 'relational' way.

To replicate such an enmeshed relationship requires a level of trust (and reciprocation) that may be more than most states could sustain, and perhaps impossible to achieve, in a fast-changing global world. Even if the

Transatlantic model is based on more than simplistic 'cultural affinity,' as some suggest, the notion that many other states could match even that first step seems unlikely. Similarly, the idea that, as states develop and become more 'advanced,' they might automatically become part of a large number of separate and intense relationships around the world does raise concerns as well as possibilities. First, historical partnerships could become burdensome as political, economic, and social realities change and those deemed allies could easily be forced, by circumstance, to change their position and thus create new conflicts. Second, intense but essentially bilateral or small group multilateral relationships may create situations in which the partners become less open to arguments or interests that run against those of their partners and therefore close themselves off to debate. Finally, such relationships may always remain in the shadows of the quintessential UK/US special relationship and be found wanting in terms of their comparatively limited power and scope, though it is possible to envisage a situation in which the idea of a strong state with 'special relationships' might continue to grow as the power of the US and the UK continues to wanes and/or increasingly looks out of place or out dated in the 'global' world that is evolving.

From Europe to Everywhere?

The study of diplomacy has undoubtedly been heavily Western-/Western European-centric, a problematic feature that is often compounded and reinforced by the tendency to privilege tactic and form over purpose and process. The 'classic' or 'traditional' narrative has a clear tendency to tell the story of diplomacy almost as an adjunct to that of the Westphalian form of the state. The paradigms of realism and liberalism provide lenses for policy discussion and debate while the debate of 'new' vs. 'old' ensures that the changes and challenges of statecraft are identified and explored. The presumption of international relations theory has generally followed the bias of the English School that the European states-system provided the basis of all states, and the features of anarchy, hierarchy, and territory apply consistently and equally to all such entities, thus ignoring two important aspects of the narrative, even within Europe itself.

First, the multilayered processes of globalization and the events of the post-Cold War era have increasingly exposed the fact that the state (at least in its Westphalian form) is changing and it is therefore only logical to assume that all the institutions based on that form of governance are also changing. So far, a common response to the debate as to the causes and effects of globalization directly on diplomacy has been scattershot and the creation of more 'adjectival' categories of diplomacy: "business, city, citizen, sub-national, non-governmental organization, civil society" (Hocking, 2012, 77) to name but a few.

Yet, even if we leave to one side the action or event-based categories of sport, dollar, and shuttle diplomacy, there are still other suggestions as to 'new' forms such as: para-diplomatic bodies for those operating below or outside state channels (Weisbrode), pluralization of actors in the diplomatic realm (Jentleson), polylateral to convey the sense that both bi- and even multi-lateral are terms now out of date with non-state actors behaving in 'diplomatic' ways (Wiseman), integrative systems that endeavor to take as many 'voices' as possible into the process (Hocking et al., 2012), and finally guerilla diplomacy that suggests more of a quick, sharp action rather than long, drawn out activities of diplomats in the past (Copeland). Intriguingly, the response of new phraseology is no more 'new' than the process of globalization itself as even the first American ambassador, John Adams, used the term "militia diplomacy" in honor of the American defeat of the British at Lexington and Concord in 1775 and to describe his own diplomatic tactics overseas (McCullough, 2001, 253–255). However, and as Brian Hocking warns, the longer we make this list, the more danger there is of losing the content we have, as he suggests that this way of dealing with change at the state and system level has the potential to "lead us down the road toward emptying diplomacy of much of its meaning" (Hocking, 2012, 77).

Second, the static nature of the traditional narrative has also meant that some of the most basic assumptions and assertions as to states-systems, international society, the development of the state itself—and, most importantly, the relationship between the state and the institution of diplomacy—have been left to atrophy. The European states-system may have been a turning point in the development of states, systems, and societies, but none of these entities have stopped evolving. The European states-system has produced two different models with consequently different forms of diplomatic interaction. The Community and Transatlantic models of diplomacy are both largely Westphalian state-based. Debate is couched in sovereign terms and hierarchy and territory, while very different in each case, remain strong drivers of action.

However, by examining the European states-system more closely and establishing the idea of the Community and Transatlantic models as steps in the evolution of the European system—and given the confident assumption that all states are, at some level, 'European' in nature, or at least 'Westphalian' by default—it may be possible to ask if other states are not also on this evolutionary trajectory and where else in the world might states become a 'community' or create the bonds of a 'transatlantic' relationship?

In this context, it is perhaps more useful to start with the Transatlantic model in that its closer adherence to the concepts of sovereignty suggest that more states are following this pattern of development. Various examples were offered such as the United States and Canada, Australia and New Zealand, or Brazil and Cuba. Unfortunately, international relations as a discipline too often ignores the evidence of such relationships unless they are between a 'great power' and a middle or small power as the asymmetry of such a relationship is of interest. At the other extreme, relations between small and medium powers are often deemed a subcategory of their own, and often discussed as part of a "jumble" and as a struggle between great and small powers (Cooper, 2013), the dynamics or "ambiguities" of being a "middle power" (Stephen 2013, Scott 2013, Behringer 2013), a form of "sub-state" diplomacy (Jones and Royles, 2012), or, more often, as a subset of American special relations and alliance theory rather than as specific relationships in their own right (Dumbrell and Schafer, 2009; and Gamble, 2003). Unfortunately, an exploration of the internal structure and shared foreign policy goals is beyond the discussion here, but it would be helpful to have more research on 'special' relations (even if they don't stretch across the Atlantic) so as to pursue the importance of embedded models of diplomatic action. Certainly, the example of the importance of the bilateral relationships that the United States has built, destroyed, and built again in the "war on terrorism" since September 11, 2001 illustrates this point aptly as close, even 'special' relationships were unable to take the strain of real-world events.

Some of the same challenges apply in any search for other states that may be developing in the direction of the Community model, though there has been a growing number of scholars seeking to understand what they see as the potential for more "regional worlds" in a more "global international relations" (Acharya, 2014) or a "decentred globalism" (Buzan, 2011) in a world without superpowers. Calls for action in both South America and Southeast Asia (as well as some moves in Africa) seem important steps towards a more community-based polity in the future, but remain nascent ideas at this point especially as the European Union, the champion of this idea, deals increasingly with a crisis of order and unity.

Conclusion

This chapter has argued that, by pushing the English School's idea of the European states-system to the next stage, it is possible to identify two models of state and diplomatic interaction and practice: Community and Transatlantic. Returning for a moment to the assumption that the European state models are the most advanced, identifying the clear difference between the two models that have evolved from this basic pattern may be helpful in that they broaden the overall assumption of uniqueness while remaining within Western parameters.

If the assertion that there are now (at least) two models in operation, and there could be at least three options in terms of the future. The first is the European states-system, a starting point for most states, and while differences have emerged, states or other entities will continue to evolve along that line of development. The assumption being that states, like children, may be very different from each other, but they 'grow up' in similar ways. The second option is that one model becomes even more prominent, perhaps even 'taking over' from the other. In current circumstances this could mean that the Community model may implode due to internal strife or the pressure of joint action. Alternatively, the Transatlantic model may 'soften' and broaden as more trade agreements create a web of connections that cannot be overcome by a fading hegemon. A third option is that the assumption that all states are somehow 'European' at the level of state DNA is flawed, but that it is not too late for non-Western states to choose to operate with a 'Western base' while (re)discovering features of other/previous systems that are more clearly aligned with their own history and culture.

In an effort to arrest the trend to name and rename the new and newer tactics of the 'old' and 'new' diplomacy, the next step here is to propose that if diplomacy is to move towards a more 'global' understanding, there must be some agreement on the process*es* of globalization and the forms of social power that created the various "polymorphous" entities of governance throughout history which have all "crystallized" in "different and competing forms" (Mann, Vol. 3, 2012, 1). In other words, before settling for one of two essentially European-centric models that are both based on a theory of diplomacy that relies on the Westphalian state rather than a broader understanding of social sources of power, the idea that other/older forms still exist and can be rediscovered and repurposed for global politics should be explored. The benefit of this option is that it seems to be the current direction of the increasing number of countries now on the rise.

CHAPTER REVIEW QUESTIONS

1. What two models have developed from the English School's European states-system?

2. What are the basic features of the Transatlantic model?
3. How does the Community model go beyond the Westphalian model on ideas of sovereignty?
4. What are the weaknesses of the Transatlantic Model?
5. Describe the challenge of the 'inner-national' level of European politics.

SEMINAR/ESSAY QUESTIONS

1. On what basis are the United Kingdom and the United States said to have a 'special' relationship?
2. Could other countries create a 'special relationship'?
3. What role does diplomacy play in these different models?
4. "The Community model is inherently weak and cannot withstand the pressure of a global world." Discuss.
5. Which of these models do you think will continue into the future and why?

References and Further Reading

Acharya, Amitav. "Global International Relations (IR) and Regional Worlds." *International Studies Quarterly*. 58 (2014): 647-659.

Allen, H.C. *Great Britain and the United States; A History of Anglo-American Relations 1783-1952*. New York: St Martin's Press, 1955.

Behringer, Ronald. "The Dynamics of Middlepowermanship." *The Journal of Diplomacy and International Relations*. Summer/Fall. 23-35 (2013): 9-22.

Bull, Hedley. *The Anarchical Society: A Study of Order in World Politics*. Basingstoke: Macmillan, 1977.

Butterfield, Herbert. "The Historical States-Systems." January 8-11 The British Committee on the Theory of International Politics. Chatham House Papers. 1965.

Butterfield, Herbert. "The New Diplomacy and Historical Diplomacy" in *Diplomatic Investigations: Essays in the Theory of International Politics*. Herbert Butterfield and Martin Wight (eds). Harvard University Press, 1968.

Buzan, Barry. "The Inaugural Kenneth Waltz Annual Lecture: A World Order without Superpowers: Decentred Globalism." *International Relations*. 25:1 (2011): 3-25.

Clark, Ian. *Globalisation and International Relations Theory*. Oxford: Oxford University Press. 1999.

Cooper, David. "Somewhere between Great and Small: Disentangling the Conceptual Jumble of Middle, Regional and 'Niche' powers." *The Journal of Diplomacy and International Relations*. Summer/Fall (2013): 23-35.

Cooper, Andrew, Brian Hocking, and William Maley (eds). *Global Governance and Diplomacy: Worlds Apart?* Basingstoke: Palgrave Macmillan, 2008.

Cooper, Robert. *The Breaking of Nations: Order and Chaos in the 21st Century*. London: Atlantic Press, 2003.

Davis, Mai'a and Jan Melissen (eds). *European Diplomacy: Soft Power at Work.* New York: Palgrave Macmillan, 2013.

Devere, Heather and Graham Smith. *Political Studies Review.* Vol. 8 (2010): 341-356.

Dumbrell, John and Axel Schafer (eds). *America's 'Special Relationships': Foreign and Domestic Aspects of the Politics of Alliance.* Abingdon: Routledge, 2009.

Gamble, Andrew. *Between Europe and America: The Future of British Politics.* Basingstoke: Palgrave, 2003.

Garten-Ash, Timothy. "The Crisis of Europe: how the Union came together and why it's falling apart." *Foreign Affairs.* September/October, 2012.

Hall, Ian. "Building the global network: The reform of the Foreign and Commonwealth Office under New Labour." *British Journal of Politics and International Relations,* Vol. 15 (2013): 228-245.

Halliday, Fred. *Rethinking International Relations.* Basingstoke: Palgrave, 1994.

Hamilton, Keith and Richard Langhorne.. *The Practice of Diplomacy: Its Evolution, Theory & Administration.* London and New York: Routledge, 1995.

Hill, Christopher. *The Changing Politics of Foreign Policy.* Basingstoke: Palgrave Macmillan, 2003.

Hocking, Brian, Jan Melissen, Shaun Riordan, and Paul Sharp. "Futures for Diplomacy: Integrative Diplomacy in the 21st Century." Clingendael: Netherlands Institute of International Relations, 2012.

Hocking, Brian. "(Mis)Leading Propositions About 21st Century Diplomacy," *Crossroads: The Macedonian Foreign Policy Journal.* Vol. III, No. 2 (April-October, 2012): 73-92.

Jentleson, Bruce. "Accepting Limits: How to Adapt to a Copernican World." *Democracy Journal.* (Winter, 2012): 38-45.

Jones, Richard Wyn and Elin Royles. "Wales in the World: Intergovernmental Relations and Sub-state Diplomacy." *British Journal of Politics and International Relations.* Vol. 14 (2012): 250-269.

Jönsson, Christer and Martin Hall. *Essence of Diplomacy.* Basingstoke: Palgrave Macmillan, 2005.

Kerr, Pauline and Geoffrey Wiseman. *Diplomacy in a Globalizing World.* Oxford: Oxford University Press, 2013.

Mann, Michael. *Volume 1. The Sources of Social Power: A history of power from the beginning to A.D. 1760.* Cambridge: Cambridge University Press, 1986.

Mann, Michael. Chapter 25: "Neither Nation-State nor Globalism" in *Globalization: Critical Concepts in Sociology Vol. II: The Nation-State and International Relations.* Roland Robertson and Kathleen White (eds). London: Routledge, 2003.

McCullough, David. *John Adams.* London: Simon & Schuster, 2001.

McGrew, Anthony. "Making Sense of Globalization" in *The Globalization of World Politics: Introduction to International Relations.* John Baylis and Steve Smith (eds). Oxford: Oxford University Press, 2011.

Neumann, Iver. "Chapter 1: Globalization and Diplomacy" in *Global Governance and diplomacy: Worlds apart?* Cooper, Andrew, Brian Hocking, and William Maley (eds). Basingstoke: Palgrave Macmillan, 2008.

Neumann, Iver B. "Euro-centric diplomacy: Challenging but manageable." *European Journal of International Relations.* 18 (2) (2012): 299-317.

Nye, Joseph. *Soft Power: The Means to Success in World Politics*. New York: Public Affairs, 2004.

Rana, Kishan. *Inside Diplomacy*. New Delhi: Manas Publications, 2014.

Rana, Kishan. *The 21st Century Ambassador: Plenipotentiary to Chief Executive*. New Delhi: Oxford University Press, 2005.

Reus-Smit, Christian. *The Moral Purpose of the State: Culture, Social Identity, and Institutional Rationality in International Relations*. Princeton: Princeton University Press, 1999.

Reynolds, David. "A Special Relationship? America, Britain and the International Order since the Second World War." *International Affairs*. Volume 62, No1, (Winter 1985-86): 1-20.

Riordan, Shaun. *The New Diplomacy*. London: Polity, 2003.

Scott, David. "Australia as a Middle Power: Ambiguities of Role and Identity." *The Journal of Diplomacy and International Relations*. (Summer/Fall, 2013): 23-35; 111-122.

Sharp, Paul. *Diplomatic Theory of International Relations*. Cambridge: Cambridge University Press, 2009.

Shaw, Martin. "The state of globalization: toward a theory of state transformation." *Review of International Political Economy*. 4:3 (Autumn, 1997): 497-513.

Shaw, Martin. *Theory of the Global State: Globality as an Unfinished Revolution*. Cambridge: Cambridge University Press, 2000.

Smith, Michael. "European Responses to US Diplomacy: 'Special relationship,' transatlantic governance and world order." Paper presented to the *European Union Studies Association*. Boston, MA March 2-5, 2011.

Stephen, Matthew. "The Concept and Role of Middle Powers during Global Rebalancing." *The Journal of Diplomacy and International Relations*. (Summer/Fall 2013): 23-35; 36–52.

Thomas, Rebecca. "Tears and Unity at Palace Tribute," BBC News Online, September 13, 2001.

Watson, Adam. "The Indian states system." British Committee on the Theory of International Politics. Chatham House Papers. April 21-23, 1967.

Watson, Adam. *The Evolution of International Society: A Comparative Historical Analysis*. London: Routledge, 1993/2002.

Weisbrode, Kenneth. *Old Diplomacy Revisited*. New York: Palgrave Macmillan, 2014.

Wiseman, Geoffrey. "Diplomatic practices at the United Nations." *Cooperation and Conflict*. April 13, 2015: 1-18.

Websites

Jewish Virtual Library: http://www.jewishvirtuallibrary.org/jsource/Holocaust/uprising1.html

Rice, Condoleezza. "Transformational Diplomacy": http://www.state.gov/r/pa/prs/ps/2006/59339.htm and "Georgetown University address": http://www.state.gov/secretary/rm/2006/59306.htm. January 2006.

UK Government Office. *Active Diplomacy for a Changing World: The UK's International Priorities*. Foreign and Commonwealth Office White Paper on International Strategy Priorities, 2006. https://www.gov.uk/government/organisations/foreign-commonwealth-office

United States Holocaust Memorial Museum. http://www.ushmm.org/

10 A Relational Model of Diplomacy

BY ALISON HOLMES

China

> *"Ici repose un géant endormi, laissez le dormir,*
> *car quand il s'éveillera, il étonnera le monde."*
>
> *"Here lies a sleeping giant, let him sleep,*
> *for when he wakes, he will shock the world."*

Almost exactly two centuries later, there is much to support Napoleon Bonaparte's oft-quoted comment as China moves slowly, but surely, from the shadows of the international community to the foreground—if relatively reluctantly. Joining the World Trade Organization in 2001 was a major step in this process, heralding the idea that China was willing to be bound by international agreement and decisions taken by an outside body. While three short years later, China moved on the cultural front both by starting the process of rehabilitating Confucius, and by creating Institutes in his name primarily in the West, but around the world. However, it is perhaps the dawning recognition of China's power, not only in its traditional sphere, but across an increasing reach in regions such as Africa where trade with China reached a new high: US$198.5 billion in 2012, with one million Chinese people living in Africa while in 2015 China pledged to invest $250 billion over the next decade in Latin America.

India

If Napoleon felt that leaving China to sleep was the prudent course of action, he had other plans for India and sought to bring its diversity and riches under French rule. His two campaigns in pursuit of that aim ultimately failed (in much the same way as the plans of many others from both the West and the East to control the subcontinent), and India continues to find its own way as the world's most populous democracy and second largest population. India, like China, also extends its reach through other means, with cities such as Bangaluru being declared by *Business Week* in 2001 to be "India's Silicon Valley," and the Confederation of Indian Industry (CII) and the World Trade organization (WTO) reporting India's investments in Africa at more than $50 billion in 2013. Yet the best is, apparently, still to come, as 2025 has been predicted as the date that India will become an economic 'superpower.'

The question for both of these ancient cultures is whether history simply finds new locations for the classic tales of expansion, over-extension and ultimate decline, or if a different path, based on different traditional values, can take these rising powers in a truly non-Westphalian direction.

International Societies of the East

Adam Watson of the English School and others have argued that the Indian and Chinese states-systems simply did not evolve in the same way as the European states-system. They further suggest that these systems did not form their own international society and, because they essentially stopped pursuing power beyond their regional base, were absorbed or overtaken by outsiders (and the European system). This may be true in various respects, but it overlooks at least the potential for these states-systems to develop their own society and a distinct form of statehood and statecraft. In short, the English School neglected the possibility that there might be other diploma*cies* based in cultures, values, and traditions beyond Europe. The suggestion here is that, just as the Community and Transatlantic models both evolved from the European states-system, it is entirely conceivable (and increasingly likely) that other states-systems may have adapted and adjusted their external relations to accommodate the overweening power of the West, but on another level, continued to operate in their own way and arguably to develop a distinct model based on a long regional history and significant cultural diffusion.

This chapter reexamines states-systems that have been effectively sidelined by mainstream interpretations of states and statecraft, and goes on to develop a non-Western 'relational' model of interaction. The argument is that the non-Western world has developed 'societies,' based not on the binary juxtapositions between anarchy and order, hierarchy and chaos, territory and center, equality and relative position, but created a model that begins with an entirely different perspective and operates with definitions of power and structure in a much more flexible way. This alternative recognizes anarchy, but allows both hierarchy and heterarchy to coexist; it envisions a hub of power that does not require rigid boundaries, but holds a center of gravity and operates through the spokes of a wheel that emanate to the 'rim' and back again; a governance structure that maintains power not solely through the threat of coercion, but through a complex system of communication, balance, and awareness of interrelated and layered interests that requires a specific and 'relational' form of diplomacy.

If the Transatlantic and Community models were built on the traditional notion of the European states-system, the Indian and Chinese states-systems suggest the possibility of a third model, one that is based on a more 'realistic realism' in that it is neither blind to the power inherent in any situation and therefore prepares for, and defends against, such encroachment, nor unaware of the complicated connections between different sources of power. In short, this model takes all these aspects into account as an integral part of the statecraft in a more holistic way than hierarchical/binary systems allow. However, to understand this alternative perspective, some structural considerations must first be taken into account before returning to the model itself.

Structure: The hegemony of hierarchy and the possibility of heterarchy

During the discussion as to the development of the state and stages in that process, there has not yet been an investigation of the underlying assumptions of such theories in terms of development and what archeologists call "social complexity." Theory is once again crucial to the outcome in that many, if not most, or even all, of our 'geometric' theories of settlement of state development are implicitly based on ideas of expansion, power, and authority. Without going too far into the world of anthropology, the point is that many such notions also have an in-built assumption of hierarchy as demonstrated by a focus on a "vertical relationship" and "chiefdom language" such as "domination, stratification, control...war, dependent, elite and prestige" (White, 1995, 103). As Carole Crumley, an archeologist and cultural anthropologist, points out, a lack of awareness as to the dominance and subordination inherent in concepts of social complexity poses two dangers both in terms of various features and structures of rank. The first problem is obvious in that such a single-minded focus can also create a blind spot both in terms of theory and understanding of real-world behavior. Second, there are actually two types of hierarchy: **scalar** (*in which any level can affect any other rather than going through a single channel*), and **control** (*levels of control and chains of causation as found in the American judicial system*). Crumley argues that these two types of hierarchy have been conflated in many different fields leading to a gap in the understanding of structure and basic misinterpretations of causal relationships (Crumley, 1995, 2).

The second problem is the juxtaposition of hierarchy with chaos or the assumption that hierarchy is somehow synonymous with order. She uses the example of an oak tree or a symphony, which are clearly not 'hierarchical,' but do have a rich and elegant structure. For the social sciences, she contends, this results in a tendency to declare a transition in the structures of hierarchy as disorder or "periods of decline or disintegration, such as the Dark Ages" rather than examining them as successive hierarchies or parallel structures. Crumley therefore puts forward the idea of heterarchy as a different **scale** or "*unit of analysis relative to the phenomenon as a whole. Effective scale is the scale at which structure among elements is perceived, and determines how they will be studied*" (Crumley, 1985, 176). Following on from the discussion of the cultural aspects of 'Time,' heterarchy presents the possibility of a more multilevel concept of order and of different spatial scales at various periods.

The term heterarchy was developed in 1945 by neurophysiologist Warren McCulloch, who observed that the human brain is not organized, as had been supposed, in a strict hierarchy, and further and even more crucially, that hierarchies and heterarchies can coexist (Crumley, 1995). His work helped to revolutionize information technology and artificial intelligence fields, but is also relevant here because it opens the idea that hierarchies are not the only alternative to egalitarian societies (O'Reily, 2003, 301). Both horizontal and vertical connections exist in social power networks, and these can be arranged and rearranged depending on the social context (Chureekamol, 2010, 47). Finally, that nonlinear and asymmetrical structures exist in which power can be ranked in a number of different ways or even "counterpoised" while still retaining what we would recognize as order (Crumley, 1985 & 1995).

Applying these ideas to ancient civilizations, Joyce White identifies four broad features of heterarchical societies: cultural pluralism; indigenous economies (household units and community-based, multi-centered, and overlapping); social status systems that include personal achievement rather than being derived solely along kinship lines; and conflict resolution and political centralization that are based on alliance formation rather than warfare—viewed as only a secondary strategy (White, 1995, 104).

International relations is not alone in generally neglecting alternative structures and, as both White and O'Reily point out, even archeology has not fully explored the effect that this kind of flexibility would have on the development of social complexity (White, 1995) or how the traditional "continuum" of social organization from the simple to the complex should be

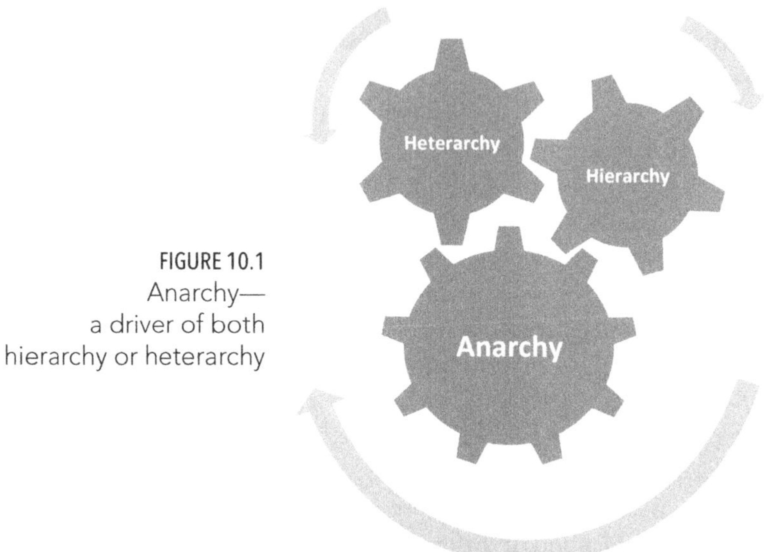

FIGURE 10.1 Anarchy—a driver of both hierarchy or heterarchy

re-visualized to incorporate the shifting power balances and coexisting hierarchies and heterarchies (O'Reily, 2003). However, and if, as Crumley suggests, heterarchy is both structure and condition and can coexist with hierarchy, the European or Westphalian concept of anarchy as currently understood is immediately called into question. (See Figure 10.1.)

In the effort to globalize our understanding of other states-systems, it may therefore be useful to suggest a reconfiguration of Watson's pendulum that swings from anarchy to empire and create, instead, a more open system that includes the potential for change and for the coexistence of different structures. As Watson's diagram suggests, the condition of anarchy may still apply, but the wheels that turn society are not limited to structures of hierarchy, and certainly not a single hierarchy built on European concepts, but a structure that could include separate, yet interacting hierarchies. The linearity of Western/European action would be replaced with multiple sites of power and interaction even if the condition of anarchy requires states to act as if they are ultimately alone.

In this light, it becomes clear as to why the mandala, outlined previously, plays a key role in Indian diplomacy, and while the mandala was also used in China, no strong connection was suggested at that point in terms of the depth of connection and the overlap between the Indian and Chinese approaches to statecraft. However, the evidence offered by anthropologists and archeologists suggests that the ancient mandala system was used throughout this region and therefore the connections they argue exist between social complexity and heterarchy to the ancient mandala system becomes very important to the development of of a relational model. As O.W. Wolters points out, "The map of earlier southeast Asia which evolved from prehistoric networks of small settlement[s] as revealed in historical records was a patchwork of often overlapping mandalas" (Wolters, 1999, 27). He goes on to suggest that these mandalas did not depend on size (though many were very large and covered a number of what today would be many different countries) or overwhelming military or physical power. Rather, each mandala viewed itself as unique and the center of their world, rather than creating a sense of being 'equal' to neighbors even despite physically overlapping spheres of influence (Wolters, 1999, 66). Mandalas relied on "networks of loyalties" to "men of prowess" (Wolters, 1999, 27), where the overlord has the prerogative to receive tribute-bearing envoys and to dispatch envoys to others in his sphere (Wolters, 1999, 28). Such men employed bards and poets in court to sing his praises as well as to disseminate information, propaganda (or what today would clearly be called 'public diplomacy') at home and abroad (Wolters, 1999, 116). Given this historical evidence, it is logical to assert the concept of heterarchy as the basis of an entirely different system or society and to connect the ancient practice of mandala governance or diplomacy to current ideas and thereby laying a foundation for a Relational model that represents and fundamental shift from the traditional or Western/European models.

The 'Traditional' Indian and Chinese States-Systems as the Basis of a Relational Model

In Part I, the idea of ancient or 'pristine' civilizations was outlined in relation to both the English School and the work of Michael Mann. However, for the purposes of exploring the Relational model, it is important to see, at least in a very broad sense, that India and China are both a part of a distinctly non-Western/European system, but more importantly have been interacting with each other as fellow great powers for centuries, thus making them part of a parallel and alternative story.

Since at least the first century, India and China engaged in trade and cultural exchange. Along the Silk Road and through Buddhist monks (as well as Hindu scholars), economic, religious, and political change and development can be traced to the early links between these two systems (Pant in Scott, 2011, 233). Chandra Bagchi suggests that India and China created "two zones of cultural influence" across eastern Asia and, given these zones were not "water-tight compartments," nor motivated by "imperialist designs" on each other, their methods were "so effective that artificial geographical and political boundaries set up during the last few centuries have not succeeded in destroying the links that connected the various groups in the past" (Wang and Sen, 2011, 183). While traditional colonial intervention and other forms of outside powers have interfered in the 'natural' development of these two rising powers there seems to be more to this story than the classic narrative would allow. For example, their recent efforts to build stronger bilateral relations, as well as the development of their own individual regional/international roles (Pant in Scott, 2011, 233), suggest that, rather than be subsumed by the traditional Westphalian/European systems or coopted into a Community or Transatlantic model, they have persistently operated a more relational style even as they continued to interact with other models on the international stage. Ironically, just as these rising powers are beginning to gain the power necessary to clearly differentiate themselves from the European models, the forces of globalization seem to be moving all states towards a more relational mode of interaction.

Ancient Indian culture moved slowly, but surely, via a number of routes—over the mountain passes to Eastern Turkestan and Tibet and over the sea to Burma, Indo-China, and Insulindia or maritime Southeast Asia, spreading Buddhist religion, art, Indian script, and Indian sciences while Sanskrit was studied by educated people in many far-flung places (Wang and Sen, 2011). In China specifically, Buddhist missionaries attracted a great deal of attention and gained followers despite, at times, being specifically prohibited by those in power. This religious channel also formed the foundation of early diplomacy as monks (Hindu and Buddhist) traveled between the courts to offer tribute, relay messages and, particularly in the case of monks in China, to translate the Sanskrit texts of Buddhism into Chinese. Blazing a trail for the Jesuit priests who would come much later, there are at least two periods of relatively intense exchange between 643-748 AD (until unrest made travel even more difficult and China lost its hold on a number of small kingdoms that had, to that point, been in their sphere of influence and helped facilitate travel), then again between 900-100 AD (Wang and Sen, 2011).

The role of Sanskrit is particularly important as it became a shared language between these two states-systems and "granted power to the royal voice" (Wolters, 1999, 118). The power of language is particularly important, according to Wolters, because the center of the mandala was both a political and a spiritual authority. Language also enabled the center to conduct the two most necessary skills: political intelligence and diplomacy. Wolters argues that the center of the mandala rests on the ability of the leader to remain connected to the entire network at all times, but, and in contrast to the

Western model, not purely to control, but primarily to communicate clearly. Context and personal relationships are crucial in the management of a mandala or heterarchy and while both cultures are largely based on the strictly hierarchical religious aspects of Hinduism or Confucianism, the relational aspect of mandala statecraft cannot be overemphasized.

Culture, Military, Politics and Economics in the Relational Model

Modern India and China are clearly not operating on some grand idea of a mandala system per se, but many scholars look to these historical traditions to explain aspects of Asian statecraft and suggest most are still present in contemporary policy. For these purposes, it is important to examine these aspects as further 'evidence' of the types of diplomacy—cultural, military, political and economic, discussed in Part II and in the context of the two models that have evolved from the European system into the foundation of much of what is considered to be the fundamental structure of international society today.

The first question that many would ask regards the importance and relevance of cultural difference, as that would seem to be the clearest point of departure from Western norms and visible in every day interaction. There is a large body of literature dealing with what is often called the 'other' or how we interact with peoples and cultures unlike ourselves at every level of society. This discussion or debate manifests itself in different disciplines in many ways. For most people, diplomacy is understood as the institution on the front line of such discussions, given its role as communicator and connector of societies. Ambassador Rana, an Indian diplomat, engages with this discussion by pointing to the ongoing question as to whether "Asian Values" (a term that was much discussed in the early and mid-1990s) really exist and what they mean for international relations and diplomatic practice. He lays out the theories of a range of scholars in areas such as cultural differences in preferred negotiating styles (Cohen in Rana, 2009), the difference between societies that have religions based on a set text such as Christianity, Islam, or Judaism and those that don't, such as Hinduism and Buddhism (Paz in Rana, 2009) and the "five yardsticks" of cultural analysis (Hofstede in Rana, 2009). Rana concludes there is no single Asian culture, but rather a "mosaic of bewildering variety," albeit one in which Rana identifies six themes or shared features (Rana, 2009, 167-173).

First, he argues that Asian cultures are *high context* in terms of negotiations, which means they are relationship- rather than results-driven.

Second, Asian cultures have a high *power distance,* which means that title and role are crucial elements and there is little or no presumed equality of power between different levels of society. The third and fourth features include a *long-term orientation* and a *consensus* style of negotiation. Fifth, they are *people-oriented,* where norms and rules are deemed relative and not as absolutes; and finally, he argues, Asian culture tends to be *pragmatic* in that principles are applied flexibly (rather than a linear culture in which principles—and sticking to them—are seen as significant).

This final feature is interesting in that Rana also highlights the work of Richard Lewis and his three "cultural value clusters": "linear active," "multi-active," and "autonomous." To Lewis, these categories basically mean that the implementation of policy or values can be gathered into groups or clusters under three specific themes. "Linear active" simply means the most direct or literal interpretation of values and goals. "Multi-active" means principles are important, but do not dominate; and finally, "autonomous" means that there is little or no necessary connection. Rana uses this approach to place both China and India firmly in the multi-active (rather than the linear) category, the dominant feature of the Western systems and bring us to the fundamental starting point of the Relational model.

In terms of military diplomacy, there have been five pan-Indian powers: the Mauryas, the Guptas, the Mughals, British India, and the Republic of India, and yet Kautilya's *Arthaśāstra* remains the most relied upon strategic work (Pant in Scott 2011, 15). Chris Ogden points to this as a key part of India's longstanding and continuing pursuit of what he calls "Great power" status. The notion of India as both "meeting point and bridge" between the West, Middle East, and Asia plays a big role in its approach to various challenges. Ogden goes on to argue that different leaders have interpreted this goal in different ways and offers two specific examples. The first is Jawaharlal Nehru, whose idea of "positive neutralism based on *purna swaraj*" or "complete independence" led him to take positions that were designed to create a self-sufficient and self-determining state, whereas Mahatma Gandhi's concept of *ahimsa* or "nonviolence" is still visible as India tends to avoid major power politics and both paths, according to Ogden, can be understood as part of an Indian vision of great power roles (Ogden in Scott, 2011). This does, however, create a dilemma in certain situations as evidenced by India's decision to conduct nuclear tests in 1998. This was widely interpreted as a direct challenge for a position of a world power (Scott, 2011, 9), yet the country was simultaneously pursuing a policy of "total diplomacy," suggesting the potential to work with anyone and everyone (Ogden in Scott, 2011).

BOX 10.1

Great Powers to Superpower

Great Powers is a phrase traditionally used for the powers of Europe deemed to have a major influence or ability to control events in their sphere. A kind of collective of would-be hegemons, Great Powers shared what was called the 'balance of power' across Europe and into the era of the United Nations as they form as the basis of the UN Security Council.

Superpower is a more recent term and is also used in a number of ways. The first and most common is to indicate the status of a state as a hegemon or dominant power in the international system and/or its ability to achieve its aims through coercion or simple implied threat given its perceived strength. Superpower is also a term used in conjunction with great, middle or small powers, which indicates other levels within the international system. Many such ideas are 'in the eyes of the beholder,' though there are a number of states who have embraced their status at one of these levels.

Ambassador Fabian, who served in the Indian Foreign Service for thirty-five years, draws on Kautilya's three types of power (intellectual, strength, and valor) as a contrast to all but the most recent Western ideas of power as being dominated by military concerns. Fabian's point is that India begins with a more holistic approach and should therefore be able to use its influence in a more balanced way (Fabian, 2012, 42), though both Harsh Pant and Jain Ragendra suggest that India has, in fact, been operating a "diplomacy of declaration" that involves a great deal of talking, but little or no action (Pant in Scott, 2011, 235). Using the case of the European Union, Ragendra in particular points out that, despite recently opening channels of communication, fundamental differences remain because "they are different levels of development, because they come from two milieu and because they have different geographical and geopolitical priorities" (Ragendra in Scott, 2011, 227).

However, such ideas are not relevant to India alone as both India and China have a general philosophical tendency to avoid dualistic conceptualizing, which has the benefit of leaving many options open and negotiation and renegotiation of the same points many times, while at the same time, creating mixed messages and the sense that there is no single message or policy line and preferring instead to believe in the complementarity of forms that require the other, if they are to exist at all (Chan, 1999, 36). For example,

China's historical tendency has been a reluctance to intervene beyond their immediate region or core, combined with a fierce defense of its own perception of its territory (Bates, 2007, 105). Bates suggests that, despite the fact that India and China did not experience colonialism in the same way, they both arrived on the international stage at a similar time, but in very different places in terms of their development and international outlook. China, for example, "did not emerge…as a confident viable nation-state in the Westphalian sense until well into the second half of the twentieth century" (Bates, 2007, 105), and wasn't brought into the United Nations until 1971.

In terms of the broader political field, modern-day commentators on relations between India and China generally highlight the **Panchshila**, *the ancient Buddhist term for five virtuous commitments as translated into the modern state context as the "Five Principles of Peaceful Coexistence"* (Rana, 2009, 163). These include: mutual respect for territorial integrity and sovereignty; mutual non-aggression; mutual non-interference in internal affairs; equality and mutual benefit; and peaceful coexistence. These were first enunciated as a shared concept in the 1954 Agreement on Tibet, and then again at the 1955 Bandung Conference. Seifudein Adem argues that this "ushered in a new era of international relations" as it really brought China back into the international community (Adem, 2013, 217). Certainly, since 1988, Deng Xiaoping and other Chinese officials in particular have looked to these five principles as both aspiration and as cover (Deng and Wang, 1999, 52), as both sides have not always upheld these intriguingly 'Westphalian' ideals. In the case of China, they also focus on the state-centrism or 'realist' approach to policy (Deng and Wang, 1999, 49). Yet, there is also a broad sense that China resists the traditional "big power politics of hegemonism" (Chan, 1999, 13) and seeks, instead, to make a connection between national interests as "the embodiment of the nation as a whole" (Deng and Wang, 1999, 50).

This analysis and effective definition of 'national interest' is also part of a concept highlighted by Gerald Chan as "comprehensive national power," or "CNP," that embraces the features of: comprehensiveness, openness, dynamism and a multilayered structure (Chan, 1999, 30). The CNP, he contends, operates at different levels; the international system, which is compared to the sky and a "holistic" idea of the system; followed by the patterns within that system, or *ge ju,* which he compares to the stars with a constant focus on the main players and their orbits in "multilayered and multidirectional patterns of conflict and cooperation" (Chan, 1999, 97); and finally, an international order, which, he argues (in keeping with Rana's presentation of Asian values) are entirely subjective whereas the first two are objective and can be observed. Interestingly, Chan links this to the work of scholar Wang Yizhou, who discusses what he calls "strategic sovereignty," outlined as having four zones: the central zone of the national capital and important economic areas; a peripheral zone that relies on the central zone; a buffer zone of neutrality and protection; and finally, a strategic zone for national outreach, and all linked and analyzed through the idea of CNP or comprehensive national power (Chan, 1999, 80). Yizhou does not claim any territorial or legal status for such zones, and despite the claim to 'newness' such zones clearly bring us straight back to a mandala understanding of enemies and friends in circles of influence around a center.

Whatever the origin, the idea of zones clearly comes through China's recent economic diplomacy and the policy of building both regional alliances with neighbors and economic partnerships with countries much further afield. Accused at one time of being a "regional power without a regional policy" (Deng and Wong, 1999, 184), China has been going to great lengths to create bilateral relations with many of the world's major players and to establish itself in both economic and security matters in a more "proactive, practical and constructive" way (Gates, 2007, 1). In the case of Africa, commonly used as an illustration of this new engagement policy, China currently has more consulates across all of Africa than the United States and sends representatives to the African Union (AU), the New Economic Partnership for African Development (NEPAD), the Common Market for Eastern and Southern Africa (COMESA), the Southern African Development Community (SADC), and the Economic Community of West African States (ECOWAS) (Adem, 2013, 234). Discussions both in and outside China increasingly revolve around the idea of the 'peaceful rise,' and by making stronger bilateral and regional connections, China continues to champion a multipower approach (Rana, 2009, 42) rather than the old, Western/European system of 'Great powers' or even superpowers.

Where some Chinese scholars may be suggesting this kind of zone system is new, others, such as Martin Jacques or Jeremy Black, delve into history to support their suggestion that this approach may be more correctly identified as a return to older style of statecraft and that China may succeed in resurrecting a new form of tributary system (Fabian, 2012, 229). Further, the point is made that the obsolescence of tributary systems have been premature as other parts of the world also maintained vassalage or suzerainty systems—though China succeeded for much longer (Black, 2010, 37), thus making Asia a key location for signs of its return and Chinese investment in African countries or Indian bilateral trade likely the site of such an approach in the future.

At this point there seem to be two options in terms of the diplomacy and the process of evolution of a states-system to a society in this alternative view.

The first is simply that India and China, as the English School and the traditional narrative suggest, were assimilated into the mainstream/Western/Westphalian approach. Their development, in this view, has essentially been a slow adaptation to the Western style and globalization, plus their current rise in economic, political, military (and cultural) power, has meant they have been effectively forced to continue that process as they wish to become more involved on the international stage.

The second is that, while the Western world became more 'powerful'—and believed the rest of the world to be following their hierarchical trajectory in terms of social complexity and development—the historical, cultural features of heterarchy or mandalas did not disappear. Other systems had to assimilate to a certain degree, but only as much or as far as was necessary to engage at whatever level was deemed relevant to their national interest. These systems were not questioned or examined directly, as they were under the influence of outside/colonial powers or communist rule and otherwise not engaged on the world stage. However, as all states have become more porous through the processes of globalization and as these specific states rise in stature as well as the increasing visibility of non-state actors in international affairs, the ancient features of this non hierarchical, non linear model and a different understanding of power and the need and role of communication come into their own through a relational model of interaction and diplomacy.

Features of the Relational Model

There are three main features of the Relational model:

1. A center-of-gravity vs. a territorial/boundary approach to power that includes the concept zones of both allies and enemies in an evolving and constantly changing formula of influence, usefulness and outcome;

2. A tendency to focus more overtly on regional/national interest when considering leadership roles rather than taking an 'international' or 'normative' approach and a relational or interactive approach to such roles when taken in terms of alliance and tribute.

3. A pragmatic or realistic approach that avoids a single hierarchy or simple dualities that may look duplicitous in the traditional, binary system, though it can also open the way for other actors and different tactics.

The Relational Model and 'Classic' Theories

The Relational model in both the Indian and Chinese context is often considered to be 'realist' in nature. However, a closer reading of the concept of the mandala and an appreciation of the constant communication needed to support a complicated system of tribute or alliance suggests that traditional realist definitions do not do justice to the subtlety of this approach. The idea of 'pragmatism' is often used instead to try and convey the sense that this kind of realism is not ideological, but more a recognition of the possible in any given situation. Crucially, when added to the idea of parallel or coexisting heterarchies, the traditional realist perspective is unable to cope with the multiple and simultaneous connections and alliances that complicate their interpretation of national interest and even power.

Perhaps these interpenetrating networks could therefore be argued as liberal systems of some kind. However, that may also stretch such definitions and interpretations beyond their limits. The multiplicity of sources of power and the close tracking of both allies and enemies might support a progressive version of statecraft. Certainly, the foreign policy of India, based on active participation in multilateral institutions and regular negotiation, or the recent increase in China's involvement in the bodies and agencies in locations where it has a range of interests, all point to a more pluralist approach to policy. However, the underlying 'reality' of national interest cannot be permanently discounted in either case, and so there is 'evidence' of both classic theories, but there are also structural issues that suggest a much older and very different approach that should give pause to those who might wish to place such countries in either category.

Strengths and Weaknesses of the Relational Model

In some ways, the Relational model is the ultimate demonstration of diplomatic purpose because, while the Westphalian system separates entities and carves out hierarchies of power using a linear understanding of time, space, and distance, the Relational model turns much of that on its head. The existence of co-existing heterarchies leaves a great deal of room for other international actors, alliances on specific events or issues, and multiple avenues for any given state or entity to participate and have a voice in the international arena.

Some may even go so far as to say that this model most closely represents the social constructivist paradigm of international relations (Yaqing, 2009), which eschews both realist pessimism and liberal institutionalism in favor of the agency of those at every level of interaction and the possibility of an entirely new international order.

Unfortunately, such optimism may be misplaced in that parallel heterarchies at the international level would also leave this model open to a problem familiar to the Community model: an inevitable lack of coordination and consistency. China's behavior in various African countries offers a possible example in that outside interpretations vary from the warmly positive to the deeply suspicious in terms of Chinese intentions. It is still early days in terms of how each country that is currently enjoying Chinese investment will fare in the longer term, but multiplicity can easily be interpreted as a lack of honesty and therefore not in any state or entity's interest.

Asia vs.? Europe

The presumption of a European 'default' pattern for modern states makes it difficult to see how the Relational model has much room for expansion. That said, there are two trends that seem to open some possibilities in this direction. First, there is growing awareness that traditional Western concepts do not apply evenly or consistently to all states. For example, scholars have recently suggested that the communist experience of China and Russia produced a very different understanding of 'soft power' for 'hard states' (Barr, Feklyunina, Theys, 2015) and China's "negative soft power" approach to President Xi Jinping's presentation of the "China Dream" (Callahan, 2015) amount to reconstructions of essentially Western concepts (Wilson, 2015).

The second trend and the alternative posed here as a new understanding or model of interaction suggests that this is not a matter of states seeking to follow or adapt to Western concepts, but part of an ongoing balancing process that engaged with Western ideas, but were never fully assimilated by them and therefore operate with very different underlying assumptions. The ancient mandala system covered vast areas of Asia and had a significant influence over the development of relations between the entities, states, and empires that came into contact with them. More recently, evidence also suggests that the idea of mandala statecraft, and the related concept of heterarchy, also provides insight to societies in Mexico and Central America in terms of their ancient cultures.

The argument posed is that the current shift in power and understanding is far more than an adaptation of Western concepts, but the (re)emergence of much older ideas and traditions. Further, it is part of the Euro-centrism of the traditional narrative of international relations that makes this more difficult to grasp. This is not to suggest that a Relational model will soon spread around the globe, but simply to offer an alternative interpretation of the traditional Westphalian hierarchy that includes more scope for non-state actors, different types and structures of power, and broader concepts of sovereignty and territory as entities or states become more 'global'. If the ancient states-systems as identified by the English School, Mann and others have not, as most assume, been absorbed or overtaken, but in keeping with other forms of entity or paradigms of analysis, have continued alongside, underneath, and around the traditional concepts, there is surely room for a relational model of diplomacy as part of that expanded international society.

Conclusion

The basic goal of this chapter has essentially been to pause and ask: Why didn't states develop in Asia in the same way they evolved in Europe? Perhaps more interesting is the question: Why does it seem so important for us to believe that they did—regardless of what seems to be important indications to the contrary? By way of beginning the process of answering such questions, the rest of the chapter presented the Relational model of diplomacy as an alternative to the dominant narrative found in the Westphalian understanding of the state, and the diplomacy that inevitably flows from that model. Rather than allowing the default assumption of European states-system dominance to entirely color the interpretation of current politics and diplomatic practice, evidence has been offered to support the idea that while the European system has continued (and evolved into two separate models), other states-systems have also survived and produced their own diploma*cies*.

Pursuing a sources of social power approach rather than a strictly hierarchical/linear one in other places, scholars have identified relational or heterarchical societies in Aztec Mexico and Peru (Black, 2010; Patterson, 1990), as well as in East Africa and the capital of Buganda (Hanson, 2009), whereas Vietnam, wedged between the mandalas of the Indian and Chinese 'zones of influence,' did manage to create a very Western sense of 'state' identity, including rigid borders and a "linear sense of history" (Wolters, 1999, 38).

There is broad spread of mandala-esque structures and yet there are also entities that insisted on a 'state' approach despite a very different system literally surrounding them? What does this mean? Does some spatial aspect or general lack of territorial compression explain why more 'state-like' entities were not the main vehicle for governance in Asia, but became universal in Europe? What about Africa's griot culture or Latin America's version of mandalas? Perhaps in places where cultures overlap in a very specific way, more 'state-like' features are needed to create an effective buffer zone? Perhaps religious culture is more directly linked to governance and politics than many theories of international relations or state development allow? This is beyond the scope presented here, but it seems clear that some states-systems, including India and China did evolve into a society of their own and that, more importantly for this examination of global diplomacy, the fundamental features of these two historically separate systems are similar enough to argue that, in today's world, they represent a model that is "a heady mix of bilateral, regional and great power diplomacy, in which the players weave bewildering nets of connections and counter-arrangements" (Rana, 2009, 213). In other words, they are Asian in culture, but relational in structure.

CHAPTER REVIEW QUESTIONS:

1. Is the mandala system unique to Asia?
2. Why is heterarchy important to the concept of a mandala?
3. What is CNP or comprehensive national power? And why is it important to China?
4. What is 'total diplomacy' for India?
5. What is the Panchshila and its importance to Asian diplomacy?

ESSAY QUESTIONS:

1. Do India and China look like 'heterarchies' in their foreign policy? Give examples.
2. Compare the Community model and the Relational model.
3. "The Relational model is more 'realist' than the Transatlantic model." Discuss.
4. "Regional diplomacy and the Relational model are the same." Discuss.
5. How do 'Asian values' support the Relational model?

References and Further Reading

Adem, Seifudein (ed). *China's Diplomacy in Eastern and Southern Africa.* Farnham Surrey: Ashgate Publishing, 2013.

Barr, Michael, Valentina Feklyunina and Sarina Theys. "Introduction: The Soft Power of Hard States." *Politics.* Vol 35, 3-4 (2015): 213-215.

Bates, Gill. *Rising Star: China's New Security Diplomacy.* Washington, D.C.: Brookings Institute Press, 2007.

Black, Jeremy. *A History of Diplomacy.* London: Reaktion Books, 2010.

Callahan, William. "Identity and Security in China: The Begative Soft Power of the China Dream." *Politics.* Vol 35, 3-4 (2015): 213-215.

Chan, Gerald. *Chinese Perspectives on International Relations: A Framework for Analysis.* London: Palgrave, 1999.

Chureekamol, Onsuwan Eyre. "Social Variation and Dynamics in Metal Age and Protohistoric Central Thailand: A Regional Perspective. *Asian Perspectives.* Vol. 49, No. 1 (Spring 2010): 43-84.

Crumley, Carole. "Pattern recognition in social science." *Social Science Newsletter.* Vol. 70, Issue 3 (1985): 176-179.

Crumley, Carole L. "Heterarchy and the analysis of complex societies" in *Heterarchy and the Analysis of Complex Societies.* R. Ehrehreich, C. Crumley and J. Levy (eds). *American Anthropological Association Archeological Papers 6.* (1995): 1-6.

Deng, Yong and Fei-Ling Wang (eds). *In the Eyes of the Dragon: China Views the World.* Boulder: Rowman and Littlefield, 1999.

Earle, Timothy. "The Evolution of Chiefdoms." *Current Anthropology.* Vol. 30, No. 1 (Feb. 1989): 84-88.

Fabian. K.P. *Diplomacy: Indian Style.* New Delhi: Har-Anand Publications Ltd, 2012.

Ogden, Chris. "International 'aspirations' of a rising power" in *Handbook of India's International Relations.* David Scott (ed). London: Routledge, 2011.

O'Reily, Dougald J. W. "Further Evidence of Heterarchy in Bronze Age Thailand." *Current Anthropology.* Vol. 44, No 2 (2003): 300-306.

Pant, Harsh. "Indian Strategic culture: the debate and its consequences" in *Handbook of India's International Relations.* David Scott (ed). New York: Routledge, 2011.

Patterson, Thomas. "Processes in the Formation of Ancient World Systems." *Dialectical Anthropology.* Vol. 15, No 1. (1990): 1–18.

Rana, Kishan. *Asian Diplomacy: The Foreign Ministries of China, India, Japan, Singapore, and Thailand.* Baltimore: Johns Hopkins University Press, 2009.

Rana, Kishan. *The 21st Century Ambassador: Plenipotentiary to Chief Executive.* Oxford: Oxford University Press, 2005.

Singh. G.P. *Political Thought in Ancient India: Emergence of the State, Evolution of Kingship and Inter-State Relations Based on the Saptā⊠ga Theory of State.* Wang, Bangwei and Tansen Sen (compilers). New Delhi: D.K. Printworld, 1993.

Bagchi, Chandra. *India and China: Interaction through Buddhism and Diplomacy: A Collection of Essays.* London: Anthem Press, 2011.

White, Joyce. "Incorporating Heterarchy into Theory on Socio-political Development: The Case from Southeast Asia" in *Heterarchy and the Analysis of Complex Societies.* R. Ehrenreich, C. Crumley, J. Levy (eds). *American Anthropological Association Archeological papers 6.* 101–123. 1995.

Wilson, Jeanne. "Russia and China Respond to Soft power; Interpretation and Readaptation of a Western Construct". *Politics.* Vol 35, 3-4 (2015): 213-215.

Wolters, O.W. *History, Culture, and Region in Southeast Asian Perspectives.* Ithaca: Cornell Southeast Asia Program Publications, 1999.

Yaqing, Qin. "Relationality and Processual construction: bringing Chinese ideas into international relations theory." *Social Sciences in China.* Vol 30 Issue 4, No 3. (11 November published online) 5–20.

Conclusion

BY ALISON HOLMES

The term 'global' has not always been used to indicate the whole world. Originally a French term, in the 1600s 'global' meant simply round or spherical. It was only in the early 1890s that it came to mean something pertaining to the earth as a whole. In the circumstances, this was hardly surprising given the 1880s and 1890s were a period when the pace of technological development and social change was intense and demanded a term to discuss these developments and their repercussions across all societies. Similarly, a century later in the 1980s, the word 'globalization' was adopted to discuss the multilayered processes of political, economic, and cultural change at the end of the twentieth century.

At the beginning of this text it was pointed out that the choice of the term 'global' was intentional and used in a slightly different way from the term's many uses in contemporary debate. The basic point was that, rather than continue to use phrases such as 'post-modern' when discussing the state or the international system, the goal should be to identify the features that actually reflect this 'global' world so as to better address current global issues. For example, human rights are a global issue. The environment is a global issue. There are local, regional, and national, even inter- and trans-national aspects to each of these areas, of course, but they are also global because they are interrelated and the separate levels within the issue are intertwined and cannot be disconnected. As former British Member of Parliament and leader of the Liberal Democrats has observed "The advent of the interconnectedness and of the weapons of mass destruction means that, increasingly, I share a destiny with my enemy" (Ashdown, 2011). To have any hope of dealing with these, and many other global issues, states must recognize not only the global nature of the problems, but also the impact of that 'globality' on their own status in the international arena. In short, states, and any other entity that would seek to change the direction of these global issues, must first learn how to operate on all levels simultaneously. Perhaps it is both a positive and a negative point of reality that such action is often achieved through the activities, offices and institution of diplomacy.

For this discussion of global diplomacy, the main line of the argument has been that, as an institution, diplomacy has existed through time, while constantly evolving to reflect and represent the entities or polities of any given period. At the most basic level, diplomacy exists because people at all times and in all places have sought to communicate with their neighbors near and far. Today, however, there is a much keener sense of awareness as to both the similarities and differences between societies: differences in the stages of development of different states, differences in the underpinnings of states-systems and regional identities, and differences in the practices that make up diplomacy and that result in different models of interaction.

The classic narrative, the international relations theory that frames that narrative, and the practices developed over time as seen from that perspective, have been laid out as the 'mainstream' approach. However, the real essence of the text has been to offer an alternative perspective that acknowledges previous traditions while, at the same time, freeing ourselves from the constraints of that historical approach while deepening our understanding of what really constitutes 'global'.

The goal has been to clarify the position of diplomacy as an inter-cultural institution in its own right—albeit one that generally operates in parallel with the state or whatever entity existed at any given point—and designed to facilitate communication in the form of dialogue representation and negotiation. Against this appreciation of the consistency in the pattern of behavior and 'type' of diplomacy across time has been laid a layer of interdisciplinarity as both sociology and anthropology have offered a complexity to 'globality.' The result is an urgent need to adapt those classical views and look for other approaches because, as Rana points out, "…'globality' is not anyone's property or monopoly. It is the objective fact of interdependence that lies at the root of this globalized world, and the choice of staying away altogether from external connections simply does not exist" (Rana, 2014, 440).

Thus, the idea was never to entirely replace these older approaches, but to move away from the idea of yet another 'new' diplomacy and thus broaden and deepen our understanding of diplomacy so as to deal more effectively with the "objective fact" of globality than is possible within those previous frames. As part of that broadening process, elements of the English School, and a 'Revised' English School were combined with a sociological/interactional perspective that frames diplomacy and diplomats as the negotiators, administrators, shepherds, and guides to the sources of social power. In this way, diplomats become instrumental actors in creating not only the governing entities of today, but whole systems and societies. Those who operate at the 'borders,' or, to recall Der Derian's and Sharp's term, on the "bridges" between 'us' and 'the other,' have the 'catbird seat' of social change and shifts in power and thus become vital witnesses to the rise and demise of societies and states.

Specifically, this alternative/global approach involved the identification of 'types' of diplomacy and the examination of diplomacy through politics, economics, culture, and the military over time. Six guest authors not only demonstrated that they could reach back in time to speak thematically about these 'types,' but they also highlighted the fact that such discussions often carry the traditional narrative with them. Much of their discussion was premised on assumptions about the centrality of the state, realist notions of power, and both hierarchical and linear time. However, in that process, they also confirmed the assertion that these types can be identified throughout the history as part of the development of diplomatic practice, thus aiding in the process of identification of the flows of power and sources of change.

Their analyses of the different types of diplomacy were then interwoven with examples of what were called the diplomacies of place. Through those very brief surveys of ancient civilizations it was possible to glimpse the way the types of diplomacy reflect and shape different forms of power while at the same time molding the entities that wield that power. In the context of these investigations, a point not previously made should now be addressed as the difference between global and universal. Indeed, if there is anything a study of global diplomacy should seek to demonstrate, it is that the assertion of universality found in the traditional narrative of diplomacy is flawed in that it posits an equality and same-ness in international relations that no longer reflects reality (if it ever did in any substantive or comprehensive manner). Thus, a significant portion of the text was dedicated to the examination of other states-systems and found that, not only did those places interact with the European states-system, but much of what we consider to be quintessentially 'European' or 'Western' actually has its origins elsewhere in the world. This point is particularly important because universality, like hierarchy and linearity, has become so much a part of Western/individualistic thinking it is all too easy to be unaware of their pervasive and distorting effects. Herein lies perhaps the main challenge to older accounts in that what is being asserted as a keystone of global diplomacy is a questioning of these fundamental, yet often unseen, biases in its recognition that other states systems did not disappear, but only became less visible in what, until very recently, has been a

Western-dominated world. Further, an appreciation of this first point supports a deeper appreciation of the fact that differences in history and culture have produced different diploma*cies* that have and continue to interact in their own ways.

Thus, to better understand the interactions of these types and diplomacies, three models or patterns of modern diplomacy have been observed in contemporary international affairs. Clearly, the Transatlantic and Community models are more familiar given the dominance of the Western/European approach in recent decades or even centuries. However, through the process of developing those models, it becomes obvious that the two basic models cannot explain all modes in the behavior of non-Western or non-European states. Thus, a Relational model was proposed so as to examine other forms of diplomacy, particularly in Asia. This last/most recent model is just now emerging with the 'rise' of India and China, and the increasing porousness of the state has forced a wider recognition of different forms of engagement. However, simple recognition is not enough. To be truly global, it is necessary to come to terms with the constant interaction between different states and models and, even more crucially, the power of the different sources of social power (cultural, political, economic and military) to alter the path of systemic development as a whole.

Similarly, the common understanding of anarchy, considered a basic building block of traditional theory, has, to date, been constrained in a two-dimensional Western form. Yet, the "objective fact" of globality presents both the possibility and the need to create a more three-dimensional concept to understand global dynamics and processes. All states may exist in a condition of anarchy, but even if they share that general reality, some are organized by hierarchy while others are governed via heterarchy; some operate on strictly linear time while others have a keen sense of cycles and movement. For some, boundaries are proxies for power, order, and control while others look to a kind of collective center for a sense of belonging and identity. Perhaps it is worth considering whether traditional ideas of dominance and subservience are as clear-cut in different places and spaces and despite the interpretations asserted by others—often outsiders.

The overall thrust of this approach is increasingly reflected in the debates currently going on in international relations in an era that has been called "late modernity." This latest phase, according to Henrik Bang, includes things such as: "replacement of hierarchy by networks...the hollowing out of the state... the increased fluidity of identity" (Marsh, Hart, and Tindall, 2010, 326), all recognized here as significant, though Bang's list is much longer. For diplomacy specifically, the focus has been on the growing propensity to add prefixes and suffixes to diplomacy such as hetero-polarity (Copeland, 2012), fragmented (Kennan, 1997), and the pluralization of diplomacy (Jentleson, 2012). Yet neither the prolonged discussion of pre and post types of state nor the creation of prefixes and suffixes for diplomacy and diplomats, do justice to the dimensionality possible through the identification of types and the creation of distinct models of interaction. The objective has been, instead, to shape a concept of the 'global' that not only offers a more complex understanding of the enduring nature of diplomacy and its role in the shaping and reshaping of international society, but also that appreciates the historical and cultural features of different diploma*cies* and seeks to understand the constant negotiation of difference and sources of social power as the real engine of change in the system.

Another recent discussion, but one that holds still more promise for this conversation, is the line being pursued by scholars such as Barry Buzan, Amitav Acharya, Iver Neumann, and others who are exploring ideas such as the decentering of the state, the growing importance of regional theories of international relations, and the role of small and middle powers and even sub-state relations in a more diffuse (and less Western-dominated) international system. The focus is increasingly on interactions and relations rather than on boundaries and units—precisely the place suggested here as being where diplomacy has always made its home. This direction seems more than compatible with the three models proposed and the suggestion that ancient texts or political philosophies such as those espoused by Kautilya or Confucius and a mandala/relational approach to neighborly relations fall directly in line with those ideas. Neumann may be right in his assertion that European diplomacy "forms the basis of global diplomacy" (Neumann, 2012, 310), but as Mann points out, it would be foolish to "fetishize the global" or fail to recognize that each society "exist[s] in particular settings" (Mann, 1986, 30).

Therefore, if this portrayal of global diplomacy is to be of use as both theory and practice, it must be allowed to have both breadth and depth and it is to this point that a third current debate in the field will be useful. What has been called the 'Practice turn' in international relations seeks to find a way to recombine the theory practice divide essentially by exploring the idea that actions are the basis of social order and that what is done in the world produces and reproduces that order (Bueger and Gadinger, 2015). The influence this may have in the area of diplomacy could be profound as it could conceivably help reconcile the deep cleavages explained at the outset as problematic to a long-term understanding of the purpose and mission of diplomacy.

The text began by asking why anyone should study diplomacy and, perhaps more relevant given the way the text unfolded, why should anyone study theories about diplomacy? The hope is that this question has been answered by offering both traditional and alternative ideas as to the international system, examining the interactions of societies, and illustrating the fact that the institution of diplomacy has proved the constant feature through time. As Clifford Geertz observes, "Thrones may be out of fashion, and pageantry too; but political authority still requires a cultural frame in which to define itself and advance its claim" (Geertz, 1993, 143). Others relate this directly to diplomacy and, as they refute the idea that a global world is one in which diplomats no longer have a role, point out that "authority is a political process made of never-ending symbolic struggles"; thus, they go on, "As much as there is a diffusion of authority and new roles for heterodox diplomatic agents, we are not moving towards a world where diplomats are rendered obsolete. For as long as there is contact between polities, there is diplomacy at work; when the character of the relations between these polities changes, so, too, does diplomatic practice" (Sending, Pouliot, Neumann, 2015, 13).

Adam Watson, practitioner and theorist of the English School, was prescient in his comment that "a global multicultural society is still something new and still experimental" (Watson, 2002, 309), while, as a former diplomat, he would surely have appreciated what Geertz calls the "fugitive truth," that:

> To see ourselves as others see us can be eye-opening... But it is from the far more difficult achievement of seeing ourselves amongst others, as local examples of the forms of human life as locally taken, a case among cases, a world among worlds that the largeness of mind, without which objectivity is self-congratulation and tolerance a sham, comes. (Geertz, 1993, 16)

Geertz was talking about interpretive anthropology, but the "fugitive truth" of diplomacy is arguably no different. To patrol the boundaries, both figurative and literal, between what we, as specific societies, deem to be 'us' and however we might define 'them' is to be constantly aware of both the case and the world, the local and the global—the single strand of wool and the overall pattern. The expectation here is that diplomacy will, as it has throughout history and through its mission of inter-cultural communication (dialogue, representation, and negotiation), continue to respond to and shape the constant interactions of global governance, leaving a densely woven pattern of peoples and societies in its wake.

References and Further Reading

Acharya, Amitav. "Global International Relations (IR and Regional Worlds)." *International Studies Quarterly*. 58 (2014): 647–659.

Adem, Seifudein (ed). *China's Diplomacy in Eastern and Southern Africa.* Farnham Surrey: Ashgate Publishing, 2013.

Ashdown, Paddy. The Global Power Shift. TedTalk. Brussels. https://www.ted.com. December. 2011.

Behringer, Ronald. "The Dynamics of Middlepowermanship." *Seton Hall Journal of Diplomacy and International Relations.* (Summer/Fall 2013): 9–22.

Bueger, Christian and Frank Gadinger. "The Play of International Practice." International Studies Quarterly. 59. 2015): 449–460.

Buzan, Barry. "The Inaugural Kenneth N Waltz Annual Lecture: A World Without Superpowers: Decentred Globalism." *International Relations.* 25:1 (2011): 3–25.

Copeland, Daryl. "Heteropoliarity, Security and Diplomacy." *Embassy.* January 18, 2012. http://www.embassynews.ca/news/2012/01/18/heteropolarity-security-and-diplomacy/42168?absolute=1

Geertz, Clifford. *Local Knowledge: Further Essays in Interpretive Anthropology.* New York: Fontana Press, 1993.

Jentleson, Bruce. "Accepting Limits: How to Adapt to a Copernican World." *Democracy Journal.* (Winter 2012): 38–45.

Jones, Richard Wyn and Elin Royles. "Wales in the World: Intergovernmental Relations and Sub-state diplomacy." *British Journal of Politics and International Relations.* Vol 14. (2012): 250–269.

Kennan, George. "Diplomacy without diplomats?" *Foreign Affairs.* Vol. 76, No. 5 (1997): 198–212.

Marsh, David, Paul t'Hart, and Karen Tindall. "Celebrity Politics: The Politics of Late Modernity?." *Political Studies Review.* Vol 8.3 (2010): 322–340.

Micklethwait, John and Adrian Wooldridge. "The state of the state: The global contest for the future of government." *Foreign Affairs.* (July/August 2014): https://www.foreignaffairs.com/articles/united-states/2014-05-29/state-state.

Neumann, Iver. "Euro-Centric diplomacy: Challenging but Manageable." *European Journal of International Relations.* 18 (2012): 299–321.

Rana, Kishan. *Inside Diplomacy.* New Delhi: Manas Publications, 2014.

Sending, Ole Jacob and Vincent Pouliot and Iver Neumann. *Diplomacy and the Making of World Politics.* Cambridge. Cambridge University Press, 2015.

Stephen, Matthew. "The Concept and Role of Middle Powers during Global Rebalancing." *Seton Hall Journal of Diplomacy and International Relations.* (Summer/Fall 2013): 36–52.

Watson, Adam. *The Evolution of International Society: A Comparative Historical Analysis.* London: Routledge, 2002.

GLOSSARY OF TERMS, PEOPLE, AND IDEAS

A

accreditation – the letter sent from a dispatching head of state to the receiving head of state for laying out the mission of their appointee, the Ambassador or Head of Mission, and usually delivered in person with varying levels of ceremony by the envoy to the host head of state as a sign of mutual respect.

Ambassador – the individual accredited to represent and act on behalf of a sovereign in a host country. Term co-opted by organizations other than the nation-state in the post-Cold War 'new' diplomacy, such as 'ambassador of sport' or 'UNICEF ambassador.'

Amphictyony – The Amphictyonic League or the 'league of neighbors,' an ancient religious association of Greek tribes, designed to defend a common religious center. More broadly a term used to indicate an association of neighboring states joined by common interest.

anarchy – a situation in which there is no higher authority than the state and which leads to the need for self-help (often interpreted as each state acting for itself or all against all).

anti-diplomacy – a term coined by James Der Derian as part of his genealogy of diplomacy the goal of which is "vertical" so as to "transcend all estranged relations."

B

basileus – Greek term of priest king and the title Greeks had used for the Persian 'king of kings.'

British Committee on the Theory of International Politics (see English School)

Bolshevism – The 1930's transition in the Russian Empire in which a combination of Russian Nationalism and anti-capitalist sentiments called for the establishment of a proletariat state. Although similar to communism, the main difference was the absence of internationalist goals.

Bretton Woods Conference (July 1944) – After the end of World War II, delegations from the Allied nations came to Bretton Woods, New Hampshire to discuss the reconstruction of Germany and Europe as a whole. This conference was the beginning of an international discussion of global political, social, and economic development. Resulting institutions included the International Monetary Fund (IMF) and the General Agreement on Tariffs and Trade (GATT, later to be called the World Trade Organization).

C

chancery – the building that houses a diplomatic mission or an embassy though it can house more than one. The term derives from chancery or chancellery, as in the office of a Chancellor—the title some states use for the head of foreign affairs or head of state. The ambassador's quarters are generally referred to as the Residence.

Clausewitz, Carl von (b. 1780, d. 1831) – a military general for the Kingdom of Prussia from 1792–1831 and also a scholar. Clausewitz is considered a realist and was greatly influenced by the Enlightenment thinkers. His most famous book, *On War*, outlines his integration of political and military analysis, but he never finished it, dying of cholera before it was complete.

Constructivism (also see social constructivism) – Based on the claim that significant aspects of international relations are historically and socially constructed, rather than inevitable consequences of human nature or other essential characteristics of world politics. During the 1980s and 1990s this became a major school of thought in the discipline of International Relations, though there are several different strands from the more mainstream to the radical.

Cobden-Chevalier treaty (1860) – A free trade agreement signed between the United Kingdom and France, named for its two authors, Richard Cobden, a Member of the British Parliament, and Michel Chevalier a French statesman. The treaty reduced French duties on most British manufactured goods to levels not above 30 percent and reduced British duties on French wines and brandy. As a result, the value of British exports to France more than doubled in the 1860s and the importation of French wines into Britain also doubled.

communication – The overall goal and purpose of diplomacy. The ability to connect using appropriate language and symbols to convey messages and be undertsood as intended.

conference diplomacy – the conduct of diplomacy by governments and other polities at international conferences.

Congress of Vienna (1814–15) – Gathering of representatives of the Great Powers of the day, to discuss aftermath of Napoleonic wars. Gives rise to diplomacy by way of 'congress' (see also Great Powers).

control – levels of control and chains of causation such as that found in a judicial system (see also hierarchy and scalar).

crisis diplomacy – the practice of diplomacy in times of acute crisis with features often determined by the compressed timeframe.

Crystal Palace (1851) – 'The Great Exhibition of the Works of Industry of all Nations' was an international fair hosted by the United Kingdom, and held in a large iron and glass structure that was erected to host the event.

Cultural Diplomacy (as adapted from Mann and used in this text) – Derived from the sociological theories of Michael Mann, and identified as ideology, but conflated here to mean 'culture.' This is based on Mann's definition of ideology as the "distinctive power... conveyed through song, dance, visual art forms and rituals."

D

dean or doyen – the unofficial 'head' of the diplomatic corps in any city or capital. Usually the most senior diplomat as determined by their date of arrival or accreditation.

Democratic Peace Theory – the idea that 'democracies don't fight with other democracies' is the main concept behind Democratic Peace Theory. Citizens of countries that identify or share the values of democracy are less likely to support taking action in armed conflict with another democracy. While empirical data on the issue is inconclusive, the commonsense appeal of democratic peace theory has ensured its popularity in government and policy-making circles.

dialogue – The process of engagement or give-and-take in the exchange of messages in a two-way exchange.

diplomacy – 1. the mediation of the sources of social power and the systems of organization and mechanisms for communication understood as dialogue, negotiation, and representation between social entities. 2. term used by James Der Derian to indicate his third paradigm, and located in the heart of the more traditional diplomatic narrative in the 17th and 18th century.

diplomatic mission or mission – term given to the undertaking of diplomacy between nation-states usually, but not exclusively headed by an Ambassador and housed in a building known as an Embassy.

discovery – term used by Paul Sharp in his theory of diplomacy to describe the process of learning and knowing more about another society or entity through regular engagement.

E

Economic Diplomacy (as adapted from Mann and used in this text) – From Michael Mann's theory of social power, economic sources of power involve both trade and exchange of all kinds and the flows that follow such exchange.

embassy – physical representation of the diplomatic process as the embodiment of one nation-state on the territory of another.

encounter – Term used by Paul Sharp in his theory of diplomacy to describe the initial meeting between one society and another.

English School – The English School of international relations theory (sometimes also referred to as Liberal Realism, the International Society school or the British institutionalists) maintains that there is a 'society of states' at the international level, despite the condition of anarchy (that is, the lack of a global ruler or world state). The English School is based on the conviction that ideas, rather than simply material capabilities, shape the conduct of international politics and deserve analysis and critique. In this sense it is similar to constructivism, though the English School has its roots more in world history, international law and political theory, and is more open to normative approaches than is generally the case with constructivism.

F

Fabians – The Fabian Society began in the late 1800s in the United Kingdom as a group who attempted to integrate socialist economics with British imperialism, though the group preferred an approach of gradual evolution towards socialism rather than revolution. The Fabians lobbied for progressive policies in the early 20th century including: establishing a minimum wage, universal healthcare, and the end of appointments to the House of Lords based on hereditary nepotism, though other ideas or policies are not regarded as progressive.

farbas – a level of commander in the Mali Empire.

Feminism – Feminism is a broad term given to works of scholars who have sought to bring gender concerns into the academic study of international politics. In terms of international relations, it is important to understand that feminism is derived from the school of thought known as reflectionism. However, it would be a mistake to think that feminist IR was solely a matter of identifying how many groups of women are positioned in the international political system. From its inception, feminist IR has always shown a strong theme in terms of thinking about 'masculinities.' Indeed, many IR feminists argue that the discipline is inherently masculine in nature. Feminist IR emerged largely from the late 1980s onwards. The end of the Cold War and the re-evaluation of traditional IR theory during the 1990s opened up a space for gendering International Relations.

The End of History – In 1992, American political scientist and political economist Francis Fukuyama published the book *The End of History and the Last Man.* In the book, Fukuyama argues that the end of the Cold War—in which capitalist ideology was left in a relatively stronger position—highlights the beginning of the end of global conflict in regards to political and economic ideologies, with the western liberal democracy as the standard. Fukuyama's book takes the position that the culture western liberal democracy produces is the final step in human evolution of economic and political institutions.

G

Gorki, Maxim (b. 1868, d. 1936) – Also known as the greatest proletarian in Russian literature, Gorki was an author, playwright and political activist whose experiences and travels through the Russian Empire greatly influenced his writing. The themes of his writings revolved around socialist realism in which communist values are placed at the center, combined with the proletariat breaking the disrupting and ending capitalism, via realistic means.

Grand Strategy, also called **high strategy** – comprises the "purposeful employment of all instruments of power available to a security community." (B.H.Liddell Hart:) [T]he role of grand strategy—higher strategy—is to coordinate and direct all the resources of a nation, or band of nations, towards the attainment of the political object of the war—the goal defined by fundamental policy (see strategy).

Grotius, Hugo (b. 1583, d. 1645) – Known as the 'father of international law,' Grotius wrote the first extensive treatment of international law that attempted to develop a systematic jurisprudence. Urged moderation of warfare and discussed war issues such as status of hostages, destruction of property, defeated peoples, and religious beliefs. Contributed new thoughts on old ideas such as neutrality, freedom of the seas, treaties, and diplomacy. Regarded war as a punitive action against state crimes. Drew distinctions between natural and voluntary law.

H

heterarchy – the idea that elements can be arranged or even 'counterpoised' without the need for rank or importance to create order.

hierarchy – the relationship between elements where certain factors are deemed to be subordinate to another and may be ranked in the mainstream/Western narrative of diplomacy as well as the primacy of the idea of anarchy (see anarchy).

historiography – the study of the dominant themes and points of view found in the writing of history.

Hoare-Laval Pact (1935) – An agreement between England, France and Italy that was an attempt at rapprochement between Italy and France and an end to the Italo-Ethiopian War. British Foreign Secretary Samuel Hoare and French Prime Minister Pierre Laval proposed the pact with the intentions of appointing large amounts of Ethiopia to Italy; the agreement never came into effect as it was met with public disapproval from both English and French constituents.

I

international society – The English School of international relations theory (sometimes also referred to as Liberal Realism, the International Society school or the British institutionalists) maintains that there is a 'society of states' at the international level, despite the condition of anarchy (that is, the lack of a global ruler or world state) that is more advanced than simply a system of states. The English School stands for the conviction that ideas, rather than simply material capabilities, shape the conduct of international politics, and therefore deserve analysis and critique.

international system – The most basic level of state interaction. All states are considered to be sovereign, and some states are more powerful than others. The system has a number of informal rules about how things should be done, but these rules are not binding. International Relations have existed as long as states themselves—though states are a relatively new innovation in 'global' issue negotiation.

J

Jomini, Antoine-Henri (b. 1779, d. 1869) – Known as one of the 'founders of modern military thought,' Swiss born Jomini served as a general in both the French and

Russian militaries. His ideas and theories on military strategy were taught in military academies around the world.

Just War Theory – When is war justifiable? How should war be fought? What is to become of enemy captives, the wounded or women and children? These are a few of the questions explored by Just War Theory. Despite the theory having its origins in Christian philosophy, it crosses religious cleavages through the recognition of the value of human life; that states have the right to defend themselves and their citizens; and violence is, at times, necessary to protect human life.

K

Kant, Immanuel (b. 1724, d. 1804) – German philosopher, considered a central figure of modern philosophy. Kant argued that fundamental concepts of the human mind structure human experience, that reason is the source of morality, that aesthetics arises from a faculty of disinterested judgment, that space and time are forms of our understanding, and that the world as it is "in-itself" is unknowable. Politically, Kant was one of the earliest exponents of the idea that perpetual peace could be secured through universal democracy and international cooperation.

L

League of Nations – intergovernmental organization founded in Geneva, as a result of the Treaty of Versailles 1919: integral to interwar multilateral diplomacy.

Lebensform – German term meaning 'form of life,' used by philosopher Ludwig Wittgenstein and others in the analytic philosophy and philosophy of language traditions. While the term is often used in various ways by Wittgenstein, it suggests the sociological, historical, linguistic, physiological, and behavioral determinants that comprise the matrix within which a given language has meaning.

Liberalism – sometimes called 'pluralism,' who believe in liberal internationalism and that people are basically good and trying to do the best they can.

M

Machiavelli, Niccolò (b. 1469, d. 1527) – Italian philosopher, politician, historian and author known for his famous book *The Prince* in which he describes the need for a strong political ruler who is not afraid to be severe with citizens and enemies both domestic and from abroad. Machiavellianism became known as the unethical behavior of corruption and ruthlessness carried out by the politicians as described in *The Prince*

mandala – Sanskrit term for 'sacred circle' or, more specifically, the *rajamandala* 'circle of kings.'

mansa – a Mandinka word meaning 'king of kings' or 'emperor' and associated with the Keita Dynasty of the Mali Empire, which dominated West Africa from the thirteenth to the fifteenth century.

Military Diplomacy (as adapted from Mann and used in this text) – From Michael Mann's sources of power approach, military diplomacy is the most 'traditional' as military and considered by both realists and Mann to be a fairly direct correlation of might and power.

Minister Plenipotentiary – minister with 'full powers' to act on behalf of their sovereign as if they were that sovereign.

Ministry of Foreign Affairs – the part of a government designated to deal with foreign policy and the conduct of diplomacy. The first was founded in France in 1626 by Cardinal Richelieu and has had near ubiquitous adoption by nation-states.

mission – more commonly known as the Embassy, the mission is seen as a physical representation of the diplomatic process as the embodiment of one nation-state on the territory of another.

model – archetype or a representation of a particular process.

multilateral diplomacy – diplomatic transactions conducted by more than two nation-states.

Münzenberg, Willi (b. 1889, d. 1940) – a political activist and a Communist in Germany. He was the first head of the Young Communist International in 1919-1920 and set up a propaganda organization Workers International Relief in 1921 that sent famine relief to Soviet Russia. He became disillusioned with Communism because of Joseph Stalin's purges and was accused of treason and condemned to death by Stalin. He left Germany for France where he led German émigré anti-fascist and anti-Stalinist groups until the Nazi invasion of France. He was later arrested by the government in France and sent to a prison camp. He escaped, but was found dead a few months later.

mytho-diplomacy – Based on James Der Derian's work, this deals with the most basic structures of identity and social values that shape the way a society governs itself and how it interacts with others. Mytho-diplomacy reflects the fundamental values of a society and the ways in which those pre-national identities shape outlook and behavior.

N

nation – an aggregate of people united by common descent, history, culture, or language.

Nation Branding – applying corporate branding techniques to countries, as a means to enhance and improve their image, thereby attracting more visitors, inward investments, and other benefits

nation-state – a geographical area that can be identified as deriving its political legitimacy from serving as a sovereign nation. A 'state' is a political and geopolitical entity, while a 'nation' is a cultural and ethnic one. The term 'nation–state' implies that the two coincide, but 'nation-state' formation can take place at different times in different parts of the world.

national interest – the overarching and deemed by many to be the most important driver in determining a course of action or a state's foreign policy strategy.

negotiation – discussion or conversation that takes place between those representing a specific position, with a view to reaching an agreement.

neo-diplomacy – a term used by James Der Derian to explain that while the old diplomacy was founded on dynastic legitimacy and the "reasons of power."

'New' Diplomacy – title given by various scholars and commentators at various times in history to denote something seemingly 'new' to diplomacy.

North Atlantic Treaty Organization (NATO; April 4, 1949) – twelve states from Europe and North America signed the North Atlantic Treaty. The Treaty created a coalition that would coordinate and participate in joint actions from external threats via political and military channels. The treaty had three objectives: discouraging Soviet growth, creating a North American presence in Europe to prevent the nationalist militarism that thrived during World War II, and finally, to promote political integration. Currently there are 28 member states, with Albania and Croatia as the most recent members, joining in 2009. NATO also has 'partner states' in every part of the world including the Mediterranean, South East Asia, and the Middle East.

nyama – a mande or Mandinka term meaning the intangible power of words and believed to live inside a griot as a wild energy and insight.

O

operations – The operational level of foreign policy is the essential crucible for the formulation of diplomatic approaches to international challenges.

P

Panchshila – the ancient Buddhist term for five virtuous commitments as translated into the modern state context as the "Five Principles of Peaceful Coexistence."

paradigms – a typical example or pattern of something; a model. In science and epistemology (the theory of knowledge), a paradigm is a distinct set of concepts or thought patterns, including theories, research methods, postulates, and standards for what constitutes legitimate contributions to a field.

Perfidious Albion – From the Latin word 'perfidia' for a person who lies or does not keep their word, while 'Albion' was the name given to Great Britain by the ancient Greeks; this term was first used as a slur against Great Britain, specifically in regards to the country's foreign policy.

Pluralists – more commonly known as 'liberals,' a paradigm that believes in internationalism and that people are basically good with a fundamental idea of progress.

Political Diplomacy (as adapted from Mann and used in this text) – Derived from the theories of Michael Mann, political diplomacy is both obvious and subtle, in that it is about relationships in their entirety not only among elites, but between the elite and the rest of society.

Polo, Marco (b. 1254, d. 1324) – an Italian merchant traveler who traveled through Asia and met Kublai Khan. He returned to find Venice at war with Genoa, and Marco was imprisoned and dictated his stories to a cellmate. He was released in 1299, became a wealthy merchant, married, and had three children. He died in 1324 and was buried in the church of San Lorenzo in Venice.

polylateralism – term coined by Geoff Wiseman, describing diplomatic processes amongst many entities not just states given multilateralism close association with inter-state relationships.

personal diplomacy – the degree to which individuals can exert their own influence on the diplomatic process, either to support a previously agreed diplomatic goal or to change the direction of the process.

plenipotentiary – means 'full powers', given as a title to Ambassadors so they can operate with 'full powers' on behalf of their sovereigns.

postcolonialism and post-colonialism – an academic field featuring methods of intellectual discourse that analyze, explain, and respond to the cultural legacies of colonialism and imperialism; and by drawing from postmodernism postcolonial studies, it analyzes the politics of knowledge (creation, control, and distribution).

post-structuralism – theory that claims "Every understanding of international politics depends upon abstraction, representation and interpretation". Scholars associated with post-structuralism in international relations include Richard K. Ashley, James Der Derian, Michael J. Shapiro, R.B.J. Walker, and Lene Hansen.

power – Power in international relations is defined in several different ways. Political scientists, historians, and practitioners of international relations (diplomats) have used the following concepts of political power: Power as a goal of states or leaders; Power as a measure of influence or control over outcomes, events, actors and issues; Power as reflecting victory in conflict and the attainment of security; Power as control over resources and capabilities; Power as status, which some states or actors possess and others do not.

practice – a specific category of action and, in contrast to theory, is understood to be a level that effectively connects the 'bottom' of strategy and the 'top' of tactics. This overlapping position is important because it is the result of the fact that practice is both strategy-driven, but also closely linked to operations/implementation.

prehistory – means literally 'before history,' from the Latin word for 'before,' præ, and historia. Prehistory covers the time since modern humans first appear, and until the appearance of recorded history and writing systems. Since both the time of settlement of modern humans, and the evolution of human civilizations, differ from region to region, prehistory starts and ends at different moments in time, depending on the region concerned. Samaria in Mesopotamia and ancient Egypt were the first civilizations to develop their own scripts and keep historical records. The neighboring civilizations of the Ancient Middle East were the first to follow. Most other civilizations reached the end of prehistory during Iron Age.

problematize – to readjust the focus of debate to different perspectives or using different assumptions.

propaganda – information that is used to deliberately influence an audience in a certain direction, generally by presenting facts selectively or using messages to produce an emotional rather than a rational response.

protohistory – refers to a period between prehistory and history, during which a culture or civilization has not yet developed writing but other cultures noted its existence in their own writings. For example, in Europe, the Celts and the Germanic tribes may be considered to have been protohistoric when they began appearing in Greek and Roman texts.

Protohistoric may also refer to the transition period between the advent of literacy in a society and the writings of the first historians. The preservation of oral traditions may complicate matters as these can provide a secondary historical source for even earlier events.

proto-diplomacy – term used by James Der Darian to indicate the period of conflict between the Holy Roman Empire and Islam, but Der Derian's point is not purely the geopolitics of that time, but the importance of the clash of these cultures and the growth of one identity at the cost of the other.

Public Diplomacy – diplomacy on behalf of a state directed at another nation-states population (rather than its counter-part government).

R

Realists – belief that human nature is basically selfish and unchangeable and that people will always take the opportunity to maximize their own interests above everything else.

reify – to create the sense that something abstract or indefinite is concrete or real.

Relationalism – applies to any system of thought that gives importance to the relational nature of reality. But in its narrower and philosophically restricted definition, relationalism refers to the theory of reality that interprets the existence, nature, and meaning of things in terms of their relationality or relatedness.

representation – communication (often by diplomats) on behalf of a constituency.

resident or permanent mission – A diplomatic mission is a group of people from one state or an international inter-governmental organization (such as the United Nations) present in another state to represent the sending state/organization officially in the receiving state. In practice, a diplomatic mission usually denotes the resident mission, namely the office of a country's diplomatic representatives in the capital city of another country. As well as being a diplomatic mission to the country in which it is situated, it may also be a non-resident permanent mission to one or more other countries. There are thus resident and non-resident embassies.

re-encounter – term used by Paul Sharp in his theory of diplomacy to convey a kind of arm's length engagement that implies a sense of having the initial contact over and over again.

Richelieu, Cardinal (b. 1585, d. 1642) – French clergyman, nobleman, and statesman, considered to be one of, if not the, founding father of modern, French Diplomacy and what is known as the 'French Method,' which spread across Europe.

S

satrapies – provinces established in an effort to make a vast territory easier to govern with its own governor or *satrap*.

scalar – system in which any level can affect any other.

scale – unit of analysis relative to the phenomenon as a whole. Effective scale is the scale at which structure among elements is perceived, and determines how they will be studied.

scapegoat – Assigning guilt, and negative treatment to persons or groups—usually minority groups—for circumstances that create uneasiness in the majority; also assigned in order to shift blame or focus from the core contradictions within an issue.

self-help (see anarchy)

sherpa – a guide who assists in the preparation and through the course of diplomatic negotiations. Adopted from the Nepalese mountain guides known as sherpas.

Shostakovich, Dmitri (b. 1906, d. 1975) – a Russian composer and pianist, and a prominent figure of 20th-century music. He achieved fame in the Soviet Union under the patronage of Soviet chief of staff Mikhail Tukhachevsky, but later had a complex and difficult relationship with the government.

Social Constructivism (see Constructivism)

Soft Power – Term adopted by Joseph Nye to describe the ability to influence others to your will by attraction rather than coercion. More broadly, the ability to convince others of the merits of your culture, values, and overall world view, with the added benefit that this translates into wider support for (foreign) policy.

sovereignty – Supreme power or authority. Authority of a state to govern itself. Jurisdiction, rule, supremacy, dominion, power, ascendancy, suzerainty, hegemony, domination, authority, control, influence.

state – territorially bounded legal entity, sovereign and equal in the world of states, strategy, sometimes called a 'grand strategy'. The entity that symbolizes the nation. And then we see the conflation of the two words—at least with a classical, Eurocentric focus—as the nation-state. Montevideo Convention on Rights and Duties of States of 1933 which determined a state had "(a) a permanent population, (b) a defined territory, (c) government, and (d) capacity to enter into relations with other States."

statecraft – the 'art' of politics or the leadership of a country and the conduct of foreign affairs.

states-system – a term common in the English School, the state- or states-system suggests a group of entities that interact, but have no or little affinity or sense of group belonging or rules and norms that are the foundation of an international society in the English School approach.

strategy – From Greek for 'art of troop leader; office of general, command, generalship' and is a high level plan to achieve one or more goals under conditions of uncertainty. Strategy is important because the resources available to achieve these goals are usually limited. Strategy generally involves setting goals, determining actions to achieve the goals, and mobilizing resources to execute the actions (see also Grand Strategy).

Structuralism – a paradigm that stresses the impact of world economic structures on the political, social, cultural and economic life of countries (see also post structuralism).

substantialist – theory about objecthood, positing that a substance is distinct from its properties. A thing-in-itself is a property-bearer that must be distinguished from the properties it bears.

summits – generally considered to be meetings between heads of state or appointed officials on a specific issue or negotiation. Increasingly the term summit is used to describe specialist meetings that involve many more international (and domestic) actors though the specificity of the topic remains the key element.

summit diplomacy – diplomacy conducted usually by heads of state or their representatives to address particular issues at a particular point and place in time.

Sun Tzu (b. 544 BCE, d. 496 BCE) – The Chinese military general, strategist, philosopher and author of *The Art of War,* an ancient text thought to be written in the late 6th century. Many contemporary military affiliated figures looked to Sun Tzu for inspiration.

superpower – an increasingly dated term, it was popular when the United States and Soviet Union dominated the world stage. The term is generally understood to refer to a state that can project its power (usually military) without challenge on a global scale.

suzerainty – system of tribute or protection where the powerful controlled their vassals in terms of their external relations, but did not seek to control their internal activities.

T

tactics – specific and direct actions taken at a given moment in time as part of an operation and/or in pursuit of a strategy.

techno-diplomacy – term used by James Der Derian to refer to the "global communication processes by which scientific or other organized knowledge is being systematically applied to, and inscribed by, power politics" and that dominate our attempts to mediate estrangement or create dialogue between states.

theory – a particular worldview and the rules by which we decide something is important or unimportant in our approach.

Thucydides (b. 460 BCE, d. 395 BCE) – the 'father of scientific history' the Greek general, philosopher of politics and author of *The History of the Peloponnesian War* which documented the conflict between Athens and Sparta from 431–404 BCE.

Track-Two Diplomacy – diplomatic negotiations conducted by semi-official or unofficial diplomats, with only nominal linkages to official state based diplomacy.

Transformational (Diplomacy) – In a speech given at Georgetown University in 2006, then Secretary of State Condoleezza Rice described Transformational Diplomacy as a way, "to work with our many partners around the world, to build and sustain democratic, well-governed states that will respond to the needs of their people and conduct themselves responsibly in the international system."

tributary state – refers to one of the two main ways in which a pre-modern state might be subordinate to a more powerful state in that a tributary would send a regular token of submission (tribute) to the superior power. Tributary relations do not involve administrative control or interference by the hegemon.

twiplomacy – diplomacy conducted via the micro-blogging tool 'Twitter.'

V

Vienna Conventions – Diplomats working in a host nation benefit from the sanctions outlined during the 1961 conventions on diplomatic relations. During the meetings countries gathered and established a protocol for the conduct a host nation should display to a foreign diplomat: freedom from coercion, granting privacy and security are just a few of the agreed upon issues. Currently 190 states have ratified the treaty.

W

World Trade Organization (WTO) – originated in 1947 as an agreement without an institution to manage it, can be seen as among the world's greatest diplomatic achievements. With competing and sometimes conflicting interests regarding international trade, the WTO brings member nations to the table to facilitate the most effective strategy to increase opportunities for free trade among the member states. From settling disputes, to pursuing international trade policies to be exercised by its member governments, the WTO's goal is to remove the barriers that prevent or create stagnation in international trade.

Z

Zheng He (b. 1371, d. 1433) – Appointed by Chinese emperors in the early 13th century, Admiral Zheng He made seven voyages with an armada of *baochuan*, or treasure ships that by some accounts had nine masts on 400-foot-long decks. The largest wooden ships ever built, they were much larger than those used by Vasco da Gama the Portuguese explorer. The fleet reached the western coast of India, and the Arabian Peninsula to as far as what is currently known as Mozambique with tens of thousands of men. The goal of the voyages was to begin in trade and display the strength of the China.

ABOUT THE GUEST AUTHORS

(in order of appearance)

Kenneth Weisbrode is Assistant Professor of History at Bilkent University, Turkey. He is a diplomatic and cultural historian, and co-founder of the Network for the New Diplomatic History. His latest book is *Old Diplomacy Revisited* (Palgrave, 2013).

Geoffrey Allen Pigman is currently a consultant specializing in international trade, political economy and global strategy. He is a Research Associate in the Department of Political Science, University of Pretoria, and a Research Associate at the Institute for Global Dialogue in Pretoria, South Africa. He is author of *The World Economic Forum (Routledge, 2006), Contemporary Diplomacy* (Polity Press 2010) and *Trade Diplomacy Transformed* (Palgrave Macmillan 2015).

Giles Scott-Smith holds the Ernst van der Beugel Chair in the Diplomatic History of Transatlantic Relations since WW II at Leiden University, the Netherlands. In 2013 he was appointed Chair of the Transatlantic Studies Association. He is co-editor for the Key Studies in Diplomacy book series with Manchester University Press, and on the editorial board of the *Journal of Contemporary History*. He is author of *Western Anti-Communism and the Interdoc Network* (Palgrave Macmillan, 2012), *Networks of Empire* (Peter Lang 2008), and *The Politics of Apolitical Culture* (Routledge 2002).

Andrew Dorman is a Professor of International Security in the Defence Studies Department, King's College London based at the United Kingdom's Joint Services Command and Staff College and the Commissioning Editor of the journal International Affairs. His books include *Providing for National*

Security and *The Future of Transatlantic Relations*, both co-edited with Joyce Kaufman (Alto, CA: Stanford University Press, 2014 & 2011), *Blair's Successful War* (Farnham: Ashgate, 2009).

Matthew Uttley holds the Chair in Defence Studies at King's College London. He has published widely on the historical and contemporary dimensions of British defence and security policy in a range of refereed journals including *International Affairs, Intelligence and National Security, Public Policy and Administration*, and *Defence and Peace Economics.*

Shaun Riordan is a Senior Visiting Fellow at the Clingendael Institute. He is also Head of Economics and Theory of Knowledge at the International College Spain in Madrid, and independent consultant to companies and sub-national governments on the analysis and management of geopolitical risk. He is the author of *The New Diplomacy* (Polity, 2003) and *Adios a la Diplomacia* (Siglo XXI, 2005).

INDEX

Lightning Source UK Ltd.
Milton Keynes UK
UKOW06f0225110516

274009UK00002B/58/P